SCAFFOLDING READING EXPERIENCES

FOR

ENGLISH-LANGUAGE LEARNERS

SCAFFOLDING READING EXPERIENCES

FOR

ENGLISH-LANGUAGE LEARNERS

by

Jill Fitzgerald

and

Michael F. Graves

Christopher-Gordon Publishers, Inc.
Norwood, Massachusetts

COPYRIGHT
ACKNOWLEDGMENTS

Every effort has been made to contact copyright holders for permission to reproduce borrowed material where necessary. We apologize for any oversights and would be happy to rectify them in future printings.

Figure from *Contemporary Educational Psychology* ©1983 reprinted with permission from Elsevier Press.

"I'm Thankful" from *The New Kid on the Block* by Jack Prelutsky, copyright © 1984 by Jack Prelutsky. Reprinted by permission of HarperCollins Publishers.

Christopher-Gordon Publishers, Inc.
1502 Providence Highway, Suite #12
Norwood, Massachusetts 02062
800-934-8322
781-762-5577

Printed in the United State of America
10 9 8 7 6 5 4 3 2   07 06 05 04

ISBN: 1-929024-60-6
Library of Congress Catalogue Number: 2003104436

 DEDICATION

Jill Fitzgerald:
To my husband, Kenneth Mabry Jackson

Michael F. Graves:
To my wife, Bonnie Graves

ACKNOWLEDGMENTS

We are grateful to several individuals for their help with this book. Bonnie Graves has been particularly helpful in suggesting children's literature. A Scaffolded Reading Experience lesson by Cheri Cooke, a teacher at Oakland Middle School in Stillwater Minnesota, is included in the book. Over the past several years, working with Greg Sales and his Seward Learning staff on a Scaffolding Reading Experience website, www.onlinereadingreseources.com, has given us an opportunity to refine and extend our thinking about Scaffolding Reading Experiences for English-language learners. We were also aided by the formal reviews of Lynn Warren, Harnett County Schools, NC; Pam Patterson, Lee County Schools, NC; Linda Higgins, Lee County Schools, NC; Mary Ramirez, School District of Philadelphia, PA; Claude Goldenberg, California State University, Long Beach; and Robert Jiménez, University of Illinois at Urbana-Champaign. Finally, we thank Hiram Howard and Kate Liston of Christopher-Gordon for their encouragement and assistance throughout the project.

Contents

FOREWORD

Promoting the growth and development of every student is a fundamental challenge for any teacher—whether in preschool or graduate school. The challenge is then amplified when a teacher has in her or his classroom students who do not know or have not fully mastered the language of instruction, which in the vast majority of U.S. classrooms is of course English. In some states and districts, teachers have been dealing with this amplified challenge for decades; in others, teachers are just now coming face to face with it. In either case, teachers need ideas and strategies they can use to help every single one of their students—ALL of them—grow and develop academically and personally.

The concept of "scaffolding," so richly described and illlustrated in this book, provides teachers with such a set of instructional tools. While educators have yet to discover or invent the magic bullet that will address all of our educational challenges and dilemmas (not that we should even expect to find one), Jill Fitzgerald and Michael Graves have done a masterful job of weaving together in this volume research, theory, and concrete applications that can go a long way toward assisting teachers to maximize instruction with all students. The authors draw on their own deep experience and knowledge as teachers and researchers to lay out a framework that will help enrich the teaching of others.

There is much we still do not fully understand about how best to help English learners succeed in U.S. classrooms. Historically, the major and most volatile debate has centered on whether we should teach non- or limited-English speaking children to read, write, compute, and learn other academic content in their home language before they begin to accomplish these tasks in English. This, of course, is the so-called "bilingual education" question. The best evidence to date suggests that learning academic skills in the home language makes a positive contribution to academic development in a second language, in addition to promoting development and maintenance of the home language. But for many English learners this is simply not an option. And even for those for whom it is, they will still require—and benefit from—the sorts of instruction described in this book. They will invariably be in instructional situations where their relatively limited knowledge of English will put them at a disadvantage, unless teachers scaffold them appropriately.

One question readers will undoubtedly have is whether these scaffolded reading experiences are just for English learners. Aren't they appropriate for all learners? In other words, isn't this "just good instruction?" Undoubtedly much of the instruction that is good and effective for English learners is also good and effective for English speakers. But as the authors make clear, English learners are probably particularly dependent on good instruction, meaning instruction that is clear, explicit, and helps them make connections between what they know and what they are being expected to learn. With English speakers we can often—not always!—assume they can make some of these connections themselves. For English learners, they are much more difficult.

Another question readers will likely ask is, "How can I find the time to do these scaffolded activities, given everything else I have to plan and do every single day?" Indeed, as the authors acknowledge some of these activities, such as modifying texts for English learners, are very time consuming. This a dilemma indeed. One possibility is to have community resource people help out. Sometimes this is possible; sometimes it is not.

The important point, however, is this: It is in teachers' and students' interest to look for ways to use many of these strategies. Doing so will help us fulfill a long-held dream of many American educators—extending the educational franchise to all.

by Claude Goldenberg, College of Education,
California State University, Long Beach

 CHAPTER 1

INTRODUCTION AND OVERVIEW

So what are we supposed to do? None of our districts have bilingual education programs. In virtually any classroom in our districts, fifteen to fifty percent of our students are English-language learners. Some of our students have never been to school before. On the other hand, some parents have told us their children excelled in their homeland schools and can read and write very well in their native languages, but they've never had a chance to learn English before. How can we teach so that our English-language learners learn well? We're not reading teachers. We just can't possibly teach all of our English-language learners how to read. Should we just drop all reading assignments, and do all teaching orally? Can the students who aren't speaking much be expected to read anything at all? How can we keep all of our students interested?

These are just some of the tough questions one of us recently fielded from a group of middle-grade teachers from four different school districts. Do the questions seem familiar to you? As the numbers of English-language learners continue to increase dramatically throughout the United States, most teachers, no matter where they live and work, now have English-language learners in their classrooms. In fact, the vast majority of English-language learners (approximately 85% of them) are educated in "regular" classroom settings where only English is spoken, with little or no added support for learning the new language (Schirmer, Casbon, & Twiss, 1996).

While teachers have always addressed classrooms filled with students having wide-ranging abilities and needs, language is increasingly becoming an additional form of diversity. Yet many teachers have received very little information or education about the English-language learner and often act on hunches or advice from other teachers, who themselves may not have had an opportunity to study and learn about assisting English-language learners with reading and writing (Constantino, 1994; Faltis & Hudelson, 1994; Garcia, Willis, & Harris, 1998). Still, many teachers have told us they want to learn as much as they can about using reading with English-language learners.

In this book, we focus on a teaching framework for planning and implementing reading activities in a wide array of situations for English-language learners. The framework is called the *Scaffolded Reading Experience.* The main purpose of a Scaffolded Reading Experience is to help English-language learners better understand, learn from, and enjoy each and every text they read. While Scaffolded Reading Experiences do not directly teach English-language learners to read, they do help students learn about many aspects of reading, such as helping them use relevant background knowledge and broadening their meaning vocabularies. Scaffolded Reading Experiences can also help English-language learners in other ways, such as ensuring that they use the many strengths they already have, assisting them in building background knowledge, and helping them become an integral part of the classroom community of learners.

We believe this book will be helpful for teachers in bilingual education programs, English-language learner resource teachers who work with second-language learners, teachers who work with English-language learners in Sheltered English settings, teachers in regular classrooms that include English-language learners and native-English-speaking students, content-area teachers who have English-language learners in their classes, as well as reading teachers, special education teachers, foreign language teachers, and others who work with English-language learners.

To provide a context for our discussion of the Scaffolded Reading Experience, we begin by briefly stating some of our basic premises about teaching English-language learners, many of which will be further explained later in this book. First, *we use the term English-language learner to refer to a wide array of language learners, including bilingual learners in the United States. Our use of the term should not be taken to mean that we advocate that students should only learn English.* To the contrary, ample evidence supports many benefits of bilingualism and biliteracy, such as enhanced cognitive ability to manipulate language (August & Hakuta, 1997; Fitzgerald & Cummins, 1999; Hakuta, 1986; Hakuta & Gould, 1987; Snow, 1987; Wong Fillmore & Valadez, 1986). We strongly endorse bilingualism, biliteracy, and bilingual education programs.

Second, *all teachers should have some basic understanding of how a second language is learned, how difficult and time consuming second-language learn-*

ing is, the relationships between first- and second-language orality and literacy, and important cultural understandings and sensibilities that vary from student to student and that are often embedded in language. We address each of these issues and more in chapter 3.

Third, *English-language learners bring a vast and rich language, background, and culture with them to our classrooms.* Our challenge as teachers is to find creative and interesting ways to open doors and make connections with these students so that they are able to use, share, and build on their language, background, and culture, and so that we can learn from them while they are learning with us.

Fourth, even when we can't see it, feel it, or hear it, *English-language learners are virtually always thinking and exerting effort to learn and understand.* Many English-language learners bring an array of emotions to our classrooms that often are not evident on the surface. The student who is afraid that his talk will sound funny to others may hide his self-consciousness. The student who does not fully understand what is said may hold a steady gaze and outwardly appear confident or even cocky. Rather than misread or misinterpret what might appear to us to be negative exterior signals, we must try to understand the sensitivities of English-language learners and then attempt to relate to those feelings and understandings.

As we wrote this book, we kept these four premises firmly in mind. We provide examples and illustrations for many types of teachers and teaching situations involving English-language learners. We discuss the most basic understandings and assumptions we think teachers of English-language learners should have, and we specifically explain how the Scaffolded Reading Experience is linked to these basic understandings and assumptions.

We assume that many readers of this book do not have strong background understandings about reading instruction, content-area reading, or English-language learners. However, those of you with expertise in these areas will find many new and powerful ideas for effective teaching. Although many of the readings and topics are targeted toward grades 3–8, we also include a few examples from earlier and later grades because the Scaffolded Reading Experience framework can be used at all grade levels. Additionally, we discuss and illustrate the use of a variety of materials, including narratives, expository materials, and high interest–easy reading texts.

As we wrote this book, we struggled with ethnic/race names. Choices of names are so important because identities are wrapped up in them. We think it is very important to use names that individuals prefer for themselves, and we also believe it is important to disentangle race and ethnicity in names as much as possible. We turned to various style sheets and educational organizations to see what guidelines were available for ethnic/race names and found that there are several different sets of guidelines and outlooks. Of the ones we considered, we thought none were perfect for our book. In the end, we made a decision to use the following names as consistently as we could in the book: Asian, Anglo (to refer to individuals primarily of European descent and who currently speak English as a native language), Black of African descent, and Latino. Our collective names are not perfect either, but we hope in our selection we have been sensitive in thinking about the ways in which names signify identity.

To offer you a glimpse of some basic understandings involved in the Scaffolded Reading Experience framework for English-language learners, we now consider what constitutes meaningful and enjoyable reading experiences. As you know from your own experience, either as a reader or a teacher, in order to enjoy reading and to get the most out of what you read, you need to be actively involved with the text. To be successful, you need to both understand and make some connections with the text. Essential to effective reading are having the prerequisite skills and background knowledge to deal with the selection you're reading, being motivated and prepared to read, and having some purpose for reading.

Say you are glancing through the newspaper and this headline catches your attention: "Middle-Grades Students Learning to Speak English Learn Social Studies and Science Through Reading." Right away you're motivated to read, although you may well be skeptical of the claim. You're a sixth-grade social studies teacher. In one of your classes, you have 28 students, 6 of whom are English-language learners who have been in the United States for less than one year. In a split second, your brain pulls out of memory the faces of those 6 students, an image of your busy classroom, and the methods and materials you've used. You're more than prepared to see what this article has to tell you about teaching them. In fact, you can't wait to get started. You want to know just what this way of reading is and whether or not it really can work with all students. Once you begin reading, you combine what you know about students, reading assignments, and classrooms with what is presented in the text, building meaning as you go. What the author says either refutes or confirms what you know. You might become intrigued, amused, discouraged, angered, or enlightened. But two things are certain—you are neither lost nor uninterested. After you read, you will be able to recall the meanings that have been presented in the text and created in your mind—to ponder them, to consider the author's arguments, and to apply or reject what you have learned.

How can we foster and encourage this kind of involvement in our English-language learners and at the same time bolster their competence as readers and their confidence in their reading ability so that they become committed, able, and lifelong readers? One way is by providing appropriate kinds of experiences before students read, while they are reading, and after they read—experiences that will ensure that they get the most they possibly can out of every reading experience, regardless of their oral or proficiency level, or whether they are reading novels or short stories, folktales or poems, chapters in textbooks, magazine articles, or cookbooks.

One very powerful approach that teachers of English-language learners can use to enable these sorts of "maximal" reading and learning experiences is instructional scaffolding. We believe that the term *scaffolding* was first used in its educational sense by David Wood, Jerome Bruner, and Gail Ross (1976), who used it to characterize mothers' verbal interaction when reading to their young children. For example, in sharing a picture book with a child and attempting to assist the child in reading the words that label the pictures, a mother might at first simply page through the book familiarizing the child with the pictures and the general content of the book. Then, she might focus on a single picture and ask the child what it is. After this, she might point to the word below the picture, tell the child that the word names the picture, ask the child what the word is, and provide him or her with feedback on the correctness of the answer. The important point to focus on is that the mother has neither simply told the child the word nor simply asked him or her to say it. Instead, she has built an instructional structure, a *scaffold*, that assists the student in learning. Scaffolding, as Wood and his colleagues aptly put it, is "a process that enables a child or novice to solve a problem, carry out a task, or achieve a goal which would be beyond his [or her] unassisted efforts." Or, to use Linda Anderson's (1989) words, a scaffold is "a temporary and adjustable support that enables the accomplishment of a task that would be impossible without the scaffold's support."

The practice of scaffolding English-language learners' reading is very important to their progress. Scaffolding and associated concepts such as *structured teaching* and plentiful *teacher guidance* are strongly advocated for use with English-language learners by many professionals (Echevarria, Vogt, & Short, 2000; Gersten & Baker, 2000; Peregoy & Boyle, 1997). Research with English-language learners supports the use of scaffolds in helping them to learn content and to progress in language learning and in reading and writing (Au & Jordan, 1981; Peregoy & Boyle, 1997; Tharp & Gallimore, 1988).

Scaffolding is not a practice that is restricted to use with English-language learners. Since its introduction in the educational literature 25 years ago, the concept of instructional scaffolding has been investigated, elaborated, related to other instructional concepts, and strongly endorsed by virtually every major reading authority. In fact, a list of the authorities strongly supporting the concept reads like a who's who of literacy education and includes Richard Anderson (Anderson & Armbruster, 1990), Arthur Applebee (Applebee & Langer, 1983), Courtney Cazden (1992), David Pearson (1996), Michael Pressley (1998), Taffy Raphael (2000), Regie Routman (2000), Catherine Snow (Snow, Burns, & Griffin, 1998), and Barbara Taylor (Taylor, Pearson, Clark, & Whalpole, 2000). Historically, studies have shown that scaffolding can be a powerful instructional technique in classrooms (Taylor et al., 2000; Warton-McDonald, Pressley, & Hampston, 1998), small groups (Brown & Palincsar, 1989; Palincsar, 1986), and one-to-one tutoring sessions (Beed, Hawkins, & Roller, 1991; Rodgers, 2000).

Although different authors define scaffolding slightly differently, three closely related features are essential attributes of effective scaffolding. First, there is the scaffold itself, the temporary and supportive structure that helps a student or group of students accomplish a task they could not accomplish—or could not accomplish as well—without the scaffold. Second, the scaffold must place the learner in what Lev Vygotsky (1978) has termed the *zone of proximal development.* As explained by Vygotsky, at any particular point in time, children have a circumscribed zone of development, a range within which they can learn. At one end of this range are learning tasks that they can complete independently; at the other end are learning tasks that they cannot complete, even with assistance. Between these two extremes is the zone most productive for learning, the range of tasks at which children can achieve *if* they are assisted by some more knowledgeable or more competent other. Third, over time, the teacher must gradually dismantle the scaffold and transfer the responsibility for completing tasks to students. As David Pearson and Margaret Gallagher (1983) have explained, effective instruction often follows a progression in which teachers gradually do less of the work and students gradually assume increased responsibility for their learning. It is through this process of gradually assuming more and more responsibility for their learning that students become competent, independent learners.

In this book, we use the concept of scaffolding to undergird the flexible instructional framework we term a Scaffolded Reading Experience. The Scaffolded Reading Experience has much in common with the *hybrid model* of instruction for English-language learners recommended by Gersten and Baker (2000). Gersten and Baker reviewed research on teaching English-language learners and interviewed professionals across the nation who work with English-language learners about their beliefs and about important instructional practices to use with English learners. Combining the conclusions from the research review and their interviews, they suggest that a "hybrid" model of instruction be used. The hybrid model consists of structured lessons during which students participate in reasonably lengthy verbal exchanges with their teachers and peers and receive clear teacher guidance. Using the model, teachers apply validated instructional approaches described in the effective teaching literature and principles of teaching emanating from advances in cognitive psychology. The Scaffolded Reading Experience framework is a well-developed, thoroughly described, and well-tested hybrid model (Cooke, 2002; Fournier & Graves, 2002; Graves & Graves, 1994; Graves & Liang, in press).

The Scaffolded Reading Experience framework suggests possible prereading, during-reading, and postreading opportunities and experiences that you as a teacher can use to empower English-language learners to successfully read, understand, learn from, and enjoy a particular selection. The process of reading a selection is somewhat like taking a journey. As with any successful journey, there are certain essentials, things that should be done before, during, and after the trip to make it a worthwhile and meaningful experience. As we will explain in chapter 2, the Scaffolded Reading Experience framework allows you to create the prereading, during-reading, and postreading experiences that will make students' journeys through selections as successful and rewarding as possible. As we will explain and illustrate throughout the book, these scaffolds present students with tasks in the zone of proximal development while gradually giving them more and more responsibility for their reading and learning. As we will also explain and illustrate throughout the book, the more unfamiliar the territory, the greater the need for substantial amounts of preparation, guidance, and follow-up. However, this does not mean that more scaffolding is better. We want to provide enough scaffolding to help English-language learners succeed while still providing enough challenges to ensure they become increasingly competent learners and readers.

The remainder of the book is divided into nine chapters. Chapter 2, "What Is a Scaffolded Reading Experience?," further defines Scaffolded Reading Experiences (SREs), gives a list and brief explanations of their components, describes the two phases of SREs, models the thinking involved in constructing an SRE for several selections, and explains what SREs are not and what other components are included in a comprehensive and balanced reading program for English-language learners.

Chapter 3 is titled "What Do Teachers Need to Know About English-Language Learners to Successfully Use Scaffolding Reading Experiences?" In this chapter, we highlight some of the most important issues surrounding English-language learners' schooling, those issues we view as most important as you work with SREs. We focus on addressing some of the most common questions that teachers have asked us, including what is known about how a second language is learned, whether second-language reading and first-language reading are significantly different processes, relationships between learning to speak and learning to read, and how culture and language are intertwined.

Chapter 4, "The Thinking Behind Scaffolded Reading Experiences for English-Language Learners," describes a variety of considerations that influenced us as we developed the SRE framework for English-language learners. These influences reflect what we have learned as we have worked with SREs, as well as discoveries and insights about reading, learning, and English-language learners—such as how literacy and orality are related—that recent research, theory and practice have revealed. The influences on the basic idea of SREs, as well as on our belief that they are likely to be useful for English-language learners, are many and varied. They include learning concepts such as scaffolding, constructs such as schema theory, concerns about English-language learners such as the importance of modulating instruction for their needs and strengths and their experiencing success in reading, and pedagogical notions such as the power of active teaching.

Chapters 5, 6, and 7 parallel each other. Chapter 5, "Prereading Activities," describes ten types of prereading activities and then gives specific examples of each of them. Chapter 6, "During-Reading Activities," describes five types of during-reading activities and then gives examples of each of these. Chapter 7 "Postreading Activities," describes and provides examples of eight types of postreading activities. Because we believe that concrete models are extremely useful in precisely conveying our meaning, we have included many detailed examples. Along with each example, we have included a discussion of the types of reading selections with which the activity would be useful and our reflections on the activity— our assessment of it, some of its unique features, and some general pedagogical considerations it raises.

Chapter 8, "Comprehensive Scaffolded Reading Experiences for English-Language Learners," begins by describing the thinking that goes into selecting a set of prereading, reading, and postreading activities that is likely to maximize the comprehension, learning, and enjoyment of English-language learners reading a particular text. The chapter then presents five examples of complete SREs, selected to convey the wide range of scaffolding possible. Each example includes a detailed description of activities of the lesson, a discussion of why we included the specific activities we did, a discussion of what some other options might be, and some general considerations the example suggests.

Chapter 9, "Incorporating Scaffolded Reading Experiences in Your Classroom With English-Language Learners," addresses some considerations to keep in mind as you begin using SREs with English-language learners. First, it describes some of the decisions you face in matters such as how frequently to use SREs and how much scaffolding to provide. Second, we emphasize that the SRE is not, in itself, a comprehensive reading program and place the SRE approach in the context of a comprehensive reading program by describing aspects of other components that are vital to English-language learners' reading successes.

In the last chapter, "Text Difficulty and Accessibility for English-Language Learners," we talk about ways of choosing appropriate reading selections for your English-language learners. We also discuss issues to think about in order to maximize English-language learners' success when reading texts of varying difficulty.

Finally, to make the book as useful and easy to use as possible, the sample activities presented are indexed by grade level, the children's literature cited is indexed by title and author, and the book itself is indexed by author and subject.

As we have mentioned, besides a general description of the scaffolded reading approach and the ideas that inform it, this book contains a number of detailed samples of SRE activities for English-language learners. These activities are designed to illustrate the general ideas we discuss, to serve as models you can use to develop similar activities for your classroom, and to suggest ways to modulate instruction for English-language learners. The activities are suggested to act as springboards for critical and creative thinking as you reflect on how these ideas might be implemented in your particular teaching situation. They are not meant to be scripts or blueprints. As you are well aware, every reading situation is slightly different from every other one. Moreover, given the dynamics of actual classrooms, even the most carefully crafted lessons have a way of taking on a new life of their own. At the same time, although your plans should and will often change as they unfold in the classroom, having carefully considered plans for facilitating your English-language learners' reading puts you in the best possible position to make informed, on-the-spot decisions as you scaffold and encourage your students in their journeys to become competent, active, purposeful, avid, and lifelong readers.

Finally, we envision teachers using this book in a variety of ways. Not all readers will want to read every page of the book. For instance, some readers will come to the book with very little knowledge about important educational issues surrounding English-language learners and about teaching reading. These readers might find each chapter of the book interesting and helpful, and they might want to read for detail. Other readers will approach this book already having considerable background knowledge about English-language learner issues and about Scaffolded Reading Experiences. These readers might prefer to glance at chapters 2 and 3 and then skim the remainder of the book. For these readers, the greatest benefit of the book might be the indices that lead them directly to particular examples of activities and books to use as they plan instruction for their students. Yet other readers may be more interested in thoroughly reading about activities in their own content area, such as science or social studies; and they might choose to just skim sample activities that do not deal with their content area in order to get ideas for activities they can use by substituting texts in their content area for the ones we have used in the activities. We hope that we have organized this book so that you find it easy to meet your personal needs and goals for improving your instruction for English-language learners.

References

Anderson, L. M. (1989). Classroom instruction. In M. C. Reynolds (Ed.), *Knowledge base for the beginning teacher* (pp. 101–115). New York: Pergamon. Excellent review of research and thinking on classroom instruction.

Anderson, R. C., & Armbruster, B. B. (1990). Some maxims for learning and instruction. *Teachers College Record, 91*, 396–408. Scaffolding is one of nine central maxims the authors see as undergirding effective instruction.

Applebee, A. N., & Langer, J. L. (1983). Reading and writing as natural language activities. *Language Arts, 60*(2), 68–175. One of the earliest articles to examine the classroom applications of scaffolding.

Au, K. H., & Jordan, C. (1981). Teaching reading to Hawaiian children: Finding a culturally appropriate solution. In H. Trueba, G. P. Guthrie, & K. H.-P. Au (Eds.), *Culture and the bilingual classroom: Studies in classroom ethnography* (pp. 139–152). Rowley, MA: Newbury House. An oft-cited study of teaching in the Kamehameha Elementary Education Program in Hawaii in which teachers implement a scaffolded way of teaching.

August, D., & Hakuta, K. (1997). *Improving schooling for language-minority children: A research agenda*. Washington, DC: National Academy Press. An ambitious review of selected research and theory on English-language learners. Suggests needed policy and research.

Beed, P. L., Hawkins, E. M., & Roller, C. M. (1991). Moving learners toward independence: The power of scaffolded instruction. *The Reading Teacher, 44*, 648–655. Discussion of the power of scaffolding in a tutoring program.

Brown, A. N., & Palincsar, A. M. (1989). Guided cooperative learning and individual knowledge acquisition. In L. B. Resnick (Ed.), *Knowing, learning, and instruction: Essays in honor of Robert Glaser* (pp. 393–451). Hillsdale, NJ: Lawrence Erlbaum. A detailed consideration of reciprocal teaching, with special attention to scaffolding.

Cazden, C. B. (1992). *Whole language plus: Essays in literacy in the United States and New Zealand.* New York: Teachers College Press. Cazden endorses scaffolding as one way in which teachers can go beyond merely immersing children in rich literacy environments, something she believes must be done if all children are to reach their full potential as readers and writers.

Constantino, R. (1994). A study concerning instruction of ESL students comparing all-English classroom teacher knowledge and English-as-a-second language teacher knowledge. *Journal of Education Issues of Language Minority Students, 13,* 37–57. An examination of teachers' knowledge about English-language learner issues.

Cooke, C. L. (2002). *The effects of scaffolding multicultural short stories on students' comprehension, response, and attitudes.* Unpublished doctoral dissertation, University of Minnesota, Minneapolis. Carefully done study, showing very positive effects of SREs.

Echevarria, J., Vogt, M. E., & Short, D. J. (2000). *Making content comprehensible for English language learners: The SIOP model.* Boston: Allyn & Bacon. Describes the Sheltered Instruction Observation Protocol model for teaching English-language learners and provides many illustrations of its implementation using classroom scenarios.

Faltis, C., & Hudelson, S. (1994). Learning English as an additional language in K–12 schools. *TESOL Quarterly, 28,* 457–468. Examines aspects of the conditions under which English-language learners study.

Fitzgerald, J., & Cummins, J. (1999). Essay book reviews: Bridging disciplines to critique a national agenda for language-minority children's schooling. *Reading Research Quarterly, 34,* 378–390. A critique of *Improving schooling for language-minority children: A research agenda* (August & Hakuta, 1997).

Fournier, D. N. E., & Graves, M. F. (2002). Scaffolding adolescents' comprehension of short stories. *Journal of Adolescent and Adult Literacy, 40,* 30–39. Experimental study showing a positive effect of SREs used with middle-school students.

Garcia, G. E., Willis, A. I., & Harris, V. J. (1998). Appropriating and creating space for difference in literacy research. *Journal of Literacy Research, 30,* 181–186. Commentary on multicultural issues in literacy research.

Gersten, R., & Baker, S. (2000). What we know about effective instructional practices for English-language learners. *Exceptional Children, 66,* 454–470. A synthesis of research and professional views on effective instructional practices with English-language learners.

Graves, M. F., & Graves, B. B. (1994). *Scaffolding reading experiences: Designs for student success.* Norwood, MA: Christopher-Gordon. The first full-length book on SREs and the underlying model for this book.

Graves, M. F., & Liang, L. A. (in press). On-line resources for fostering understanding and higher-level thinking in senior high school students. In *National Reading Conference yearbook.* Multifaceted study showing positive effects of SREs.

Hakuta, K. (1986). *Mirror of language: The debate on bilingualism.* New York: Basic Books. Argues for benefits of bilingualism.

Hakuta, K., & Gould, L. J. (1987). Synthesis of research on bilingual education. *Educational Leadership, 44,* 38–45. Critiques selected studies on bilingual education programs.

Palincsar, A. S. (1986). The role of dialogue in providing scaffolded instruction. *Educational Psychologist, 21*(1 & 2), 73–93. A detailed look at dialogue as scaffolding.

Pearson, P. D. (1996). Reclaiming the center. In M. F. Graves, P. van den Broek, & B. M. Taylor (Eds.), *The first R: A right of all children* (pp. 259–274). New York: Teachers College Press. Includes a strong endorsement for scaffolding and the Scaffolded Reading Experience itself.

Pearson, P. D., & Gallagher, M. (1983). The instruction of reading comprehension. *Contemporary Educational Psychology, 8,* 317–344. An insightful view of comprehension instruction.

Peregoy, S. F., & Boyle, O. F. (1997). *Reading, writing, & learning in ESL: A resource book for K–12 teachers* (2nd ed.). New York: Longman. Provides ideas for teaching English-language learners.

Pressley, M. (1998). *Reading instruction that works: The case for balanced teaching.* New York: The Guilford Press. An excellent review of much of the research on reading instruction and a strong endorsement for scaffolding.

Raphael, T. M. (2000). Balancing literature and instruction: Lessons from the Book Club project. In B. M. Taylor, M. F. Graves, & P. van den Broek (Eds.), *Reading for meaning: Fostering comprehension in the middle grades* (pp. 70–94). New York: Teachers College Press. Scaffolding is one of the cornerstones of Raphael's Book Club approach.

Rodgers, E. M. (2000). Language matters: When is a scaffold really a scaffold? *Forty-ninth yearbook of the National Reading Conference* (pp. 78-90).

An exploration of the concept of scaffolding. Chicago: National Reading Conference.

Routman, R. (2000). *Conversations*. Portsmouth, NH: Heinemann. Presents strategies for teaching, learning, and evaluating.

Schirmer, B. R., Casbon, J., & Twiss, L. L. (1996). Innovative literacy practices for ESL learners (diverse learners in the classroom). *The Reading Teacher, 49*, 412–414. Discusses reading and writing instruction for English-language learners.

Snow, C. E. (1987). Beyond conversation: Second language learners' acquisition of description and explanation. In J. P. Lantolf & A. Labarca (Eds.), *Research in second language learning: Focus on the classroom* (pp. 3–16). Norwood, NJ: Ablex. Presents research results on English-language learners' English development.

Snow, C. E., Burns, M. S., & Griffin, P. (Eds.). (1998). *Preventing reading difficulties in young children*. Washington, DC: National Academy Press. Seminal review of research on what makes early reading instruction and experiences effective.

Taylor, B. M., Pearson, P. D., Clark, K. F., & Walpole, S. (2000). Beating the odds in teaching all children to read. *Elementary School Journal, 101*, 121–165. A national study highlighting scaffolding as one of the most effective instructional approaches.

Tharp, R., & Gallimore, R. (1988). *Rousing minds to life: Teaching, learning and schooling in social context*. New York: Cambridge University Press. Explores issues and practices in teaching English-language learners and bilingual learners.

Vygotsky, L. S. (1978). *Mind in society: The development of higher psychological processes*. Cambridge, MA: Harvard University Press. The source of the zone of proximal development concept.

Wharton-McDonald, R., Pressley, M., & Hampston, J. M. (1998). Literacy instruction in nine first-grade classrooms: Teacher characteristics and student achievement. *Elementary School Journal, 99*, 101–128. Empirical study revealing the scaffolding provided by effective teachers.

Wong Fillmore, L., & Valadez, C. (1986). Teaching bilingual learners. In M. C. Wittrock (Ed.), *Handbook of research on teaching* (pp. 648–685). New York: Macmillan. A critical review of research on the education of bilingual students.

Wood, D. J., Bruner, J. S., & Ross, G. (1976). The role of tutoring in problem-solving. *Journal of Child Psychology and Psychiatry, 17*(2), 89–100. An introduction to the concept of *scaffolding* and an insightful examination of parent–child interactions.

CHAPTER 2

What Is a Scaffolded Reading Experience for English-Language Learners?

In this chapter, we explain what a Scaffolded Reading Experience for English-language learners is and how you create one. We also discuss some matters that are likely to be particularly important when creating Scaffolded Reading Experiences for English-language learners, and we give you some examples. A Scaffolded Reading Experience (SRE) is a set of prereading, during-reading, and postreading activities specifically designed to assist English-language learners in successfully reading, understanding, and learning from a particular selection. You create an SRE by first considering your students, the text they are reading, and what you want them to gain from their reading. Then, you consider a range of options you might use and prepare for your students a set of prereading, during-reading, and postreading activities that will assist them in successfully reading the text and achieving the purposes you have set.

Below, we list the options for creating an SRE. As you can see, the list includes 10 types of prereading activities, 5 types of during-reading activities, and 8 types of postreading activities. On the following pages, we say a few words about prereading, during-reading, and postreading activities generally, and then describe each of the sorts of activities that you might use before students read, as they are reading, and after they read. Three issues are important to keep in mind as you consider the SRE framework and the activities. First, the framework presents a list of options. No single SRE will contain all of the activities. Second, the purpose of the list is to suggest a wide variety of activities. It is certainly not intended to limit the activities you might use or to suggest that you need to rigidly classify activities into one category or another. Moreover, activities listed in one part of the framework can sometimes be useful in other parts. For example, *relating the reading to students' lives* could be something you do after students read a selection as well as before they read it. Similarly, although we list *writing* as a postreading activity, it can be used as a prereading or during-reading activity as, for example, when students write a list of what they know about a topic before reading or take notes while reading. Additionally, two of the activities listed as prereading activities— *using students' native language* and *involving English-language learner communities, parents, siblings*—are every bit as appropriate when used as during-reading or postreading activities. We don't list them again in those sections simply to avoid redundancy. Third, our examples are mainly from trade books, but the SRE framework and most, if not all, of the activities we suggest are also applicable to other types of texts—basal series, textbooks, high interest–easy reading series, magazine articles, and so on.

**Possible Components of a Scaffolded
Reading Experience for English-Language Learners**

Prereading Activities
    Motivating
    Relating the reading to students' lives
    Building or activating background knowledge
    Providing text-specific knowledge
    Preteaching vocabulary
    Preteaching concepts
    Prequestioning, predicting, and direction setting
    Suggesting strategies
    Using students' native language
    Involving English-language learner communities, parents, siblings
During-Reading Activities
    Silent reading
    Reading to students
    Supported reading
    Oral reading by students
    Modifying the text
Postreading Activities
    Questioning
    Discussion
    Writing
    Drama
    Artistic, graphic, and nonverbal activities
    Application and outreach activities
    Building connections
    Reteaching

Prereading Activities

Prereading activities prepare English-language learners to read the upcoming selection. They can serve a number of functions, including getting students interested in reading the selection, reminding students of things they already know that will help them understand and enjoy the selection, and preteaching aspects of the selection that may be difficult. While prereading activities are important for all students, they are likely to be particularly important to many English-language learners because often such students are not experienced with the topics in texts used in U.S. schools and because the vocabulary and idioms in the materials they encounter may be new to them. Providing adequate preparation is a good way to help to ensure that English-language learners participate in the most enjoyable, rewarding, and successful reading experience possible (Echevarria, Vogt, & Short, 2000; Perez & Torres-Guzman, 1992).

Prereading activities are widely recommended for English-language learners (e.g., Echevarria et al., 2000; Gersten & Baker, 2000; Perez & Torres-Guzman, 1992; Rousseau, Tam, & Ramnarain, 1993) and for students in general (e.g., Aebersold & Field, 1997, Ciborowski, 1992; Fountas & Pinnell, 1996; Readence, Moore, & Rickelman, 2000; Schoenbach, Greenleaf, Cziko, & Huriwtz, 1999; Yopp & Yopp, 1992). A number of different types of prereading activities have been suggested. In creating the list of possible prereading activities for SREs, we have attempted to list a relatively small set of categories that suggest a large number of useful activities teachers and students can engage in. As we have noted, we list 10 categories of prereading activities.

By *motivating* activities we refer to any activity designed to interest students in a selection and entice them to read it. For example, to motivate students, a teacher might make statements and pose questions such as "We're going to read about the solar system—about the Earth and other planets. Why do you suppose it would be important for you to know about the solar system?"

In many cases, motivational materials can accomplish some other purpose besides motivating students. As in the above example, questions may serve both to motivate students and to focus their attention as they read. We list *motivating* activities as a separate category, however, because we believe that they should be a very frequent part of an SRE. Motivating activities are likely to be particularly important when introducing material to English-language learners because such students frequently have to devote so much attention to understanding new concepts and vocabulary, as well as to general language processing, that the learning and reading activity can seem daunting to them. By using motivational activities, teachers can spark interest in students, and this interest can sustain them when the reading is challenging.

Relating the reading to students' lives helps students to make the text more meaningful by thinking about the text in relation to some personal meaning. Many English-language learners will not automatically see the relevance to their lives of the selections they read. Therefore, relating the reading to students' lives can be extremely important. For example, if you're in California and your newly arrived Asian students are reading Betsy Byers' *Sam's Story*—which deals with a boy's bravery when a tornado hits his home in the Midwest—you might point out to your students that, while they are unlikely to experience tornadoes, they may have to deal with earthquakes or floods. Or, for instance, before reading a new text, a teacher might say, "We are going to read about how the president of the United States gets the job. If you have lived in another country, can you tell me about how the leader there gets the job?" Then, the teacher might ask students to read to find out how it is the same or different in the United States. Or, after reading a text, the teacher might ask students if there were any characters or events in the text that they especially identify with. By relating the text content to something similar in students' own lives, students can use what they know from their own experiences to better understand the new information. They can also use what they learn in texts to help them think about their own lives and problems.

Building or activating background knowledge is often necessary for English-language learners to get the most from what they read (Gersten & Baker, 2000; Saunders, O'Brien, Lennon, & McLean, 1998). When you *build* background knowledge, you introduce concepts that are central to the meaning of the text—concepts that students don't know in advance, but are helpful to understanding the text. For instance, if your English-language learners are about to read about animal life in circuses, but have never encountered the concept CIRCUS, then it will be important to build their background knowledge about circuses.

When you *activate* background knowledge, you prompt students to bring to consciousness already known information that will help them to understand the upcoming text. For example, let us say a group of your sixth graders is researching the plight of migrant workers. Before these students read a story you have recommended from *The Circuit*, Francisco Jiménez's award-winning collection of stories based on his own experiences as a child migrant worker in California, you might encourage them to discuss what they have already learned about migrant workers from their previous reading or experience.

In addition to activating background knowledge, it is sometimes necessary to build background knowledge, knowledge that the author—

usually tacitly—has presupposed readers already possess. For example, in reading the stories in *The Circuit*, you might find that Jiménez presupposes some specific knowledge of California geography, knowledge that you're pretty sure your English-language learners lack. In this case, supplying the information would make good sense.

In contrast to activities that build or activate background knowledge, activities that *provide text-specific knowledge* give students information that is contained in the reading selection. Providing students with advance information on aspects of the content of a selection is certainly justified if the selection is difficult or densely packed with information. For many English-language learners, even materials that you might normally consider "reader friendly" may present many unfamiliar concepts. For these children, providing the concepts orally or visually in advance of the reading may not only be justified, it may be imperative.

Preteaching vocabulary and *preteaching concepts* are closely related activities and thus can be conveniently considered together. We list these two as different activities to contrast two ideas: teaching words that are merely new labels for concepts that students already know versus teaching words that represent new and potentially difficult concepts. For English-language learners, it is often difficult for teachers to know when words are labels for concepts already known and when the concept itself must be taught. For example, a fourth-grade teacher can just about always assume that all of her students, including her English-language learners, understand the concept of RED, and so teaching the word *crimson* would be giving a new label to a known concept. However, suppose the three English-language learners in her class recently arrived from a small pueblo in Guatemala where they attended 2 years of school and lived with no running water or electricity. She would probably assume the word *igloo* represents a known concept for her other fourth graders, but she could reasonably wonder if her English-language learners would already understand the concept of IGLOO or even those of SNOW and ICE.

When the basic concepts are known, up to a half dozen or so new words can easily and quickly be presented before students read an upcoming selection. However, when the basic concepts are not known, teaching them usually takes significant amounts of time and requires powerful instruction. This generally means that at most only two or three words representing new concepts can be taught before students read a selection.

We have listed *prequestioning, predicting, and direction setting* activities together because we see them as three methods of accomplishing the same task. With any of them, you are focusing students' attention and telling them what is important to look for as they read. Such focusing is often necessary because without it students, especially English-language learners, may not know what to attend to.

In *suggesting strategies* the key word is *suggesting*. SREs are not designed to *teach* reading strategies, for example, to teach students how to make inferences or how to summarize a selection. Helping English-language learners to develop strategic thinking is addressed in the national *ESL (English-as-a-Second-Language) Standards for Pre-K–12 Students* (Teachers of English to Speakers of Other Languages, 1997). Many English-language learners who are devoting a lot of their mental energy to language processing may have difficulty initiating an active role in using reading strategies. Especially for these students, as part of an SRE you may want to alert students when a particular strategy they have already been taught is likely to be useful, perhaps saying something like "Since this chapter has a lot of new information, it would be a good idea to write a four- or five-sentence summary of it soon after you've read it." For more information on why you might want to teach strategies even though doing so is not part of the SRE framework, we suggest you read chapter 7 of *Reading Instruction That Works* (Pressley, 2002) and the RAND Reading Study Group report (2002) For specific information on how to teach strategies, we suggest chapter 7 of *Teaching Reading in the 21st Century* (Graves, Juel, & Graves, 2004).

Our next category of activities is *using students' native language.* When the going gets tough, when the gulf between students' proficiency in English and the task posed by the reading becomes wide and deep, one extremely helpful alternative is likely to be to use students' native language. Strategic use of native language is highly recommended by many professionals who work with English-language learners (Gersten & Baker, 2000). You might, for example, present a preview of a book like Seymour Simon's *Earthquakes* in Spanish. Or you might give your Spanish-speaking students directions for reading *Earthquakes* in Spanish. As we said earlier, we have not listed *using students' native language* in our lists of during-reading or postreading activities in order to avoid redundancy. It is important to remember, however, that employing students' native language is just as viable an option as they are reading a text or after they have read a text as it is before they read. Thus, you might want to give Filipino students a study guide in Tagalog, or you might want to allow Hmong students to sometimes respond to what they read in Hmong.

There are other ways to bring students' native language into the classroom as well. That's where *involving English-language learner communities, parents, siblings* becomes tremendously valuable. In all probability, other students in your class, students in other classes in your school, and people out in the community do speak the language or languages spoken by your English-language learners. Getting help from these children and adults has tremendous advantages. The most obvious of these is that they can communicate effectively with your students who are not yet proficient in English. Another advantage is that, by helping your students, your resource people—if their English is not well developed—will improve their own English abilities. Still another advantage is the satisfaction, sense of belonging, and sense of pride that the resource people will get from assisting in your classroom. It is often difficult to convey to parents who are not proficient in English that they are welcome at school, that you really want to work with them to help their children succeed. By bringing parents into the school as resource people, you convey to them that they are not only welcome but needed! It is, to use a phrase that's trite but really does fit here, a "win–win" situation. Again, as is the case with using students' native language, engaging people resources is just as viable an option while students are reading a text or after they have read a text as it is before they read.

During-Reading Activities

During-reading activities include both things that students themselves do as they are reading and things that you do to assist them as they are reading. Like prereading activities, during-reading activities are frequently recommended for English-language learners (e.g., Echevarria et al., 2000; Gersten & Baker, 2000; Peregoy & Boyle, 1997) and for learners in general (e.g., Aebersold & Field, 1997, Bean, Valerio, & Stevens, 1999; Beck, McKeown, Hamilton, & Kucan, 1997; Ciborowski, 1992; Fountas & Pinnell, 1996; Richardson, 2000; Schoenbach et al., 1999; Wood, Lapp, & Flood, 1992; Yopp & Yopp, 1992). In creating the list of possible during-reading activities for SREs for English-language learners, we have again attempted to list a relatively small set of categories that suggests a large number of useful activities that will help your students to gain more from what they read. In this case, we describe five categories of activities.

We list *silent reading* as the first during-reading activity because we believe strongly that silent reading should be the most frequently used during-reading activity for English-language learners. The central long-term goal of reading is to prepare students to become accomplished lifelong readers, and most of the reading students do in life—in the upper elementary grades, in the middle grades, in secondary school, in college, and in the world outside of school—will be silent reading. While more than practice is required to develop proficient readers, it is both a basic rule of learning and everyday common sense that one needs to repeatedly practice the skill he or she is attempting to master. In general, if teachers choose appropriate selections for students to read and have adequately prepared them to read the selections, then students will often be able to silently read the selections on their own. Also, many English-language learners are much more comfortable reading silently than reading aloud, or at least reading silently *before* reading aloud.

For English-language learners, choice of material—including whenever possible ensuring that the reading level of the material is matched to the reading level of the learner—and your support, including adequate preparation, are likely to be especially important keys to a successful silent reading experience. It is also important for teachers to keep in mind that English-language learners are often more proficient at reading than at listening.

Reading to students can serve a number of functions. Depending on the oral English levels of your students, hearing a story or expository material read aloud can be a very pleasurable experience for many youngsters. It also serves as a model of good oral reading. Reading the first few paragraphs of a piece to English-language learners can help ease them into the material and serve as an enticement to read the rest of the selection on their own. For students whose oral English abilities outpace their English-reading abilities, reading to them can make texts that otherwise might be inaccessible to them quite accessible. Also, some texts really come alive when they are read aloud. In these instances, reading aloud, or playing an audiotape for the same purpose, may be particularly appropriate. The power of Martin Luther King Jr.'s "I Have a Dream" speech, for example, is certainly better understood when listening to an actual recording of the speech than when reading the material silently. Also, many English-language learners at more advanced levels find audiotapes useful because they can replay sections to better hear and understand what is said. Of course, reading some or all of the text to your English-language learners in their native language or having more advanced students or other resource people do so is another option.

Supported reading refers to a broad range of activities. It includes any activity that you use to focus students' attention on particular aspects of a text as they read. Professionals who work with English-language learners tend to recommend supported reading as a very important aspect of English-language learner instruction (Gersten & Baker, 2000). Supported reading can be used to assist students in such thought-demanding activities as selecting main ideas, focusing on specific themes, and forming generalizations. Supported reading often begins as a prereading activity, perhaps with you setting directions for reading, and is then carried out as students are actually reading. For example, to help students understand ethnic stereotypes, you may have them jot down some of the adjectives used to describe individuals of different ethnicity as they read and compare two articles on the same current event written in *Ebony* and *Newsweek*. Such supported reading activities can help students really learn from their reading.

To be sure, one long-term goal of schooling is to enable and motivate students to read without your assistance. Thus, with less challenging selections and as students become increasingly competent over time, your support can be less specific and less directive and perhaps consist only of a suggestion such as "After reading this chapter, I have an idea for you. Try reading it with a partner and stopping after each section to take notes. This should help you understand and remember the material better."

Oral reading by students is a relatively frequent activity in some classrooms but a much less frequent one in others. As we previously mentioned, most of the reading students will do in their lives is silent reading. Nonetheless, oral reading has its place. Oral reading is needed in the early stages of play production. Also, poignant or particularly well-written passages of prose are often appropriate for oral reading. Reading orally can also be helpful when the class or a group of students is studying a passage and trying to decide on alternate interpretations or on just what is and is not explicitly stated in the passage. Additionally, students often like to read their own writing orally. Moreover, oral reading is extremely useful for diagnosing students' reading proficiency. Thus, while oral reading need not be a frequent activity, it can be a useful one and something to include among the many alternatives you offer students.

However, we strongly recommend that oral reading in front of classmates be reserved for those English-language learners whose English reading fluency is well developed. For English-language learners who do not yet read English fluently, oral reading in front of peers may be a difficult and even painful experience. Pronouncing English words in ways that are dialectically similar to peer native-English speakers can be extremely difficult, and many second-language speakers, especially adolescents, are very self-conscious about pronunciation. Consequently, reading orally in front of peers can be a risky situation for many English learners.

When English-language learners do read orally, it is best to de-emphasize pronunciation. Instead, as students are learning to read English, it is likely to be a good idea to ignore pronunciation errors and support their movement toward understanding what they read (Nurss & Hough, 1992). Also, many English learners move through a silent period, a phase during which they can understand somewhat but choose not to make an effort to speak (Terrell, 1981). Teachers can expect students in such a "silent period" to continue to learn and grow, but they should also respect that many students need to have time to gain more confidence and to realize that others in the classroom will support and encourage their oral language growth.

Modifying the text is sometimes necessary to make the reading material more accessible to English-language learners. This is likely to be especially true for English-language learners in the early stages of their

English development. For example, if a chapter in a social studies or science textbook is particularly lengthy and contains many concepts that will be new to students, you might want to select parts of the chapter to read. For some English-language learners, you might even rewrite the text to simplify it, perhaps making an outline-like version for them to read. Although this is not something most teachers have the time to do very often, it can be an excellent task for community resource people.

Another way to modify the text is to draw a pictorial or graphic representation of the main ideas and ask students to examine these representations. Or you might modify a text by substituting a version in the students' native language for the English version. Still another means of modifying a text is to find an alternative text that better matches your students' proficiency. Suppose, for example, some of your eighth-grade English-language learners have difficulty reading the history text your class is using. You may want to have them read a parallel chapter from a fifth-grade U.S. history text in lieu of your eighth-grade book. At other times, you may feel your textbook's treatment of a topic is inadequate and you choose to find supplemental readings to help develop your students' understanding. Each of these cases represents an example of modifying the text to increase the possibility that your students will have successful reading experiences.

Postreading Activities

As is the case with prereading and during-reading activities, postreading activities serve a variety of purposes for English-language learners. They provide opportunities for students to synthesize and organize information gleaned and created from reading the text and to understand and recall important points and details. They provide opportunities for students to respond to and evaluate information and ideas, the author's stance, their own stances, and the quality of the text itself. They provide opportunities for students to respond to a text in a variety of ways, for example, to reflect on the meaning of the text, to compare differing texts and ideas, to imagine themselves as one of the characters in the text, to synthesize information from different sources, to engage in a variety of creative activities, and to apply what they have learned within the classroom walls and in the world beyond the classroom. You can also use postreading activities to evaluate your students' understandings and responses.

Not surprisingly given their many functions, postreading activities are widely recommended for English-language learners (e.g., Echevarria et al., 2000; Peregoy & Boyle, 1997) and for other learners (e.g., Aebersold

& Field, 1997; Alvermann, 2000; Bean et al., 1999; Ciborowski, 1992; Fountas & Pinnell, 1996; Gambrell & Almasi, 1996; Schoenbach et al., 1999; Wood et al., 1992; Yopp & Yopp, 1992). In most classrooms, they are very frequently used. In creating the list of possible postreading activities for SREs, we have again attempted to list a relatively small set of categories that suggests a large number of useful activities, in this case eight categories of activities.

Questioning, either orally or in writing, is a frequently used and frequently warranted activity. Some teachers use questions almost exclusively as a means of assessing students' understanding. While this is one valid use of questions, it is important to realize that there are many *instructional* functions wrapped up in questions that can greatly benefit students. Questions can encourage and promote students' higher order thinking, and they can nudge students' interpretations, analysis, and evaluation of the ideas created and gleaned from reading. Questions can also elicit creative and personal responses, such as when you ask "How did you feel when . . . ?" "What do you think would have happened in the experiment if . . . ?" Of course, teachers are not the only ones who should be asking questions after reading. Students can ask questions of each other, they can ask you questions, and they can ask questions they plan to answer through further reading or by searching the Internet.

Some sort of *discussion,* whether it is discussion in pairs or small groups or discussion involving the entire class, is also very often appropriate. Although the research so far on discussions with English-language learners has been scant and not overwhelmingly positive (Echevarria, 1995), discussions are generally considered to be good ways of helping English-language learners, but only if the learner feels comfortable and safe in the group and is able to take risks with his or her developing language (Goldenberg, 1992–1993). When a discussion is well structured, it can reinforce the main points of the material, thereby helping students who may have had difficulty understanding some of basics of the material. It also gives the teacher an opportunity to extend and raise the level of all students' thinking about the material. Equally importantly, discussion gives students opportunities to offer their personal interpretations and responses to a text and to hear those of others. Discussion is also a vehicle for assessing whether or not reading goals have been achieved and to evaluate what went right about the reading experience, what went wrong, and what might be done differently in the future.

Writing is a postreading task that probably should be used frequently with English-language learners. In recent years, a good deal of well-warranted emphasis has been placed on the fact that reading and writing are complementary activities and ought often to be dealt with together. Writing can be used to help English-language learners discover and learn ideas, understandings, and their own responses, to reinforce concepts gleaned and created during reading, and to assist later recall of those ideas, understandings, and concepts.

Writing can be particularly useful for assisting English-language learners, especially those in the earlier phases of English development. When teachers consistently use writing as a means of instruction, students are often more comfortable using writing than they are with responding aloud. Also, for those who are in the early phases of English learning and have some native-language writing facility, encouraging writing in the native language is likely to be extremely beneficial. Of course, if you can't read or speak the students' native language, you must rely on the students' own incentives and accuracy. However, even though this situation is less than optimal, writing in the native language without feedback is probably more beneficial than not writing at all. To make writing more feasible for students with very minimal English skills, you may sometimes have to ask students to write texts of just a few words until they gain more proficiency.

Drama offers a range of opportunities for English-language learners to get actively involved in responding to what they have read. By drama, we refer to any sort of production involving action and movement. Given this definition, short plays, skits, and pantomimes are among the many possibilities. Drama often gives English-language learners a special boost in learning and participating in a class because ideas and concepts in the reading materials become more evident through facial expressions, gestures, and other movements. Additionally, practicing the lines of a play is a wonderful situation for building fluency.

Artistic, graphic, and nonverbal activities constitute additional possibilities for postreading endeavors. In this broad category, we include visual art, graphics, music, dance, and media productions such as videos, slide shows, and audiotapes, as well as constructive activities that you might not typically think of as artistic. Probably the most frequent members of this last category are graphics of some sort—maps, charts, time lines, family trees, symbols, diagrams and the like. Other possibilities include constructing models or bringing in artifacts that are somehow responses to the selection read.

Artistic and nonverbal activities allow English-language learners to think and work in ways that fully engage their capacities without having to use oral or written language (Gersten & Baker, 2000). Artistic and nonverbal activities are also particularly useful because they are fun, may be a little different from typical school tasks, and provide opportunities for students to express themselves in a variety of ways, thus creating situations in which students of varying talents and abilities can excel. This is not to say that such activities are frills, something to be done just to provide variety. In many situations and for many students, including English-language learners, artistic and nonverbal activities offer the greatest potential for learning information and for responding to what they have read.

In the *application and outreach activities,* we include both concrete and direct applications, such as conducting a survey after reading about simple survey methods, and less direct ones, such as having students work together to change some aspect of student interaction in your classroom after reading about summits and councils on racial tensions in the United States. Here, we also include activities that extend beyond the campus. For instance, English-language learners might interview their older relatives to see if things in their native country were actually the way they are described in the text they read in class. Obviously, there is a great range of application and outreach options.

Building connections is a tremendously important part of making reading meaningful for students, and with English-language learners connections that would be automatically made by native speakers may have to be explicitly pointed out (Gersten & Baker, 2000). Only by helping students build connections between texts and between the ideas they encounter in reading and other parts of their lives can we ensure that they to come to really value reading, read enough that they get to be really proficient readers, and create, remember, and apply important understandings from reading.

Several sorts of connections are important. These include relating the material to students' lives, current issues, and previously learned material. For example, after a group of Somali youngsters living in New York City read a description of the daily life of youngsters in a small town in the Midwest, they could compare these youngsters' daily lives to their lives in New York and their lives in Somalia.

Reteaching is also an important activity for teachers of English-language learners. Because students' learning is a joint responsibility between the teacher and students, and because the best planned lessons sometimes go awry, it is important for us to always keep the idea of reteaching in our minds. Did the student attain our goals in the lesson? If not, we need to think about the reasons and try to rework our lessons so that students do achieve success.

Planning Scaffolded Reading Experiences for English-Language Learners

We have described a fairly lengthy list of possible activities; in fact, as we have already noted, far too many to be used with a single selection. Again, however, this is a list of *options*. From this set of possibilities, you choose only those that are appropriate for your particular students reading a particular text for a particular purpose. Suppose, for example, you are an English-language learner teacher working with some fourth- and fifth-grade students in a pullout setting. In their classrooms, the teachers want all of their students to learn about selected features of Native American life. They have introduced the first chapter of Michael L. Cooper's *Indian School*, and their goal is for the students to learn the most important information presented in this chapter. You decide to strongly support your English-language learners in learning the content. You might provide prereading instruction that includes a motivational activity, the preteaching of some difficult vocabulary such as *interpreter* and *proposition*, and a questioning activity—an activity in which students pose *who*, *when*, *where*, *what*, *how*, and *why* questions they expect to be answered in the chapter. Next, for the during-reading portion of the lesson, you might read part of the chapter orally and then have students read the rest silently, looking for answers to their questions. Finally, after students have finished the chapter, they might answer the questions they posed during prereading. Here is a list of the activities for this SRE for this group of English-language learners reading the first chapter of *Indian School:*

Prereading:	Motivating
	Preteaching vocabulary
	Questioning
During Reading:	Reading to students
	Silent reading
Postreading:	Questioning
	Discussion

There are two characteristics of this example particularly worth recognizing at this point. For one thing, this combination of prereading, during-reading, and postreading activities is only one of a number of combinations you could have selected. For another, you selected the activities you did based on your assessment of the students, the selection they were reading, and their purpose in reading the selection.

We can again highlight the fact that SREs vary considerably by giving another example. Suppose the same fourth- and fifth-grade English-language learners are reading something in their classroom that you think is relatively easy for them, something like Andrew Clements' award-winning *Frindle*. Suppose further that their primary purpose for reading the story is simply to enjoy this thought-provoking yet fast-paced, humorous tale. In this case, your prereading instruction might consist of only a brief motivational activity, the during-reading portion might consist entirely of students reading the novel silently, and the postreading portion might consist of their voluntarily discussing the parts of the story they found most humorous or interesting. Here is the list of activities for this SRE for *Frindle:*

Prereading:	Motivating
During Reading:	Reading to students
	Silent reading
Postreading:	Optional small-group discussion

It is, as you can see, much shorter than the one for *Indian School.* It's short because neither your students, the story itself, nor the purpose for reading the story requires a longer and more supportive SRE.

Now consider a third example, one which allows us to introduce the concept of DIFFERENTIATED SCAFFOLDED READING EXPERIENCES. This time let's say you are the regular classroom teacher in a fifth-grade class that includes four English-language learners whose English reading skills are considerably less well developed than those of the native-English speakers. The class is reading *Frindle,* and your goal is the same as it was before: for all of your students to enjoy this thought-provoking, fast-paced, and humorous tale. However, the four English-language learners in your class are not going to enjoy it unless you give them some additional assistance—*more scaffolding.* You provide this scaffolding by giving these four students additional activities as part of their SRE. This more powerful version of the SRE might look like this, with the added or modified activities shown in bold:

Prereading:	Motivating
	Preteaching vocabulary
	Preteaching concepts
During Reading:	Reading to students
	Supported reading
Postreading:	**Large group discussion**
	Questioning
	Reteaching

In this SRE designed to more fully support your English-language learners, you have added two prereading activities: preteaching vocabulary, because the story contains some labels the students don't know, and preteaching concepts, because the story contains some words that represent new concepts. Then, in the during-reading portion of the SRE, you have substituted supported reading for silent reading, perhaps by giving students a set of questions that highlight the important parts of the story to answer as they read. Finally, in the postreading portion of the SRE, the four English-language learners join you in a group discussion, you guide them through and help them answer the questions you gave them as supported reading, and you do any reteaching that seems needed. The result of the extra support provided by the more powerful version of this differentiated SRE is that your English-language learners have a more successful, more enjoyable, and more rewarding reading experience than they would have had without the extra support.

We will provide a number of examples of differentiated SREs in chapters 5 through 8. At this point, however, we want to return to our discussion of the basic plan for an SRE. We can make the basic plan for an SRE more tangible and perhaps more memorable with the aid of the diagram below.

**Two Phases of a Scaffolded Reading
Experience for English-Language Learners**

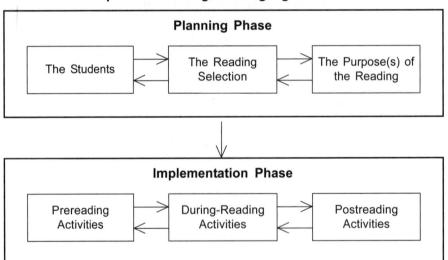

As shown in this diagram, a Scaffolded Reading Experience has two phases. The first phase is the planning phase, during which you design the entire experience. The second phase is the implementation phase and includes the activities you and your students engage in as a result of your planning.

Planning takes into account the students, the reading selection, and the reading purpose. Suppose you are a social studies teacher and you have a group of sixth graders, five of whom are English-language learners, and all of whom read in English at least at grade level. You want them to develop some fairly deep knowledge of river ecology, and the text you have chosen is quite demanding. Or consider a very different situation. Suppose you are working with these same sixth graders, your purpose is to have them read a humorous short story for the pure enjoyment of it, and you have chosen a fairly easy reading selection.

In both of these situations, your planning leads to the creation of the SRE itself and to its implementation. As shown in the lower half of the figure, the components of the implementation phase are prereading, during-reading, and postreading activities. With the river ecology text, we have already suggested that you want students to develop some fairly deep knowledge. This means that your SRE for the river ecology text is likely to be a substantial one, with prereading activities that prepare students to read the difficult text, during-reading activities that lead them to interact and grapple with the text in ways that help them understand and learn from it, and postreading activities that give them opportunities to check their understanding of the text and solidify their learning. Consequently, the class might spend 4 or 5 days reading the chapter and completing the learning activities you have assembled.

Conversely, with the humorous short story and the major goal of students being to simply enjoy the reading experience, your SRE is likely to be minimal. Prereading might consist of a brief motivational activity, students might read the story silently to themselves, and postreading might consist of an optional discussion. Consequently, the class might spend only a day or so reading and responding to the short story.

In addition to recognizing that the SRE framework results in very different SREs for different situations, it is important to recognize that the components of each phase of the SRE are interrelated. Consider the three components of the planning phase—the students, the text, and your purposes. Once you decide which students you're going to work with, there are only some texts you can use and some purposes you can expect to accomplish. Once you decide which text you are going to use, there are only some students who will be able to read it and some purposes you can hope to achieve with it. And once you decide what your purposes are, there are only some texts you can use to accomplish those purposes and some students who will be able to achieve them. The same sort of interdependency holds with the three components of the implementation phase. For example, if decide you are going to have some very challenging postreading tasks, you'll want to include prereading activities and during-reading activities that thoroughly prepare students to accomplish those challenging tasks.

Sample Planning Experience for an SRE

Consider the planning you might do and the SRE you might construct for a chapter on waves in a fifth-grade science text. Your students are fifth graders of average to high ability, and the class includes two English-language learners who have attended your school since first grade. The English-language learners are well on their way to becoming fluent in English, but they need plenty of time if they are working with technical and academic language, a need shared by most of your native speakers. After reading the chapter, you decide the important reading purposes are for students to understand the concept of waves, note some of the properties of waves, describe several different types of waves, and come away with the understanding that waves are important physical phenomena, a scientific topic they will meet again and learn more about in later grades.

Thinking again about your students, you decide that they can handle the chapter, with your help. You also decide that both your native speakers and your English-language learners will profit from a good deal of help, and you do not need to construct a differentiated SRE. Again considering the chapter, you identify the concepts you want to stress, and you note that the chapter contains some material students do not need to deal with at the present time. You also note that the chapter is 10 pages and about 3000 words long, and you estimate that it will take students 20 to 30 minutes to read through it once.

All of this thinking—these considerations about your students, the chapter, and reading purposes—are in your mind as you plan the SRE. (As a matter of fact, in actually planning an SRE, you would probably consider more factors than we have listed in this brief example.) With those considerations firmly in mind, you come up with pre-, during-, and postreading activities. Here is an outline of what the SRE might look like.

SRE for "Waves" Chapter

Planning

Students:	Selection:	Purpose:
Fifth-graders of average to high ability; the class includes two English-language learners	Chapter titled "Waves" in fifth-grade science text.	To understand and recall the concept of waves, some wave properties, and types of waves

(Continued on next page)

SRE for "Waves" Chapter (*Continued*)

Implementation		
Prereading Activities	**During-Reading Activities**	**Postreading Activities**
Motivating: Acting out the motion of a wave	**Reading Aloud:** Read first section aloud to students.	**Discussion:** Small groups discuss chapter and add information to outline.
Preteaching Concepts: Teaching the concepts AMPLITUDE and FREQUENCY	**Manipulating Medium:** Tape chapter and make tape available to ESL students.	**Reteaching:** Reteach and extend central concepts as necessary.
Building Text-Specific Knowledge: Using the headings in the chapter to preview and predict its contents.	**Silent Reading:** Students read chapter on their own.	**Writing:** Have students write an imaginative tale in which a wave goes berserk.

For prereading, you decide to include a motivational activity that will relate the topic of waves to students' lives and preteach the concept. You include motivation because you believe that some sort of motivation is almost always a good idea and because students will not automatically be interested in waves. You have students demonstrate a wave by arranging themselves in a line across the front of the room and then successively standing up and sitting down—much as fans do at a football game. Following this demonstration (students will probably have to practice the wave several times before it becomes rhythmic and looks very much like a wave), you point out various attributes of their wave and of waves generally. For example, their wave and all waves are rhythmic and have amplitude and frequency. You might go on to explain these related concepts and then have students again demonstrate several different wave forms, changing the amplitude of their wave by raising both hands rather than standing up and changing its duration by standing up and sitting down or raising and lowering their hands at different rates. Finally, you might draw several wave forms on the board to illustrate the rhythmic patterns and the different amplitudes and durations waves can have.

Motivating students might also include stressing that the study of waves is an important science topic, reminding them that they are already familiar with some sorts of waves, such as those in oceans or lakes, and asking them what other sorts of waves play parts in their daily lives. Microwaves and TV waves are likely responses.

Next, because the chapter contains several difficult concepts, more really than you would like, you decide to preteach two of the most important ones. These are the concepts of AMPLITUDE and FREQUENCY as they apply to waves. You begin by writing the words on the board. Then, you define each of the concepts. As you give the definitions, you try to act out the meaning with gestures, and you also draw pictorials on the board at the same time. The amplitude of a wave is the height of the wave from its origin to its crest. You draw a picture of a wave, and as you draw a line from the inception of the wave to the crest, you say and point to the word *amplitude*. The frequency of a wave is the number of cycles of the wave that pass through a point in a certain amount of time. This one is harder to show. You show the students an extended "slinky." You draw a line on the board and, with a student's help, gradually draw the slinky through it, counting each "circle" on the slinky as it crosses the line. When you finish counting, you point to and say the word *frequency*. Next, you remind students that their own wave had amplitude and frequency; its amplitude was perhaps a foot or two, and its frequency might have been 10 cycles a minute. After this, you might show a video that illustrates the two concepts. Finally, you could ask students if they know of other words or phrases that express concepts similar to those expressed by *amplitude* and *frequency*—*height, size,* and *how often something happens* are possible responses. Of course, these brief activities have not fully taught the concepts, but students will be better prepared to understand them when they come up in the chapter.

To prepare students to deal with both the content and the organization of the chapter, you next write the headings and subheadings from the chapter on the board, being sure to preserve the features of the text used to show subordination—for example, the superordinate topics might be in all capital letters and left justified, while the subordinate topics might have just the first letter of each word in capitals and be indented. Then, you ask students to identify the superordinate and subordinate topics by noting their placement and the type of letters used. Finally, you ask students to brainstorm what they can learn just from the headings. For example, the first heading "HOW DO WAVES TRANSFER ENERGY?" clearly indicates that one thing waves do is transfer energy. You write this on the board and continue through the rest of the outline with the class, jotting down similar information students glean from the outline.

For during-reading activities, you decide to make an audiotape of the chapter for your English-language learners, and you ask these students to follow along in the book as they listen to the tape. The tape is carefully prepared so that you are reading slowly and enunciating clearly. Your plan also includes reading the first section of the chapter aloud to all students to ease them into the chapter. After the first section, the English-language learners will listen to the tape, and the rest of the class will finish the chapter by reading silently to themselves. Before students begin their listening or reading, however, you remind them that they shouldn't try to learn everything in the chapter, but should focus their attention on the topics discussed in the outline—the properties of waves and the different sorts of waves described. You ask the English-language learners to write down five words they think are the most important words in the chapter.

In deciding on postreading activities, you would probably take into account the fact that the chapter is challenging and that you definitely want students to remember the major concepts dealt with in the chapter. You might, therefore, hand out a discussion guide that parallels the chapter outline you wrote on the board and offer students 20 minutes to discuss these concepts in small groups. Each group is asked to focus on a particular concept and to decide one or two important things about that concept that they will "teach" to the rest of the class. You are careful to place the English-language learners in groups with students who will be supportive of their participation. After that, the class could come back together, and each group could report one piece of information they discovered about waves. Also, it is likely that some of your students will need extra work with concepts such as AMPLITUDE and FREQUENCY, and you might offer to join a group of students if there are any that would like to further consider these ideas. Finally, because many of your students have a creative bent and because you believe that WAVES and related concepts might prompt interesting fantasy tales, you suggest that students work alone or in small groups to create stories, sketches, or poems in which waves play central roles. Then, once students have completed their creations, they can either present them orally or post them around the room.

All in all, your students might spend 3 or 4 days with this SRE. Your purpose in designing these activities, and the purpose in planning and carrying out any SRE, is a straightforward one: You want to do everything possible to ensure that students have a successful reading experience. As we suggested before, we believe that a successful reading experience is one in which students glean and create meaning from the selection, learn from it, respond to it, and enjoy it. Moreover, our goal includes students realizing that they have been successful and recognizing that they have dealt competently with the selection. We want students to become successful lifelong readers, that is, persons who voluntarily choose to read in order to better understand themselves and their world, gain and create information, and experience the joy of reading. If students are to become lifelong readers, the vast majority of their reading experiences must be successful ones.

What a Scaffolded Reading Experience for English-Language Learners Is Not

To conclude our explanation of what a Scaffolded Reading Experience is, we want to briefly explain what an SRE is *not* and what goals SREs are not designed to achieve. First, and most importantly, a Scaffolded Reading Experience is not a complete plan for a reading program for English-language learners. Compared to a comprehensive reading program for both native-English speakers and English-language learners, it does not deal at all with emergent literacy skills such as phonological awareness or reading words from left to right. Nor does it deal with word identification skills such as phonics, structural analysis, using context, cross-checking, or monitoring. It does not provide a systematic program of vocabulary meaning instruction. It does not, as we have already noted, provide *instruction* in reading comprehension strategies. And it does not take the place of recreational reading, independent reading, or free reading programs.

As compared to a comprehensive English-language program for English-language learners, it lacks both these and other components. For example, an SRE does not include systematic instruction in oral English, specific instruction in pronunciation, and systematic instruction in a basic English vocabulary. SREs are not intended to be comprehensive reading or language programs for English-language learners.

SREs are only one part of a reading program for English-language learners. However, SREs can be a tremendously important part of a reading program. SREs assist English-language learners in understanding, enjoying, and learning from the material they read. Repeatedly successful experiences in reading will produce students who are more knowledgeable and in all likelihood students who are more interested in learning. Success breeds success! The SRE is our attempt to provide you with an instructional framework that will assist you in leading all of your students to the success they need and deserve.

Concluding Comments

In this chapter, we have attempted to give you a thorough overview of a Scaffolded Reading Experience for English-language learners. In doing so, we have defined an SRE, listed its components, briefly described each of them, introduced the concept of differentiated SREs, and discussed other matters important when creating SREs for English-language learners. We have also given examples of SRE activities and how we would go about planning them, and directly explained what SREs are and are not intended to accomplish. In the next chapter, chapter 3, we discuss some issues surrounding English-language learners that are important to consider as you plan SREs. In chapter 4, we examine the thinking that prompted us to develop the general notion of the Scaffolded Reading Experience for both English-language learners and native-English speakers.

References

Aebersold, J. A., & Field, M. L. (1997). *From reader to reading teacher: Issues and strategies for second language classrooms.* Cambridge, UK: Cambridge University Press. This very useful text on teaching reading to second-language learners deals largely with a prereading, during-reading, and postreading framework.

Alvermann, D. E. (2000). Classroom talk about texts: Is it dear, cheap, or a bargain at any price? In B. M. Taylor, M. F. Graves, & P. van den Broek (Eds.), *Reading for meaning: Fostering comprehension in the middle grades* (pp. 136-151). New York: Teachers College Press. Highlights the strengths and some possible weaknesses of small-group discussion.

Bean, T. W., Valerio, P. C., & Stevens, L. (1999) Content area literacy instruction. In L. B. Gambrell, L. M. Morrow, S. Newman, & M. Pressley (Eds.), *Best practices in literacy instruction* (pp. 175–192). New York: Guilford Press. Advocates a before-reading, during-reading, and after-reading framework to provide students with assistance as they read in various content areas.

Beck, I. L., McKeown, M. G., Hamilton, R., & Kucan, L. (1997). *Questioning the author: An approach for enhancing student engagement with text.* Newark, DE: International Reading Association. Detailed description of a during-reading discussion technique designed to yield deep understanding of a text.

Ciborowski, J. (1992). *Textbooks and the students who can't read them: A guide to teaching content.* Cambridge, MA: Brookline Books. Describes an approach to teaching less able readers that employs a before-reading, during-reading, and after-reading format.

Echevarria, J. (1995). Interactive reading instruction: A comparison of proximal and distal effects of Instructional Conversations. *Exceptional Children, 61,* 536–552. A study of the effectiveness of the Instructional Conversation format.

Echevarria, J., Vogt, M. E., & Short, D. J. (2000). *Making content comprehensible for English language learners: The SIOP model.* Boston: Allyn &

Bacon. Describes the Sheltered Instruction Observation Protocol model for teaching English-language learners and provides many illustrations of its implementation using classroom scenarios.

Fountas, I. C., & Pinnell, G. S. (1996). *Guided reading: Good first teaching for all students.* Portsmouth, NH: Heinemann. Describes a lesson framework for small-group instruction of primary-grade readers. Like the SRE, guided reading is one part of a reading program.

Gambrell, L. B., & Almasi, J. E. (1996). *Lively discussions! Fostering engaged reading.* Newark, DE: International Reading Association. This collection contains 18 chapters focusing on discussion.

Gersten, R., & Baker, S. (2000). What we know about effective instructional practices for English-language learners. *Exceptional Children, 66,* 454–470. A synthesis of research and professional views on effective instructional practices with English-language learners.

Goldenberg, C. (1992–1993). Instructional conversations: Promoting comprehension through discussion. *The Reading Teacher, 46,* 316–326. Describes a format for holding discussions.

Graves, M. F., Juel, C., & Graves, B. B. (2004). *Teaching reading in the 21st century* (3rd ed.). Boston: Allyn & Bacon. In this elementary reading methods text, we describe the components of a comprehensive and balanced reading program, including an approach to teaching comprehension strategies.

Nurss, J. R., & Hough, R. A. (1992). Reading and the ESL student. In S. J. Samuels & A. E. Farstrup (Eds.), *What research has to say about reading instruction* (pp. 277–313). Newark, DE: International Reading Association. Summarizes instructional implications from research and theory with English-language learners.

Peregoy, S. F., & Boyle, O. F. (1997). *Reading, writing, & learning in ESL: A resource book for K–12 teachers* (2nd ed.). New York: Longman. Provides ideas for teaching English-language learners.

Perez, B., & Torres-Guzman, M. E. (1992). *Learning in two worlds: An integrated Spanish/English biliteracy approach.* New York: Longman. Explicates how teachers can organize curriculum and learning environments to facilitate student growth in Spanish and English literacy, emphasizing the native-Spanish-speaking students' needs. The authors approach the practices of teaching literacy within a broad social and cultural network of understandings.

Pressley, M. (2002). *Reading instruction that works: The case for balanced teaching* (2nd ed.). New York: Guilford Press. Excellent discussion of what constitutes balanced reading instruction.

RAND Reading Study Group. (2002). *Reading for understanding: Toward an R&D program in reading comprehension.* Santa Monica, CA: RAND Education. Excellent review of what we know and need to know about comprehension instruction.

Readence, J. E., Moore, D. W., & Rickelman, R. J. (2000). *Prereading activities for content area reading and learning* (3rd ed.). Newark, DE: International Reading Association. This useful resource, now in its third edition, presents a variety of activities for preparing students to read as well as strategies students can use independently as they approach content-area reading selections.

Richardson, J. S. (2000). *Read it aloud: Using literature in the secondary content classroom.* Newark, DE: International Reading Association. Suggests the value of reading literature aloud in various content areas, with the major goal of spreading the "joy of reading."

Rousseau, M. K., Tam, B. K. Y., & Ramnarain, R. (1993). Increasing reading proficiency of language-minority students with speech and language impairments. *Education and Treatments of Children, 16,* 254–271. A study of different methods of vocabulary instruction with English-language learners.

Saunders, W., O'Brien, G., Lennon, D., & McLean, J. (1998). Making the transition to English literacy successful: Effective strategies for studying literature with transition students. In R. Gersten & R. Jiménez (Eds.), *Effective strategies for teaching language minority students* (pp. 99–132). Belmont, CA: Wadsworth. A research study on effective instruction with English-language learners.

Schoenbach, R., Greenleaf, C., Cziko, C., & Hurwitz, L. (1999). *Reading for understanding: A guide to improving reading in middle and high school classes.* San Francisco: Jossey-Bass. Here two teachers and two staff developers describe their approach to a reading course designed for urban middle-school and high-school students.

Teachers of English to Speakers of Other Languages (TESOL). (1997). *ESL standards for pre-K–12 students.* Alexandria, VA: Author. TESOL is a major international organization devoted to advancing the learning and instruction of individuals learning English as a new language. This document lists and explains the standards and goals enumerated by the organization for English-language learners.

Terrell, T. D. (1981). The natural approach in bilingual education. In California Office at Bilingual-Bicultural Education (Ed.), *Schooling and language minority students: A theoretical framework* (pp. 117–146). Los Angeles: California State University. Describes how to use authentic activities to help English-language learners' develop both their native language and English.

Wood, K. D., Lapp, D., & Flood, J. (1992). *Guiding readers through text: A review of study guides.* Newark, DE: International Reading Association. A detailed, lucid, and very useful description of 17 types of study guides that teachers can use to focus students' attention and guide them toward learning and understanding as they are reading.

Yopp, R. H., & Yopp, H. K. (1992). *Literature-based reading activities.* Boston: Allyn & Bacon. Describes pre-, during-, and postreading activities for literary selections.

Children's Literature Cited

Byers, B. (1985). Sam's story. In *QUEST.* New York: Scholastic. 10 pages.

Clements, A. (1998). *Frindle.* New York: Aladdin. 104 pages.

Cooper, M. (1999). *Indian school: Teaching the white man's way.* New York: Clarion Books. 103 pages.

Hackett, J. K., & Moyer, R. H. (1991). Waves. In *Science in Your World,* Level 6. New York: Macmillan/McGraw-Hill.

Jiménez, F. (1999). *The circuit.* Boston: Houghton-Mifflin. 144 pages.

King, M. L., Jr. (1997). *I Have a Dream.* New York: Scholastic. 40 pages.

Simon, S. (1991). *Earthquakes.* New York: Morrow Junior Books. Unpaged.

CHAPTER 3

WHAT DO TEACHERS NEED TO KNOW ABOUT ENGLISH-LANGUAGE LEARNERS TO SUCCESSFULLY USE SCAFFOLDED READING EXPERIENCES?

In this chapter, we summarize key issues related to English-language learners that are especially important when using Scaffolded Reading Experiences (SREs). We want to emphasize the words *summarize* and *key*. In this brief chapter, we cannot cover everything that teachers should know about teaching reading to English-language learners. Nor can we offer thorough and comprehensive explanations of the topics we cover. Instead, we focus on the major issues that teachers raise with us and with issues that directly relate to implementing SREs.

In many ways, research and theory about English-language learner's reading are in their infancy, and many issues are yet to be settled. As we discuss issues in this chapter, we note whether consensus or conflicting opinions surround the issue and whether evidence is available. As we write, we are also thinking about the important differences between what *can* happen in a learner's reading development and what *must* or *should* happen. For instance, some research suggests that first-grade English-language learners *can* learn to read well in English in situations where they are immersed in English-only (or other new-language) settings (Araujo, 1997; Fitzgerald & Noblit, 1999, 2000; Geva, 1999; Geva, Wade-Woolley, & Shany, 1993; Geva, Yaghoub-Zadeh, & Schuster, 2000; Weber & Longhi, 1996). However, this does not mean that students *must* or *should* learn to read English in all-English settings to achieve optimal reading levels or that such a setting is the best one for achieving optimal reading levels. Nor does it mean that such a setting is the best one for developing other desirable learner and cultural characteristics, such as a positive attitude toward school or pride in one's heritage.

In the following pages, we address questions about how a second language is learned, the extent to which second-language reading processes are potentially significantly different from first-language reading processes, relationships between learning to speak and learning to read and write, whether native-language reading *must* precede learning to read in English, the extent to which "special" reading instruction methods are *necessary* for second-language learners, and ways in which culture and language are intertwined. Then, we suggest how our discussion of these issues is related to implications for classroom reading instruction, and we close by specifically pointing to ways in which these issues are related to using SREs in your classroom. Teachers who are interested in greater detail about research and theory on English-language learners' reading may find reviews by one of the authors (Fitzgerald, 1995a, 1995b, 2001), García (2000), and Gersten and Baker (2000) helpful starting places.

How Is a Second Language Learned?

Most research and theory on second-language learning has focused on oral language development and, consequently, that is our focus in this section, though literacy development is also mentioned. Since our book is about reading, you may be wondering why we are including information about oral language development. We include it because oral language, reading, and writing are inextricably intertwined. Oral development can be considered as one form of language development and reading as another form. Second-language learners' oral development can be directly related to their reading development, and therefore, you need to understand certain issues about oral language and how it relates to what you do with reading in their classrooms.

As you read this chapter, it is important to recognize that second-language acquisition is a complex process that requires consideration of many factors, including phonological, semantic, syntactic, morphological, pragmatic, and social and cultural features as well as accounting for learner differences in areas such as age and native language (August & Hakuta, 1997). Indeed, the complexity of learning a new language has been documented by research findings on the length of time for learners to reach proficiency levels comparable to native-language counterparts. For instance, on average, it may take about 2 years to learn conversational English at a level comparable to native-English speakers, and as many as 8 years may be needed for learning more formal or academic language, the language required to read and learn in school (Collier, 1987, 1989; Collier & Thomas, 1989; Cummins, 1981; Krashen & Biber, 1988).

Currently, no "grand" theory explains everything involved in oral and literate second-language learning and, indeed, controversy has arisen over which of several theories of second-language learning is, or are, most appropriate (Mitchell & Myles, 1998). In the following sections, we first explain just two, among several, positions that are related to second-language learning. These are *positions*, not theories *per se*. But they are important positions for teachers to know about because they have implications for how we teach English-language learners. After that, we briefly describe just three, among many, second-language learning theories. These positions and theories have important implications for classroom instruction. If you are interested in more detail about theories and research on learning a second language you might find the Mitchell and Myles' book a useful starting place. Later in the chapter, we explicitly discuss the instructional implications in more detail.

Two Important Positions Related to Second-Language Learning

Two positions emerged in the late 1970s and 1980s, have been supported by quite a bit of research, and continue to be important in the field today. These two positions underscore two very important points about cognitive aspects of second-language learning: The *way* cognitive understandings of a second language are learned is highly similar to the way they are learned in a first language, and *what* is learned in one language is usually shared in the other (Hakuta, 1986; Krashen, 1991; Snow, 1992).

It is important to understand both of these points because they will help you better appreciate how you can create reading lessons that capitalize on English-language learners' native and new oral language strengths, how reading can help develop English-language learners' native and English oral language, and how learning a new language can constrain an English-language learners' reading and academic development.

The first position (Chomsky, 1980) suggests that the ability to learn any language (first or second) is innate and that individuals all over the world have a "universal grammar" built into our minds that allows us to learn language. The "universal grammar" works for any language. Thus, according this outlook, all language learning tends to have something in common and tends to happen in similar ways. Again, it is important to keep in mind that the referent point of this position is cognitive learning and, even more specifically, grammar learning.

The second position is represented in the Common Underlying Proficiency (CUP) Model of how two languages are related (Cummins, 1978, 1979). The CUP Model posits that a common set of proficiencies (generally interpreted as cognitive proficiencies) underlies both the first and second languages. If you learn something in one language, it will likely transfer to another language. Additionally, using a skill or strategy in one language is pretty much the same process as in another. Importantly, according to the CUP Model, several reading abilities are considered to be common across languages. These include conceptual knowledge, subject-matter knowledge, higher order thinking skills, and reading strategies. Cummins (1981, 1989) has also proposed that successful transfer of knowledge and expertise across languages is dependent on the development of cognitive proficiency in one language and that the knowledge, skills, and expertise can first be developed in either the native or the new language so that once learned, they can be transferred to the other language (Fitzgerald & Cummins, 1999).

Three Second-Language Learning Theories

Two, among several, second-language learning theories that were developed in the late 1970s and 1980s continue to be widely recognized in the field today. These are the Monitor Model (e.g., Krashen, 1977, 1985; Krashen & Terrell, 1983) and Cognitive Theory (McLaughlin, 1987). Because features of these two theories are frequently referenced in contemporary literature, we briefly describe them here. The third position we consider here is a sociocultural view of language learning. Second-language learning theory based in a sociocultural outlook has a long tradition, but received a lot of emphasis in the 1990s (Mitchell & Myles, 1998).

The Monitor Model (Krashen, 1985) has been very popular among U.S. second-language teachers (Johnson, 1992), though it has not been without critics (e.g., Gregg, 1984; McLaughlin, 1987). Briefly stated, one salient point of the model is that individuals learn to acquire the new language through efforts to understand and be understood in meaningful situations. Among some of the more specific claims derived from the model are that language acquisition occurs through meaningful interaction in a natural setting, that learning is a "conscious process that results in knowing about language," and that individuals acquire language by receiving "comprehensible input" (Krashen, 1985).

What does understanding the Monitor Model have to do with English-language-learner reading instruction? One implication is that the more the teacher can involve English-language learners in reading and writing in "authentic" ways—such as involving the student in personal responses to texts and in bringing student-to-student conversations to bear on texts that are read—the more the teacher will be supporting the students' language and academic learning. Another implication is that in order for students' language to grow, texts must be comprehensible. When texts are not comprehensible, teachers' scaffolding must work to enhance the comprehensibility of the text. So teachers who help their students to read in texts that are at their "instructional" reading level also make the students' learning more comprehensible.

Cognitive Theory (McLaughlin, 1987) focuses on the internal mental processes of the learner. According to Cognitive Theory, a learner acquires a second language through gradual accumulation of subskills. *Subskills* refer to procedures such as using strategies for selecting appropriate vocabulary or using grammar rules. At first, the subskills require the learner's concentration, but with time, they become automatic. Automaticity is achieved through practice.

One way in which understanding Cognitive Theory is important to teachers using SREs is that some of these subskills can be built through activities like SREs. For example, when teachers carefully teach critical new vocabulary in a reading selection, they help students not only to learn the academic content of the text, they also help develop the students' oral language abilities. Another way in which understanding Cognitive Theory is important to teachers is that the theory points to the constraints under which many English-language learners must work when they are learning a new language. These constraints, such as the gradual accumulation of skills and abilities, suggest that teachers must not expect "all or nothing" of these students. Rather, they can structure reading activities in ways that afford English-language learners opportunities to learn about *parts* of the text content and that enable gradual approximations toward ultimate learning goals.

Second-language learning theory based in a sociocultural outlook reflects a stance on learning that is different from those just discussed in that while cognitive learning is still considered important, the social and cultural nature of learning receives more emphasis (Lantolf, 1994; Lantolf & Appel, 1994). That is, in this outlook, language learning is quintessentially social rather than individual in nature. It happens first between and among individuals and within the individual (in the mind) (Mitchell & Myles, 1998). That learners co-construct their own learning environments and their own learning is taken as an important premise. The contexts for learning, including the classroom, school, and wider sociopolitical climate, are taken as influential in the language learning process.

Among the most important implications of sociocultural outlooks on second-language learning for teachers of English-language learners is that the teacher plays a critical role in structuring lessons so as to scaffold learners, working with them to construct activities and lessons in ways such that English-language learners can move forward. We will talk more in chapter 4 about the idea of scaffolding and specifically about how SREs can help with this. Another important implication of a sociocultural outlook is that communities of learners can serve to create mutual learning environments so that English-language learners can learn from peers as well as the teacher. A final implication is that the political climate of the classroom and school can have far-reaching effects on English-language learners' progress. We will reiterate throughout this book that when teachers and school personnel embrace the rich backgrounds, beliefs, values, and understandings that English-language learners bring to school with them, when teachers and school personnel work to create caring, concerned, and open communities, and when teachers and school personnel work with English-language learners' families, all students can flourish.

Are Second-Language Reading Processes Significantly Different From First-Language Reading Processes?

We do not have a definitive answer about the extent to which second-language and first-language reading processes are similar or different. Some scholars have argued that theories about learning to read in a first language are applicable to second-language learners (e.g., Carrell, Devine, & Eskey, 1988). Some have also pointed to the theoretical similarities between first- and second-language reading. For instance, Heath's (1986) idea of transferable generic literacies and Krashen's (1988) reading hypothesis both assume that second-language reading entails the same basic processes as first-language reading (Hedgcock & Atkinson, 1993). Others contend that preexisting reading theories do not sufficiently address specific aspects of second-language reading or that second-language reading is actually "a different phenomenon" from first-language reading (Bernhardt, 1991, p. 226).

Considering just U.S. studies of English-language learners' cognitive English reading processes, one of the authors (Fitzgerald, 1995a) found support for the position that the cognitive reading processes of English-language learners in the United States are substantively the same as those of native-English speakers, at least with regard to the categories of reading processes that have mainly been used in the research. Minimally, the processes appear more alike than they are different. We should keep in mind, however, that these conclusions were reached after reviewing reading research done *only* with individuals in the United States and with a focus on *English* reading. Different results could occur for other second-language speakers and in other situations. Also, the central features of research interest have been cognitive processes. Affective and social variables and their interplay in English-language learners' reading have not been well addressed in research.

At the same time, results from several studies (e.g., Chikamatsu, 1996; Koda, 1993) suggest that second-language readers definitely rely on their native language in ways that both facilitate and interfere with their second-language processing (Bernhardt, 2000), suggesting that native language should be taken into account in theories and models of second-language reading.

Much work needs to be done to develop theories about the extent to which second-language reading processes are similar to, and different from, native-language reading processes (Bernhardt, 2000; Fitzgerald, 2003). The reason this is important is that theory tends to underlie instruction. If second-language reading processes are significantly different from native-language reading processes, then the way in which teachers teach English-language-learner reading would need to be quite different from the way they teach native-language reading. We will return to the practical implications of theory development in a later section in this chapter, called "Are Special Reading Instruction Methods *Necessary* for English-Language Learners?"

Relationships Between Learning to Speak and Learning to Read and Write

Language Is Language

In many ways language is language—some language is oral and some involves print (or other symbols such as pictures or gestures). Here, we focus just on the psycholinguistic aspects of language, that is on the cognitive features of language, and not on social, political, or cultural aspects of language. In doing so, we are taking a narrow, but useful, outlook on the relationship between oral language use and written language use in classrooms. It is an oversimplification, but we find it helpful to use the metaphor of a tree as we think about language from a cognitive perspective. The roots of the cognitive aspects of language can be described as syntactic, semantic, phonologic, pragmatic, and metalinguistic. *Syntax* refers to acceptable orders of words in sentences and orders of chunks in longer discourse, such as a story beginning, goal, action, outcome, and moral. *Semantics* refers to meaning, word meaning and meanings of connected text, whether the text is oral or printed. *Phonology* refers to sounds in language—hearing separate words, chunks in words, and individual sounds in words.

Pragmatics has to do with the functions or purposes and intentions of language. *Metalinguistics* refers to knowing about what you know and don't know about language use and being able to manipulate language through the use of terms referring to language.

The roots of language may also be considered to be the invisible understandings about language an individual has. These understandings become visible in the tree's branches as an individual speaks, listens, reads, and writes. Viewed in this way, speaking, listening, reading, and writing are different expressions of commonly rooted understandings.

This is not to say that oral and literate language are exactly the same. They aren't. We won't enumerate their differences here, but we will give one very important example. Unlike oral language, printed texts must stand on their own without the aid of the supporting gestures and facial expressions that are frequently present in oral interchanges (Snow, Tabors, Nicholson, & Kurland, 1995). This means that reading and writing present some challenges seldom encountered when speaking and listening.

Reading Can Help English-Language Learners' Oral/Aural Development

So how does the tree metaphor help us? It pushes us to think about helping English-language learners to develop cognitive language abilities that are wrapped up in the "roots" and to consider the visible branching manifestations as different avenues through which the abilities can be developed and manifested. From this standpoint, activities like SREs can help English-language learners not just to learn the content of texts, but also to develop their general language abilities. A good deal of research shows that second-language reading can assist learners' second-language oral/ aural development as well (e.g., Anderson & Roit, 1996; Elley, 1981; Elley & Mangubhai, 1983; Gersten, 1996; Klingner & Vaughn, 1996).

There are many reasons why reading might help English-language learners' oral/aural language development. Here are some of them:

 + Reading can provide a supportive context that doesn't always exist in oral situations. For instance, listening to someone talk about something without the aid of pictures or print can be much harder than reading about it.

 + A printed text can be arranged to present a topic or theme more clearly.

 + Pictures, diagrams, graphs, and other visuals can assist the learner.

✦ Print can give clues to sounds, and white spaces separate words. So students can see what the words are; and for many English-language learners, this can ease the struggle of trying to sort out words and sounds from the stream of oral language.

✦ For some English learners, some native-language words are very similar to English words—*cognates.* For instance, in Spanish the word for *idea* is *idea*, even though it is pronounced differently in Spanish than it is in English. So Spanish speakers can look for words that look like words they already know how to read in Spanish, and this can assist their learning and understanding.

✦ It is well known that for monolinguals wide reading is associated with enhanced knowledge of word meanings (Anderson, 1996; Graves, 2000). It is likely that a similar relationship exists for bilinguals, so it is very important for teachers to involve English-language learners in reading so that they can begin to achieve the same benefits.

Is Some Optimal Level of Oral English *Necessary* Before Students Begin Reading English?

Whether students *must* be at least somewhat fluent in oral English in order to begin English reading is another controversial issue (Fitzgerald, 2001). Some educators have argued that, for English-language learners, some degree of oral English fluency *is* a prerequisite to learning to read in English (e.g., Snow, Burns, & Griffin, 1998; Wong Fillmore & Valadez, 1986). However, others have argued that English oral proficiency *is not* a prerequisite to English reading (e.g., Anderson & Roit, 1996; Barrera, 1984; Fitzgerald & Noblit, 1999; Gersten, 1996), even for students with learning disabilities (Klingner & Vaughn, 1996).

The extent to which oral proficiency is necessary may be related to the grade level or age of the student. For instance, young learners, such as kindergarten through second-grade children, may not need much new-language oral proficiency as they begin to learn to read in English because the texts they are reading are "easier" than those in the higher grades. Also, at the lower grade levels, teachers are attempting to help youngsters, including native-English speakers, to develop linguistic awareness, most especially phonological awareness. In other words, at the lower grade levels, the overall classroom goals for native-language speakers for language development in general and for reading development in particular coincide, or at least overlap, nicely with those for second-language learners. On the other hand, at higher grade levels, texts are written with more linguistic complexity, and they have more complicated content. Classroom teachers' reading and content-area instruction for native-English speakers are not at the levels of a novice English-language learner's needs. Consequently, perhaps at least some minimal degree of oral proficiency in advance of reading is more important for older learners than for younger learners.

Our position is that when teachers use activities such as SREs with English-language learners—even those who are just beginning to develop oral English proficiency—they ease the many complexities involved in new-language reading, in ways that provide more benefits to the students than not having the students read at all. We have alluded to some of these benefits elsewhere, such as assisting students' oral/aural language development. Another way in which activities like those in SREs can help English-language learners is that as part of scaffolding students' reading you can draw attention to particular words, showing words and saying them at the same time. By connecting the visual appearance of the word to the sound of the word, you are not only helping the student with reading, you are likely to be helping the student to learn something about the English sounds. In other words, calling attention to the visual word can support the student's aural language development.

Must Native-Language Reading Precede Learning to Read in English?

The role and timing of native-language reading and English reading for English-language learners is still another debated issue. While we endorse bilingual education, we also understand that there are many situations in the United States where bilingual programs are not in place. Many teachers in all-English situations wonder whether they can help students to learn in their content areas and develop students' English reading skills when the students have developed little or no native-language reading skills. Our position is that teachers can and should use activities such as SREs to assist English-language learners in general, including those who have not developed optimal levels of native-language reading.

Are "Special" Reading Instruction Methods *Necessary* for Second-Language Learners?

We make the following statement guardedly because so little theory development has been done about what second-language reading looks like, because so little research has been done on this question, and because it is clear that native language does play a role in second-language reading. If we focus only on the cognitive aspects of reading and learning to read and only on U.S. studies, we find very little evidence to support the need for a *dramatically* different or entirely different vision of second-language learner reading instruction (Fitzgerald, 1995b). For instance, some limited research findings on instruction with second-language readers support this contention (Fitzgerald, 1995b). Some explicit-instruction studies with English-language learners tend to replicate earlier research paradigms done with monolingual subjects—studies on expository text structure, building background knowledge, and metacognitive/strategy training (e.g., Au, 1979; Carrell, 1987; Carrell, Pharis, & Liberto, 1989; Floyd & Carrell, 1987; Johnson, 1982). However, most professionals agree that, at the very least, reading instruction must be modulated for English-language learners (Gersten & Baker, 2000). Authors of earlier reviews (e.g., Fitzgerald, 1995a, 1995b; García, 2000; Gersten & Baker, 2000) have suggested that teachers should be especially aware of some areas that might deserve extra consideration when teaching second-language learners so that instruction is modified for them. We enumerate some of these later in this chapter.

Culture and Language Are Intertwined

For each of us, our own language, our dialect, and our "ways of talking and naming" are parts of our individual and cultural identities. Cultural ways are embodied in language. Here are two examples, both taken from the work of Shirley Brice Heath (Heath, 1986; Heath & Mangiola, 1991). In some communities, adults often ask children many questions to which the adults already know the answer. In these communities, such question–answer routines may occur in almost any context. They may begin in early childhood and last into puberty. "Where are your eyes?" "Can you tell Aunt Jessie what you did last night?" By contrast, in some groups, such questions seem silly, and telling something you know others already know may even invite ridicule, censure, or punishment from adults. Or consider this example. In some groups, elders talk about "raising," "bringing up," or "training" their children, imbuing adults with particular powers and responsibilities for the actions and learning of their children. In other groups, views of adult power are replaced by the ideas of children's "self-development" or "self-fulfillment." In this example, we see that adults in different communities may have critically different understandings of how children learn or are taught, and we see that children acquire the understandings from their particular understandings from their own group's perspectives.

Teachers cannot possibly know all of the nuances of the varied cultural backgrounds their students bring to classrooms. Here, we want to point to just five kinds of understandings about culture that can help you set the stage for working with diverse students.

First, we need to *realize* that language embodies culture and that each of us may have understandings that seem so "real" to us that our own "reality" also seems "right." At the same time, the social expectations and understandings that are tied up in our language are so natural to us that they may be invisible. It is often hard for us as teachers to examine events as they appear to students who come from families and communities where there are different lenses for learning, lenses that are not consonant with those used in schools for seeing, knowing, and telling. As a consequence, we teachers must be vigilant in seeking to understand and see from our students' perspectives. That "wrong" response or "bad" behavior may not be so "wrong" or "bad" when we understand how the student sees and thinks. Instead, the unexpected in the classroom may signal an important cultural disjuncture between the teacher's or school's ways of knowing and a student's ways of knowing. Being alert to such disjunctures is one way teachers can begin to connect with their students so that learning is enhanced (Heath & Mangiola, 1991).

Second, when students perceive their teachers as making an effort to connect with them, to support them, and to "see through their eyes," they are more likely to be engaged in the classroom and tend to make more gains in academic and language proficiency than others (Hakuta, Ferdman, & Diaz, 1987). You can enhance students' perception of your support by making it a definite point to show respect for and appreciation of their cultures and by repeatedly demonstrating your understanding of how difficult it is to learn a new language and be in a new environment.

Third, background knowledge is closely tied to language and culture. Students who are learning English may not have learned many concepts necessary in U.S. classrooms. Research has documented that English-language learners often know less about topics in typical English-language texts than do native-English speakers (Droop & Verhoeven, 1998; García, 1991; Jiménez, García, & Pearson, 1995, 1996). At the same time, English-language learners may understand a concept, but their understanding may not be the same understanding as the teacher's. For instance, in one study, Indians who read a text in English about a North American wedding tended to make events consistent with those of Indian weddings, effecting distortions (Steffensen, Joag-Dev, & Anderson, 1979). Consequently, for English-language learners, it is especially important that teachers provide orientations to classroom values and behaviors. It is equally important to make sure that students have the background knowledge needed to understand concepts in texts and class discussions. Moreover, the teacher who sees from the student's perspective invites English-language learners to elaborate on their own understandings of given concepts in their own cultures in order to enrich the teacher's and classmates' views.

Fourth, teachers can consider ways to "bridge" incongruencies between home and school cultures. Some have argued that the work of bridging may be the most important way to help language-minority students. In general, such bridging can occur through incorporation of students' languages and cultures into the school culture, modification of the school culture to enhance respect for the language-minority culture, implementation of pedagogical empowerment strategies, and parental and community involvement in students' school experiences (Cummins, 1989). As for incorporating students' language and cultures into schools, it would seem that bilingual programs would offer the greatest potential for this. However, even where bilingual programs do not exist, teachers can still encourage and support students' use of native languages, and home and native cultures can be respected, read about, talked about, and in other ways brought into schools.

One pedagogical empowerment strategy is to change aspects of classroom routines to make them more compatible with home patterns familiar to the children. Of course, this is easier said than done! Often it is impossible to figure out exactly what is incongruent. However, sometimes teachers can notice natural language patterns by watching students at play or working with peers (Cazden, 1988). Sometimes teachers learn about particular cultural features or patterns through reading about specific cultures or attending workshops. Where classroom modifications are reasonable, it is likely they would positively affect students' learning. An example of such a modification comes from the Kamehameha project in Hawaii. Some researchers realized that Hawaiian children learn at home through *talk-story,* that is, through communal oral participation in narratives quite unlike the discussions in traditional classrooms. When teachers of Hawaiian children modified their reading lesson formats to allow children to participate in the lessons as they did in their home narratives, students spent more time on the reading task, gave more correct responses, and discussed more of the text content (Au & Mason, 1983).

There are many ways to involve parents and families in students' schooling. For example, Luis Moll and his colleagues (Moll & González, 1994) have asked teachers to go into the children's homes to survey the kinds of literacy activities and events that occur there. These activities and events then become the basis for classroom and school instruction in reading and writing. Bringing parents into the classroom as resources of information about their culture is another good way to "bridge" between home and school.

Fifth, most English-language learners' lives and worlds are transnational in nature, and not much research and theory has explored this (Jiménez, 2003). Consequently, we know little about what such a way of living means for how we teachers interact with English-language learners and how we build instructional situations for them. At the very least, teachers who are aware that some students can live in two different cultures— their U.S. situation and their homeland situation—more willingly see that English-language learners not only hold great promise as learners but also face considerably different challenges than many other learners. Such teachers can become advocates for English-language learners, helping them to voice their opinions and beliefs, to maintain their cultural heritage, and to bring new horizons to other students in the classroom and school.

Some Implications for the Classroom

Research and theory on special issues related to working with English-language learners along with our own experiences have led us to some understandings about teaching English-language learners. In this section, we summarize the major inferences about implications for classroom practice that arise from our understandings. As we discuss these implications, we look back at each of the issues we've discussed in this chapter.

Because language learning is so complex, English-language learners have to attend to many features in a new language. You can assist them by highlighting important features and calling attention to them. For instance, by speaking more slowly, you can help new-language learners' phonological awareness development. That is, you can help new-language learners perceive the separations between words and thus hear the words and sounds in words better. You can also support new-language learners by using easier syntax and using gestures.

Also, the complexities of language learning are related to the contexts within which the language is learned. Many students, especially adolescents, may tend to be self-conscious and anxious about how they sound to others and about how their work is perceived. So it is particularly important that in the beginning, you—not the student—be willing to assume the responsibility for most of the work of deciding what and how much can be learned and at what pace. One way you can shoulder most of the work is through using activities such as those in SREs.

Somewhat similarly, it is vital that you reach out and initiate, show students you want to connect with them, and do all of this without putting undue pressure on students. Moreover, through these demonstrations, you are modeling attitudes and ways of assisting new-language learners that can be used by your native-English speakers. English-language learners' peers can alleviate the pressures on new-language learners by accepting them and their language, by showing interest in them, by learning from and with them, and by trying to help them through their work—in short, by demonstrating a caring attitude.

The fact that conversational English develops far more rapidly than academic English means that we must be careful when generalizing about a student's language abilities from one domain to another. For instance, many times a student who seems fluent in English does not have sufficient technical or academic vocabulary or does not use or understand enough of the more formal syntactic patterns in the new language to work comfortably in content areas. Unfortunately, we sometimes mistake this slower progress in a content area or in reading or writing as a "disability." This often leads to misclassification of second-language learners in one of the various "disability" categories. For instance, even in the early 1970s, there were between three and four times as many Blacks of African heritage and Latino students in classes for the educable mentally retarded than would be expected based on their proportion in the school population (Mercer, 1973). In Texas in the 1980s, researchers found a threefold overrepresentation of Latino students labeled *learning disabled* (Ortiz & Yates, 1983), and authors of a recent study reported that the numbers of language-minority students in special education classes in Texas rose by 11.7% from 1997 to 1999 (Johnson & Supik, 1999).

It is vital that we be sensitive to the varied kinds of language use (particularly conversational and academic) that English-language learners are developing so that we do not mistakenly refer English-language learners for special education. We should be careful and thoughtful about making referrals for special testing for disabilities for second-language learners. This is not to say that referrals should not be made, but rather when considering referrals for English-language learners, we should be particularly thoughtful about the complexities and length of time it takes to learn a new language in various settings.

Another implication of knowing that students can appear to be fluent in conversational English but not be as fluent in academic English is that we should make every effort to support the new-language learner in content areas. This is especially true when the English-language learner appears to be struggling in a content area.

There are many implications of the selected theories we presented on how second languages are learned. One especially important one that arises from Krashen's Monitor Model is that, particularly in the beginning stages of second-language learning, teachers should try to focus on "big things," like overall meaning, rather than "smaller things," like correct pronunciation or correct syntax in speech. For learning in content areas and for reading and writing tasks, one way to think about this is to ask students to achieve a subset of goals, rather than all of your goals for the rest of the class, or to do just parts of activities, rather than all of them. For instance, you might have a set of goals in mind for a given lesson with a group of diverse students. For the beginning English-language learners in the group, you might choose just one or two of the most important goals. Similarly, you might ask new-language learners to do some portion of an activity, rather than the complete activity. An implication of McLaughlin's Cognitive Theory is also that narrowing goals or activities is likely to assist English-language learners by focusing their attention on specific ideas or features of language.

The ideas of focusing on "big things" at first and narrowing goals and activities are also consistent with McLaughlin's theory that language is learned through gradual accumulation of subskills. Everything that needs to be learned about language, and by extension about content areas, cannot be learned at once. However, when teachers "approximate" goals for students' language and content learning and narrow activities, they support students' gradual accumulation of knowledge and experience; they encourage "successive approximations" on the road to a grander set of goals.

The Monitor Model, Cognitive Theory, and theory based on a sociocultural outlook imply that language is learned through use. Consequently, working with peers in small groups to encourage conversation and doing as much reading and writing as possible is likely to help the new-language learner to achieve automaticity for selected subskills sooner. Similarly, both drama and role playing can be very useful in moving English-language learners toward fluency and automaticity.

Theory of second-language learning based in a sociocultural outlook leads us to say again that scaffolding learning is extremely important and that creating a caring and respectful learning environment cannot be emphasized enough. Also, a favorable political climate of the school and community can strongly influence English-language learners' progress, and teachers who advocate for English-language learners' needs can participate in creating a positive climate.

Based on what we know about the relationships between literate and oral language, we believe that reading and writing are fantastic avenues for new-language learners' development of content-area understandings as well as for their language development in general. Moreover, we think sufficient theory and research exist to support early immersion in reading and writing for the new-language learner as long as expectations for what is read and written are reasonable for the student's new-language developmental reading and writing levels. For instance, students cannot immediately read and write texts at grade level in a new language. However, they can look for words that look like words they know in their native language in the new text, and they can be encouraged to write their main ideas in their native language or, if in English, without being held to the spelling, phrasing, syntax, and punctuation standards to which native-English speakers might be held.

From the research that has addressed the issue of whether teachers must use very different teaching methods for helping second-language learners to read, we believe that teachers should consider modulating their instruction to accommodate English-language learners. For instance, teachers might display even more than normal patience. They might also take extra care when wording questions and making comments in order to maximize the opportunity for implementing deeper thought processes. Additionally, teachers might pay even more attention to readers' development of topic knowledge and vocabulary meanings for specific reading selections. Where cognates exist, students are likely to benefit from explicit instruction in how to capitalize on these when reading in the new language (Jiménez, 1997). For those of you in situations in which you can teach reading lessons, we suggest that you identify the instructional reading level of the student in the new language and teach the student the critical features associated with that level so as to help him or her move to the next developmental level. Modifications such as ones we've already suggested in this chapter should certainly be made.

Perhaps the main implication we take from the work on the relationships between culture and language is that teacher sensitivity to difference in language and its accompanying cultural understandings is critical. Teachers who understand the transnational lives and worlds of many English-language learners seek to understand what is new and unknown to them and who reach out to new-language learners are more likely to help facilitate and enhance their students' learning. They also can become advocates for English-language learners in their schools and communities, supporting their cultural heritage and their education.

Returning to SREs

In closing, in this chapter we have provided brief summaries of salient issues related to second-language learning including the following:

+ How a second language is acquired or learned,

+ The extent to which second-language reading processes are different from first-language reading processes,

+ The relationships between orality and literacy,

+ Whether an optimal level of oral English is *necessary* before students can begin reading in English,

+ Whether native-language reading must precede learning to read in English,

+ Whether reading instruction for second-language learners must be very different from that for native speakers' reading instruction, and

+ How culture and language are related.

We now turn back to the main purpose of this book—learning about how to structure and restructure classroom lessons using SREs. As we reconsider the content of this chapter in relation to SREs, we point to ways in which SREs are an excellent means of assisting English-language learners.

One reason SREs are particularly beneficial to English-language learners is that they provide a means for breaking down the complexity of the reading task. Splitting a lesson into before- during-, and after-reading activities can substantially reduce the cognitive demands on English learners.

SREs provide a mechanism that empowers teachers to plan and initiate lessons in ways that enable them to shoulder the main responsibility for students' learning. In this way, teachers alleviate what can be overwhelming pressures on English-language learners.

SREs can facilitate learning in general, and content learning in particular. They take on special significance for the English-language learner because of the length of time new-language learners need to become proficient with academic English. One of the ways we all learn new vocabulary, content, concepts, and understandings in our first language is through wide reading. This is likely to be similarly true for English-language learners—especially for those in English immersion situations. When English-language learners are not reading, the gap between their knowledge and understandings and their monolingual peers' may widen. Without teacher support, English learners may be hesitant to attempt reading, especially in the beginning. SREs provide much of the needed support.

We have spoken in this chapter about the reasons for narrowing goals and activities with many English learners. SREs are excellent vehicles for providing this narrowing. In other chapters in this book, we give abundant examples of just how it can be done.

Two crucial areas that need extra attention for second-language learners are background knowledge and vocabulary meanings. The before-reading menu in SREs provides for a wide array of activities that can be used to facilitate instantiation of important background knowledge for a reading selection. Likewise, SREs can be used to enhance vocabulary knowledge. Teachers can also teach students how to use cognates within the SRE structure.

References

Anderson, R. C. (1996). Research foundations to support wide reading. In V. Greaney (Ed.), *Promoting reading in developing countries* (pp. 57–77). Newark, DE: International Reading Association. Presents research that supports the far-reaching effects of wide reading.

Anderson, V., & Roit, M. (1996). Linking reading comprehension instruction to language development for language minority students. *Elementary School Journal, 96* (3), 295–310. Presents research on links between reading and oral language for second-language learners.

Araujo, L. (1997, December). *Making the transition to English literacy.* Paper presented at the annual meeting of the National Reading Conference, Scottsdale, AZ. A study of young English-language learners' English-reading development.

Au, K. H. (1979). Using the experience–text–relationship method with minority children. *Reading Teacher, 32,* 677–679. Describes teaching reading lessons so as to involve children in ways that are consistent with oral language patterns in their native-language cultures.

Au, K. H., & Mason, J. M. (1983). Cultural congruence in classroom participation structures: Achieving a balance of rights. *Discourse Processes, 6,* 145–167. A study of teachers' modification of reading lesson structures to make them more compatible with students' natural talk patterns.

August, D., & Hakuta, K. (Eds.) (1997). *Improving schooling for language-minority children: A research agenda.* Washington, DC: National Academy Press. Reviews research on second-language learning and suggests research directions.

Barrera, R. (1984). Bilingual reading in the primary grades: Some questions about questionable views and practices. In T. H. Escobedo (Ed.), *Early childhood bilingual education: A Hispanic perspective* (pp. 164–184). New York: Teachers College Press. Examines issues involved in teaching reading to bilingual students.

Bernhardt, E. B. (1991). *Reading development in a second language: Theoretical, empirical, and classroom perspectives.* Norwood, NJ: Ablex. This book won an American Educational Research Association book award. The author details a theory of reading in a second language and reviews research.

Bernhardt, E. B. (2000). Second-language reading as a case study of reading scholarship in the 20th century. In M. L. Kamil, P. B. Mosenthal, P. D. Pearson, & R. Barr (Eds.), *Handbook of reading research* (Vol. III, pp. 791–811). Hillsdale, NJ: Lawrence Erlbaum. An excellent critical study of the history of second-language reading scholarship.

Carrell, P. L. (1987). Facilitating ESL reading by teaching text structure. *TESOL Quarterly, 19,* 727–752. Presents a study on teaching text structures to English-language learners.

Carrell, P. L. , Devine, J., & Eskey, D. E. (Eds.) (1988). *Interactive approaches in second language reading.* New York: Cambridge University Press. Describes a theory of second-language reading and classroom approaches consistent with the theory.

Carrell, P. L., Pharis, B. G., & Liberto, J. C. (1989). Metacognitive strategy training for ESL reading. *TESOL Quarterly, 23,* 647–678. Reports a study of teaching English-language learners to use metacognitive strategies.

Cazden, C. B. (1988). *Classroom discourse: The language of teaching and learning.* Portsmouth, NH: Heinemann. Examines classroom language.

Chikamatsu, N. (1996). The effects of L1 orthography on L2 word recognition: A study of American and Chinese learners of Japanese. *Studies in Second Language Acquisition, 18,* 403–432. A study of whether and how second-language learners use their knowledge of word patterns in their native language when they read words in a new language.

Chomsky, N. (1980). *Rules and explanations.* New York: Columbia University Press. This famous linguist describes rules of language learning.

Collier, V. P. (1987). Age and rate of acquisition of second language for academic purposes. *TESOL Quarterly, 21,* 617–641. A frequently referred to study of the length of time it takes to learn aspects of a new language.

Collier, V. P. (1989). How long? A synthesis of research on academic achievement in a second language. *TESOL Quarterly, 23,* 509–531. Reviews research on the length of time it takes to learn aspects of a new language.

Collier, V. P., & Thomas, W. P. (1989). How quickly can immigrants become proficient in school English? *Journal of Educational Issues of Language Minority Students, 5,* 26–38. A frequently referred to study of how long it takes to learn English in the academic setting.

Cummins, J. (1978). Educational implications of mother tongue maintenance in minority-language groups. *The Canadian Modern Language Review, 34,* 395–416. Discusses issues around maintaining one's native language abilities while learning a new language.

Cummins, J. (1979). Linguistic interdependence and the educational development of bilingual children. *Review of Educational Research, 49,* 222–251. A classic exposition of the relationships between first- and second-language learning with special emphasis on educational settings.

Cummins, J. (1981). Age on arrival and immigrant second language learning in Canada: A reassessment. *Applied Linguistics, 2,* 132–149. A frequently cited article on the length of time it takes to learn a new language, focusing on the Canadian setting.

Cummins, J. (1989). *Empowering minority students.* Sacramento: California Association for Bilingual Education. Discusses issues related to second-language learning.

Droop, M., & Verhoeven, L. (1998). Background knowledge, linguistic complexity, and second-language reading comprehension. *Journal of Literacy Research, 30,* 253–271. Reports a study of the interrelationships among knowledge, language, and reading.

Elley, W. B. (1981). A comparison of content-interest and structuralist reading programs in Niue primary schools. *New Zealand Journal of Educational Studies, 15*(1), 39–53. Presents a study of different forms of instruction for second-language learners.

Elley, W. B., & Mangubhai, F. (1983). The impact of reading on second language learning. *Reading Research Quarterly, 19,* 53–67. Presents a study of second-language learners' reading.

Fitzgerald, J. (1995a). English-as-a-second-language learners' cognitive reading processes: A review of research in the United States. *Review of Educational Research, 65,* 145–190. An integrative research review of studies on U.S. students learning to read English as a second language.

Fitzgerald, J. (1995b). English-as-a-second-language reading instruction in the United States: A research review. *Journal of Reading Behavior, 27,* 115–152. An integrative review of research on U.S. reading instruction for English-as-a-second-language learners.

Fitzgerald, J. (2001). English language learners' reading: New age issues. In P. R. Schmidt & P. B. Mosenthal (Eds.). *Reconceptualizing literacy in the new age of pluralism and multiculturalism.* Greenwich, CT: JAI Press. Discusses common questions asked by teachers about working with English-language learners. Focuses on settings where only English is used for instruction.

Fitzgerald, J. (2003). New directions in multilingual literacy research: Multilingual reading theory. *Reading Research Quarterly, 38,* 118–122. Explores ways in which theory development might benefit research and instruction in multilingual reading.

Fitzgerald, J., & Cummins, J. (1999). Essay book reviews: Bridging disciplines to critique a national agenda for language-minority children's schooling. *Reading Research Quarterly, 34,* 378–390. Reviews August and Hakuta's book (1997) on *Improving Schooling for Language-Minority Children.*

Fitzgerald, J., & Noblit, G. (1999). About hopes, aspirations, and uncertainty: First-grade English-language learners' emergent reading. *Journal of Literacy Research, 31,* 133–182. A study of two Latino children's English-language reading development during their first-grade year with the first author as their teacher.

Fitzgerald, J., & Noblit, G. (2000). Balance in the making: Learning to read in an ethnically diverse first-grade classroom. *Journal of Educational Psychology, 92,* 1–20. A study of children's reading development in the first author's first-grade balanced reading program. Half of the children in the class were Latino.

Floyd, P., & Carrell, P. L. (1987). Effects on ESL reading of teaching cultural content schemata. *Language Learning, 37,* 89–108. Presents a study of instructional effects on English-language learners' reading.

García, G. E. (1991). Factors influencing the English reading test performance of Spanish-speaking Hispanic children. *Reading Resarch Quarterly, 26,* 371–392. Details a study of explanations for Latino children's English reading test performance.

García, G. E. (2000). Bilingual children's reading. In M. Kamil, P. B. Mosenthal, P. D. Pearson, & R. Barr, (Eds.) *Handbook of reading research* (Vol. III, pp. 813–834). Hillsdale, NJ: Lawrence Erlbaum. An integrative review of research on bilingual reading.

Gersten, R. (1996). Literacy instruction for language-minority students: The transition years. *The Elementary School Journal, 96*(3), 228–244. Examines the importance of reading instruction for second-language learners.

Gersten, R., & Baker, S. (2000). What we know about effective instructional practices for English-language learners. *Exceptional Children, 66,* 454–470. A study of the knowledge base of effective instruction for English-language learners in elementary and middle school grades.

Geva, E. (1999). Learning to read in a second language: Implications for assessment and instruction. In T. Nunes (Ed.), *Integrating literacy, research and practice* (pp. 343–368). Dordrecht: Kluwer. Reports research on second-language reading especially as it relates to diagnosis and instruction of reading.

Geva, E., Wade-Woolley, L., & Shany, M. (1993). The concurrent development of spelling and decoding in two different orthographies. *Journal of Reading Behavior, 25,* 383–406. Found only weak relationships between second-language oral proficiency and second-language word recognition measures for young school children.

Geva, E., Yaghoub-Zadeh, Z., & Schuster, B. (2000). Understanding individual differences in word recognition skills of ESL children. *Annals of Dyslexia, 50,* 123–154. The authors studied the reading and oral language development of English-language learners and native-English-speaking children during their first- and second-grade years in all-English classrooms. They found similar profiles across the two groups on all but the oral English language measure.

Graves, M. F. (2000). A vocabulary program to complement and bolster a middle-grade comprehension program. In B. M. Taylor, M. F. Graves, & P. van den Broek (Eds.), *Reading for meaning: Fostering comprehension in the middle grades* (pp. 116–135). New York: Teachers College Press. Presents a full-fledged vocabulary program for students in the middle grades.

Gregg, K. R. (1984). Krashen's Monitor and Occam's razor. *Applied Linguistics, 5,* 79–100. Critiques the Monitor Model.

Hakuta, K. (1986). *Mirror of language: The debate on bilingualism.* New York: Basic Books. Discusses issues about bilingualism.

Hakuta, K., Ferdman, B. M., & Diaz, R. M. (1987). Bilingualism and cognitive development: Three perspectives. In S. Rosenberg (Ed.), *Advances in applied psycholinguistics: Reading, writing, and language learning* (Vol. II, pp. 284–319). New York: Cambridge University Press. Discusses interrelationships between language, bilingualism, and cognitive growth.

Heath, S. B. (1986). Sociocultural contexts of language development. In *Beyond language: Social and cultural factors in schooling language minority students* (pp. 145–186). Los Angeles: California State University Evaluation, Dissemination, and Assessment Center. Discusses a wide array of factors important to second-language learners' school success.

Heath, S. B., & Mangiola, L. (1991). *Children of promise: Literate activity in linguistically and culturally diverse classrooms.* Washington, DC: National Education Association. Examines the importance of language and cultural identity in learning.

Hedgcock, J., & Atkinson, D. (1993). Differing reading–writing relationships in L1 and L2 literacy development? *TESOL Quarterly, 27,* 329–333. Discusses the links between reading and writing in native language and in second language.

Jiménez, R. T. (1997). The strategic reading abilities and potential of five low-literacy Latina/o readers in middle school. *Reading Research Quarterly, 32,* 224–243. Reports on a case study of reading achievement for low-literacy middle-school Latino learners.

Jiménez, R. T. (2003). New directions in research: Literacy and Latino students in the United States: Some considerations, questions, and new directions. *Reading Research Quarterly, 38,* 122–128.

Jiménez, R. T., García, G. E., & Pearson, P. D. (1995). Three children, two languages, and strategic reading: Case studies in bilingual/monolingual reading. *American Educational Research Journal, 32,* 31–61. Describes research on second-language learners' reading progress.

Jimenez, R. T., García, G. E., & Pearson, P. D. (1996). The reading strategies of bilingual Latina/o students who are successful English readers: Opportunities and obstacles. *Reading Research Quarterly, 31,* 90–112. Reports a study of bilingual Latino students' reading strategies.

Johnson, K. E. (1992). The relationship between teachers' beliefs and practices during literacy instruction for non-native speakers of English. *Journal of Reading Behavior, 24,* 83–108. Examines the extent to which teachers' beliefs about English-language learners and their instruction are related to teachers' practices.

Johnson, P. (1982). Effects on reading comprehension of building background knowledge. *TESOL Quarterly, 17,* 503–516.

Johnson, R., & Supik, J. D. (1999, September). More students served in bilingual and ESL programs but more LEP students assigned to special education. *IDRA Newsletter* (http://www.idra.org/Newslttr/1999/Sep/Roy.htm). Provides statistics on bilingual student services in schools.

Klingner, J. K., & Vaughn, S. (1996). Reciprocal teaching of reading comprehension strategies for students with learning disabilities who use English as a second language. *The Elementary School Journal, 96*(3), 275–294. Presents a study of a particular form of reading instruction and its effects on English-language learners with learning disabilities.

Koda, K. (1993). Transferred L1 strategies and L2 syntactic structures in L2 sentence comprehension. *Modern Language Journal, 77,* 490–499. A study of second-language learners' use of the native language in understanding a new language.

Krashen, S. (1977). The Monitor Model for second language performance. In M. Burt, H. Dulay, & M. Finocchairo (Eds.), *Viewpoints on English as a second language.* New York: Regents. Presents a view of second-language learning that was widely embraced in instructional settings.

Krashen, S. D. (1985). *The input hypothesis: Issues and implications.* London: Longman. Presents a widely embraced view of aspects of second-language learning.

Krashen, S. D. (1988). Do we learn to read by reading? The relationship between free reading and reading ability. In D. Tannen (Ed.), *Linguistics in context: Connecting observation and understanding: Advances in discourse processes* (Vol. 2, pp. 269–298). Norwood, NJ: Ablex. Discusses the importance of wide reading to improve one's reading ability.

Krashen, S. (1991). *Bilingual education: A focus on current research.* (Focus Occasional Papers in Bilingual Education Number 3). Washington, DC: The George Washington University and Center for Applied Linguistics. Examines current research on bilingual education.

Krashen, S., & Biber, D. (1988). *On course: Bilingual education's success in California.* Sacramento: California Association for Bilingual Education. Provides evidence of the success of bilingual education.

Krashen, S., & Terrell, T. (1983). *The natural approach: Language acquisition in the classroom.* Hayward, CA: Alemany Press. Presents an instructional approach to support second-language learners.

Lantolf, J. P. (1994). (Ed.) Sociocultural theory and second language learning: Special issue. *Modern Language Journal, 78.* An informative collection of articles on second-language learning studies based in sociocultural theory.

Lantolf, J. P., & Appel, G. (1994). (Eds.) *Vygotskian approaches to second language research.* Norwood, NJ: Ablex. Presents a sociocultural outlook for second-language learning.

McLaughlin, B. (1987). *Theories of second-language learning.* Baltimore, MD: Arnold. Presents and discusses outlooks on how a second language is learned.

Mercer, J. (1973). *Labeling the mentally retarded.* Los Angeles: University of California. Provides statistics on children with special needs.

Mitchell, R., & Myles, F. (1998). *Second language learning theories.* London: Arnold. An excellent presentation and balanced critique of different theoretical outlooks on second-language learning.

Moll, L., & González, N. (1994). Lessons from research with language-minority children. *Journal of Reading Behavior, 26,* 439–456. Reports ways of teaching based on improved understandings of children's home cultures.

Ortiz, A. A., & Yates, J. R. (1983). Incidence of exceptionality among Hispanics: Implications for manpower planning. *NABE Journal, 7,* 41–54. Provides statistics on special education Latino learners.

Snow, C. E. (1992). Perspectives on second-language development: Implications for bilingual education. *Educational Researcher, 21,* 16–19. Examines research on second-language learning and presents implications of different perspectives.

Snow, C. E., Burns, S., & Griffin, P. (Eds.). (1998). *Preventing reading difficulties in young children.* Washington, DC: National Academy Press.

Snow, C. E., Tabors, P. O., Nicholson, P. A., & Kurland, B. F. (1995). SHELL: Oral language and early literacy skills in kindergarten and first-grade children. *Journal of Research in Childhood Education, 10,* 37–48. Presents a study of young children's oral language and reading abilities.

Steffensen, M. S., Joag-Dev, C., & Anderson, R. C. (1979). A cross-cultural perspective on reading comprehension. *Reading Research Quarterly, 15,* 10–29. A classic study on the effects of cultural knowledge on reading comprehension.

Weber, R. M., & Longhi, T. (1996, December). *Moving into ESL literacy: Three learning biographies.* Paper presented at the National Reading Conference, Charleston, SC. Studies three first-grade English-language learners' English reading progress.

Wong Fillmore, L., & Valadez, C. (1986). Teaching bilingual learners. In M. C. Wittrock (Ed.), *Handbook of research on teaching* (pp. 648–685). New York: Macmillan. Reviews research on instruction for bilingual students.

CHAPTER 4

THE THINKING BEHIND SCAFFOLDED READING FOR ENGLISH-LANGUAGE LEARNERS

The Scaffolded Reading Experience approach is rooted in a substantial body of theory and research, some of which has been done with English-language learners, and much of which has been done with native-language learners. In this chapter, we discuss the ideas that most influenced us as we considered using SREs with English-language learners. Some of these ideas are formal and properly deserve the term *theories*. Others are much less formal and are better termed *notions*. Some are complex and require serious study. Others are more easily grasped. All in all, it is a diverse set of ideas, linked by a single unifying theme: Each of these ideas makes a direct and practical statement about what can be done to assist English-language learners in reading and enjoying specific selections.

We have already introduced some of these ideas—the concept of SCAFFOLDING and the related concepts of the ZONE OF PROXIMAL DEVELOPMENT and the GRADUAL RELEASE OF RESPONSIBILITY MODEL. The concept of SCAFFOLDING is at the center of the plan we are presenting, and we want to amplify on what we said earlier here at the beginning of this chapter. Later in the chapter, we'll say more about the zone of proximal development and the gradual release of responsibility model.

In chapter 1, we defined a scaffold as a temporary supportive structure that enables a child to successfully complete a task he or she could not complete without the aid of the scaffold. Here, we want to modify that definition slightly by adding that, in addition to helping English-language learners complete tasks they could not complete without the aid of the scaffold, scaffolding can aid students by helping them better complete a task, complete a task with less stress or in less time, or learn more fully than they would have without the aid of the scaffold.

Training wheels for young children's bicycles are an excellent example of a scaffold used to assist youngsters in mastering a challenging physical task. Training wheels are temporary, they are supportive, they can be adjusted up or down to provide more or less support, and they allow a child to ride a bicycle with fewer falls, with less stress, and in a shorter amount of time than they would be able to do without the scaffold. This is very similar to the function that an SRE serves in supporting students' reading. An SRE maximizes the chances that students will understand the reading, learn from it, find it a nonthreatening experience, and generally enjoy both what they read and the experience of reading it.

In the remainder of this chapter, we have grouped the other ideas underlying the Scaffolding Reading approach for English-language learners under five headings: Student Engagement, Cognitive-Constructivist Learning Concepts, Sociocultural Outlook, Instructional Concepts, and Pedagogical Orientations. We have grouped our ideas under these five headings to avoid giving you one long list of topics. We stress, however, that the topics included in one of these areas could in some cases have been placed in another, and that the collection of topics within a single area is sometimes quite diverse. Grouping the topics is in fact a form of scaffolding that should aid you in understanding them and in remembering them.

Student Engagement

The theme of this section is that English-language learners' reading abilities can grow in direct proportion to the extent to which they are engaged in the reading they do. To be engaged, they need to see reading as an activity that they succeed at, an activity that is under their control and something they can improve at, and an activity that is a worthwhile and enjoyable. Being tightly engaged in reading has been shown to increase English-language learners' reading achievement (Waxman, de Felix, Martinez, Knight, & Padron, 1994). In elaborating on the theme of engagement, we consider three topics: the critical importance of success, attribution theory and learned helplessness, and the significance of creating a literate environment that will nurture English-language learners' reading and writing development.

Success

The dominant thought motivating not just this section of the chapter but the whole of this book is the overwhelming importance of success. As both the professional judgments of teachers and research have repeatedly verified (Brophy, 1986; Guthrie & Alvermann, 1999; Guthrie &

Wigfield, 2000; Pressley, 2002), if students are going to learn to read effectively, they need to succeed at the vast majority of reading tasks they undertake. Moreover, if students are going to become not only proficient readers but also avid readers—children and later adults who voluntarily seek out reading as a road to information, enjoyment, and personal fulfillment—then successful reading experiences are even more important.

Reading experiences can be successful in any of a variety of ways. Several of them deserve special consideration. First, and most importantly, a successful reading experience is one in which the reader understands what he or she has read. For some English-language learners in the beginning and middle phases of learning to read in English, "success" may depend on the teacher asking the student to target just a subset of text ideas. Or understanding may take more than one reading. It may require your assistance or that of other students, and it will sometimes require the reader to actively manipulate the ideas in the text—summarize them, discuss them with classmates, or compare them to other ideas. Second, a successful reading experience is one that the reader finds enjoyable, entertaining, informative, or thought provoking. To be sure, not every reading experience will yield all of these benefits, but every experience should yield at least one of them. Finally, a successful reading experience is one that prepares the student to complete whatever task follows the reading.

To some extent, children's success in reading is directly under your control. You can select, create, and encourage your students to select materials that they can read. You can "simplify" the student's reading goals to bring successful understanding into the reach of a student. To the extent that the material they read presents challenges, you can provide support before, during, and after they read that will enable them to meet those challenges. Additionally, you can select and help them select postreading activities that they can succeed at.

Doing this—targeting "just right" goals for learning from the reading, choosing selections, arranging activities, and selecting doable postreading tasks so that students are successful in their reading—is the essence of the Scaffolded Reading approach for English-language learners. Here, we give three brief examples of ways in which you can help ensure students' success. Suppose you have a group of English-language learners who read at about 100 words a minute and a 15-minute period in which they will be reading. Giving students a selection slightly shorter than 1,500 words will ensure that they at least have time to complete it, while giving them a selection much longer than 1,500 words is very likely to leave them frustrated and all but ensure failure.

As another example, suppose you have a group of students, including English-language learners, who will be reading a science chapter on the ecology of freshwater lakes but who have virtually no concept of ECOLOGY, who have never even thought about the relationships among organisms and their environment. Preteaching the concept of ecology—quite possibly in a fairly extensive lesson—will greatly increase the possibilities that students will understand the chapter and not simply flounder in a sea of new ideas.

As a third example, suppose that you have a group of students for whom the questions at the end of a social studies chapter on Reconstruction are likely to present too great a challenge. In such a case, you might cue students to the places where the questions are answered in the text. Or you might work through the first few questions as a group to get students off to a good start. The point, once again, is to do everything possible to ensure success.

In concluding this discussion of success, we want to point out an extremely important qualification. Beginning, and even middle-level, English-language learners *do* need an incredible amount of teacher support. But teachers should also be sensitive to trying to help each student to become an independent learner to the greatest extent possible. The goal of self-reliance should always be in sight. Teachers who gradually decrease the amount of their scaffolding and gradually increase the learners' responsibility are more likely to help their students to move toward independence. Unless readers undertake some challenging tasks, unless they are willing to take some risks and make some attempts they are not certain of and get feedback on their efforts, there is little room for learning to take place. Moreover, as Mihaly Csikszentmihalyi (1990) has discovered in more than three decades of research, facing significant challenges and meeting them is one of the most fulfilling and rewarding experiences a person can have. To develop as readers, English-language learners need to be given some challenges. However, it is vitally important to arrange and scaffold reading activities so that students can meet these challenges.

Attribution Theory and Learned Helplessness

Attribution theory deals with students' perceptions of the causes of their successes and failures in learning. As Michael Pressley (2002) explains, in deciding why they succeed or fail in reading tasks, students can attribute their performance to ability, effort, luck, the difficulty of the reading task, or a variety of other causes. On many occasions, English-language learners might rightly attribute a failure to a mismatch between their English-reading level and that required by the text or to teacher demands for learning that far exceed their English-reading level. However, often children who have repeatedly failed in reading wrongly attribute their failure to factors that are beyond their control—to an unchangeable factor such as their innate ability or to a factor that they can do nothing about such as luck. Once this happens, children are likely to lose their motivation to learn to read generally, and they are likely to doubt their capacity to successfully read and comprehend specific selections. From their perspective, there is no reason to try because there is nothing they can do about it. Moreover, as long as they do not try, they can't fail. You can't lose a race if you don't enter it.

As Peter Johnston and Peter Winograd (1985) have pointed out, one long-term outcome of children's repeatedly wrongly attributing failure in reading to forces that are beyond their control is their falling into a passive failure syndrome. Children who exhibit passive failure in reading are apt to be nervous, irritable, withdrawn, and discouraged when faced with reading tasks. They are unlikely to be actively engaged in reading, to have goals and plans when they read, to monitor themselves when they are reading to see if the reading makes sense, or to check themselves after reading to see if they have accomplished their reading goal. Finally, even when they are successful—and this is not likely to be very often—children who are passive failures are likely to attribute their success to luck, or their teacher's skill, or some other factor they have no control over.

Obviously, we need to break this cycle of negative attributions and learned helplessness. Here, we suggest three approaches. The first, and almost certainly the most powerful, is something we just stressed: Make reading a successful experience; make it so frequently successful for a student that he or she will be compelled to realize that it is himself or herself and not some outside force that is responsible for the success. Second, tell students that their efforts make a difference, and when they are successful in a reading task, talk to them about the activities they engaged in to make them successful. If, for example, after reading an informational piece about dinosaurs students successfully answer several questions about dinosaurs that they generated before reading the selection, discuss how generating those questions beforehand helped them focus their attention so that they could find the answers to the questions as they read. Third, try to avoid competitive situations in which students compare how well they read a selection to how well others read it and instead focus students' attention on what they personally gained from the selection. Even just a few words or a smile from you to an English-language learner about the positive things she did for the reading selection might provide encouragement and some measure of feeling successful. Finally, provide a number of reading activities in which the goal is to enjoy reading, have fun, and experience something interesting and exciting rather than only offering reading activities that are followed by discussion or some other sort of external accountability.

A Literate Environment

The phrase *literate environment* describes a classroom, school, and home environment in which literacy is fostered and nurtured (Goodman, 1986; Graves, Juel, & Graves, 2001). Probably the most important component of a literate environment is the modeling done by people children respect and love. In the richest literate environment, children's teachers, principals, parents, brothers and sisters, and friends read a lot and openly display the pleasure reading gives them, the fact that reading opens up a world of information to them, the value they place in reading, and the satisfaction they gain from reading. Also, many bilingual families and teachers read and tell stories in their native languages a lot.

To be most effective, this modeling should occur not just once but repeatedly—all the time, really. Also, this modeling should include both repeated demonstrations—your reading along with students during a sustained silent reading period, you looking up an answer to a question children have in a book, and your sharing a favorite poem with your class—and direct testimonials—"Wow! What a story." "I never knew what fun river rafting could be till I read this article; I sure wish I'd read it sooner." "Sometimes I think the library is just about my favorite place."

Another important component of a truly literate environment is the physical setting in which children read; for teachers, this generally means the classroom. In a highly literate environment, the classroom is filled with books, books that are readily accessible for students to read in school or take home. The walls are covered with colorful posters that advertise books and the treasures they offer. And there are several comfortable and inviting places to read—a carpeted corner of the room where children can sit on the floor and read without interruption, bean bags or other comfortable chairs that entice young readers to immerse themselves in a book, places where students can gather in groups to read to each other or discuss their reading, and some tables for students to use when reading prompts them to write.

Still another component of a rich literate environment is the content of the books, magazines, and other reading materials that are available to students. The reading materials you have available for your students need to reflect the diversity of your classroom—the range of abilities, interests, and cultural, linguistic, and social backgrounds of your students—as well as the diversity of the larger society outside your classroom. What students read must connect with their individual experiences if reading is to have meaning for them. What students read must connect them to the larger society if both students and the larger society are to prosper.

A final and equally important component of a literate environment is the atmosphere in which children read. For teachers, this again means the classroom. In the richest literate environment, everything that happens in the classroom sends the message that reading—learning from what you read, having personal responses to what you read, talking about what you read, and writing about what you read— is fantastic! In such a classroom, children are given plenty of time to read, they are given ample opportunities to share the information they learn and their responses to what they have read with each other, they are taught to listen to and respect the ideas of others, and they learn that others will listen to and respect their ideas. A literate atmosphere is a thoughtful atmosphere in which values and ideas are respected—values and ideas in books, one's own values and ideas, and other people's values and ideas.

In concluding this section on student engagement, we emphasize that the concepts described here—success, attribution theory and learned helplessness, and literate environment—are interrelated. Frequent success is crucial, and one of the most fulfilling sorts of success is achieving at challenging tasks. One reason that success is crucial is that it precludes learned helplessness; successful students are simply not faced with the repeated failures that lead them to attribute failure to factors beyond their control. Finally, a literate environment both nurtures success and provides students a secure place that enables them to deal positively with the small failures they will inevitably encounter from time to time.

Cognitive-Constructivist Learning Concepts

After reviewing research on instruction with English-language learners and consulting with professionals who work with English-language learners, Gersten and Baker (2000) concluded that instruction should incorporate principles that emanate from advances in cognitive psychology. Cognitive psychologists view the mind as central to learning and the study of learners' thought processes as a central focus of their work. They also view learners as active participants who act on rather than simply respond to their external environment as they learn. More recently, certainly by the 1980s, constructivism became a prominent force in psychology, particularly educational psychology; and as we begin the 21st century, may educators see themselves as constructivists. Five concepts that have emerged from what might be called the *cognitive-constructivist* (Graves et al., 2004) orientation—schema theory, the interactive model of reading, automaticity, constructivism, and reader response theory— are particularly important to understanding the reading process, reading instruction, and the SRE approach.

Schema Theory

Schema theory is concerned with the way knowledge is represented in our minds and its importance to learning. Knowledge is packaged in organized structures termed *schema*. According to David Rumelhart (1980), schema constitute our knowledge about "objects, situations, events, sequences of events, actions, and sequences of actions." We have schema for objects such as a house, for situations such as being in a class, for events such as going to a football game, and for sequences of events such as getting up . . . eating . . . showering . . . and going to work. We interpret our experiences—whether those experiences are direct encounters with the world or vicarious experiences gained through reading—by comparing and in most cases matching those experiences to an existing schema. In other words, we make sense of what we read and of our experiences more generally by a tacit process that in essence tells us "Ah ha. This is an instance of such and such."

Quite a few studies have been done on English-language learners' use of schema. Most of the studies have used methodologies patterned after studies done with native-English speakers (Fitzgerald, 1995), and most were done with adults. Only a few explored schema issues at the seventh grade or lower. Collectively, the studies suggest that English-language learners use schema to affect their comprehension and recall, just as native-English speakers do (Fitzgerald, 1995).

Both what we learn and the ease or difficulty of the learning are heavily influenced by our schema. The more we know about something, the easier it will be to deal with that topic and learn more about it. Three sorts of schema that children possess to varying degrees are particularly important to consider as we plan reading instruction. One of these is knowledge of the world and its conventions—knowledge about the makeup of families, about daily events such as children going to and returning from school and adults going to and returning from work, about institutions such as churches and the government, about holidays such as Memorial Day and Martin Luther King's birthday, about places such as zoos and the beach, and about a myriad of other events, places, institutions, objects, and patterns of behavior. Children acquire a good deal of this knowledge simply by growing up in and experiencing the world. This knowledge will generally serve students well in understanding narratives—stories, plays, and novels—because this is the principal sort of knowledge that narratives require. However, if children grew up in a culture different from that depicted in the narrative, as often happens with English-language learners, then the world and conventions they understand may be different from those depicted in the narrative, and they will need some help developing appropriate schema for the narrative. Additionally, of course, if your classroom includes students representing several cultural backgrounds, you will want to take into account students' cultural backgrounds when you choose reading selections and deliberately choose some selections particularly appropriate for each of the cultural groups represented in the class.

Another sort of schema that children possess to varying degrees is schema about the ways in which different types of texts are organized. Many children have relatively well-developed schema for the organization of narratives because most narratives mirror the temporal order of the world they live in and most narratives have a similar structure. Most narratives have a beginning, a middle, and an ending; most have characters that are involved in a plot that includes some sort of complication; and most end with some sort of resolution to the complication. Moreover, most children have had numerous experiences with narratives both in school and at home (RAND Reading Study Group, 2002). However, it is important for teachers to understand that some English-language learners may bring with them schema that are different from the ones we typically expect as native-English speakers. For instance, students from Spain or Central and South American countries may have been exposed to written and orally recounted stories that have "surreal" qualities and event orders which to native-born North Americans are unusual. If students have had considerable acquaintance with such stories, they might find stories we consider "typical" as "strange," and as a consequence they might encounter difficulties in understanding the sequence and content of such stories (see Steffensen, Joag-Dev, & Anderson, 1979). So even in the case of narrative texts, it is a good idea for teachers to "check out" the English-language learners' understanding and to use SREs to help students acquire the schema in the narratives that are used in class.

Unfortunately, most children do not have well-developed schema for the structure of expository material, the informational material they encounter in social studies, math, science, health, and the like (RAND Reading Study Group, 2002). This is true because children often have not had much experience with expository material, because expository material can have a number of different structures, and unfortunately because a good deal of the expository material children read is not very well structured (Chambliss & Calfee, 1998). Many times students will benefit from additional help in dealing with expository material.

The third sort of schema that children possess to varying degrees are schema for the content of various subjects—knowledge about science, about history, and about geography. Most of this knowledge does not come from simply living in the world. Much of it comes from formal schooling. Each year, teachers help students build their knowledge in such areas as history, health, math, and science. Until students develop their schema for various content areas, they will often need assistance in successfully reading in these areas.

As a final comment on the importance of schema in reading, we quote a particularly eloquent statement by Marilyn Adams and Bertrand Bruce (1982): "Without prior knowledge, a complex object such as a text is not just difficult to interpret; strictly speaking, it is meaningless."

Interactive Model of Reading

The interactive model of reading serves to remind us that both the reader and the text play important roles in reading. In arriving at the meaning of a text, Rumelhart (1977) has explained, readers use both their schema and the letters, words, phrases, sentences, and longer units in a text. Moreover, they use these various sources simultaneously and in an interactive fashion. They do not, for example, look at a sentence with no idea what it will be about, zero in on the first word, first recognize the letter *t* and then the letter *h* and then the letter *e*, decide that the word is *the*, and then move on to do the same thing with the next word. Instead, readers begin a passage with some idea of what it will be about, encounter the letter string *t-h-e* and decide that it is the word *the* partly because it's followed by the noun *cat* and partly because *the* is fairly frequently the first word in a sentence, and determine that the third word in the sentence is *meowed* partly because that's what cats do, partly because of its spelling, and partly because it makes sense in the sentence.

Many researchers and theoreticians have based their studies of English-language learners' reading in the interactive view of reading (Fitzgerald, 1995). Some have detailed why the interactive model of reading is applicable for English-language learners (Carrell, Devine, & Eskey, 1988).

Good readers need to rely appropriately on the texts they are reading and their background knowledge to arrive at meaning, and teachers need to provide them with the sorts of texts and tasks that promote their doing so. For English-language learners who are reading in English, this is likely to be especially true. For example, giving students who are in the early stages of learning English a selection that deals with a largely unfamiliar topic and that includes a lot of difficult vocabulary may force them to give undue attention to the individual words they encounter, to neglect summoning up their prior knowledge to bear on their understanding of the text. More seriously, having students do a lot of oral reading, emphasizing their being 100 percent correct in their oral reading, and putting them in a position where they face a penalty for being incorrect will almost certainly force them to give undue attention to the text and focus on words and letters rather than sentences, paragraphs, and ideas. For example, having students who read at low levels or new English learners read orally in front of their peers without adequate preparation for doing so is likely to lead them to focus almost all their attention on correctly pronouncing individual words and thus give little attention to meaning.

Conversely, having children only read silently and providing no follow-up to what they read, or having them repeatedly engage in postreading discussions that are only vaguely related to what they read, may encourage students to give too little attention to the text itself. In such situations, some students may largely ignore the words and sentences on the page, frequently guess at the meaning of what they are reading, and make little use of the text in confirming their guesses. For example, giving students a steady diet of individualized reading may not provide them with sufficient opportunities to check their understanding of what they have read with you or with other students, and without such checks they may fall into a habit of guessing a great deal. Again, an appropriate balance of attention to the text itself and to prior knowledge is the goal.

Automaticity

An automatic activity is one that we can perform instantly and with very little attention. As David LaBerge and S. Jay Samuels (1974) pointed out in their pioneering work on automaticity in reading, the mind's attentional capacity is severely limited; in fact, we can only attend to about one thing at a time. If we are faced with a task in which we are forced to attend to too many things at once, we will fail. For example, a number of people have reached a level of automaticity in driving a stick shift car. They can automatically push in the clutch, let up on the accelerator, shift gears, let out the clutch, and press on the accelerator; and they can do all this while driving in rush-hour traffic. Beginning drivers cannot do all of this at once; they have not yet automated the various subprocesses, and it would be foolish and dangerous for them to attempt to drive a stick shift car in rush-hour traffic.

Reading includes a number of subprocesses that need to take place at the same time—processes such as recognizing words, assigning meanings to words, constructing the meanings of sentences and larger units, and relating the information gleaned from the text to information we already have. Unless some of these processes are automated, readers simply cannot do all of this at once. Specifically, readers need to perform two processes automatically: They need to recognize words automatically, and they need to assign meanings to words automatically. For example, if a student is reading and comes across the word *imperative*, he or she needs to automatically recognize the word and automatically—immediately and without conscious attention—know that it means "absolutely necessary." If the student needs to pause very often and go through this sort of mental process to recognize and assign meanings to words, reading will be difficult and laborious, and the student will not understand much of what he or she is reading.

Achieving automaticity can be a particular challenge for English-language learners in the beginning and middle stages of learning English. When students are learning to read in English, they must focus on so many facets of the reading process that attaining automaticity in any of the subprocesses of reading can be strenuous. Not surprisingly, some research indicates that many English-language learners at various stages of learning to read English take more time than do native-English speakers for some subprocesses, such as using metacognitive strategies and monitoring their own comprehension, and they tend to read more slowly (Fitzgerald, 1995).

The road to automaticity can require considerable patience for English-language learners and their teachers. To become automatic at an activity, we need to practice the activity a lot in nontaxing situations. To become automatic in reading, students need to do a lot of reading in materials they find relatively easy, understandable, interesting, and enjoyable; and they need to do that reading in situations that are nontaxing, that is, in situations in which they can read for enjoyment and not be faced with difficult questions or requirements based on the reading. One way to assist students with automaticity is encouraging them and giving them a lot of opportunities for independent reading in material they find interesting and enjoyable (Pressley, 2002). Another way is to provide them with classroom reading materials that are at their instructional reading level in English and their native language.

Unfortunately, in content areas in the upper grades, matching classroom reading materials to the instructional levels of new English learners is usually very difficult. Fortunately, though, it is still possible for content-area teachers to help English-language learners to move toward automaticity in English reading. One way is to encourage students to read in native-language material they feel competent with, since skills and strategies learned in the native language often transfer to English reading. When English-language learners do have to cope with English content-area texts at their frustrational levels, it is important to remind them that automaticity takes time when learning in a new language and you're not expecting them to cope with the *whole* text and *all* of the ideas in it. In the beginning, for example, asking the student to become automatic with a handful of the new vocabulary words in a text may be the best way to move toward automaticity.

Constructivism

Constructivism is a philosophical and psychological position that holds that much of the meaning of a text is constructed by the individual (Cunningham & Fitzgerald, 1996). As Dennis Phillips (1995, 2000) notes, constructivism is a diverse construct with a number of roots, and exactly how much texts shape and constrain meaning is a matter of debate. However, most constructivists place a good deal of emphasis on the reader's contribution. Many constructivists also hold that the social world in which we live heavily influences our interpretations (Gergen, 1985). These two views—the belief that much of the meaning a reader arrives at when reading a text is actually constructed by the reader and the belief that social interactions heavily influence readers' constructions—have important implications for reading instruction. Here, we discuss three of them.

Most obviously, constructivism serves as a direct reminder that comprehending a text is an active, constructive process. Constructivists often use the phrase *making meaning* to emphasize the reader's active role in comprehending texts. Students cannot just passively absorb meaning from texts. A truly passive reading would leave the reader simply having turned the pages. Instead, readers must actively engage with the text, consider what they are reading, and link the information they are gleaning from the text with ideas, topics, and events they already know. Moreover, the more difficult a text becomes for students—the more new and challenging information it presents—the more actively engaged readers must be.

As we just noted, in addition to emphasizing the active nature of reading, constructivism adds a new point to the view of the reading process we are describing: The meaning one constructs from a text is subjective, the result of that particular reader's processing of the text. Just as no two builders will construct exactly the same house from a blueprint, so no two readers will construct exactly the same meaning from a text. A particular reader's processing is influenced by the sum total of her experience as well as by her unique intellectual makeup. Because of this, each reader constructs a somewhat different interpretation of the text, the text as he or she conceptualizes it (von Glaserfeld, 1984). One reader's conceptualization of a text will never be precisely that of another.

Finally, an implication of the constructivist tenet that readers create meaning with texts as a social process is that teachers can use group projects and group discussion as a means of helping students to become better meaning makers. Students need to be given opportunities to work together in preparing to read texts, in considering alternate interpretations of texts, in writing about what they read, in preparing and delivering oral presentations on their reading, and in completing projects prompted by the reading. Group work is likely to be especially beneficial for English-language learners, especially when groups are mixed by native language. Group work gives students chances to talk through and gradually build up their interpretations of a text in a nonthreatening setting. Group work also gives students opportunities to teach each other, to learn from each other, to get actively involved in learning, and to learn that others often have alternate interpretations of texts. More generally, as many educators are currently noting (e.g., Johnson, Johnson, & Holubec, 1994; Slavin, 1991), group work gives students the opportunity to learn to work together, a skill that is becoming increasingly important in today's interdependent world. At the same time that we endorse group work, we want to note that not all group work is constructivist (Marlowe & Page, 1998) and not all group work is productive (Anderson, Reder, & Simon, 1998). *Circles of Learning* (Johnson et al., 1994) contains a number of sound ideas for orchestrating effective group work.

Reader Response Theory

Reader response theory has much in common with constructivism. However, reader response theory differs from constructivism in that it has different roots than constructivism and deals specifically with reading, particularly with reading literature. Reader response theory originated in the work of I. A. Richards (1929) and Louise Rosenblatt (1938/1995) more than half a century ago, but it was slow to influence classroom instruction. During the past 30 years, however, it has had a very prominent influence on literature instruction (Beach, 1993; Galda & Guice, 1997; Marshall, 2000). Reader response theory puts a good deal of emphasis on the reader. It stresses that the meaning one gains from text is the result of a transaction between the reader and the text and that readers will have a range of responses to literary works (Rosenblatt, 1938/ 1995, 1978). When reading complex literary texts, students will derive a variety of interpretations. Many literary texts simply do not have a single correct interpretation; and readers should be allowed and encouraged to construct a variety of interpretations—if they can support them.

At this point, a caution is in order: One very important fact to keep in mind when considering reader response theory is that it applies primarily to certain types of texts and certain purposes for reading. As part of explaining when and where reader response theory applies, Rosenblatt (1978) points out that there are two primary types of reading: *efferent* or informational reading and *aesthetic* reading. In efferent reading, the reader's attention is focused primarily on what he or she will take from the reading—what information will be learned. Much of the reading that both students and adults do is done for the sake of learning new information, answering questions, discovering how to complete a procedure, or gleaning knowledge that can be used in solving a particular problem. Much of the reading done in such subjects as health, science, math, and geography is informational reading. These texts, unlike many literary texts, often constrain meaning substantially, do not invite a variety of interpretations, and should yield quite similar interpretations for various readers (Stanovich, 1994).

The other sort of reading Rosenblatt considers, *aesthetic* reading, is quite different. In aesthetic reading, the primary concern is not with what students remember about a text after they have read it but with what happens to them as they are reading. The primary purpose when reading aesthetically is not to gain information but to experience the text. Although the aesthetic reader, like the reader whose goal is gaining information, must understand the text, he or she must "also pay attention to associations, feelings, attitudes, and ideas" (Rosenblatt, 1978, p. 25) that the text arouses. For the most part, literature is written to provide an aesthetic experience. Most adults read literature for enjoyment; they do not read literature to learn it. Students need to be given opportunities to do the same.

In considering how this distinction between aesthetic and informational reading affects what you do in the classroom, several points should be kept in mind. First, reader response theory does not imply that one sort of reading is superior to the other. Students need to and deserve to become adept at reading as an aesthetic experience; students also need to and deserve to become adept at reading to gain information. Second, although much of the reading students do in textbooks and in other material used in content areas is informational reading and much of the reading they do in the novels and short stories they encounter is aesthetic reading, literary texts often contain useful information and informational texts can often yield aesthetic enjoyment and pleasure. Finally, as noted earlier, in order to have an appropriate aesthetic response, some understanding of a text is necessary; if youngsters read John Steinbeck's *The Red Pony* and do not understand that Jody feels partly responsible for the pony's death, it would be very difficult for them to have a full response to the piece. Moreover, if students are to learn about literary texts, to learn how literary texts are constructed and how to better understand and more fully enjoy literary texts, students need to sometimes treat literary texts as information to be studied.

In concluding this section on cognitive-constructivist learning concepts, we very briefly review the major educational implications of each concept. Schema theory emphasizes the importance of making sure that students have the background knowledge to read the texts you assign. The interactive model of reading reminds us that the reader needs to use both the text and his or her background knowledge in understanding selections. The notion of automaticity signals the importance of students doing a lot of reading that is relatively easy for them—the sort of reading we as adults do when we read the newspaper, a magazine, or a popular novel—so that they can become automatic. Constructivist theory highlights the fact that reading is an active constructive process, explains that constructing meaning for a text is a subjective process, and underscores the values of group work. Finally, reader response theory stresses the value and appropriateness of personal responses to literature.

Sociocultural Outlook

The SRE is based in part on a sociocultural outlook. The term *sociocultural* refers to a family of theories with roots in the writings of Vygotsky (1978) (cf. Forman, McCormick, & Donato, 1998). We will talk more about Vygotsky and some of his ideas later in this chapter. For now, the most important thing to understand is the basic idea of a sociocultural outlook as it applies to SREs for English-language learners—that language and literacy, meanings and understandings, are inseparable from the cultural and social contexts in which they occur. The cultural and social contexts can be immediate, as in the small group students are working in, or they can be more distanced, as in the context of the whole school climate or local communities' attitudes and beliefs.

For an example, consider two classroom scenarios as our sociocultural context. When a teacher stands in front of a class and lectures just about the whole time, she creates a classroom culture in which students and the teacher alike assume that the teacher's knowledge about the topic is more important than what the students know, and that the students need to absorb and *ventriloquate* (Bakhtin, 1981) what the teacher knows and says. Students learn that the teacher's role is powerful and that their own social role is to be a recipient who should internalize the teacher's ideas and language. Sometimes, such absorption and ventriloquism is just what is needed in a classroom, but we do not think it should dominate in classrooms with English-language learners, especially those who are just beginning to learn English.

Now imagine another classroom scenario, one in which the teacher regularly uses SREs. Today, she begins by presenting important vocabulary for a new reading selection, asks the students what they already know about this topic, has them read a few pages, and then asks them to discuss the main ideas of what they read in small groups. This teacher's classroom culture reveals different understandings about learning and about language. Students in this classroom are more likely to assume that they should bring their own knowledge to bear as they create new understandings, that they learn about ideas and language by interacting with the teacher and one another, and that they have some power over their own learning.

Do you see how the way in which the teacher sets up the lesson has social and cultural implications? Our position is that, although some kinds of learning are best achieved through lecture, others are best achieved through other means, and using SREs is one way to effect a classroom environment in which English-language learners learn that a teacher cares about them and their learning, that their voice is important, and that what they already know from their own lives and prior schooling is not only useful, but valued.

As shown in the heuristic for thinking about comprehension created by the RAND Reading Study Group (2002), students, tasks, and activities all exist within a sociocultural context. Thoughtful use of SREs can help make your classroom a place where all participants, their ideas, and their efforts are valued and supported.

A Heuristic for Thinking About Reading Comprehension

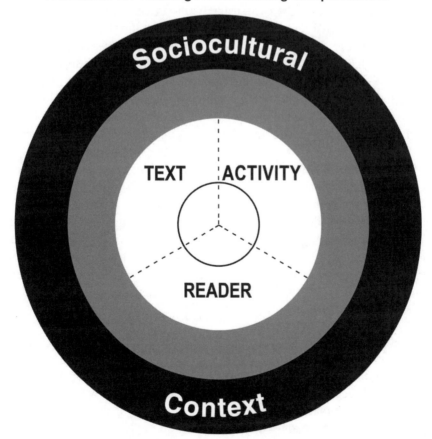

Instructional Concepts

In this section of the chapter, we consider six instructional concepts that are especially relevant to English-language learners and the use of SREs: modulated instruction, the "hybrid model" of teaching, active teaching, active learning, the zone of proximal development, and the gradual release of responsibility model. Together, these ideas suggest some very powerful approaches to instruction for English-language learners.

Modulated Instruction

When Russell Gersten and Scott Baker (2000) conducted their review of studies on effective instruction with English-language learners, they did a unique thing. They simultaneously held five nationwide professional work group meetings to find out what experienced practitioners and researchers working with English-language learners saw as promising and productive practices. They called their study "multivocal" research. A major finding from their meetings with the professionals was that, although the professionals thought principles of effective instruction in general were important considerations when working with English-language learners, they also consistently stressed that instruction needed to be *modulated* for English-language learners. Gersten and Baker provide a metaphor to explain what the professionals meant, saying: "Effective instruction for English-language learners is . . . teaching that is tempered, tuned, and otherwise adjusted as a musical score is adjusted, to the correct 'pitch' at which English-language learners will best 'hear' the content (i.e., find it most meaningful)."

We think that SREs are useful with English-language learners because they are rooted at least in part in the more general literature and theory related to effective instruction, but SREs can be adapted in so many ways that they are a model of the concept of modularity. You can plan and conduct lessons with goals for specific students in mind and easily adapt the lessons, either by doing something for a whole class or by doing one part for some class members while other class members do something else. Matching activities to specific student goals for learning is central to the idea of SREs.

Hybrid Model of Teaching English-Language Learners

Another result of Gersten and Baker's (2000) review of instructional research and meetings with professionals was that they were able to describe a model of teaching with English-language learners that represents a good deal of consensus. They called this the *hybrid model*. The hybrid model of good teaching for English-language learners has three main characteristics: Teachers employing the hybrid model use (1) structured dynamic teaching, which involves students in fairly long, complex verbal exchanges with their teachers and peers and also involves plentiful teacher guidance; (2) instructional approaches described in the effective teaching literature; and (3) principles of teaching derived from advances in cognitive psychology. As they talked about this model, professionals also emphasized that an important goal of the hybrid model of teaching is that students develop both language proficiency and academic knowledge.

We believe that SREs illustrate the critical features of the hybrid model. They are structured; require dynamic and not static or routinized teaching; engage students with texts, teachers, and peers; involve lots of teacher guidance; and are based in instructional principles that have emerged from both the effective teaching literature and from advances in cognitive psychology. Moreover, development of both language proficiency and academic performance are at the heart of SREs.

Active Teaching

The term *active teaching* refers to a set of principles and teaching behaviors that teacher effectiveness research has shown to be particularly effective. As noted by Brophy (1986), teachers who engage in active teaching are the instructional leaders of their classrooms; they are fully knowledgeable about the contents and purposes of the instruction they present and about the instructional goals they wish to accomplish. Active teachers do a lot of teaching. Although they use discovery learning for some purposes, they do not generally rely on students discovering what it is they are supposed to learn. Similarly, although they use a variety of materials as part of their teaching, they do not rely on materials to do the teaching. Often, they directly carry the content to be learned to students in short presentations, discussions, and demonstrations. When active teachers use cooperative groups, they make certain that each group is made up of students who can and will work together, that students have the training necessary to work cooperatively, that group members have clearly defined goals, and that each group has definite goals. When active teachers have students work on projects, whether in groups or alone, they make certain that students understand their goals at the outset, monitor students' work, and give them periodic feedback as they work to accomplish those goals.

Active Learning

In discussing constructivism, we noted that comprehending text is an active, constructivist process. Here, we want to stress that all learning is the result of active, constructive processes. Just as it is vital that the teacher be actively involved in teaching, it is also vital that the learner be actively involved in learning (Brophy & Good, 2003). The learner must do something with the material he or she is studying if he or she is to truly learn from it. As David Perkins (1992) points out, "Learning is a consequence of thinking." The learner must somehow think about—mentally manipulate—the material to be learned. This mental manipulation can take a variety of forms: The learner might apply the new information, as for example a science student does when he or she develops a theory about the flow of electricity and designs a circuit to test that theory. The learner might compare or contrast the information to already known information. Or he or she might use the new information in a creative endeavor such as writing a story. These are just a few of the myriad possibilities for active learning; there are countless others. But some type of involved mental activity is absolutely necessary. As Ernest Boyer (1988) put it after observing that not much active learning was taking place in the classrooms,

> If students are to excel, they must be actively engaged in learning. The mastery of subject matter is essential. But unless students are creative, independent thinkers, unless they acquire the tools and motivation to go on learning, the prospects for excellence will be enormously diminished.

Zone of Proximal Development

The concept of the ZONE OF PROXIMAL DEVELOPMENT is primarily attributed to the Russian psychologist Lev Vygotsky (1978). The notion places major emphasis on the interactive nature of learning, stressing that learning is very much a social phenomena. We learn much of what we learn in our social interchanges with others. That is, much learning is constructed through the interplays between individuals. According to Vygotsky, at any particular point in time, children have a circumscribed zone of development, a range within which they can learn. At one end of this range are learning tasks that they can complete independently; at the other end are learning tasks which they cannot complete, even with assistance. Between these two extremes is the zone most productive for learning, the range of tasks at which children can achieve *if* they are assisted by some more knowledgeable or more competent other.

Teachers' understanding of the zone of proximal development is likely to be especially critical when students are learning a second language. While all students learn best if teachers can help to negotiate their learning within the "zone," English learners are especially overwhelmed by the myriad of reading processes they are trying to acquire or stabilize. Understanding each learner's knowledge level for the particular content and understanding each learner's English instructional reading level are likely to be extremely important for effectively moving English learners along.

If left on their own, for example, many third graders—native English speakers and English-language learners alike—might learn very little from a *National Geographic World* article on the formation of thunderstorms. Conversely, with your help—with your spending some time getting them interested in the topic, focusing their attention, preteaching some of the critical concepts such as the effects of rising heat, and arranging small groups to discuss and answer questions on certain parts of the article— these same students may be able to learn a good deal from the article. However, with other topics and other texts—for example, with a chapter on gravity from a high school text—no amount of outside help, at least no reasonable amount of outside help, will foster much learning for these third graders. The topic of gravity and its presentation in the high school text is simply outside the third graders' zone of proximal development.

Outside of school, many people can and do serve as more knowledge- able or more competent others—parents and foster parents, brothers and sisters, relatives, friends, and clergy. As a teacher creating scaffolded read- ing activities, you may occasionally be able to bring in outside resources to assist students. If there are English learners in your class, involving adult resources from their native lands and adults who speak their native languages is a good way to show respect for the diverse cultures and lan- guages and to particularly pique the English learners' interest. Moll and González (1994) conducted studies in which Latino adults became re- sources for Latino students' classroom instruction. You may wish to read about some of the ways in which this kind of work was accomplished.

Often, however, you will arrange reading situations so that you serve as the more knowledgeable other who assists students in successfully read- ing selections they could not read on their own. Additionally, in many cases students will be able to pool their resources and assist each other in dealing with reading selections they could not successfully handle alone.

The Gradual Release of Responsibility Model

The gradual release of responsibility model depicts a progression in which students gradually assume increased responsibility for their learning. The model was first suggested by Joseph Campione in 1981, and since that time it has had a very significant effect on reading in- struction. David Pearson and Margaret Gallagher (1983) presented a particularly informative visual representation of the model, and we have included a slightly modified version of it here.

Gradual Release of Responsibility Model

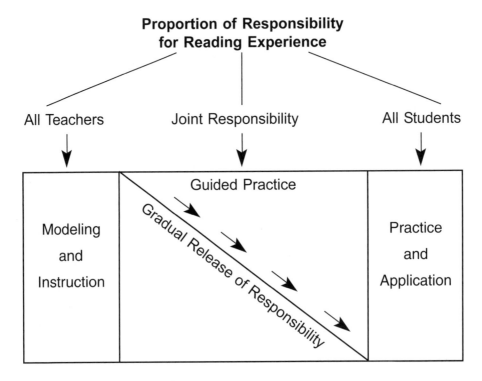

The model depicts a temporal sequence in which students gradually progress from situations where the teacher takes the majority of the responsibility for their successfully completing a reading task (in other words, does most of the work for them), to situations where students assume increasing responsibility for reading tasks, and finally to situations where students take total or nearly total responsibility for reading tasks.

Here, we give several concrete examples to illustrate these notions. Consider a kindergarten or first-grade teacher in early October seated in a circle with a group of children and displaying a big book—a book large enough that a group of children can all see the pictures and the print. The book has a colorful cover with a picture providing some good clues to what the book is about and a similarly revealing title. The teacher reads the title aloud and talks a little bit about what it and the picture on the cover make him think of. Then, he asks the children what the title and picture make them think of and what the book might be about. After listening to students' responses and trying to emphasize and highlight those that are likely to help students understand the story, the teacher begins reading. Even though there are only a handful of words on each page and even though the story is a very simple one, the teacher stops every two or three pages, asks students what has happened, summarizes the story up to that point if children's responses suggest a summary is necessary, and perhaps asks students what they think will happen next. After completing the story, the teacher may ask students a few questions to see if they understood it. Or he may get some other sorts of responses from them—how they felt about one of the characters, if they have had any experiences similar to those in the story, or what emotions the story aroused in them. He might also share his understanding of the story and some of his personal responses to it. But whatever he does afterwards, he will try to ensure that each student has gotten something from the story and leaves the experience feeling good about it.

At home, many of the children will tell their parents what they did in school, and many will say that they read a story. But of course they really didn't read a story on their own. The teacher selected the book, gathered the children together, previewed the story and built their interest for it, read it to them, checked on their understanding and summarized events when necessary, and engaged them in postreading tasks they could accomplish. Appropriately, the teacher took a huge proportion of the responsibility for their "reading" the story.

Now consider this same teacher and class in January. During the past four months, the teacher has continued to take much of the responsibility for students' reading. He has done a lot of building interest, reading to students, checking on understanding, and the like. Additionally, over this same period, he has gradually introduced children to longer and more challenging books. At this point, when students go to read something like the very simple picture book they read in October, he will let them handle it largely on their own, perhaps having children self-select books and then pair off to read and share them. With the more challenging books, however, the teacher will continue to scaffold activities.

This same process of gradually releasing responsibility holds for older students—for fourth graders, for eighth graders, for high school students, and even for college students. It holds for English-language learners as well. As students progress through school, they assume increased responsibility for their learning. As English-language learners continue to grow, whether they are learning in their native language or in English, they assume increased responsibility for their learning.

The gradual release of responsibility model emphasizes that over time the goal is to dismantle the scaffolds we have built to ensure children's success. However, children do not repeatedly deal with the same sorts of text over time. Instead, over time, students deal with increasingly challenging texts and with a broader range of topics. Moreover, the English-language learner may encounter added challenges such as when texts they read contain culturally unfamiliar material, when texts are organized in a way that is not compatible with the types of organization known in their home language, or when the student is beginning to learn to read in English.

At any particular point in time, English-language learners are likely to be—and probably should be—dealing with some texts that are more challenging and some that are less challenging. For instance, some fourth-grade English-language learners who have been schooled in the United States and reading in English for quite some time will be able to take full responsibility for reading an easy novel such as *Skinnybones* by Barbara Park. These same students may need you to assume some of the responsibility for their successfully dealing with a somewhat challenging historical novel such as *Pedro's Journal* by Pam Conrad, and they may require you to assume a great deal of the responsibility for their successfully dealing with an expository article on acid rain. Some eighth-grade English-language learners may be able to take full responsibility for dealing with an article on acid rain much like the one fourth graders needed your help with, but they may need you to assume some of the responsibility for their successfully dealing with a thought-provoking novel such as Steinbeck's *The Red Pony*. You might also assume a great deal of the responsibility for their successfully dealing with a challenging short story such as Ray Bradbury's "The Foghorn."

In considering the gradual release model as it applies to scaffolding reading activities, we emphasize three ideas: The first idea is that SREs are completely compatible with the concept of GRADUAL RELEASE. When teachers do prereading, during-reading, and postreading activities with students, they are essentially shouldering much of the work involved in the reading assignment. The second idea is that the gradual release model inherently points to the importance of the roles of text difficulty in relation to students' developmental reading levels and content-area knowledge in deciding on how much responsibility is appropriate for teachers and how much is appropriate for students. As grade levels increase, and as students participate in more and more intense content learning, you will generally encounter classes in which some students—English-language learners and others—are mismatched with the required texts. In these cases, SREs provide ways to support students in spite of the mismatch because by selecting activities from SRE menus, you can take up more of the responsibility for structuring learning and then, by selecting different activities, gradually turn over more of the responsibility to students. The third idea relates to the recursive nature of the gradual release model; that is, you and your students will cycle through the model many times.

For instance, some students will need more support for certain types of content material than for others. SREs are flexible so that you can choose more or less structured activities as they are needed.

As we did with the previous section, we conclude this one by briefly reviewing the instructional implications of each of the concepts presented. The concept of modulated instruction suggests that much instruction that is effective with native-English speakers is generally effective with English-language learners, but that instruction will often have to be fined tuned so that it is fully appropriate for English-language learners. The hybrid model of teaching indicates that instruction for English-language learners is structured and dynamic, is consistent with the effective instruction literature, and incorporates more recent advances from cognitive psychology, for example, scaffolding. The concept of active teaching makes it clear that teaching is not a passive endeavor; teachers frequently need to carry the content to be learned to the students. The concept of active learning makes it similarly clear that learning is not a passive process; the learner needs to be involved in the learning process and mentally manipulate the material to be learned. The concept of the zone of proximal development indicates that there is a circumscribed range within which children can learn, that the assistance of a more knowledgeable or competent other person extends this range, and that instruction should be targeted to present learning tasks that are within this range. The gradual release of responsibility model indicates that for English learners who are beginning to learn to read in English and for more advanced English learners who are dealing with new and difficult material, the teacher might begin instruction by doing all or most of the work and, to the extent possible, end with students doing all or most of the work. The gradual release of responsibility model also indicates that when the learning task becomes really difficult, virtually any learner will benefit from the aid of a skillful teacher.

Pedagogical Orientations

In this last section of the chapter, we discuss four pedagogical orientations, four contemporary stances toward teaching and learning that apply to English-language learners. These include reflective teaching, literature-based instruction, making use of the relationship between reading and writing, and teaching for understanding.

Reflective Teaching

The concept of teacher reflection was first introduced by John Dewey (1909/1933), who saw the reflective teacher as a person who deliberately and consciously reflects on his or her instruction and its effects on students. Somewhat more recently, the concept of reflection was revived and elaborated on by Donald Schön (1983), who examined the place of reflections in professionals such as engineers, architects, and managers. The concept continues to be an influential one today (Eby, Herrill, & Hicks, 2002).

As applied to teaching, reflection is a cyclic process in which teachers repeatedly view their ongoing instruction and the results of that instruction as a series of problems to be examined and temporarily solved. We say *temporarily* solved because a central tenet of reflective teaching is that there is no single or ultimate solution to instructional questions; the context in which instruction takes place will heavily influence what is appropriate in any particular case. In reaching these temporary solutions, reflective teachers use knowledge they have acquired formally in their own education, their experience and intuitions, and the ongoing events of the classroom. A reflective teacher consciously reflects on all aspects of the learning situation—the students, the materials, the learning activities, and what is learned—the aspects of learning considered in the Scaffolded Reading approach. Additionally, one very important object of reflection is the values inherent in what is being taught and in the teaching itself (Calderhead, 1992).

Three considerations are essential to optimizing your ability to create the best possible reading experiences for students: considering all aspects of the learning situation, observing the experience as it unfolds in the classroom, and evaluating that experience. Moreover, to the extent that you share your reflections with students, you will not only be honing your own teaching but assisting them in becoming more conscious about what does and does not work for them as they are reading.

Suppose, for example, that your class is reading a selection about world hunger, a selection that you judged to be fairly easy for all the students in your class, including your English-language learners. Also suppose you assumed that the selection would easily gain their attention. So you consequently did little prereading preparation. A few minutes after students begin reading, however, you notice that some of them are not engaged in the reading. A few students are talking, a few heads are nodding, and quite a few pairs of eyes look a bit glazed. A reflective teacher would first notice the situation and then decide what to do about it. The decision, of course, could only be made in the context of a specific class reading a specific selection. One alternative, however, would be to interrupt the class at that point and attempt to kindle or rekindle interest and commitment in the topic. Another would be to decide that an interruption at that point would be counterproductive and instead make alternative plans for students' next encounter with a similar topic. If the latter were your choice, further reflection might focus on whether you could find texts that were intrinsically more interesting, or whether with such topics you need to include more motivational and interest-building activities as part of prereading instruction. Finally, the fact that the topic of world hunger and the materials and approach used in presenting the topic did not result in much engagement on the part of students would itself be a matter for reflection.

As another example, suppose you plan a set of activities for a health lesson on communicable diseases and decide that many of the concepts are difficult ones for many students in your class, including your advanced English-language learners, and you will therefore need to do a lot of preteaching of concepts and building background knowledge. Consequently, you prepare a substantial set of prereading activities. However, when you begin the prereading activities, you quickly learn that your initial assessment of students' knowledge on communicable diseases was incorrect; your students in fact know a lot about the topic. Of course, one appropriate step here is to truncate the planned prereading instruction and let students get on with the reading itself. Beyond that, however, as a reflective teacher you would want to consider what led you to underestimate students' knowledge in the first place and make a conscious effort to avoid doing so in the future.

Importantly, a central tenet of reflective teaching is that such reflection should be a continuing process for all teachers, that it is not something that you only do until you get it "right" or something only new teachers do. The complexities of the classroom—the ever changing combination of students, texts, learning activities, and goals—require that reflection be an ongoing part of teaching.

Literature-Based Instruction

Two very prominent principles of literature-based instruction are (1) that children ought to enjoy reading and become lifelong, dedicated readers who view reading as a rich source of information and insight, and (2) that enjoyment is every bit as important as becoming competent in the cognitive practice of reading. We strongly endorse both of these principles. Students succeeding at reading and realizing that they have succeeded are major goals of every SRE.

Another literature-based principle is that the situation in which children learn and use their literacy skills is crucial to their success. The supportive and encouraging "literate environment" described earlier in the chapter is the type of setting in which literacy flourishes.

Still another principle is that risk taking is a necessary part of learning to read. We have already noted the importance of risk taking in qualifying our emphasis on the importance of success with the caution that students need to face some challenges if their reading and other literacy skills are to grow. Also, considering students' zone of proximal development and providing the support they need to achieve at the outer limits of their competence is one method of encouraging and supporting risk taking.

The final principle we highlight, and one we will return to, is that reading and writing are supportive skills that should often be integrated with each other. We discuss the close relationship between reading and writing in the next section.

Advocates of literature-based instruction such as Leslie Morrow and Linda Gambrell (2000), children's literature scholars such as Lee Galda, Gwynne Ash, and Bernice Cullinin (2000), and the vast majority of reading educators place special emphasis on the value and importance of quality children's literature in the reading program. Good literature is seen as particularly valuable and supportive of children's growing competency in reading because it deals with important and widely applicable themes. Good literature often has great emotional appeal and thus has the potential to foster students' love of reading—to create readers who are both competent and motivated to read. This is likely to be especially true for English-language learners when they see themselves and their cultures represented in the books they read. Some good literature for young children uses repetitive refrains, parallel sentence structure, and is highly predictable. This is probably particularly helpful for the beginning English-language learner. Other good literature can present challenges to the new English learner when sentence structures are complex and new or difficult vocabulary meanings are plentiful. For more advanced English learners, such books can stretch children's growing competence with language and serve as models for their own writing.

Finally, it is worth noting that quality children's literature includes both narratives and exposition. To be sure, a lot of good literature consists of narratives—stories. Narratives offer a particular advantage to beginning readers because they follow an organizational structure that children are already familiar with. They involve a setting, a cast of characters, a plot with some sort of complications, and a resolution to those complications. Such familiar structures nourish children's understanding and memory for what is read and thus make the task of learning to read easier. However, children also need to read and learn from expository material—informational materials, including textbooks. Scaffolded Reading activities are designed to support both reading narrative literature and reading expository material, such as textbooks, informational trade books, magazine articles, and the like.

Making Use of the Relationship Between Reading and Writing

Reading and writing are related in many ways (Fitzgerald & Shanahan, 2000). For instance, reading is an excellent prompt for writing. Frequently, one of the biggest problems facing students as they begin to write is having something to write about. But reading often solves that problem. The student who has just finished Avi's *The True Confessions of Charlotte Doyle* is likely to have an easy time writing about how he would feel if he suddenly found himself in Charlotte's shoes, alone on a ship with a cruel and murderous captain and a crew bent on reaping their revenge before the voyage ends. And fiction is not the only sort of reading that can stimulate writing. The student who has studied a chapter dealing with black widow spiders has gained a lot of information that could be used in writing a descriptive piece about some creepy and crawling creature she has encountered.

Another way in which reading and writing are related is that writing complements and aids students with their reading. The student who writes about how he would feel if he were in Charlotte's place is learning to relate to fictional characters, empathize with them, and consider how their experiences are similar to and different from his own. The student who writes the descriptive piece prompted by what she has read about black widows is engaged in generative learning, establishing a relationship between information in a text and her existing knowledge and experiences. The writing should improve both her understanding of what she has read and her memory for the information. More generally, writing is an excellent study technique, one that is by its nature active and constructive.

For English-language learners, writing has the added advantage of forcing attention to the relationships between sounds in the language and letters and spelling rules as well as to syntactical structures. Again, for the beginner English learner, there is so much to attend to that the teacher must be careful about what is required of the student.

Still another advantage of linking reading and writing is that students can learn a lot about reading from writing. As Robert Tierney and David Pearson (1983) have explained, it is useful to view reading as a composing process, as a situation in which a reader must actively construct meaning. Particularly for students who are not active readers, the process of composing may serve as a cue to the importance of getting actively involved in their reading. Additionally, students can learn a lot about reading from writing because both processes employ the same organizational structures. A student who has just written a narrative and has found that organizing the piece was almost automatic is in an excellent position to discuss just what constitutes the narrative form and to realize that most narratives follow a prototypic form. Conversely, a student who has just written an informational piece and found that he or she had to struggle with a number of different ways of organizing the piece is in a good position to recognize the fact that expository writing can have many structures and that dealing with the organization of expository materials when reading them may be a demanding task.

Finally, reading, writing about what they read, and sharing that writing with other students allows students to appreciate a host of complex features of reading and writing. Writers usually write for some purpose; they have information they want to communicate, a position they want to support, or an idea or feeling they wish to convey. Readers usually read for some purpose; they may want to learn something, they may wish to be entertained, or they may seek an aesthetic experience from reading. Writers often have to strive to convey their messages, and despite the attempt not all messages are successful. Authors must write in different ways for different readers; what will inform or please one reader will not necessarily satisfy another. Different readers will come away from the same text with quite different messages and quite different responses. The list of subtleties to be learned is nearly endless, and such subtleties will not be learned simply because reading and writing are taught and practiced together, but combining experiences in reading and writing can certainly help to promote such learning.

Teaching for Understanding

During the past decade or so, a number of educators and researchers have given considerable attention to teaching for understanding (Graves, 1999; Graves & Liang, in press). Particularly useful from a classroom teacher's perspective is the work of Fred Newmann (Newmann, Secada, & Wehlage, 1995), Grant Wiggins and a colleague (Wiggins & McTighe, 1998), and David Perkins and his colleagues (Blythe, 1998; Perkins, 1992; Wiske, 1998). Perkins' approach is the one that has been described most completely in the literature and the one we describe here. However, we stress that each of these approaches has a number of exciting and innovative features and that you might want to look at the work of all three of these authorities.

An important prelude to understanding Perkins' notion of teaching for understanding and its importance is the realization that in some ways schooling is not going well even for our best students, that all too few students attain the deep level of understanding critical in today's world (Bransford, Brown, & Cocking, 2000; RAND Reading Study Group, 2002; Shavelson & Towne, 2002). Recent reports suggest that many students in the upper elementary and secondary grades are not able to fully understand much of the material they read (Clinton, 2002; Sum, Kirsch, & Taggart, 2002). Such results bode extremely poorly for students' success in the information age.

Students need to be able to deeply understand what they read. They must, for example, be able "to explain, muster evidence, find examples, generalize, apply concepts, analogize, represent in a new way, and so on" (Perkins, 1992, p. 13). To teach for understanding, Perkins explains, we must go beyond simply presenting students with information and ensure that they accomplish three tasks:

1. They must understand topics deeply.

2. They must retain important information.

3. They must actively use the knowledge they gain.

Not all SREs can or should be designed to lead students to such deep understanding. For your English-language learners, it will be especially important to make sure that you fit the goal to the particular learner so that the student is challenged to progress toward deep understanding, but isn't overwhelmed and frustrated because too much is asked of her. Sometimes your purpose for reading a selection will be for students to simply enjoy it. But at other times, you definitely want to foster deep understanding; and SREs can help foster that understanding. Appropriate prereading, during-reading, and postreading activities can help students understand topics deeply. Appropriate postreading activities—particularly activities in which students actively investigate, manipulate, and transform the information they have learned—will lead to retention of important information. Other appropriate postreading activities—particularly activities that give students opportunities to apply what they have learned from reading to their lives and the world they live in—will prepare them to actively use the knowledge they gain from reading.

As with the two previous sections, we end this one with educational implications. Because the four notions presented—reflective teaching, literature-based instruction, making use of the relationship between reading and writing, and teaching for understanding—are pedagogical concepts, the implications are straightforward. As teachers, we need to be reflective; we must continually examine our teaching and its results and attempt to make our instruction and our students' learning more and more effective. First-rate literature, exposition as well as narratives, should be a major component of every reading program. Reading and writing belong together and mutually support each other, and the two should frequently be intertwined in SREs and other classroom activities. Finally, while the goals of SREs are as varied as your students and the texts they read, teaching for deep understanding is one particularly important goal.

Concluding Comments

In this chapter, we have described much of the thinking that prompted us to develop the Scaffolded Reading approach and that has continued to shape the approach. The ideas that motivated us have, as we noted earlier, been diverse. They include affective concerns such as the importance of success, concepts from cognitive psychology such as the importance of prior knowledge, a sociocultural outlook in which language and learning are viewed as inseparable from their social and cultural contexts, general instructional concepts such as the gradual release of responsibility, and current ideas about teaching and learning such as the value of integrating reading and writing instruction. While a narrower range of underpinning concepts for SREs might at first seem desirable, we have decided that this is not the case for two reasons. First, the Scaffolded Reading approach is itself diverse and multifaceted because it is designed so that you can tailor activities to a wide array of students, texts, and purposes of reading. It is not surprising that a diverse set of concepts is needed to underpin such a flexible plan. Second, we very much believe that a variety of perspectives offer useful ideas about teaching and learning and that no single perspective or small set of perspectives can offer all the background teachers need to meet the challenging goal of SREs: to make each and every reading experience a successful one for each and every student, including of course English-language learners.

References

Adams, M., & Bruce, B. (1982). Background knowledge and reading comprehension. In J. A. Langer and T. M. Smith-Burke (Eds.), *Reader meets author: Bridging the gap* (pp. 2–25). Newark, DE: International Reading Association. A brief and very readable discussion of the importance of background knowledge to reading comprehension.

Anderson, J. R., Reder, L., & Simon, H. A. (1998). Radical constructivism and cognitive psychology. In D. Ravich (Ed.), *Brookings papers on educational policy, 1998* (pp. 227–278). Washington, DC: Brookings Institution Press. Three eminent psychologists' carefully crafted response to what they see as the excesses of radical constructivism.

Bakhtin, M. M. (1981). *The dialogic imagination: Four essays by M. M. Bakhtin* (M. Holquist, Ed.; C. Emerson & M. Holquist, Trans.). Austin: University of Texas Press.

Beach, R. W. (1993). *A teacher's introduction to reader-response theories.* Urbana, IL: National Council of Teachers of English. A thorough and quite sophisticated introduction to reader response.

Blythe, T. (1998). *The teaching for understanding guide.* San Francisco: Jossey-Bass. A very practical, teacher-oriented guide to teaching for understanding as developed by David Perkins and his colleagues.

Boyer, E. L. (1988). *College: The undergraduate experience in America.* New York: Perennial Library. Influential critique of undergraduate education.

Bransford, J. D., Brown, A. L., & Cocking, R. R. (Eds.) (2000). *How people learn: Brain, mind, experience, and school* (expanded ed.). Washington, DC: National Academy Press. A major synthesis of what we know about teaching and learning based on work commissioned by the National Research Council.

Brophy, J. (1986). Teacher influences on student achievement. *American Psychologist, 41,* 1069–1077. Concise summary of the findings of the teacher effectiveness research.

Brophy, J., & Good. T. (2003). *Looking into classrooms* (9th ed.). Boston: Allyn & Bacon. Chapters 3 and 4 provide detailed information on the authors' position on active teaching and effective instruction generally.

Calderhead, J. (1992). The role of reflection in learning to teach. In L. Vali (Ed.), *Reflective teacher education: Cases and critiques* (pp. 139–146). New York: SUNY Press. A lucid treatment of the importance of reflection in becoming an effective teacher.

Campione, J. (1981, April). *Learning, academic achievement, and instruction.* Paper presented at the second annual Conference on Reading Research of the Center for the Study of Reading, New Orleans, LA. The original source of Campione's widely endorsed and very useful gradual release of responsibility model.

Carrell, P. L., Devine, J., & Eskey, D. E. (1988). *Interactive approaches to second language reading.* New York: Cambridge University Press. Describes a theory of second-language reading and classroom approaches consistent with the theory.

Chambliss, M. J., & Calfee, R. C. (1998). *Textbooks for learning: Nurturing children's minds.* London: Blackwell Publishers. A truly insightful book on improving learning by improving textbooks.

Clinton, P. (2002, September/October). Literary in America: The crisis you don't know about. *Book*, L4–L9. Discussion of the reading problems of middle-grade and secondary students

Csikszentmihalyi, M. (1990). *Flow: The psychology of optimal experience.* New York: Harper & Row. This popular book summarizes Csikszentimahalyi's three decades of work on optimal human experiences—the joy, creativity, and total involvement he terms *flow.*

Cunningham, J. W., & Fitzgerald, J. (1996). Epistemology and reading. *Reading Research Quarterly, 31,* 36–60. Discusses epistemologies underlying various views of reading.

Dewey, J. (1909/1933). *How we think.* Lexington, MA: D. C. Heath. Dewey's classic text on the relationship of reflective thinking to effective teaching.

Eby, J. W., Herrell, A. L., & Hicks, J. L. (2002). *Reflective planning, teaching, and evaluation, K–12* (3rd ed.). Upper Saddle River, NJ: Merrill/Prentice Hall. Well-known text with reflection as a central theme.

Fitzgerald, J. (1995). English-as-a-second-language learners' cognitive reading processes: A review of research in the United States. *Review of Educational Research, 65,* 145–190. An integrative research review of studies on U.S. students learning to read English as a second language.

Fitzgerald, J., & Shanahan, T. (2000). Reading and writing relations and their development. *Educational Psychologist, 35,* 39–50. Survey of research on this topic.

Forman, E. A., McCormick, D., & Donato, R. (1998). Learning what counts as a mathematical explanation. *Linguistics and Education, 9,* 313–339. One view of a sociocultural perspective.

Galda, L., Ash, G. E., & Cullinin, B. E. (2000). Children's literature. In M. Kamil, P. Mosenthal, P. D. Pearson, & R. Barr (Eds.), *Handbook of reading research* (Vol. 3, pp. 361–379). New York: Longman. Major review of the research on children's literature.

Galda, L., & Guice, S. (1997). Response-based reading instruction in the elementary grades. In S. A. Stahl & D. A. Hayes (Eds.), *Instructional models in reading* (pp. 311–330). Mahwah, NJ: Lawrence Erlbaum. An overview of the reader-response approach.

Gergen, K. J. (1985). The social constructionist movement in modern psychology. *American Psychologist, 40,* 266–275. One of the most readable introductions to social constructionist thinking.

Gersten, R., & Baker, S. (2000). What we know about effective instructional practices for English-language learners. *Exceptional Children, 66,* 454–470. A study of the knowledge base of effective instruction for English-language learners in elementary and middle school grades.

Goodman, K. (1986). *What's whole in whole language?* Toronto, Canada: Scholastic TAB. A concise overview of the whole-language approach by one of the founders of the movement.

Graves, M. F. (1999, October). Fostering high levels of reading and learning in secondary students [40 paragraphs]. *Reading Online* [on-line journal]. Available: http://www.readingonline.org/articles/graves1/.

Graves, M. F., Juel, C., & Graves, B. B. (2004). *Teaching reading in the 21st century* (3rd ed., Chap. 2). Boston: Allyn & Bacon. Chapter 2 of this comprehensive elementary reading methods text includes a description of what constitutes a literate environment.

Graves, M. F., & Liang, L. A. (in press). On-line resources for fostering understanding and higher-level thinking in senior high school students. *Fifty-first National Reading Conference Yearbook*. Chicago: National Reading Conference. Empirical study of SREs that stress higher-order thinking.

Guthrie, J. T., & Alvermann, D. E. (1999). *Engaged reading: Processes, practices, and policy implications.* Newark, DE: International Reading Association. An edited collection of chapters on reading engagement and related topics.

Guthrie, J. T., & Wigfield, A. (2000). Engagement and motivation in reading. In M. Kamil, P. Mosenthal, P. D. Pearson & R. Barr (Eds.), *Handbook of reading research* (Vol. 3, pp. 403–422). Mahway, NJ: Lawrence Erlbaum. A contemporary review of research on engagement, motivation, and related factors.

Johnson, D. W., Johnson, R. T., & Holubec, E. J. (1994). *The new circles of learning.* Alexandria, VA: ASCD. A concise yet very complete description of what cooperative learning is and how to prepare students to succeed in cooperative learning groups.

Johnston, P. H., & Winograd, P. N. (1985). Passive failure in reading. *Journal of Reading Behavior, 17,* 279–301. A powerful and important explanation of this very destructive phenomenon.

LaBerge, D., & Samuels, S. J. (1974). Toward a theory of automatic information processing in reading. *Cognitive Psychology, 6,* 293–323. The original description of this simple yet powerful concept.

Marlowe, B. A., & Page, M. L. (1998). *Creating and sustaining the constructivist classroom.* Thousand Oaks, CA: Carwin Press. A brief book on constructivist instruction.

Marshall, J. (2000). Response to literature. In M. Kamil, P. Mosenthal, P. D. Pearson, & R. Barr (Eds.), *Handbook of reading research* (Vol. 3, pp. 381–402). Mahwah, NJ: Lawrence Erlbaum. A thoughtful overview and analysis of reader-response research.

Moll, L. C., & González, N. (1994). Critical issues: Lessons from research with language-minority children. *Journal of Reading Behavior: A Journal of Literacy, 26,* 439–456. Some research findings on working with English-language learners.

Morrow, L. M., & Gambrell, L. B. (2000). Literature-based reading instruction. In M. Kamil, P. Mosenthal, P. D. Pearson, & R. Barr (Eds.), *Handbook of reading research* (Vol. 3, pp. 563–586). Mahwah, NJ: Lawrence Erlbaum. Major review on literature-based instruction.

Newmann, F. M., Secada, W. G., & Wehlage, G. G. (1995). *A guide to authentic instruction and assessment: Vision, standards and scoring.* Madison, WI: Wisconsin Center for Educational Research. An overview of Newmann's authentic instruction approach.

Pearson, P. D., & Gallagher, M. C. (1983). The instruction of reading comprehension. *Contemporary Educational Psychology, 8,* 317–344. Still a useful summary of the research on teaching reading comprehension.

Perkins, D. (1992). *Smart schools: From training memories to educating minds.* New York: Free Press. A well-written, engaging, and comprehensive consideration of teaching for understanding.

Phillips, D. E. (1995). The good, the bad, and the ugly: The many faces of constructivism. *Educational Researcher, 24* (7), 5–12. Explores several meanings of this complex and often difficult to pin down concept.

Phillips, D. E. (Ed.). (2000). *Constructivism in education.* Chicago: National Society for the Study of Education. A recent analysis of constructivism as it applies to education.

Pressley, M. (2002). *Reading instruction that works: The case for balanced teaching* (2nd ed., Chap. 8). New York: Guilford Press. An extremely thorough review of the research on elementary reading instruction. Chapter 8 deals specifically with motivation.

RAND Reading Study Group. (2002). *Reading for understanding: Toward an R&D program in reading comprehension.* Santa Monica, CA: RAND Education. Excellent report on the research on comprehension and comprehension instruction.

Richards, I. A. (1929). *Practical criticism.* New York: Harcourt Brace. An early influence on contemporary response theory.

Rosenblatt, L. (1938/1995). *Literature as exploration.* New York: Appleton-Century. Rosenblatt's original presentation of her response theory.

Rosenblatt, L. (1978). *The reader, the text, the poem: The transactional theory of the literary work.* Carbondale, IL: Southern Illinois University Press.

Another presentation of Rosenblatt's response theory; both this and her 1938 book have had enormous influence on the teaching of literature.

Rumelhart, D. E. (1977). Toward an interactive model of reading. In S. Dornic (Ed.), *Attention and performance* (Vol. 6, pp. 573–603). Hillsdale, NJ: Lawrence Erlbaum. The original description of the interactive model, done by one of the major researchers in the area.

Rumelhart, D. E. (1980). Schemata: The building blocks of cognition. In R. J. Spiro, B. C. Bruce, & W. F. Brewer (Eds.), *Theoretical issues in reading comprehension* (pp. 33–58). Hillsdale, NJ: Lawrence Erlbaum. One of the original descriptions of schema theory, done by a pioneer researcher on the topic.

Schön, D. (1983). *The reflective practitioner*. New York: Basic Books. The book that first prompted current interest in the importance of teacher reflection.

Shavelson, R. J., & Towne, L. (2002). *Scientific research in education*. Washington, DC: National Academy Press. Examines methods in educational research and some of the reasons educational research is so important.

Slavin, R. E. (1987). *Cooperative learning: Student teams* (2nd ed.). Washington, DC: National Education Association. A brief overview of several of Slavin's approaches to cooperative learning.

Stanovich, K. E. (1994). Constructivism in reading education. *The Journal of Special Education, 28,* 259–274. Notes that texts vary markedly in the extent to which they constrain meaning.

Steffensen, M. S., Joag-Dev, C., & Anderson, R. C. (1979). A cross-cultural perspective on reading comprehension. *Reading Research Quarterly, 15,* 10–29. A classic study on the effects of cultural knowledge on reading comprehension.

Tierney, R. J., & Pearson, P. D. (1983). Toward a composing model of reading. *Language Arts, 60,* 568–580. A cogent perspective on reading as an active, constructive process.

Sum, A., Kirsch, I., & Taggart, R. (2002). *The twin challenges of mediocrity and inequality: Literacy in the U.S. from an international perspective*. Princeton, NJ: Educational Testing Service. A sobering look at literacy in the U.S.

von Glaserfeld, E. (1984). An introduction to radical constructivism. In P. Watzlawick (Ed.), *The invented reality* (pp. 17–40). New York: W. W. Norton. An introduction to radical constructivism and a defense of it.

Vygotsky, L. S. (1978). *Mind in society.* Cambridge, MA: Harvard University Press. One of Vygotsky's classic texts, probably best known for its description of the zone of proximal development.

Waxman, H. C., de Felix, J. W., Martinez, A., Knight, S. L., & Padron, Y. (1994). Effects of implementing classroom instructional models on English language learners' cognitive and affective outcomes. *Bilingual Research Journal, 18,* 1–22. A study of different types of instruction with English-language learners.

Wiggins, G., & McTighe, J. (1998). *Understanding by design.* Alexandria, VA: Association for Supervision and Curriculum Development. The basic description of Wiggins' approach to teaching for understanding.

Wiske, M. S. (Ed.). (1998). *Teaching for understanding: Linking research with practice.* San Francisco: Jossey-Bass. A detailed look at teaching for understanding by the participants of the Harvard Teaching for Understanding research group.

Children's Literature Cited

Avi. (1990). *The true confessions of Charlotte Doyle.* New York: Orchard.

Bradbury, R. (1990). The foghorn. In *The stories of Ray Bradbury.* New York: Alfred A. Knopf.

Conrad, P. (1991). *Pedro's journal.* Honesdale, PA: Boyds Mills.

Park, B. (1982). *Skinnybones.* New York: Alfred A. Knopf.

Steinbeck, J. (1955). *The red pony.* New York: Bantam.

CHAPTER 5

PREREADING
ACTIVITIES

The first set of optional activities for a Scaffolded Reading Experience (SRE) prepares English-language learners for a successful reading experience before they begin reading. Taking time to adequately prepare English-language learners before they read will likely pay big dividends in their reading fluently, understanding what they read, learning from what they read, and finding reading an enjoyable and rewarding experience. In chapter 2, we described the ten categories of prereading activities listed below. As we have noted, the last two categories apply as well to during-reading and postreading activities. However, we will not repeat these two categories in the following chapters.

PREREADING

1. Motivating
2. Relating the reading to students' lives
3. Building or activating background knowledge
4. Providing text-specific knowledge
5. Preteaching vocabulary
6. Preteaching concepts
7. Prequestioning, predicting, and direction setting
8. Suggesting strategies
9. Using students' native language
10. Involving English-language learner communities, parents, siblings

Here, we elaborate on these descriptions and give examples of activities in each of these categories. Before doing so, we should point out that it might be useful to think of these categories as serving four different purposes. Activities in the first two categories, motivating and relating the reading to students' lives, serve primarily to get students interested and even excited about reading the upcoming selection. Activities in the next four categories—building and activating background knowledge, providing text-specific knowledge, preteaching vocabulary, and preteaching concepts—build students' knowledge, providing them with a sturdy base for understanding the text. Activities in the next category—prequestioning, predicting, and direction setting—key students to what they are to attend to as they read. The eighth category—suggesting strategies—gives you an opportunity to remind students of strategies they already know that will be particularly useful in the upcoming selection. Finally, the last two categories draw on your English-language learners' strengths in their native languages and bring their cultures into the classroom.

The different types of prereading activities described in detail in this chapter are intended to prompt you to consider a wide array of activities as you plan effective prereading instruction. As you consider the various types of activities, you will find that a number of them overlap. That's fine. We created the categories to suggest the range of options available, not so that you could neatly classify each activity you create as this or that.

As we explained in chapter 2, in planning an SRE you initially consider three factors: the students, the selection, and the purpose or purposes for which students are reading. After either you or your students have selected the text to read and after you have read through it and identified topics, themes, potentially difficult vocabulary, and other salient features of the material, you begin to map out the entire SRE. What is your students' overall goal for reading? Is it primarily for an aesthetic experience, or is it to gain information or insights? Will getting the gist of the material be sufficient, or do students need to gain a deep and thorough understanding of it? The kinds of activities students will be involved in before, during, and after reading will reflect these goals.

As you continue planning prereading activities, ask yourself questions such as "How can I get these students really interested in this selection? What sort of background knowledge do they have on this topic? What might they need to know to profit most from their reading? Is there anything in the material I can relate to their lives? Are there any concepts or vocabulary in the selection that students might benefit from working with? Could they use any of their repertoire of reading strategies to help them better understand the material?" The answers to these questions will guide you in planning an effective SRE for your class.

Prereading Activities in Chapter 5

Motivating	*Frindle*
	Sporting Life
	Survival Kit
Relating the Reading to Students' Lives	*Common Threads*
Building or Activating Background Knowledge	*Places, Events, and Times*
	Think About It!
Providing Text-Specific Knowledge	*In a Nutshell*
Preteaching Vocabulary	*Paired Questions*
	Word Clues and Cognates
Preteaching Concepts	*Living Words*
	Is It? Or Isn't It?
Prequestioning, Predicting, and Direction Setting	*What Do You Want to Know?*
	I Predict
	Looking for Old, Looking for New
	Looking for Answers
Suggesting Strategies	*A Quick Look*
Using Students' Native Language	*Helping Hands*
Involving English-Language Learner Communities, Parents, Siblings	*What Does a Word Mean?*

Motivating

A big part of preparing students to read is motivating them. Whatever the task, it is always more interesting, exciting, and meaningful if we have a good reason for wanting to do it. Think about yourself and your own reading. What motivates you to pick up the evening newspaper, to read an article in *The Instructor*, or to read a mystery novel? Is there a particular purpose you have in mind? Do you read to be informed, enlightened, inspired, or entertained? We all read for a combination of reasons, but usually because we expect the text is going to give us something we need or want—information, inspiration, entertainment, whatever. Many of you reading this book are native-English speakers, and your motivations may be quite different from those of young English-language learners. To ensure a successful reading experience for all students, we need to be sure that all students are really motivated to read.

Motivational activities are just that—activities that incite enthusiasm, an eagerness to delve into the material. Sometimes, you will undoubtedly use activities that serve primarily to motivate students. However, motivational activities frequently overlap with other kinds of prereading activities, such as activating background knowledge, relating reading to students' lives, and preteaching concepts. In general, motivational activities will draw on the interests and concerns of the particular students doing the reading. Puppets and puppies might be part of a motivating activity for first and second graders, a rap song or challenging puzzle for fourth, fifth, and sixth graders. You know many of the things that interest and excite your students, and you can find out more about what interests and excites your English-language learners. You can learn more about your English-language learners' backgrounds, culture, and interests by reading, by perusing the Internet and other media, and by talking with your students and their families. And you can learn still more by participating in events in the students' communities, such as shopping in their neighborhood stores, at least occasionally attending their neighborhood churches, visiting their homes, and attending community public celebrations. Use what you know and what you learn to motivate your English-language learners as they read.

Motivational activities often involve "hands-on" experiences, active student participation, drama, and intrigue:

> "Feel this fabric and tell me what it makes you think of and how it makes you feel."

> "Think of your favorite color. Walk around the room and touch three things that have that color in them."

> "Guess what's in this box?"

> "Look at this picture. Imagine you are there. What are you doing? How are you feeling?"

Now, once students' interest is piqued, comes the next step—transferring that interest to the reading material.

> "Jorge, the little boy in the story you will read today, has a special blanket made of the cloths you were feeling— flannel and satin."

> "*Hailstones and Halibut Bones* is a poem all about colors. . . . "

> "I guess my clues were good ones, and you're pretty good detectives. What was in the box is pumice, and we'll be

reading about it and other kinds of rocks, called igneous rocks, in our science chapter today."

"The picture you were looking at shows the village of San Paulo in Argentina. Pedro, the main character in the story you will be reading, lives in a village very much like it. Have any of you lived in a village that looks like the one in the picture, or have you seen one like it?"

Motivating Sample Activity for *Frindle*

In the next several paragraphs, we give a detailed example of a motivational activity. Lauren Moser used this activity with a group of fourth graders in a Midwestern suburb. We modify it here to specifically address benefits for the activity when some English-language learners are in the class. The selection the students were about to read was *Frindle* by Andrew Clements. In this award-winning middle-grade novel, Nick is intrigued by how words are created and decides to create a new word for *pen*. He calls it a *frindle* and tries to get others to call it that as well. Soon the new word spreads from the school, to the town, and across the country. Mrs. Moser's purpose for this prereading activity was to pique her students' interest and to build on their concept of how objects get named, a central theme in the novel.

This novel also provides an excellent opportunity for the class to talk about language—how it works, what names and words really mean, and to explore similarities and differences in words and meanings across different languages. Classroom talk about language can be especially important for English-language learners because it can raise students' awareness of important features of language. It also helps all the students in the class to consider what language and speech signify about identity and culture, and such discussion in turn can help students who speak different native languages to better understand the challenges presented in learning a new language. Does it matter what something is called? Could you change your name and have the new name encompass all the meanings of the old name, like changing Jorge to George? So the book becomes an excellent vehicle for building common understandings among English-language learners and other children.

Mrs. Moser began by taking several items out of a bag and placing them on a table in front of her students: a chalkboard eraser, a book, an orange, a painter's cap, and a pen. Without saying anything, she wrote the word *lollop* on the board. She pointed to the word *lollop* and said to her the students, "What if I told you one of these things is a lollop. Which one do you think it is?"

The students looked puzzled, but intrigued, and offered their guesses. Then, she said to the students, "What if I told you this is a lollop? (She holds up the chalkboard eraser.) This is a vole. (She holds up the book.) This is a grinderfife. (She holds up the orange.) This is a weedle-wizenbracker. (She puts on the cap.) And this one, my friends, is a frindle! (She holds up the pen.) What would you say?"

"Maybe you're talking in another language," one student offered.

"You're trying to trick us," said another.

After a few more students gave their opinions, Mrs. Moser asked, "How do things get the names we give them anyway? Why do we call an orange an *orange* and not a *grinderfife*?" After students gave a few suggestions, Mrs. Moser pulled a dictionary from her bag and began to thumb through it, reading a few words and their definitions. "There are thousands of words in the English language that are found in this dictionary. How did they get there?"

Next, Mrs. Moser gives some examples of word labels from different languages, including languages from children in her classroom. Holding up a pen, she asks, "Julia, how do you say *pen* in Spanish? Tu-Ken, how do you say *pen* in Chinese?" After students answer, she asks, "Why are there different words in different languages? Does it matter? When? Why or why not?"

After a brief discussion, Mrs. Moser wrote *frindle* on the board. "Could you invent a new word for pen, could you call it a *frindle* and get it in the dictionary?" She then pulled another book from her bag—*Frindle*—and showed the students the cover illustration, which shows the hand of a boy holding a pen. "That's just what Nick, the fifth grader in this story, wanted to find out. He wanted to call a pen a *frindle* and see if he could get his new word in the dictionary. Do you think he was able to do it? When you read the book *Frindle* you'll find out!"

As Mrs. Moser's lesson aptly illustrates, motivating activities should be fun. They get students interested and involved. They also direct their thinking toward the themes, topics, and concepts of the material you are preparing them to read and relate to the types of during-reading and postreading activities that students will do as well. Moreover, using the theme of this particular book is directly pertinent to the English-language learners and other children because of their everyday challenges and possibilities in using different languages with one another.

In the next section, we present two additional motivational activities, this time using the format we will use for most sample activities. Each description begins with a heading showing the type of activity and giving the specific activity a name. Then comes a one- or two-sentence description of the activity. Next come sections on the selection, the students for whom the activity was written, the reading purpose, goals of the activity, a rationale for the activity, the procedures to be followed, and a note on adapting the activity. At the end of this and of each sample activity in this book, we have included a section called "Reflections." This section serves a function somewhat similar to that of dialog journals. Dialog journals, as you know, are used to share a common interest or to work out a common problem with someone else. Unfortunately, a book format doesn't allow us to hear your responses. However, what these reflection sections do allow is for us to expand on ideas and issues that emerge from the activities in a conversational style. In these informal remarks, we have tended to do two different things. Most of the time, we comment on the activity itself—what it did, what it did not do, how it might be changed, and the like. Less frequently, we comment on a general principle the activity reminds us of. We hope you find our reflections helpful and that they encourage your own reflection.

MOTIVATING Sample Activity 2: *Sporting Life*

Sporting Life inspires students to think about the ways in which sports figures can contribute to their heritage and to their own lives.

Selection: *¡Béisbol!: Latino Baseball Pioneers and Legends* by Jonah Winter. Winters compellingly presents major Latino baseball figures' achievements in a way that even students who are not interested in sports or baseball in particular are likely to find fascinating. Each tribute is one page long, and on the facing pages are stunning full-page portraits of the personae. Not only does the author inform the reader about the specific sports characters, he also paints an historical tapestry by positioning the players vis-à-vis racial and ethnic precedents and by showing these great athletes as pioneers both in the United States and in several Latin American countries. The book is probably written at about a fourth-grade English reading level, but it is likely to be interesting to students at lower and much higher grade levels.

Students: Ten seventh- through ninth-grade Latino English-language learners in a Sheltered English class. Their English reading levels range from third through fifth grade. The teacher has selected this text to help develop their English reading and to interest them in history lessons.

Reading Purpose: To relate personal background to textual information and to encourage literal and inferential thinking.

Goal of the Activity: To motivate students to read this and other selections related to significant ethnic sports figures.

Rationale: Asking Latino students to think about how historic Latino sports figures might have paved the way for other Latinos and minorities in sports can lead students to consider their heritage and its effects on themselves. It can also encourage them to consider how their own actions can be related to ethnic pride. In this activity, the form of the activity itself and the text selection combine to generate some very substantial motivation.

Procedure: Tell the students that they will be reading parts of a book about famous Latino baseball players. Select a player who has a national origin that is the same as most of the students. For instance, tell them one of the Cuban players is José Méndez, also known as "El Diamant Negro" or "The Black Diamond." Slowly read the following excerpt from the book while showing the students the picture of José Méndez:

> Barred from the major leagues because of his dark skin, the Black Diamond nonetheless sparkled in Cuban baseball and Negro Leagues in the United States. During the first quarter of the 20th century, there was no better pitcher. That was the opinion of many, including the great major league manager John McGraw. Although McGraw did not hire Méndez to pitch on his all-white team, he did secretly hire the Cuban pitcher to coach his own pitchers.

Ask the students the following questions, moving from the more literal to the more inferential:

> What does this mean—"barred from the major leagues"?
>
> What years would be in the "first quarter of the 20th century?"
>
> How do you think Méndez felt to "secretly" coach other pitchers for McGraw?
>
> How do you think McGraw felt to "secretly" hire Méndez?

Next, prompt the students to discuss ways in which Méndez's actions as a player and "secret" coach were "historic." Possible prompts include these: How were Méndez's actions "historic?" Why do you think the author included him in this book? Méndez died almost 100 years ago. Can you think of him as a person today? How do you feel about him? Do you think he knew he was affecting history? If you had to write a "moral of the story" for other students your own age, what would it be?

Finish reading the entire page on Méndez aloud to the class and discuss any other features the class wants to talk about. Then ask the class to select another player from the book to read about and ask them to read that selection silently to note one or two aspects they would like to discuss.

Adapting the Activity: This activity could easily be adapted for any informational or fiction book involving sports figures. While the selection in our example is about Latinos and focuses in part on ethnic pride, the activity could as well be about understanding how sports figures can impact society in positive ways as well as how sports can be overemphasized and impact society as entertainment. The activity could also be used as a postreading discussion. In all cases, the use of sports figures or sporting activities can be motivational if you have students consider their relationship to their own lives as well as society in general.

Reflection: *In addition to motivating the students to want to read more of this book, the activity also helps them to learn about unfamiliar history and challenges them to* *consider their own lives in relation to those of the characters. Another "plus" in the activity is the use of a text that is interesting to the students because it is about their own ethnic heritage, is very well written, and yet is written at a low enough reading level that these older students can read it themselves.*

MOTIVATING Sample Activity 3: *Survival Kit*

Survival Kit motivates students to think about the items they would need to survive in the Arctic wilderness.

Selection: *Frozen Fire* by James Houston. This exciting adventure novel tells the story of Matthew Morgan and his Eskimo friend Kayak, who battle to stay alive while attempting to rescue Matthew's father and a helicopter pilot who are lost in the Canadian wilderness.

Students: Fourth and fifth graders of average to high reading ability, including a few advanced English-language learners.

Reading Purpose: To understand and enjoy an exciting survial story.

Goal of the Activity: To motivate students to want to read this novel, to activate their prior knowledge about the arctic, to consider what items might be needed for survival in the arctic wilderness, and to gain practice in making decisions.

Rationale: Planning for an imaginary journey to a potentially dangerous and exciting locale is an activity students find engaging. Also, having students think about what items they might need to survive in a frozen wilderness area will help focus their attention on one of the main themes of this story—survival. Moreover, if you are teaching Alaskan students, these children might be especially interested in the story because they might "see themselves" in it or easily relate to Kayak.

Procedure: Ask students to imagine that they are going to take a trip to the northern Canadian wilderness. Locate northern Canada and Frobisar Bay on a map or globe. (The story's setting is in the vicinity of Frobisar Bay in northeastern Canada.) Discuss what the climate might be like and what sort of terrain they would expect to find there. Discuss what the word *Eskimo* means and what it is like to live in an Eskimo culture. How might Kayak's home life be similar to or different from our lives (all of us in the class)?

Ask students to think about what kinds of things they might need to take in order to survive in an extremely cold and isolated environment. Beginning with the letter *A,* have students suggest one item that begins with that letter to take on their trip, then continue through the rest of the alphabet (*ax, bedding, can opener,* etc.). After 26 items have been named, tell students you are going to ask them to think about which 10 items they would most want to have if stranded in the Arctic wilderness. Organize students into groups of three or four to decide which 10 items they would choose. Appoint a facilitator and recorder for each group. Allow students about 10 minutes to meet and discuss their choices.

When students have finished making their choices, call on the recorders to name the choices their groups made. Write these on the chalkboard. Compare and contrast the items in each group's list.

After students finish the book, it would be worthwhile to repeat this activity. Students may have quite a different perspective on the most important things necessary for survival in the Arctic once they have finished the book. It will be interesting for them to see how their perceptions have changed.

Adapting the Activity: *Survival Kit* can be adapted to use for any reading selection in which the protagonist or protagonists find themselves in a setting away from home. For example, this activity can be used before reading in a story about kids going to camp (what sorts of items might they want most at camp?), kids visiting grandparents and/or a dad or mom they don't live with. With English-language learners, it's important to use some selections that show their homelands. This activity can also be used before reading a social studies text such as the expeditions of Lewis and Clark or pioneers on the Santa Fe Trail (what sorts of items might Lewis and Clark take or the pioneers?). *Survival Kit* can also be adapted as a motivational activity for any selection in which the protagonist is trying to achieve a goal or solve a problem. For example, if the main character wants to win a new friend, students can think of what he or she might need in a "survival kit" to make that happen. Students might suggest qualities such as friendliness, honesty, cooperation, and so forth. *Survival Kit* could also be used as a postreading activity in science. After reading about various careers in science, students might pack survival kits for geologists, oceanographers, or astronomers.

You can also reverse the *Survival Kit* activity. Instead of having students suggest items for a survival kit, you can do the selecting and present these to the students. For example, let's say students are going to read *Charro: The Mexican Cowboy* by George Anaconda. You can identify words that name things that are critical for a Mexican cowboy to have, for example, *rope, horse, muscles*, and *courage*. Write your words on cards in English and, if you can, in the languages of the English-language learners in your class, use pictures, or even supply the real things and put them in a prop such as a saddlebag or backpack to add interest. Then let students guess who might need these things in a survival kit and why.

Reflection: *As you may have noticed, in addition to motivating students to want to read a selection, this activity builds and activates students' background knowledge of its content and themes. It can also help students to build their knowledge of unfamiliar geography and customs. It challenges their thinking. Considering just what someone might need to survive, endure, or triumph in various life situations requires higher order thinking skills.*

Note that it isn't always necessary that they come up with a word for every letter of the alphabet. Better to keep the activity lively and focused than to have students labor over a letter or offer inappropriate words. It's important to keep in mind that the idea of the activity is to motivate students to be excited about reading the upcoming selection, not as a word play or thinking activity in and of itself.

Finally, we want to emphasize that students need to get interested and actively involved with ideas that will help them as they read. It is extremely important that motivating activities do direct students' attention to the themes, topics, and concepts in the upcoming reading. With motivating activities, we are not just trying to get students interested and excited, we are trying to get them interested and excited about the upcoming selection.

Relating the Reading to Students' Lives

Relating the reading to students' lives can be an extremely powerful approach for getting students to commit themselves to a text, to claim ownership of it. If we can see how something relates to our lives, then we are making a personal connection. We suddenly have a vested interest. Let us say you have a class of third graders and you run across an engaging story about a boy and his new puppy. One of your students, Fernando, just got a puppy for his birthday, and you realize this would be a great book for Fernando. To prepare him to read the story, you might get him to talk about his puppy, what he feeds it, where it sleeps, who takes care of it, and how he feels about it. Getting Fernando to think about his own experiences with a puppy will help him better appreciate the events that take place in the story and the actions and emotions of the main character.

You can also relate the topics of expository material to students' lives. Say, for instance, your fifth-grade students are going to read about electricity in their science texts that day. As a prompt for their journal writing that morning, you might write on the board, "Write about the different ways you used electricity so far today." Or, "Imagine your electricity went out this morning. Describe what your morning was like without it." Writing in general, and journal writing in particular, is an effective way to build or evoke background knowledge.

Relating the reading to students' lives includes any kinds of activities that help students understand how what they read has meaning for the world they live in.

RELATING THE READING TO STUDENTS' LIVES
Sample Activity: *Common Threads*

In *Common Threads,* the teacher helps bridge the gap between the characters in a story and the students' experiences by having them think about experiences in their own lives that are similar to the ones faced by the story's protagonist. She also helps children within the class understand one another better.

Selection: *First Apple* by Ching Yeung Russell. Set in China, nine-year-old Ying lives with her Grandmother's family. She wants to give her grandmother a very special birthday present and sets her heart on an apple, a rare and expensive delicacy where Ying lives. Ying sets out to buy an apple, but along the way, she encounters many obstacles. Her cousin makes her work in the garden, a boy in her class bullies her, and she is accused of stealing. This poignant tale is based on the author's own childhood in China.

Students: Sixth graders of mixed reading abilities. Most of the students are Anglo. A few are Black of African descent. Three students are English-language learners from China who have been at this school since the beginning of fourth grade.

Reading Purpose: To appreciate a well-written piece of fiction that portrays life in another place and time.

Goals of the Activity: To bridge the gap between readers' lives, one to another, and to bridge the gap between the readers' lives and the story's main character and setting by helping them make meaningful connections to their lives. Another goal is to introduce the basic elements of plot: problem, solution, and change.

Rationale: The setting and situation described in this novel are very different from what most of the young readers in the class will have personally encountered. However, although Ying's problems may be far removed from those of most of today's 10- to 13-year-old readers, what lies at the heart of her story remains the same—resourceful and determined individuals courageously find ways overcome obstacles. Focusing on this universal theme and having students discover examples from their own experiences can bridge the gap between themselves and the main character and promote a deeper understanding of the text. The activity also helps students focus on some of the primary elements of fiction—a character with a problem, actions taken to solve the problem, and the character's change or reaction.

Procedure: Begin by inviting an adult with a Chinese background to class to tell about her childhood life in China. Hold a question/answer session. On another day, tell students that the reason you're having them think about aspects of Chinese life is that they will be reading *First Apple*, a story of a young girl living in China. They will learn just what her situation is when they read the book, but first you want them to think about their own experiences with unusual and difficult situations. Doing this will help them understand and enjoy the novel more. Ask the students to talk about any situations they have found themselves in when they wanted to do something for someone else but couldn't or if they have ever been accused of doing something bad when they were innocent.

Write these headings on the board.

Problem	**Solution**	**How Changed?**

Next, hand out sheets of paper and have students fold them into thirds and write each of the headings in a column.

Before asking students to write their responses in each of the columns, model the activity by giving an experience from your own life and recording your responses on the board. Elaborate orally on these responses as you write them. Tell students that you are writing quickly and not worrying about spelling or using complete sentences and that they can do the same with their responses. What you want to get down is the gist of the idea.

Problem	**Solution**	**How Changed?**
When I was 4, I took a children's book from the grocery store when my mom was shopping. At home, my mom found the book!	My mom took me back to the store and made me give the book back and say I was sorry	learned what "stealing" meant. I was embarrassed, but felt proud I could fix the problem

After this have students write their own problems, solutions, and changes. After they have had a chance to record their own responses, let students voluntarily share them with the rest of the class. With students' permission you may want to record some on the board or a chart.

Problem	Solution	How Changed?
Came to live in a country where I don't know any-body and don't know the language.	Went to school, sat by myself	I haven't changed me. I still don't think most people care about me. I don't know what to do sometimes. But I under-stand more and I have two good friends now.
Got separated from parents in downtown San Francisco	Started roaming the streets, cried, and found a policeman who found my parents	More careful to stay with parents when in a strange place, no longer afraid of policemen

After ample discussion, hold up a copy of *First Apple* and read the title and the author's name. Explain that Ying Yeung is the main character in the story, and have students predict from the cover illustration—which shows Ying holding a red apple—what they think Ying's problems might be. Explain that Ying does face a number of problems in the story. When they finish reading, you will talk about those difficulties, Ying's responses to them, and in what ways she changed.

Adapting the Activity: *Common Threads* can be used as a prereading activity for any novel, story, or biography in which the main character is faced with numerous problems to solve or obstacles to overcome. Literature abounds with these kinds of situations—realistic and historical fiction, biographies, and fantasies all contain nu-merous stories of heroes who triumph over difficulties. Examples include *The True Confessions of Charlotte Doyle* by Avi, *Hatchet* by Gary Paulsen, *The Boxer* by Kathleen Karr, *Rachel Chance* by Jean Thesman, *Behind the Mask: The Life of Queen Elizabeth I* by Jane Resh Thomas, *China's Bravest Girl: The Legend of Hua Mu Lan* by Charlie Chin, and *Maniac Magee* by Jerry Spinelli. Also, instead of doing this as a whole group activity, you might have students work in groups of four to six.

Reflection: Many students are usually eager to talk about themselves, but some will have a tendency to ramble and need to be encouraged to stick to the main topics of problem, solution, and change. Some English-language learners may not want to talk about themselves or their families. Although teachers should try to include English-language learners in lessons like this, they should also be careful not to force them to participate. Also, an activity such as this one begins as a prereading activity but is continued through the other two phases of reading. While they read, students might record problems, solutions, and changes in the main character. Then after they have finished the novel, they can discuss with each other what they discovered about problems, solutions, and change.

As in the case when motivating students, in relating a selection to students' lives, it is important to remember that the focus needs to be on the aspects of students' lives relevant to the targeted selection. As a colleague pointed out, introducing a science selection about the ocean by asking whether students have ever been to the ocean and then presiding over a discussion of vacations at the seashore will be of minimal benefit to students understanding the concepts in the chapter.

Building or Activating
Background Knowledge

No text contains all the information necessary for a reader to understand it. All texts leave out a tremendous amount of information and rely on readers to fill in that information from their background knowledge. Thus, understanding any text requires a huge store of knowledge. All students come to school with a vast repertoire of concepts that teachers can tap into, but some students have different knowledge than others and some have more knowledge than others. Some students have rich stores of knowledge relevant to what they read in school from having read widely themselves, been read to, traveled a good deal, lived in various locations, taken trips to museums, gone on nature outings, and belonged to groups such as Boy Scouts, Campfire Girls, and the YMCA that provide a variety of experiences. Other students, including those from other countries and other cultures, have had equally rich experiences but sometimes not experiences relevant to what they read in school, not the experiences assumed by the authors of many of their school texts. Still other students have not had the benefits of these types of rich experiences. A few studies suggest that bilingual students tend to know less about topics in school texts than their same-age native-language-speaking peers (Droop & Verhoeven, 1998; García, 1991; Jiménez, García, & Pearson, 1995, 1996). Building and activating background knowledge have been shown to be particularly important when teaching English-language learners (Gersten & Baker, 2000; Saunders, O'Brien, Lennon, & McLean, 1998).

Even when English-language learners appear to have acquired good conversational English, teachers should be aware that they may not have the requisite background understanding for a specific text, and if at all possible teachers should always try to find that out. Also, teachers can remind their students to think about what they know that is related to the topic. Results of one study suggested that teachers of bilingual students did not routinely encourage students to use their personal knowledge as they read (Delgado-Gaitán, 1989). In another study, when teachers asked children to relate their personal lives to what was being read, the students' participation levels increased (Thornburg, 1993). Thinking about these results can raise our awareness of the need to make sure we encourage English-language learners to bring all that they can to bear on their constructions of text meanings. It is also important that teachers embrace and appreciate the background knowledge that English-language learners do carry with them to the reading.

Since background knowledge is one of the most important factors influencing students' ability to comprehend and learn from a text (Bransford,

Brown, & Cocking, 2000; RAND Reading Study Group, 2002), one of your most important tasks is to be sure that all students have the background knowledge to read the texts you ask them to. This means carefully considering the text and the knowledge it assumes, carefully considering your students and the knowledge they have, and being sure that those who do not have that knowledge get as much of it as possible.

Sometimes that means you are going to have to build students' background knowledge. If, for example, your seventh graders are going to read an article on poverty in Appalachia and the author of the article assumes that readers already know quite a bit about Appalachia—where it is located, how populated the area is, what sorts of people live there—you are going to have to teach that information before they read the article. At other times, students actually have the relevant information to read an upcoming selection, but don't realize that they have it or don't think in a way that allows them to summon it. In these cases, you are going to have to assist them in activating their prior knowledge. Activating prior knowledge means providing students with prereading experiences that prompt them to bring to consciousness information they already know. Sometimes students might write about what they know, other times talk about it. If this information is shared in a class discussion, it will then be available for both the students who produced it and others in the class. Having this information readily available will help students make connections with similar ideas when they meet them in the text.

BUILDING BACKGROUND KNOWLEDGE
Sample Activity 1: *Places, Events, and Times*

In *Places, Events, and Times,* you provide background information on the setting, events, and time frame of a selection.

Selection: *Number the Stars* by Lois Lowry. In Denmark, 10-year-old AnnMarie and her family help their neighbors, the Rosens, flee to Sweden in order to escape Nazi persecution. The teacher has copies of the book printed in Spanish and is using only the Spanish version for this class. The title in Spanish is *Quien Cuenta Las Estrellas*. All discussions about the book are conducted in Spanish. We write here only in English so that readers who do not understand Spanish can follow.

Students: Fifth and sixth graders—Anglo, Black of African descent, and Latino—in a bilingual education classroom.

Reading Purpose: To understand, enjoy, and appreciate a well-written historical novel.

Goal of the Activity: To provide students with information on the geographic and historical setting of the novel so that they can better understand and appreciate the situation faced by the main characters.

Rationale: The location and situation faced by the characters in *Number the Stars* may be quite unfamiliar to many students. Providing them with information regarding the setting, historical events, and time frame of this particular period in history will help them better conceptualize the people, places, and events in the story. Having this information before they read will give students a solid foundation on which to build meaning as they read.

Procedure: Begin by writing *1943 Copenhagen, Denmark,* on the board. Then, write *Germany.* Tell students that something very tragic was happening in Germany in 1943. If students are familiar with the Nazis, Hitler, and the Holocaust, let them discuss what they know. If not, briefly explain the situation to them. Tell them that during this time German troops began to "relocate" all of the Jews of Denmark—to take them to concentration camps. Locate Germany, Denmark, and Copenhagen on a map.

Tell students that the story they will be reading, *Number the Stars* or *Quien Cuenta Las Estrellas,* by Lois Lowry, takes place in Copenhagen, Denmark, in this period in history. Explain that the main character AnnMarie isn't Jewish, but her best friend Ellen is. You also may want to give some background information on the Jews and the Jewish religion. Explain that it was because of where the Jewish people in the novel lived and because they lived during this period of time that they had to face situations calling for personal sacrifice, daring, and courage.

Adapting the Activity: Giving information on places, events, and time frames before students read a selection is appropriate any time these elements play key roles in a story or expository piece and are therefore important to students understanding and appreciating the ideas presented. Many selections, fiction as well as nonfiction, revolve around important historical events and figures. A few of the selections you might choose to use for the *Places, Events, and Time* activity are *¡Béisbol!: Latino Baseball Pioneers and Legends* by Jonah Winter, selected parts of chapters in *Harvest of Empire: A History of Latinos in America* by Juan Gonzalez, *Shh! We're Writing the Constitution* by Jean Fritz, *Sitting Bull and His World* by Albert Marrin, *The Two Mountains: An Aztec Legend,* retold by Eric A. Kimmel, *Smoke and Ashes: The Story of the Holocaust* by Barbara Rogasky, *Jackie Robinson: He Was the First* by David Adler, *The Great American Gold Rush* by Rhoda Blumberg, and *George Midgett's War* by Sally Edwards. This activity could also easily be used with selections from texts in reading series, such as *SRE Open Court Reading* published by SRA/McGraw-Hill.

Reflection: As you probably noticed, this activity is simple and straightforward. Nevertheless, the information will be quite helpful to some students and crucial to others in their understanding and appreciation of many historically based texts. Sometimes, students have little or no knowledge about the places, events, and time frames in the selections they are asked to read. At other times, students may have misconceptions about these elements. And even those students who do have fairly well-developed, accurate views can benefit from further information or new insights. Accurate information on places and events can bolster each student's reading experiences with historically based texts, connect their reading to geography and history themes, and provide them with valuable information about the world in which they live.

ACTIVATING BACKGROUND KNOWLEDGE
Sample Activity 2: *Think About It!*

Think About It! uses cooperative learning groups as a forum for students sharing knowledge about a topic in order to stimulate interest and activate prior knowledge.

Selections: *The Ultimate Field Trip 3: Wading Into Marine Biology* by Susan Goodman; *Exploring the Deep, Dark Sea* by Gail Gibbons; *The Oceans Atlas* by Anita Ganeri; *Down, Down, Down in the Ocean* by Sandra Markle; and other books that explore the wonders of the ocean.

Students: Fourth graders of average to high Spanish and English reading ability. Eighty-five percent of the class consists of Latino students and 15 percent are Anglo and Black of African descent. All of the students were in bilingual education programs in first through third grade and are now transitioned into an all-English setting. The books used and the classroom language of instruction are English.

Reading Purpose: To add to old knowledge and gain new information about the ocean's features, ocean life, and protecting the ocean.

Goal of the Activity: To pique students' interest in learning more about the ocean prior to a four-week unit on "Exploring the Ocean," to activate their prior knowledge, and to give specific information about the topics of these texts.

Rationale: Sharing what they know about a topic can serve to stimulate interest, activate prior knowledge, and focus students' attention on the material that will be covered in the selections they read.

Procedure: Write the unit topic and subtopics on the chalkboard.

EXPLORING THE OCEAN

Ocean Features   Ocean Life   Protecting the Ocean

Following a motivational activity the day before involving a marine biologist who brought in slides and ocean artifacts, tell students that they will have an opportunity to learn more about the ocean in the next few weeks. They are going to read several books that talk about the features of the ocean, ocean life, and protecting the ocean. Point out that they know something about the ocean from what they learned from the guest marine biologist and from what they've read or from trips to the ocean. Explain that you'd like them to share that knowledge with each other.

Divide the class into groups of about six students each and appoint a facilitator and recorder for each group. Before the groups meet, talk about what they are to discuss—what they *know* about each of the three topics.

Ocean Features

Ocean Life

Protecting the Ocean

Explain that the facilitator will call on people to tell what they know about each of the topics and the recorder will write down the information that students share. Briefly review the topics with students, and discuss some of the things they will want to think about for each. For example, you might write these prompts on the board:

Ocean Features: Think about what you would see if you could drain all the water from the ocean.

Ocean Life: Think about all the different kinds of living things that live in the ocean.

Protecting the Ocean: Think about the things that can be harmful to the ocean.

After discussing the prompts, give students about 10 minutes to discuss the three topics. At the end of the discussion time, let the recorder for each group read the responses for each topic. Also, spend a little time evaluating the activity, what worked, what didn't, and how they can improve on the activity.

Adapting the Activity: *Think About It!* can be used to activate knowledge for any selection with a topic or theme that is somewhat familiar to students—for example, you could use *Think About It!* before your ethnically diverse fifth graders read Russell Freedman's *Immigrant Kids,* before your California fourth graders read *Earthquakes* by Seymour Simon, or before curious and scientifically inclined third graders read *Forest in the Clouds* by Sneed B. Collard, III.

Reflection: *After reading through the sample, you may wonder why we included it under activating background knowledge rather than providing text-specific knowledge. Obviously, the activity serves both of these functions. In fact, it serves as much to evoke and build knowledge as it does to activate it. It could also be considered a motivational activity since any sort of social interaction is highly motivating for most students, particularly gregarious 10-year-olds. Having students' thinking stimulated and challenged by their peers is an excellent way to pique their curiosity and get them interested and actively involved with a topic. Remember, the categories of activities we suggest here are meant to suggest many different sorts of activities and are not in any way intended to be restrictive. Some activities fall into several categories, and that's just fine.*

Providing Text-Specific Knowledge

In the previous activity, we assumed that the students had some *background knowledge* relevant to the topic of the upcoming selection and our task was to activate it. In building text-specific knowledge, we assume that students do not have the *specific information in an upcoming text* and need some of that information to deal with it adequately. For instance, if they are going to read a chapter on electricity in a science text, they will probably have some general understanding of electricity but won't know the precise topics covered or how they are organized. In this situation, you might tell them what those topics are and how the author has organized and structured the text. Or perhaps students are going to read the time-travel books of *The York Trilogy* by Phyllis Reynolds Naylor. To fully understand and enjoy these stories, students will need to know something about how time-travel is portrayed in the stories. Giving them a few details about the sort of time-travel that takes place in the stories can be easily accomplished in a brief prereading discussion.

One way to build text-specific knowledge is to give students a preview of the material they are going to read, a procedure that has been effective with English-language learners (Chen & Graves, 1998) as well as with native speakers of English (Graves, Prenn, & Cooke, 1985). A preview of a reading selection is similar to previews you see of movies and TV shows and can be used with both expository and narrative texts. A preview of an article, textbook chapter, or informational book could include information about the topics, events, people or places covered, and unusual or difficult vocabulary. In a preview of a novel or short story, you might introduce the setting, characters, and something about the plot.

Building text-specific knowledge can be achieved in a variety of different ways. Here, we present one way of doing so.

PROVIDING TEXT-SPECIFIC KNOWLEDGE Sample Activity: *In a Nutshell*

In a Nutshell uses an outline and deductive and inferential questioning to familiarize students with the content of the text.

Selection: "Waves," a chapter in *Science in Your World*. This chapter from an elementary science text discusses the physical phenomenon of waves as rhythmic disturbances that transfer energy—mechanical waves involve matter, and electromagnetic waves involve electric and magnetic fields. Some of the topics covered are how waves transfer energy, the properties of waves, and electromagnetic waves, which include radio waves, infrared waves, light, ultraviolet waves, X-rays, and gamma rays.

Students: Fifth-grade students of mixed reading abilities in a suburban setting, one English-language learner who just arrived from Southeast Asia a few months ago and is in the very beginning phase of learning English.

Reading Purpose: To gain new understanding about the properties and functions of waves, both mechanical waves and electromagnetic waves.

Goal of the Activity: To give students information on the topics and structure of the text so that they will have a schema in place that includes both the concepts presented in the chapter and how the chapter is organized. This will be an extremely difficult topic and lesson for the English-language learner. At this point in time, she cannot be expected to understand a lot from the chapter. However, some goals such as the following could be set for her: (1) to learn one main concept—there are physical waves and other waves; (2) to learn two key vocabulary words in English—waves and light; and (3) to try to participate in the class session in some way.

Rationale: Giving students an outline of the material they are going to read provides them with a conceptual framework for understanding and remembering what they read. Also, having them explain what information the outline reveals stimulates inferential and deductive reasoning—a kind of thinking that will serve them well in life as well as with the many other texts.

Procedure: Before the lesson, either on a transparency or the chalkboard, write the chapter title and subtitles.

WAVES

How Do Waves Transfer Energy?

Electromagnetic Waves

Radio Waves

Higher Frequency Waves

Infrared Waves

Light

Ultraviolet Waves

X-Rays and Gamma Rays

Lasers

For the English-language learner, next to the title word *Waves* draw a picture of waves. Point to pictures from the book that help to define waves. Next to the word *Light* place a picture of a light bulb and two contrasting pictures showing a room with a light on and a dark room, putting a big "X" over the dark room.

Tell students that today you're going to take a look at the topics and subtopics from the chapter on waves before reading it. Tell them that noticing how a chapter is organized can help them understand the ideas the author is presenting.

Draw students' attention to the outline, and challenge them to pick out the three major topics. Call on a volunteer to read them (*How Do Waves Transfer Energy?, Electromagnetic Waves, Lasers*). Ask students to explain how they determined that these were the main topics. (*They are written in large print and are not indented. Some have subtopics written below them.*) Make it a point to look at your English-language learner and emphasize the words *waves* and *light* each time they are said.

Next, ask students to identify which of the main topics have subtopics. (*Electromagnetic Waves has the subtopics Radio Waves and Higher Frequency Waves. Subtopic Higher Frequency Waves has the subtopics Infrared Waves, Light, Ultraviolet Waves, and X-Rays and Gamma Rays.*) If students are unable to come up with the correct responses, be sure to praise their efforts anyway, then show them the correct responses and how you arrived at them. (*Main topics are in larger type than subtopics. Subtopics are indented under the main topic. Sometimes subtopics have subtopics of their own which are also indented. Subtopics are details that explain more about a topic. For example, a main topic might be compared to a house, subtopics to the rooms in a house, and further subtopics to the objects in the room.*)

After this, explain to students that now that they have identified the topics and subtopics in the chapter on waves, they are going to see how much information the author has given on the topic in just these few words. Tell them that they may be surprised at just how much they already know. Starting with the first main topic, guide students to the following conclusions.

Q — What do we know about waves from the statement "How Do Waves Transfer Energy"?

A — Waves transfer energy.

Q to the English-language learner – (Pointing to the word *Waves*) What is this word?

A — Waves.

Q to the English-language learner – (Pointing to the word *Light*) What is this word?

A — Light.

Q — What do we know about waves from the topic "Electromagnetic Waves"?

A — Some waves are electromagnetic.

Q — What do we know about waves from the subtopic "Radio Waves"?

A — Some waves are called radio waves.

Q — What do we know about waves from the subtopic "Higher Frequency Waves"?

A — Waves have different frequencies, some higher and some lower. Radio waves probably have a low frequency since they are not listed under the subtopic "Higher frequency Waves."

Q — What do we know about waves from the subtopics "Infrared Waves," "Light," "Ultraviolet Waves," and "X-Rays and Gamma Rays"?

A — Infrared, light, ultraviolet, x-rays and gamma rays are all names for high-frequency rays because they are listed as subtopics under "Higher Frequency Waves." Infrared waves probably have the lowest frequency of these waves because they are listed first in the sequence and gamma rays probably have the highest because they are listed last. (This sequence from lowest to highest can be deduced from the fact that radio waves are listed as a separate topic before the higher frequency waves, and therefore waves listed earlier probably have lower frequencies than the others.)

Q — What do we know about lasers from the topic "Lasers"?

A — Lasers have something to do with waves since they are listed as a topic in the chapter on waves.

Keep the questioning lively. Encourage students to keep thinking and to make inferences from the information given. Praise their participation, and tell them that their efforts now will pay off in their understanding and learning from the chapter on waves.

Adapting the Activity: This activity can be used prior to reading any material that outlines easily or in which the author has organized the material into topics and subtopics—textbook chapters, informational trade books, and articles. Chapter 1, for instance, from *Garbage! The Trashiest Book You'll Ever Read* by Suzanne Lord would work well for this activity. The titles and subtitles for this chapter are:

Garbage: The Never-Ending Story

What Do We Mean by Garbage?

How Long Has Garbage Been Around?

A Short History of Garbage

What Kinds of Garbage Are There?

Natural Garbage

Personal Garbage

Industrial Garbage

Hazardous Garbage

Space Garbage

There is, however, one thing to be on the lookout for in selecting material. Check to see that the heading and subheadings accurately reflect the material the text contains. In some cases, headings turn out not to be good guides to the content of selections.

Reflection: As you probably noticed, there are some difficult concepts presented in this outline. Sometimes the materials your students will be reading offer real challenges. When this is the case, you want students to know that material sometimes is challenging, but not impossible. When you introduce students to difficult vocabulary and concepts, go out of your way to encourage them not to feel defeated if they don't immediately understand all of the concepts. Explain that the author wrote this in a way that's "dense," and they will be learning fuller meanings of these terms as they read, that now they are just getting a head start in understanding the material. Also, some students may tend to be complacent and let their classmates do all the talking and all the thinking. Encourage the more reluctant participants, the drifters and dreamers, to participate in the activity by saying something like "There are some good thinkers in this class we haven't heard from yet. Not everyone may get the chance to speak their answers, but everyone can think their answers. If you're thinking along with us, then you're doing your part." If your English-language learners are comfortable in your class, try to find some ways to include their responses, such as asking a question and suggesting the English-language learner answer in native language (even if you can't understand that language), point to an answer on the board, or write a word or two as an answer and then have a buddy read it aloud. If you look for the kinds of things that beginning English learners can do, you will often find at least some ways to help them learn something new. At the same time, you signal to everyone in the class ways to be an inclusive community.

In showing students the structure and content of the Waves chapter in *In a Nutshell*, we used a standard outline. Alternately, we could have presented the information as a graphic organizer, a frequently recommended visual display for which Richard and Jo Anne Vacca (1993) provide a convenient description. A possible graphic organizer for the "Waves" chapter is shown below.

WAVES

How Do Waves Transfer Energy?   **Electromagnetic Waves**   **Lasers**

Radio Waves	**Higher Frequency Waves**
	Infrared Waves
	Light
	Ultraviolet Waves
	X-Rays and Gamma Rays

There are at least two reasons you might want to use a graphic organizer rather than a standard outline. One is that the graphic organizer may be more informative. In the case of the "Waves" example, the graphic organizer very clearly shows that the topic of "Higher Frequency Waves" receives a good deal of attention. Another reason you might want to occasionally use a graphic organizer instead of an outline is simply to provide some diversity. Sometimes, varying the way you present information can spark interest in both you and your students.

Preteaching Vocabulary

One important part of the background knowledge English-language learners possess has to do with their word knowledge. Research findings, professional wisdom, and common sense all suggest that preteaching critical vocabulary is incredibly helpful to English-language learners (García & Nagy, 1993; Gersten & Baker, 2000; Nagy, García, Durgunoğlu, & Hancin-Bhatt, 1993; Rousseau, Tam, & Ramnarain, 1993). The words students encounter while they are reading fall on a continuum from those they can read and understand easily to those they can't even pronounce much less associate with a meaning. For instance, most third graders could decode and understand the meaning of the word *garden*, but very few would be able to pronounce *gargoyle*, much less understand its meaning.

In one study investigating Latino students' English reading test performance, unfamiliar vocabulary was found to be the major linguistic factor that adversely affected their performance (García, 1991). English-language learners may be able to look at a word in a text and say it, but they may not know its meaning, either in their native language or in English. Sometimes English-language learners know the meaning in their native language, but not in English. Structuring English-language learners' acquisition of new word meanings is one of the most helpful things a teacher can do.

In Chapter 2, we defined vocabulary instruction as instruction on words that are new labels for concepts that students already have—for example, teaching *gregarious* to students who already know what *friendly* means.

That is the sort of learning task we deal with here. For English-language learners, we are now talking about students who know the meaning of a concept and have a label for it in their native language (e.g., for friendly), but have no label for it (either friendly or gregarious) in English. Sometimes researchers and theorists refer to an individual's "depth" of word knowledge (e.g., Nagy & Scott, 2000). What we are talking about at this point can be thought of as "depth" of word knowledge. "Depth" of word knowledge has to do with the idea that really "knowing" a word can be quite complex. For instance, you might "know" a word's literal meaning, its connotations, the kinds of syntactic uses it has, whether it can have different affixes, and an array of semantic relationships, including synonyms, anonyms, and so on. Results of at least one study suggest that acquiring "depth" of word knowledge can be difficult for second-language speakers, even for frequently occurring words (Verhallen & Schoonen, 1993).

A special word is in order here about students' use of cognates—words that are similar in two languages—for cross-linguistic transfer. Many students automatically make use of cognates to figure out a word meaning in English (García, 1998; Nagy et al., 1993). However, other students tend to underutilize cognates as a means of accessing word meanings that are already known in their native language (García & Nagy, 1993). Helping English-language learners to use cognates where possible can help them by aiding their understandings as well as by providing them with a strategy to use in other reading situations.

Activities for preteaching vocabulary focus on helping students pronounce and define words as they are used in the upcoming selection. The purpose of such activities is to provide students with this information before they read so that when they meet these words in the text they don't have to focus on deciphering individual word meaning but can focus their attention on the ideas the author is presenting. For example, before fourth graders, including advanced English-language learners, read the "August" entries in Pam Conrad's *Pedro's Journal,* you might plan vocabulary activities that enable students to pronounce and learn a basic meaning for the words *mandarin, rosary, rudder, boatswain, and chaukers.*

There are any number of vocabulary activities you can engage students in prior to their reading a selection. We include two samples here.

PRETEACHING VOCABULARY Sample Activity 1: *Paired Questions*

In *Paired Questions* targeted words are presented in pairs of questions, one that can be answered affirmatively and the other negatively. This activity is based on vocabulary instruction suggested by Kameenui, Carnine, and Freschi (1982).

Selection: *Vietnam: A Portrait of the Country Through Its Festivals and Traditions*, a book in the *Fiesta* series by Grolier. *Fiesta* is a series of books with each book focusing on a country. *Vietnam* is probably easily read by students who can read at the third- or fourth-grade level. Short selections portray traditions, main religions, songs, folk tales, and more, with beautiful accompanying photographs and drawings. The selection chosen for this activity is about paper blossoms. Students learn that at the Tet festival, spring blossoms fill the streets and houses because the people believe that flowers welcome good spirits. In two steps, students are shown how to make simple paper blossoms out of tissue paper and then attach them to a branch of a tree for decoration.

Students: Third-grade native-Vietnamese English-language learners who have second-grade-level English reading abilities in a pullout class with the school's teacher of English-language learners. The classroom teacher has asked the ELL teacher to help these students to choose something from this book to share with the rest of the class. The classroom teacher asks that the students prepare to "teach" the rest of the class about something Vietnamese. These students have chosen to teach about the importance of blossoms during the Tet festival as well as how to make the blossoms.

Reading Purpose: This book is just a little too hard for these students to read on their own, so the ELL teacher will read the selection the students have chosen about "paper blossoms" to them. Her main reading goal is for the students to learn the English words *blossom* and *tissue.*

Goal of Activity: To increase students' understanding and enjoyment of a selection by ensuring that they know challenging words and to increase their knowledge and appreciation of word meanings. Another goal is to nurture the students' understandings of their own heritage.

Rationale: *Blossom* and *tissue* are two words that may pose difficulties for these students—words that may be in the students' native-language oral vocabularies but are not likely to be in their English oral or reading vocabularies, or words for which they have an available concept but not a label. Having students pronounce, read, and think about some of the words used in an upcoming story makes the reading task easier and more enjoyable. Also, an activity such as this one, which requires students to apply their knowledge of words to novel situations, encourages critical thinking and appreciation of words.

Procedure: Select up to three or four words that might be stumbling blocks for some of your students and develop paired questions using these words: One question should yield an affirmative answer, the other a negative answer. Write the paired sentences on the chalkboard:

> **Easier:**
>
> Do flowers have a blossom?
>
> Do dogs have a blossom?
>
> Can a tissue tear?
>
> Can a tissue cry?
>
> **Harder:**
>
> Can a person blossom?

Can a book blossom?

Can a tissue be made of cloth?

Can a tissue be made of paper?

Read the sentences to students or have volunteers read them. Have students think about these questions, answer them for themselves, and then discuss the answers together. As a whole-group activity or in pairs or trios, have students compose paired sentences of their own that can be answered "yes" or "no" for each. Write these sentences on the board. For example, for *tissue*, students might suggest:

Can you use a tissue when you sneeze?

Can you write with a tissue?

Adapting the Activity: This activity is readily adaptable to any selection—narrative or expository—that contains words that are in your students' oral vocabularies but perhaps not in their reading vocabularies or words for which they have an available concept but not a label. For instance, you might introduce *independent*, *survive*, *sovereign*, *scoffed,* and *legislature* in paired sentences before your fifth graders read the first few pages of Jean Fritz's *Shh! We're Writing the Constitution.* Or, you might introduce *gremlin, shrug, detective,* and *imagine* before your second- or third-grade English-language learners read Bonnie Graves' *Mystery of the Tooth Gremlin.* If you can speak the native language of your English-language learners, you should relate the English words to the words in the native language. Where cognates exist, always try to help the students to see the cognate relationships and to use cognates as a strategy to learn new words in English. A parent or assistant who speaks the native language of your English-language learners could also help here.

Reflection: We have found that students really enjoy vocabulary activities, especially when they are fun and offer some challenges too. Paired Questions gives students a chance to be a bit silly and have some fun with words, while at the same time giving them new insights into word meaning and an appreciation of words themselves. Experimenting with words in this way also helps students realize that words are not just printed marks on a page, but compact capsules of meaning that can be interesting and fun to work with.

PRETEACHING VOCABULARY Sample Activity 2: *Word Clues and Cognates*

Word Clues and Cognates introduces potentially difficult vocabulary using context-rich sentences in teacher-created worksheets and points out cognates for Latino learners who can read in Spanish.

Selection: "Thomas Nast: Political Cartoonist Extraordinaire" by Lynn Evans. Bavarian-born Thomas Nast is responsible for creating some of our most notable and enduring political symbols—the Republican elephant, the Democratic donkey, and Uncle Sam. As a young student, Nast did poorly in all subjects except art, and at 15 he began work as a draftsman for *Frank Leslie's Illustrated Paper.* In 1859 he began his 30-year partnership with *Harper's Weekly,* and together they became a powerful force against political corruption. Fiercely Republican in his views, Nast is credited with the election of many Republican candidates, that is, until 1884 when

Nast and *Harper's* supported a Democrat for the first time, presidential candidate Grover Cleveland. In 1886, Nast and *Harper's* ended their association and the political influence of both declined.

Students: Eighth graders who are Latino and Anglo. The native-English speakers in the class read at or slightly below grade level. There are five English-language learners in the class who have been in the school system since first grade. These five can read at or slightly below grade level in English and cannot read in Spanish. There are two Latinos who recently arrived. The two recent arrivals can read Spanish at grade level. The classroom teacher has some limited knowledge of Spanish and has purchased a Spanish-English dictionary for the classroom.

Reading Purpose: To understand and recall some of the important highlights of an historical figure's life and work in the United States. To assist the Latino learners in learning to use cognates to create word meanings.

Goal of Activity: To introduce potentially difficult vocabulary and to give students practice in using context clues to unlock word meaning. Also, in this selection, all of the students learn about an immigrant's contributions to U.S. politics, so a goal is for all of the students to be more aware of the roles immigrants can play in their contemporary U.S. life. An additional goal for the newly arrived Latinos is to learn to use cognates to assist word meaning development.

Rationale: This piece, as will be the case with many content-area selections, contains vocabulary that will prove difficult for some native English speakers and for a number of English-language learners. To give them practice in using context clues to unlock word meaning as well as learn the meanings of some key words, a worksheet activity that requires students to focus on context clues is a helpful aid. Many words in the piece have cognates in Spanish, and helping the newly arrived Latino learners to locate and use these cognates provides them with an immediate strategy to use in all of their English reading. It will also help them realize that the teacher is making a concerted effort to be a good teacher to them. Although the newly arrived Latinos cannot be expected to complete the worksheet, by teaching them about cognates, the teacher signals them about the importance of their place in the classroom community as well as her belief that they can make contributions to it.

Procedure: Before the lesson, select five to seven words you suspect some of your students may have trouble reading and that are important to understanding the selection.

From the Thomas Nast selection, the teacher chose the following words. The newly arrived Latinos in the class will not be able to read this selection, but the teacher can capitalize on their Spanish reading strengths by helping them to locate words that are cognates in Spanish. After she chooses the words that she thinks are most critical to the selection, she looks each up in her Spanish-English dictionary to see if there are Spanish cognates for any. She finds cognates for six of the seven words. We note the cognates in the following list in parentheses.

1. *draftsman*—This is a relatively easy word for sixth to eighth graders to pronounce, but because students may not be familiar with this occupation and because it is central to understanding the article, we have included it.

2. *emigrate (emigrar—to emigrate)*—This polysyllabic word is less easily pronounced. Many students will probably have some idea of its meaning when seen in context.

3. *reform (reformar—to reform)* 4. *endorse (endosar—to endorse)* 5. *symbol (simbolo)*—These are probably fairly easy words to pronounce. However, understanding their meaning is critical to appreciating the substance and thrust of Nast's career.

6. *corruption (corrupción)* 7. *critical (critico)*—These words may prove difficult for both pronunciation and meaning, although most students will have a basic notion of the concepts they represent.

For each of the words you select, present the word in a context-rich sentence or paragraph that provides clues about the word's meaning. Following this sentence or sentences, create two items that will give the student practice in using context clues for unlocking the word's meaning. Two examples are given next:

1. Target word—*draftsman*

Mr. Jones called on his best *draftsman* to sketch plans for the new ice arena.

- Based on the sentence above, a draftsman would probably use pencils and rulers in his or her job.

  true   false

- Draftsman probably means someone who

  a. runs

  b. draws

  c. teaches

  d. rides

2. Target word—*emigrate (emgrar—to emigrate)*

Thomas Nast *emigrated* to the United States in 1840 when he was just six years old. He and his mother and sister settled in New York City.

- Based on the sentences above, Thomas Nast probably left his home country and came to live in the United States.

  true   false

- Emigrated probably means

  a. took clothes and food to poor people

  b. left one country to settle in another

  c. ran a very difficult uphill race

  d. borrowed enough money to buy a house

Before giving students the worksheet, write all the target words (including the cognates) and the first item from the worksheet on the board. Explain that these are some of the words they will be encountering in their reading selection. Turn to the newly arrived Latino students and while speaking slowly, point to the English word and then the cognate word. Say each word. For Latino students who understand

English well enough, explain that some English words have similar counterparts in Spanish and that it's good for readers who know Spanish to look for these kinds of words. Read the English words out loud again for the whole class. Tell the students you will give them a worksheet that will help them unlock the meaning of these words. Also tell them that knowing these words will make the article more interesting and understandable and that the items on the worksheet will look something like what you have printed on the board. Read the target word and the sentence. Ask what words or phrases provide clues about the underlined word's meaning. After a brief discussion, complete the true–false and multiple-choice items, explaining the thought processes you go through in deciding which is the correct choice and being sure that all students understand each word's meaning. Take advantage of the presence of émigrés in the classroom by saying something like "Juan and Rosalía recently emigrated to the United States."

Ask if there are any questions, then distribute the worksheets. Ask the newly arrived Latinos to make a list of cognate words from the text. You can use gestures and demonstrate what you want the students to do by starting a list for them. After students have completed the worksheet and the cognate lists, briefly discuss their answers and look at the cognate lists.

Adapting the Activity: In place of individual worksheets, present the material to the whole class using a transparency and overhead projector. Also, instead of using the *Paired Questions* activity to introduce *independent*, *survive*, *sovereign*, *scoffed*, and *legislature* before your fifth graders read the first few pages of Jean Fritz's *Shh! We're Writing the Constitution*, you might choose to get students involved in creating *Word Clues* themselves. After students have become familiar with the activity, choose less difficult words and let students create their own worksheet items that help unlock word meanings; then let them try out their items on each other. For Latino students who can read in Spanish, you might provide them some time to talk together about each cognate word, asking them to tell each other the meanings of the words in Spanish.

Reflection: For the context clue part, on the one hand, since this type of activity takes quite a bit of teacher preparation time, you will probably want to use it primarily with those students who need the practice in using context clues. On the other hand, since using context clues to unlock word meanings is such a useful skill and since many students would profit from becoming more adept with context clues, you may choose to use it fairly frequently. As we noted, students can learn to create instructional items like these themselves. Moreover, letting them do so gives them practice with specific words, practice with context clues, and a chance to write for a real audience—other students. Sometimes you may want to take advantage of these benefits by having your students write vocabulary items of this sort for students in lower grades or by asking teachers with upper-grade classes if their students would be interested in developing "word clue" vocabulary items for your class. For the part about learning to use cognates, there are ample opportunities to incorporate such learning in your classroom and doing so does not consume much time either during planning or during instruction. Moreover, the benefits of teaching about cognates go beyond helping students to learn word meanings in English. Even though some students might not know the meanings of all of the cognates in Spanish, they quickly learn that the teacher values their knowledge and appreciates their efforts to learn and become part of the classroom community.

Preteaching Concepts

As we noted in chapter 2, what distinguishes preteaching vocabulary from preteaching concepts is that vocabulary instruction teaches new labels for known concepts, while concept instruction focuses on words that represent new and potentially difficult ideas. When we talk about preteaching concepts, we are referring to occasions when English-language learners do not know the concept, either in their native language or in English. *Metamorphosis,* for example, is a word that would probably represent a new concept for most third graders whether they are English-language learners or not; and *recession* is a word that would probably represent a new concept for fifth and sixth graders, both native-English speakers and English-language learners.

In addition to thinking about teaching new concepts, it is also important to think of ways to further extend and refine some of the concepts students already know. Knowing a concept is not an on/off matter. Students first develop relatively simple and unsophisticated understandings of a concept and then gradually refine and extend their knowledge of that concept.

Ideally, your students will be reading material composed largely of vocabulary they can handle comfortably, yet at the same time offering some opportunities to learn new words and add to the depth of knowledge of words and concepts they already know. For example, most of the words and concepts in *Number the Stars* by Lois Lowry are within the reach of competent fifth or sixth graders. Yet these same readers might need help with such terms as *Nazi occupation* and the *Resistance.* Also, the vocabulary of Beverly Cleary's *Ramona* books is probably in the comfort zone of competent fourth graders, yet offers opportunities to deepen their knowledge of concepts such as *responsibility, indignant,* and *reassurance,* to name a few.

However, in many classroom situations the ideal "just right" amount of new vocabulary doesn't exist for English-language learners. Often, especially in situations where native language is not supported in the school, English-language learners are confronted with a new vocabulary load that is far beyond their reach. Even in these situations, though, classroom teachers can structure their lessons in ways that can help the students, sometimes to a great extent, sometimes only to a small extent, but always to some extent. Preteaching concepts is one of the ways classroom teachers can ease the burdens of overwhelming vocabulary loads for English learners.

When thinking about preteaching concepts, what you need to do is decide when and where it's appropriate to do so. If your students are going to read *Number the Stars,* they are going to need some prior knowledge of the Nazi occupation and the Resistance in order to fully understand and appreciate the events in the story and the motivations and emotions of the characters. In this situation, you will need to supply the necessary information by explaining these terms. Or, perhaps your students could benefit from expanding their knowledge of the concept *responsibility.* Maybe *responsibility* has even become an issue in your classroom because of certain behaviors of your students. In this situation, presenting the word before students read, brainstorming its probable meanings, and then having students notice how the word is used in *Ramona Forever* will help them understand the concept more fully.

The way you will go about presenting concepts before students read will depend on how familiar they are with the concepts and how well they need to know them in order to achieve their reading goals. We give additional information on preteaching concepts and the differences between various word-learning tasks in Graves (2000). On the next several pages, we give two detailed examples of activities for preteaching concepts.

PRETEACHING CONCEPTS Sample Activity 1: *Living Words*

Living Words uses charades and word clustering to activate prior knowledge of concepts as well as to add to students' understanding of those concepts.

Selection: *Harriet Tubman: Call to Freedom* by Judy Carlson. This biography chronicles the extraordinary life of Harriet Tubman, a woman of African heritage who had been enslaved herself. She was a person of invincible spirit and determination who worked unceasingly to bring freedom and justice to slaves. Harriet was born in Maryland in 1820 or 1821 and died in Auburn, New York, in 1913. For almost a century, Harriet fought for the ideals she believed in: human dignity, justice, and equality. Strong in body and spirit and empowered by an unshakable faith in God, Harriet led hundreds of slaves to freedom through the underground railroad, was an eloquent antislavery spokesperson, worked in the Union army as a nurse and a scout, established schools and homes for the poor, and supported the rights of individuals from African heritage and women to vote.

Students: Sixth graders of low to average English reading ability. Four of the students are English-language learners who have been in the school system for two years and have excellent conversational English.

Reading Purpose: To understand and relate to the incidents of Tubman's life and the injustices she fought and triumphed over.

Goals of the activity: To get students actively thinking about three concepts central to the Tubman biography—freedom, slavery, and justice—and to build on their existing knowledge of these concepts.

Rationale: To fully understand and appreciate what motivated Tubman to risk life and limb for her own freedom and that of other slaves, students need a good understanding of freedom, slavery, and justice. Activating and building on their knowledge of these concepts will help them make stronger and more lasting connections with the text when they read it. An activity such as charades requires students to think critically and creatively about words in order to dramatize them in a way that others will be able to understand their meaning. The second part of the activity, word clustering, requires students to think about what they know and organize that thinking. Both of these activities will help students better understand Tubman's motivations and actions when they read the biography and prepare them to add to their understanding of freedom, slavery, and justice.

Procedure: Before the lesson, write the words *freedom* and *slavery* on two separate slips of paper to give to the students for charades. On another sheet of paper, jot down as many words and phrases that you can think of that describe or relate to freedom, slavery, and justice. This is to help you prepare for the word-clustering part of the activity.

To begin, tell your students that they are going to play a short game of charades and that the words you have chosen for the game are very important in a book they will be reading. If they don't know how to play, explain that in charades one person tries to convey the meaning of a word or phrase by acting out its meaning while the members of his or her group call out their guesses. If their group guesses correctly within the allotted time (two minutes), that group gets a point. Give a sample word such as *beautiful* and let a few students demonstrate how they would act out the word. Next, divide the class into two groups and choose someone to go first. Show that person a slip of paper with the word *freedom* written on it. Give them about 30 seconds to think about what they will do, then have them act out the word while their group tries to guess it. If they can guess it in the two minutes time, their group gets a point. If not, give the same word to the first charader in the second group and let him or her act out the word. If group 2 cannot guess the word, let another person in group 1 act out the word. (Of course, the first person who knows the word cannot guess.) Keep going until the word *freedom* is guessed. Write that word on the chalkboard. Next, show the slip of paper with the word *slavery* on it. Proceed in the same manner as with the word *freedom*.

After the words *freedom* and *slavery* have been guessed and you have written them on the chalkboard, add the word *justice* to the board. Point to the word *freedom* and ask students to give words or phrases that they think of when they hear the word. Write their responses on the chalkboard in clusters as shown below. Then, fill in any gaps in the students' knowledge with the words and phrases you jotted down prior to the lesson. Next, explain how these words and phrases relate to or describe freedom, slavery, and justice.

going where you want	eagle	doing what you want
saying what you want	**FREEDOM**	happiness
the flag	having fun	equality

not doing what you want	no pay	
not going where you want	chains	hard work
being afraid	**SLAVERY**	wrong
bad	terrible	unfair
	not free	

lawyer		right
blind	**JUSTICE**	judge
fairness	trial	jury

After the students have given their responses and you have included yours, review the concepts. For some English-language learners, it will be important to give at least a brief synopsis of the U.S. history of slavery. Tell the students that freedom, slavery, and justice are ideas that are central in the biography of Harriet Tubman. Explain that Harriet, who was born in 1820 or 1821, was a slave in Bucktown, Maryland, until she ran away to Philadelphia when she was a young woman. Harriet returned to the South many times to help other slaves escape to the northern states and Canada. (Point out these locations to your students on a map.) In fact, Harriet spent her entire life serving the poor and enslaved. Harriet abhorred the idea of slavery and used every ounce of her intellect and energy to make freedom and justice not just words, but a reality.

Adapting the Activity: *Living Words* is an activity that can be used any time you want your students to have a good grasp of concepts that are central to appreciating and understanding the selection that they are going to read. For example, before third or fourth graders read *Sarah, Plain and Tall*, you might have them act out and do a word clustering for *mother, father, wife, husband, and children,* because these roles and relationships play an important part in the novel and expanding their understanding of them will add to your students' appreciation of the story.

Reflection: *The concepts of freedom and slavery may prove difficult for some students to act out by themselves. Sometimes it's helpful to let small groups of students, rather than individuals, dramatize these concepts for other groups of students to guess. In this situation, the students would be allowed a few minutes to prepare their charade. Additionally, you will want to make it clear to students that the reason they are thinking about these concepts is that they are important to the biography they are going to read. Knowing what they mean will help them better understand and enjoy the biography.*

PRETEACHING CONCEPTS Sample Activity 2: *Is It? Or Isn't It?*

With *Is It? Or Isn't It?* students use their prior knowledge to expand, elaborate, and refine a concept by identifying and creating examples and nonexamples of that concept.

Selection: "Rainy Season" by Nikki Grimes, from *Is it Far to Zanzibar?*

Students: Fourth graders of mixed reading abilities. One-third of the students are English-language learners of mixed oral English fluency and mixed English reading levels.

Reading Purpose: To visualize, understand, and enjoy a humorous poem.

Goal of the Activity: To help students enjoy the humor in the "Rainy Season" and to introduce the concept of EXAGGERATION as a literary device.

Rationale: Expanding and enriching students' understanding of the concept EXAGGERATION is a worthwhile activity in order to appreciate the humor in this poem.

Procedure: Say to your students, "I was so sleepy when I woke up this morning it took half an hour to open my eyes. Then my cat meowed so loud that he woke up my sister in California. When I finally got out of bed, I tripped over a pile of dirty clothes five feet tall that my husband left on the floor!" For your less proficient English-language learners, you can act out some of what you're saying as you say it. You'll probably get a few odd looks and a couple of snickers from your students. Good. They're listening. Talk about what you said and why some people laughed. (*It sounded silly. A pile of laundry wouldn't be five feet high. Cats don't meow that loudly.*) If the word *exaggeration* doesn't come up, write it on the chalkboard. Make sure that the English-language learners are looking at the word as you say it. If you know the word in their native language, say it. Explain to the students that you are exaggerating what really happened that morning. You made everything "bigger" than it really was. Authors sometimes do that to make a point or to add humor to their writing. Draw some pictures on the board to represent the concept of exaggeration. For instance, you might draw a stick figure with a normal sized head, and then next to it, draw the same body with a huge head. Or you might draw a cat's face, and then next to it, draw the same face but with a huge mouth. The drawings will help the English-language learners. Also, again if you point to the pictures and the written word while saying the word, that will also help the English-language learners to understand.

Next, show students how to change factual statements into exaggerations. First ask them to give some factual statements, and write these on the chalkboard. For example:

> Drew invited lots of people to his party.
>
> Sidelia loves the water.
>
> Mrs. García wears big earrings.

Then show how to make these statements into exaggerations by taking the truth in these statements and stretching it. For example:

> Drew invited the whole world to his party.
>
> Sidelia's in the water so much she's grown gills.
>
> Mrs. García wears earrings the size of wagon wheels.

After giving these examples of exaggeration, write a few nonexamples of exaggeration on the chalkboard and have *students* suggest how you might turn these statements into exaggeration.

> Tania has a huge bug collection.—*Tania has a bug collection the size of a house.*
>
> The baby cried.—*The baby cried buckets of tears.*
>
> Damien likes ice cream cones.—*Damien would walk 100 miles across a hot desert for an ice cream cone.*

Tell students that Nikki Grimes, author of a book of poetry called *Is it Far to Zanzibar?,* uses exaggeration in many of her poems. The poem "Rainy Season" is a good example. When students read the poem, they will discover how she uses exaggeration.

Adapting the Activity: This activity can be modified to use before reading almost any selection with an important central concept—either a literary device such as exaggeration or irony, or a concept such as friendship or honesty. For example, before reading Bruce Brooks' *Everywhere,* Nina Ring Aamundson's *Two Short, One Long,* Margaret Wild's *The Very Best of Friends,* or Bonnie Graves' *The Mystery of the Tooth Gremlin,* students could create examples and non-examples of the concept *friendship.* Giving examples and nonexamples of *tragedy* could help to increase students' perceptions and understanding of the novel *Cousins* by Virginia Hamilton or *Bridge to Terabithia* by Katherine Paterson. Before reading an informational article on drug abuse, students might list examples and nonexamples of drugs. Sometimes the concepts you might choose to have students work with will appear in the piece itself, and sometimes they won't. For example, the word *exaggeration* doesn't appear in "Rainy Season," and such words as *discrimination, freedom,* and *justice* may or may not be used in a story that illustrates those ideas.

Reflection: Having students engage in this kind of activity where they are giving examples and nonexamples of a concept not only provides an opportunity to expand their understanding of that concept but also gives them the chance to practice using their analytical and critical thinking skills. First they must think about the attributes of a concept (analyze it), then come up with some examples that clearly represent or illustrate that particular concept and others that clearly do not. Additionally, as Dorothy Frayer and her colleagues (1969) have shown in her excellent model for teaching concepts, truly understanding what something is entails understanding what it is not. Thus, giving students opportunities to consider both examples and nonexamples of concepts will sharpen their understanding of key concepts and begin to give them a sense of what it means to know a concept well.

Prequestioning, Predicting, and Direction Setting

Prequestioning

Posing questions before reading a selection gives students something to look for as they read. Thus, questions both direct attention and prompt students to be active, inquisitive learners. For example, one student might pick up the novel *Miracles on Maple Hill* by Virginia Sorenson, read the title, and ask himself, "I wonder what kind of miracles could happen on Maple Hill? What's Maple Hill anyway? A hill? A town? What?" Of course, others students may pick up the same novel and begin reading without posing any sorts of questions. Initially, teachers need to prompt these students with questions, partly to help them deal with the upcoming selection and partly to model the process of asking questions. The long-term goal, of course, is to get students in the habit of asking questions.

In chapter 7, Postreading Activities, we discuss in detail the various kinds and levels of questioning you might involve students in after they read a selection—questions that prompt students to demonstrate an understanding of what they read; questions that ask students to apply, analyze, synthesize, or evaluate information or ideas; and questions that encourage creative, interpretive, or metacognitive thinking. Questions posed *before* students read a selection can also prompt them to think on these various levels. In the sample activity that follows, questions asked before students read a selection encourage them to think analytically, critically, and creatively.

PREQUESTIONING Sample Activity: *What Do You Want to Know?*

In *What Do You Want to Know?* students generate their own questions about a story and then write their personal responses to a teacher-generated question on a reader response chart.

Selection: *Journey* by Patricia MacLachlan. *Journey* is a compact, well-crafted novel about an 11-year-old boy whose anger and grief over his mother's abandonment is eventually replaced by acceptance and trust. When Journey's mother leaves him and his sister Cat to live with their grandparents, he is deeply hurt by her abandonment and struggles to understand her motivation. With the help of his grandfather's photography, as well Journey's own detective work with a box of torn photographs, Journey is able to piece together his past. These photographs help him understand the present and give him hope for the future.

Students: Fifth and sixth graders of average to high reading ability in a bilingual education class. About half the students are Latino and one-fourth are Anglo and one-fourth Black of African heritage. The students have been in bilingual education since kindergarten. The text is written in English, and the teacher conducts the entire lesson in English.

Reading Purpose: To read and enjoy a sensitive, well-crafted piece of literature and to make personal connections with the thoughts and emotions of the main character.

Goal of the Activity: To focus students' attention by having them generate their own questions about the text and to also consider a specific question for the reader response chart that will help them connect with the thoughts and emotions of the main character.

Rationale: Having students generate their own questions about a story establishes a strong, well-motivated purpose for reading. Also, encouraging students to give their personal responses to a teacher-posed question about a piece of literature can serve a number of other purposes, but there are three primary objectives of this particular activity. One is to help students feel secure in their response to a particular work and not be dependent on someone else's response. Another is to encourage respect for the unique responses of others. A third is to help students recognize the common elements in people's responses to the same piece of literature.

Procedure: Prior to students reading the novel, bring in a camera and some pictures of yourself and your family. Show the camera and photos to your students and explain that a camera and photographs play a significant role in Patricia MacLachlan's novel *Journey*. Mention also that you will be using both a camera and photographs for a classroom literature project.

Explain that two of the main characters in *Journey* have unusual names. The protagonist, an 11-year-old boy, is in fact named Journey, and his older sister's name is Cat. They live on a farm with their grandmother and grandfather. Ask students to speculate on why a camera and family photographs might be important to the characters in the story. After students have discussed their ideas, tell them that when they go home that day you want them to look through their family photos and bring in a favorite picture of themselves to school. Tell them that you also will be taking their picture at school. Explain that the photos they bring in and the pictures you take will be used for a special project. At this time, display the reader response chart illustrated below.

Reader Response Chart for *Journey*

Tell students that the chart will give them an opportunity to share their responses to *Journey* and to other stories and poems they read. The chart will also let them see how other people respond. The question they are going to consider is. "How did photographs help Journey?"

Next read the following two quotes found at the beginning of the novel.

It is our inward journey that leads us through

time—forward or back, seldom in a straight line,

most often spiraling.

Eudora Welty,

ONE WRITER'S BEGINNINGS

Photography is a tool for dealing with things every-

body knows about but isn't attending to.

Emmet Gowin, in

ON PHOTOGRAPHY

by Susan Sontag

After you read the quotes, read the one-page introduction that precedes the first chapter. This describes the scene in the barn in which Journey's mother leaves Cat and Journey. She tells Journey that she will be back; but after she has gone, Journey's grandfather tells him that his mother won't return. Journey then hits his grandfather.

Have students generate questions from this scenario that they hope will be answered in the story. Write their questions on the board. Some questions might include these: Why was Journey's mother leaving? Why did Journey hit his grandfather? How did Cat feel? What is grandfather going to do?

Adapting the Activity: Having students generate their own questions prior to reading is an activity that can be used before reading any kind of selection—narrative or expository. The reader response chart can also be used to publish student responses to any kind of reading material. Questions can focus on feelings: "What part of the story made you feel saddest and why?" "How do you think the character felt when . . . ?" or speculation, "Why do you think the author . . . ?" "If there were another chapter in the book, what do you think the main character would do?" or interpretation, "What do you think is the story's main theme?" The questions, whatever they are, should function to get students to *think* and respond.

Reflection: *As you may have noticed, this activity accomplishes a number of prereading functions that lead up to the question-generating activity and the reader response chart. First, you do a bit of* motivating *with props (photos and a camera), then you* provide text-specific knowledge *with a short preview of the book and ask students to* predict *how a camera and photographs might be important in the story. Next you* relate the reading to the students' lives *by asking them to bring photos of their own family to school to share. And, by introducing the reader response chart, you are also preparing the foundation for during-reading and postreading activities. As we noted at the beginning of the chapter, when planning and implementing scaffolded reading activities, this kind of overlapping will very often occur, and it should.*

Predicting

Consider again the novel *Miracles on Maple Hill,* which we mentioned in discussing prequestioning. Let us say the student who selected this novel from your library shelf reads the title and looks at the cover illustration. "Hmm," he thinks to himself. "*Miracles on Maple Hill.* I bet the miracles have something to do with maple syrup." That student, of course, is making a prediction about the story. When he reads, he will be looking to see if he is correct, if the miracles do indeed have something to do with maple syrup.

Predicting activities encourages students to speculate about the text based on various prompts—illustrations, titles or subtitles, key words from the text, character names or descriptions, or short excerpts from the text. After students make their predictions, one of their reading purposes will be to see if their predictions are accurate.

Encouraging students to make predictions about an upcoming selection is a worthwhile prereading activity. Not only does it focus their attention and give them a purpose for reading, it also models a useful reading strategy, one they can employ on their own with a variety of texts. Of course, the goal is to encourage reasoned predictions based on the information available, not wild guessing. Thus predicting should often be accompanied by thoughtful discussion of what prompted the predictions and how certain or speculative the predictions are. Beginning English learners will have difficulty because they will not understand much of the conversation and will not be able to say much. It is still possible, however, for them to make some kind of prediction during the lesson, perhaps by pointing, by drawing, or by writing a single word. Also, encouraging them to state predictions in their native language (even if you don't understand it) is one way to include them, to support their thinking, and to respect their native language.

PREDICTING Sample Activity: I Predict

I Predict uses visual cues from illustrations to stimulate students' curiosity and assist them in making predictions about a text's content and in setting purposes for reading.

Selection: *Starfish* by Edith Thacher Hurd. *Starfish* is a science concept book suitable for children in kindergarten through second grade. It tells about where starfish can be found, how they move, eat, and grow.

Students: First graders of mixed reading abilities. One-third of the students are English-language learners of Asian background.

Reading Purpose: To gain appreciation for the unique qualities of the starfish.

Goal of Activity: To pique students' interest and to encourage them to make predictions about the book so they will have some definite purposes for reading.

Rationale: Predicting content is a natural and very appropriate prereading strategy for many informational selections. This science picture book is no exception. Students' inherent curiosity about animals can be easily channeled toward the selection's content by asking appropriate questions and leading students to make their own predictions. These predictions then become the purposes for students' reading.

Procedure: Before students read the book, hold up the picture on the cover showing a starfish on a rock or piece of coral surrounded by other sea creatures and plants. Cover up the title of the book, and ask students to predict what the book is about. (*Starfish.*) Uncover the title of the book, *Starfish*, and say the word as you underline it with your finger.

Next, ask students what they might expect to learn in a book about starfish and what they predict this book will be about. Write students' responses on the board under the heading WHAT WE MIGHT FIND OUT ABOUT STARFISH. Here are possible some responses:

WHAT WE MIGHT FIND OUT ABOUT STARFISH:

What they eat

Where they live

What they do

How big they are

As students give responses, act out ones which are amenable to that. For example, when a student says, "what they eat," you can pantomime eating. Open the book to one of the early pictures, call on one of the English-language learners, and ask, "Is a starfish big (pantomiming "big") or little (pantomiming "little")? What do you think?"

After several predictions have been made, ask students what it is THEY would most like to know about starfish. Give them a few minutes to think about this, and then review the predictions you have written on the board. Then, tell students you are going to read the book aloud to find out how accurate their predictions were. Say that after you are done reading, you will talk about what they found, to find out if their predictions about what they would learn were accurate.

Adapting the Activity: Using the cover illustration from a book, or other visual aids, to stimulate students' curiosity about a reading selection in order to make predictions about that selection is a technique that can be used effectively for almost any type of reading material. And, of course, using illustrations is something that puts English-language learners on a more even playing field. If appropriate illustrations don't accompany the selection itself, you can provide other types of materials— magazine illustrations, slides, photos, and concrete objects. For example, before students read Paul Goble's *Her Seven Brothers*, the Native American tale of a quill-working girl and her seven brothers who make bags, furniture, and clothing beautiful with embroidery of dyed porcupine quills, you might want to bring in porcupine quills or perhaps even an actual example of something embroidered with porcupine quills. The students might then predict why porcupine quills might be important to the story or why anyone would want to beautify objects with porcupine quills. Or students might look at the jacket cover of *The Great Gilly Hopkins* by Katherine Paterson (which pictures Gilly with a huge bubble gum bubble about to burst and cover her face) and predict what kind of a person Gilly is.

Reflection: Ideally, predicting activities such as this one will prompt students to make similar kinds of predictions when reading on their own. You can encourage such predicting by saying things such as "making predictions before reading and while you read can make reading more fun because predicting is kind of like playing a guessing game. Maybe you're reading a story in which the author shows a character running a lot. When it comes to a point in the plot when a race is about to take place, you make a prediction based on what you know. 'I bet that character will win the race because she's had so much practice.' After she does win, you can congratulate yourself. 'Nice job. I was right!'" You can encourage predicting by English-language learners by using reading selections about topics with which they are familiar.

Direction Setting

Direction setting is a third alternative to use as a focusing activity. Direction setting typically comes at the end of your prereading activities and functions as the final word of direction and encouragement you give readers. Direction setting activities tell students what it is they are to attend to while they read. Sometimes they will be oral instructions, "Read the story to find out if your predictions are correct." Sometimes they will be written on the board, a chart, or a handout so students might reflect on them or refer back to them.

As the following two activities illustrate, direction setting activities often follow other prereading activities and are typically brief and to the point.

DIRECTION SETTING Sample Activity 1: *Looking for Old, Looking for New*

Looking for Old, Looking for New is designed to follow the *Think About It!* activity (discussed earlier) and focuses students' attention on finding examples of topics they discussed in their groups and new information presented in the reading selections.

Selection: *Exploring the Deep, Dark Sea* by Gail Gibbons, *The Ultimate Field Trip 3: Wading Into Marine Biology* by Susan Goodman, *The Oceans Atlas* by Anita Ganeri, and other books that explore the wonders of the ocean.

Students: Fourth graders of average to high Spanish and English reading ability. Eighty-five percent of the class consists of Latino students and 15 percent are Anglo. All of the students were in bilingual education programs in first through third grade and are now transitioned into an all-English setting.

Reading Purpose: To add to old knowledge and gain new information about the ocean's features, ocean life, and protecting the ocean.

Goal of the Activity: To increase comprehension by having students connect what they have learned in the *Think About It!* prereading activity to what is presented in the texts.

Rationale: After having engaged in the *Think About It!* activity, students are aware of the topics discussed in these trade books. However, they will still benefit from an additional reminder of what to attend to as they read. Giving students specific directions as to what they should look for *just before* they begin reading is another way to reestablish a purpose for reading and focus their attention on salient aspects of the text. Doing so will help improve both understanding and recall.

Procedure: After you have completed the *Think About It!* activity, give each student a sheet of lined paper which they are to fold in half, making two columns. At the top of the left-hand column have them write "Old Information." At the top of the right-hand column, have them write "New Information." Tell students as they read their first ocean book (the choice is theirs to make which book they read first) that "they are to look for those features they discussed in their groups and ideas that are new ones, ones they didn't discuss." Encourage students to jot information down in the appropriate column as they read—previously discussed ideas in one column and new information in the other. Tell them they will have a chance to discuss their findings when they finish reading the book.

Proceed in a similar manner with the remaining two ocean books, discussing what students discovered in their reading and evaluating the importance of the features and issues they discussed beforehand and those found in the selection.

Adapting the Activity: *Looking for Old, Looking for New* can be used as a direction setting activity any time the prereading activity includes having students discuss or write about what they know about the topics of a selection before reading it. As we mentioned in the *Think About It!* activity, you could also use *Looking for Old, Looking for New* when your ethnically diverse fifth graders read Russell Freedman's *Immigrant Kids,* your California fourth graders read *Earthquakes* by Seymour Simon, or when curious and scientifically inclined third graders read *Forest in the Clouds* by Sneed B. Collard, III.

Reflection: This activity provides a good opportunity for students to work on critical thinking skills. When you discuss what students have recorded, they should be encouraged to look carefully and thoughtfully at the information they have chosen to record, identify what is more and less important in what they have recorded, and discuss why some information is more important than other information.

DIRECTION SETTING Sample Activity 2: *Looking for Answers*

Looking for Answers follows the *What Do You Want to Know?* activity (discussed earlier) and serves to focus students' attention on finding answers to the questions they generated prior to reading the story and toward considering the question posed for the reader response chart.

Selection: *Journey* by Patricia MacLachlan. As we have noted, *Journey* is a compact, well-crafted novel about an 11-year-old boy whose anger and grief over his mother's abandonment is eventually replaced by acceptance and trust. When Journey's mother leaves him and his sister Cat to live with their grandparents, he is deeply hurt by her abandonment and struggles to understand her motivation. With the help of his grandfather's photography as well as Journey's own detective work with a box of torn photographs, Journey is able to piece together his past. These photographs help him understand the present and give him hope for the future.

Students: Fifth and sixth graders of average to high reading ability in a bilingual education class. About half the students are Latino, one-fourth Anglo, and one-fourth Black of African heritage. The students have been in bilingual education since kindergarten. The text is written in English, and the teacher conducts the entire lesson in English.

Reading Purpose: To read and enjoy a sensitive, well-crafted piece of literature and to make personal connections with the thoughts and emotions of the main character.

Goal of the Activity: To improve understanding and enjoyment of the story by focusing on finding answers to student-generated questions and to focus student thinking along the lines of the story's theme.

Procedure: After you have finished with the *What Do You Want to Know?* activity, tell students to read the first chapter of *Journey* to find out the answers to their questions (which you have written on the board). Ask them to jot down answers as they run across them in the text. After students have finished the first chapter, give them the chance to discuss whether or not their questions were answered and if they were answered in the way they expected them to be. This discussion might take place in a large group, small groups, or pairs.

   At the end of the discussion on the first chapter but before students begin to read the remainder of the novel, remind them that as they read the novel they should be thinking about the question "How did photographs help Journey?" so that when they finish they can write a short response for the reader response chart. Tell them to pause after each chapter and reflect on that question, writing down any ideas they have, either in journals or on a sheet of paper you provide for that purpose.

Adapting the Activity: *Looking for Answers* can be used any time questions—either student generated or teacher generated—have been posed prior to reading a selection. Sometimes you may want to give general directions such as having students pause at the end of a section or chapter to think about or write down their answers. Other times you may want to give more specific guidance by giving page numbers or even specific paragraphs that contain the information that students are looking for. The more difficult or obscure the text, and the less open to interpretation the questions, the more helpful specific directions will be.

Reflection: You will probably have noticed that while this activity is quite simple and straightforward, it also overlaps, not only with another prereading activity, but also with during-reading (silent reading) and postreading (discussion after reading the first chapter) activities as well. While all pre-, during-, and postreading activities are tied to each other in one way or another, it is particularly difficult to describe direction setting activities without also describing what precedes and follows. Also, as we mentioned at the beginning of this section, direction setting activities are often quite brief. One purpose they serve is to remind students of what they have done previously, whether it is to find out how the questions they posed are answered, whether or not their predictions are accurate, or how a selection's topic or theme relates to their lives. If they have asked the questions, "Why was Journey's mother leaving? Why did Journey hit his grandfather? How did Cat feel? What is Grandfather going to do?" then a direction setting activity will encourage them to look for answers to these questions in the text.

Suggesting Strategies

It is essential that English-language learners acquire useful learning and reading strategies (Teachers of English to Speakers of Other Languages, 1997). During the past two decades, a number of reading comprehension strategies have been identified as valuable for understanding, remembering, and enjoying text (National Reading Panel, 2000; Pressley, 2000; RAND Reading Study Group, 2002). Some of these include using prior knowledge, asking and answering questions, determining what is important, imaging, summarizing, dealing with graphic information, and monitoring comprehension. As we noted in chapter 2, teaching students to use reading strategies is an important part of reading instruction, but it is not a part of SREs and therefore not a topic we discuss in this book.

However, sometimes as a prereading activity you will want to review one or more strategies that students have already learned and suggest that they employ these while reading a specific selection. Such activities encourage students to engage in previously taught strategies while they read. Already, we have alluded to several strategies in our prereading activities—using prior knowledge, making inferences, determining what is important, using context clues to unlock word meaning, asking and answering questions, and making predictions.

Prereading activities that we have labeled as suggesting strategies remind students to use strategies that they have been taught before. For instance, you might suggest that students should be on the lookout for cognates, or words that look similar to known words in their native language; that they use imaging as they read, consciously creating pictures in their heads of the people and events in the story; or, if there are illustrations in the text, to look carefully at those. Or, if they are reading material that is going to be important for them to remember, you might have them summarize after each paragraph or subtopic. You might also have them look for the most important point in each section of an article or textbook chapter.

Suggesting strategies to students by no means takes the place of strategy instruction. Teaching students about strategies, what they are and when and where to use them, and providing practice in their use requires in-depth, long-term instruction for both English-language learners and native-English speakers alike. However, once students have learned strategies, they should be encouraged to apply them when appropriate. The next sample activity in the chapter encourages students to use strategies they have been taught previously.

SUGGESTING STRATEGIES Sample Activity: *A Quick Look*

With *A Quick Look* students skim a selection in order to build a conceptual framework before reading it.

Selection: "Communities," chapter 5 in the informational trade book *The Wigwam and the Longhouse* by Charlotte and David Yue. This chapter gives a substantial amount of information about the Woodland Indians' communities, focusing on the types of settlements they had, the organization of their families, the food they ate and how it was obtained and prepared, their clothing, recreation, art and technology, festivals and work, and warfare.

Students: Fifth graders of average English reading ability. Half of the students are English-language learners with different ethnicities, all of whom have been educated in the United States since at least third grade.

Reading Purpose: To understand and remember the important aspects of the community life of the Woodland Indians.

Goal of the Activity: To encourage students to use skimming as a prereading strategy for understanding and remembering information.

Rationale: In many informational texts, the large number of names, dates, and facts can overwhelm readers. Establishing a framework for these facts and figures before tackling the text itself can aid students in making sense of the material as well as remembering it. One strategy for building this framework is to skim through the material before reading to try and determine the general thrust of the selection and some of its major topics.

Procedure: Before students read the chapter, remind them that it is sometimes helpful to skim through a chapter before reading it. In skimming, they should look for clues such as headings, boldface type, pictures, graphs, and other information that stands out or looks important. Remind them that they are trying to find out what sort of information is being presented before they actually read the chapter. Explain that doing this will help them better understand and remember the material.

Have students turn to the chapter in their books. Ask for a volunteer to read the chapter title, and write the title "Communities" on the board. Tell the students that chapter titles help point our attention in the right direction, and ask them what the title alone tells them about what they might learn in this chapter. Then write their responses on one side of the board and explain that you will compare these with what they actually find in the chapter.

Tell students to take a few minutes now to skim the entire chapter, and explain that after they have finished they will have the chance to discuss their findings. They might also want to jot down some notes.

After students have skimmed the chapter, call on a volunteer to find and read the first heading ("Settlements"). Write that heading on the board. Then ask other students for the remaining headings and put those on the board also. Be sure to arrange things so that some of your English-language learners will be able and confident enough to volunteer some headings. This may mean preparing them to do so before this activity begins.

Communities

Settlements

Families and Kinships

Food

Clothing

Art and Technology

Recreation

Festivals and Work

Warfare

Ask students what else besides headings suggest the chapter's content. Some of their responses should be drawings and illustrations. Ask them to briefly explain what these items told them about the chapter's content. (*The drawing on page 51 shows how a typical settlement was set up; the illustrations on page 70 identify and name the various types of games the woodland Indians had, etc.*)

Review the expectations students had given from the title alone (those written on one side of the board) and supplement or modify these with the new information students gleaned from skimming the chapter. Then, have students read the chapter, fitting specific information from the chapter into the framework they have created for understanding it.

Adapting the Activity: Skimming a selection before reading it is particularly useful when the text is divided into sections with titles and subtitles or has illustrations, graphs, sidebars, or other types of supplementary material that highlight important information. This means that skimming is appropriate for a lot of the expository material students read in school—articles, textbook chapters, biographies, informational books. "Your Body Systems and Health" from *Health: Focus on You* (Meeks & Heit, 1990) is an example of an excellent chapter for skimming because it outlines with its subheadings, accompanying photos, and diagrams each of the body's nine systems. With just a brief skimming of the chapter, students will have a framework in place to learn about the nine body systems: the skeletal system, the muscular system, the integumentary system, the nervous system, the endocrine system, the digestive system, the circulatory system, the respiratory system, and the urinary system.

Reflection: *Here we make three points. First, you may have noticed some similarity between this surveying activity and the* In a Nutshell *described earlier. Both include an outline of the major topics of a selection. However, in* In a Nutshell *the teacher produces the outline, whereas in* A Quick Look *students use the strategy of surveying to create their own outline. Second, surveying is an excellent and very widely applicable activity. In fact, if students are reading expository material, if they are reading it to learn something and not just to be entertained, and if they want to be*

*efficient in their learning, then surveying is definitely called for. Trying to glean infor-
mation from a text without first getting an idea of what information it contains and
how the text is organized is nearly futile. Third, even though the activity we present
here is a fairly lengthy one that might take 30 to 40 minutes of class time, we still
view the role you are playing here as that of suggesting a strategy rather than initially teaching it. Teaching students who do not know how to survey to become
skilled at surveying requires much more protracted and rich instruction than that
described here, whether or not they are English-language learners.*

Using Students' Native Language

As we have previously discussed, encouraging students to use their native
language in your classroom is helpful for many reasons including these:
It provides students with an available means of thinking about the concepts you are discussing, it shows respect for their background and culture, and what students learn while using their native language can transfer
to their thinking in English (Gersten & Baker, 2000). In all of these ways,
by encouraging students to use their native language, you are supporting
the development of their thinking and their interaction in your classroom. What students know and can discuss and think about in their native language is a valuable asset, a rich resource, to both students and
teachers.

In the following, we focus on the particular situations in which students are in all-English settings, situations in which the teacher does not
speak the student's native language. We list some of the ways in which
you can capitalize on students' native language strengths, not just during
prereading, but during and after reading as well. You can teach students
to look for cognates; provide students with the book (or a similar book
on the same topic) written in their native language; encourage students
to respond in writing in their native language; hook "newer" English-
language learners up with others who speak the same native language
but are more experienced in English. You can also have them work together so that one can "translate" for the other and locate volunteers or
bilingual teacher assistants who can assist English-language learners. The
following sample activity is called *Helping Hands,* and as is the case with
all of the activities in this chapter it's a prereading activity. While we speak
here of using students' native language during prereading, clearly similar
ideas can be used for during-reading and postreading activities as well.

USING STUDENTS' NATIVE LANGUAGE Sample Activity: *Helping Hands*

Helping Hands involves a prereading at home before the book is read in class. In
Helping Hands, the teacher locates multiple sets of a book that is written in both

English and the student's native language. As a prereading activity, she asks children to take the book home and have a parent or other relative read the book aloud in the student's native language. She also asks children to interview the person who read the book aloud prompting with the question "Is there anything in the book that felt 'true' to your own experience?"

Selection: *The Upside Down Boy, El niño de cabeza*, written by award-winning poet Juan Felipe Herrera and illustrated by Elizabeth Gomez, is formatted such that both English and Spanish appear practically side by side across pages. The story is a recounting of the year the author's migrant family settled down so that he could go to school for the first time. Juanito is confused by the new school and misses the solace of country life. Everything makes him feel out of sync—upside down. A sensitive teacher and a loving family help him to find a place in the life of his new world. The language of the book is delightfully playful and offers a fertile ground for both youngsters and adults alike to explore word meanings and turns of phrases in both Spanish and English. This is a great book to use for those who are native-English speakers as well as those who are native-Spanish speakers.

Students: The students are fourth graders in a bilingual education classroom. Most of the students are native-Spanish speakers who have lived in the United States for varying numbers of years. Some were born in the United States, some went to school in the United States for one or two years, and a few are recent arrivals to the United States. The other students are Anglos and Black of African descent. The students' reading levels in English and Spanish are diverse, ranging from first-grade level to fifth-grade level.

Reading Purpose: To become familiar with the main ideas of the book, to relate the content to the students' own lives and their families' lives, and to understand that reading in the native language can help reading in the new language.

Goal of the Activity: To encourage students to relate their experiences to the content of a book, to perceive and value the reading strengths and world knowledge of members of their own family, and to value reading in their own language as they are learning to read a new language.

Rationale: Many students feel isolated and confused as they enter new situations. This activity is intended to help students to understand that reading is a way of helping them to understand themselves and their families. The activity also helps students to feel the strength of hearing words and learning in their native language as they are learning in the new language.

Procedure: Speaking in either English or Spanish, hand out the books and introduce the title, author, and illustrator. Ask the students what they think the book might be about. Have them flip through the pages to see that this book is written in both Spanish and English. Tell the students that we're going to read the book and discuss it together in class, but that first, you want them to take it home and have an adult read it to them. They should have an adult read it to them in their native language. Have the class write down the following prompt to ask the adult after reading: "Did you ever feel like Juanito?" Ask the students to make a few notes at home about the adult's answer, and tell them that we're going to start our reading together in class by sharing the answers they heard.

Adapting the Activity: *Helping Hands* can be used with many books, including books that are not written in two languages. Students can be given a book that is written in their native language and asked to do the activity, with the idea of helping them to use their native language as they learn to read in a new language.

Reflection: Helping Hands *is a good way to encourage children to value and use their native language as they are learning English, but in some families the parents may not be able to read well enough in the native language to read the text to the students. In these cases, if another adult is called on, it is important for teachers to make sure that the parents' roles are not eliminated and that the parents' esteem and knowledge is not diminished in the children's eyes. Even if parents can't read the selection, they can still listen to the text and respond to the prompt question from the student. In this way, the parent's view and knowledge are still valued, and the student learns about his heritage and commonalities that run across generations.* Helping Hands *is also an activity that cuts across both "Using Students' Native Language" and the following category, "Involving English-Language Learner Communities and Families."*

Involving English-Language Learner Communities, Parents, and Siblings

Involving English-language learners' communities and families in your classroom life is perhaps one of the most important ways in which you can help all of the students in your care, English-language learners and native-English speakers alike. When students believe their teacher respects them, cares for them, and is trying to understand them and their situations in life, they tend to perform better academically (Hakuta, Ferdman, & Diaz, 1987). Also, when the social atmosphere in the classroom reflects such caring and respect, students tend to be more motivated and engaged in the classroom (e.g., Ryan & Patrick, 2001). Moreover, there is some evidence that when teachers and administrators hold themselves accountable to meeting the needs of English-language learners' families, they are more successful in involving the families in their children's school lives, and such involvement tends to be related to increased effectiveness in children's learning (Lopez, Scribner, & Mahitivanichcha, 2001).

There are countless ways to involve your English-language learners' communities and families in your classroom. Here, we mention just a few ways to consider when you choose prereading activities: Bring in English-language learners' relatives to show and talk about issues or concepts as a way to build knowledge for a particular text; where community opportunities exist that are related to text topics, make a class visit to those community centers (e.g., neighborhood markets or restaurants) or you visit and take photos; interview family members on topics they know about that are related to text content; and make home visits to learn about your children's families' interests. We know one principal who requires all the teachers in her school to ride all of the buses her children go on at least once during the fall so that she can experience the trip in the same way that her students do and so that she can see where each student lives, how students are greeted at the door or the bus stop, and who appears to arrive home alone. In our last sample activity in this chapter, we show just one example of family involvement in a prereading activity. As we mentioned at the beginning of this chapter, involving students' families and communities in their classroom learning doesn't just apply to prereading. There are many ways to involve them in during-reading and postreading activities as well.

INVOLVING ENGLISH-LANGUAGE LEARNER COMMUNITIES, PARENTS, AND SIBLINGS Sample Activity: *What Does a Word Mean?*

In *What Does a Word Mean?* family elders are interviewed about one or two word meanings. The teacher selects a word or two that are central to the meaning of a particular text the children are about to read. She gives the students three or four prompt questions and asks the students to interview an elder in the student's family. If students can, they also tape record the interview. If they cannot tape record it, they make notes and try to write quotes from the interview.

Selection: Chapters 1 and 2, "Responsabilidad" and "Respeto," in *It's All in the Frijoles*, by Yolanda Nava. The book is a unique compendium of inspiring recollections and stories by 100 well-known and beloved contemporary and historic Latino figures, from Jaime Escalante, the sensitive and courageous teacher in the movie *Stand and Deliver*, to actor Hector Elizondo, to Benito Juarez, president of Mexico in the mid-1800s, and many others. The arrangement of the topics in the book reveals something of the author's sense of Latino values. For instance, the first two chapters are titled "Responsabilidad" and "Respeto," or "Responsibility" and "Respect," and from their early placement, we might intuit that Ms. Nava believes these play a primary role in Latino cultures. As she says in the introduction to the book, her upbringing was filled to overflowing with a sense of values that contributed to her own character. Yolanda Nava has named and arranged these values in a way that transcends the personal and moves to the more general human and cultural values.

Students: The students are in an eighth-grade all-English language arts class. About one-fourth of the students in the class are English-language learners of Latino descent, one-half are of Anglo and Black of African descent, and one-fourth are English-language learners of Asian descent. The students' English reading levels are mixed, ranging from second-grade level to high school level. Some Latino students can read at or near grade level in Spanish.

Reading Purpose: A main purpose for reading the selections is for students to better understand some of the values the author portrays as central to Latino cultures and to explore the extent to which the same values have similar places and meanings in both the lives of students in the classroom and of elders from cultures other than Latino cultures.

Goal of the Activity: A main goal of the activity is for students to understand how language in general and word meanings in particular are often imbued with cultural understandings. Printed and spoken words can stand for wide-ranging denotative and connotative meanings, and sometimes the denotative meanings cut across cultures, while the connotative meanings may not.

Rationale: Students may not have an appreciation of how word meanings can be cultural, and they may also not have an appreciation of values that are commonly attributed to Latino cultures. *What Does a Word Mean?* can help students explore connotations of words. As well, it can help students from a variety of cultural backgrounds to consider both synonymous and asynchronous views and values across their own and their peers' lives.

Procedure: The teacher explains that the class is going to read the first two chapters from the book *It's All in the Frijoles*. He also gives a brief overview of the book, its contents, and why Ms. Nava wrote the book. He explains that Ms. Nava's mother was dying, and Ms. Nava took care of her during this time. She gradually understood that her own character was largely shaped by her mother's wisdom and that her mother had viewed certain values as central to Ms. Nava's upbringing. The teacher introduces the titles of all the chapters in the book and tells the students that before reading the first two chapters, he wants them to interview at least one *elder* in their families. He asks what the word *elder* means and explains it as needed after hearing students' responses. He asks them to tape record the interview if at all possible and to bring the tape to class. If the students cannot tape record the interview, they should write notes about the interview, including as many quotes as possible. At the beginning of the interview, each student should tell the elder the reason for the interview and ask permission to use the answers in class. If an audiotape is done, the student should also ask permission to play it in class. Then the student should ask the following prompt questions: What does the word "responsabilidad/responsibility" mean to you? How did you learn about "responsabilidad/responsibility?" "What would you like me to know about "responsabilidad/responsibility?" "On a scale of 1 to 10, with 10 being the most important, how important is "responsabilidad/responsibility" in our family?" Then the four questions are repeated for the word "respeto/respect."

When students have completed the interviews, the teacher divides the class into small groups of three, so that the groups are mixed by ethnicity. Within each group, by question, students tell how their elders answered the three questions. If they tape recorded the interview, they should play at least part of the tape and, where necessary, translate for their peers. Then as a whole group, the teacher asks the students to tell what they most want to share from each small group meeting, making notes on the board so as to group "like ideas" together, such as "doing what your mother and father tell you to do," "owning up when you've done something wrong," and "doing your very best on your schoolwork." Next, the students meet in their original trios to complete the following chart:

RESPONSABILIDAD/RESPONSIBILITY Means:

Two or three of us think or our elders thought that "responsabilidad" means:	One of us thinks or the elder thought, that "responsabilidad" means:

Then as a whole group, the teacher asks the students to tell what's on their lists, and he makes one new list compiling the students' ideas. Next, he summarizes the ideas of denotation and connotation.

Adapting the Activity: This activity could be adapted in many ways. Instead of doing the activity as a prereading activity, it could be done as a postreading activity, comparing the elders' outlooks to those in the book. Alternatively and as a postreading activity, students could read a selection from the first chapter to an elder, and ask the elder to comment. The comments could then be shared in class. Another adaptation would be for a few elders from different ethnic backgrounds to come to class to give their opinions. Still another would be to invite students from different ethnic backgrounds to elicit *dichos* (sayings), anecdotes, or short stories from elders in their families and then to write them. A class collection could be made, in parallel fashion to Nava's book, but for one chapter, and representing a multicultural outlook on the meaning of the word/topic. The class could then come up with a good title for the collection.

Reflection: What Does a Word Mean? *can help students to both "play" with a word and to understand the serious cultural connotations that can be imported to word labels. Helping students to discover the ways in which words convey and embody cultural meanings is one way to help them to see similarities in word meanings across cultures. Involving elders from multiple ethnicities is also a way to help students to understand the meanings of different values in their own lives. Additionally, comparing elders' meanings to the youngsters' meanings can be a way of exploring how we sometimes modulate inherited word meanings, either willfully or not.*

Prereading Activities: A Final Word

As we said at the outset, prereading activities serve to motivate and prepare students to read. They can be particularly helpful for English-language learners. Sometimes just one brief prereading activity will be sufficient to ensure a successful reading experience for your particular group of students with the specific selection they will be reading. At other times you may want to provide your students with several prereading activities. Still other times, you may want to do one type of prereading experience for some students in the class and a different type of prereading experience for your English-language learners. As always with SREs, what you plan will be determined by the selection itself, the *overall* purpose for reading the selection (information, enjoyment), your specific purposes for English-language learners in your class, and your students' strengths and needs. Of course, prereading activities must be coordinated with the activities students will be doing during and after reading also.

The more students *want* to read, the better their understanding of the *purposes* for which they are reading, the more *background information* they have to bring to a text, the more they will both contribute to and take from what they read. Reading experiences may still be very difficult for many English-language learners, but when teachers do prereading experiences and always keep their English-language learners in mind, they maximize the possibilities of easing the readers' burdens and improving the possibilities for all students' learning.

References

Bransford, J. D., Brown, A. L., & Cocking, R. R. (2000). *How people learn: Brain, mind, experience, and school* (expanded ed.). Washington, DC: National Academy Press. A major synthesis of what we know about teaching and learning based on work commissioned by the National Research Council.

Chen, Hsiu-Chieh, & Graves, M. F. (1998). Previewing challenging reading selections for students for whom English is a second language. *Journal of Adolescent and Adult Literacy, 41,* 370–371. Reports on the effectiveness of previews for helping English-language learners with reading.

Delgado-Gaitán, C. (1989). Classroom literacy activity for Spanish-speaking students. *Linguistics and Education, 1,* 285–297. A study of literacy activities experienced by Latino students.

Droop, M., & Verhoeven, L. (1998). Background knowledge, linguistic complexity, and second-language reading comprehension. *Journal of Literacy Research, 30,* 253–271. Reports on a study of the interrelationships among knowledge, language, and reading.

Frayer, D. A., Fredrick, W. C., & Klausmeier, H. J. (1969). *A schema for testing the level of concept mastery* (Working Paper No. 16). Madison: Wisconsin Research and Development Center for Cognitive Learning. The original source of the Frayer model for teaching concepts.

García, G. E. (1991). Factors influencing the English reading test performance of Spanish-speaking Hispanic children. *Reading Research Quarterly, 26,* 371–392. Details a study of explanations for Latino children's English reading test performance.

García, G. E. (1998). Mexican-American bilingual students' metacognitive reading strategies: What's transferred, unique, problematic? *National Reading Conference Yearbook, 47,* 253–263. A study of Mexican-American students' use of metacognitive strategies.

García, G. E., & Nagy, W. (1993). Latino students' concept of cognates. In D. J. Leu & C. K. Kinzer (Eds.), *Examining central issues in literacy research theory, and practice: Forty-second yearbook of the National Reading Conference* (pp. 367–373). Chicago: National Reading Conference. A study about Latinos' use of cognates for reading.

Gersten, R., & Baker, S. (2000). What we know about effective instructional practices for English-language learners. *Exceptional Children, 66,* 454–470. A synthesis of research and professional views on effective instructional practices with English-language learners.

Graves, M. F. (2000). A vocabulary program to complement and bolster a middle-grade comprehension program. In B. M. Taylor, M. F. Graves, & P. van den Broek (Eds.), *Reading for meaning: Fostering comprehension in the middle grades* (pp. 116–135). New York: Teachers College Press. Presents a full-fledged vocabulary program for students in the middle grades.

Graves, M. F. , Prenn, M. C., & Cooke, C. L. (1985). The coming attraction: Previewing short stories to increase comprehension. *Journal of Reading, 28,* 549–598. A clear description of how to write previews and a summary of much of the research on previewing.

Hakuta, K., Ferdman, B. M., & Diaz, R. M. (1987). Bilingualism and cognitive development: Three perspectives. In S. Rosenberg (Ed.), *Advances in applied psycholinguistics, Vol. II: Reading, writing, and language learning* (pp. 284–319). New York: Cambridge University Press. Discusses interrelationships between language, bilingualism, and cognitive growth.

Jiménez, R. T., García, G. E., & Pearson, P. D. (1995). Three children, two languages, and strategic reading: Case studies in bilingual/monolingual reading. *American Educational Research Journal, 32,* 31–61. Describes research on second-language learners' reading progress.

Jiménez, R. T., García, G. E., & Pearson, P. D. (1996). The reading strategies of bilingual Latina/o students who are successful English readers: Opportunities and obstacles. *Reading Research Quarterly, 31,* 90–112. Reports a study of bilingual Latino students' reading strategies.

Kameenui, E. J., Carnine, D. W., & Freschi, R. (1982). Effects of text construction and instructional procedures for teaching word meanings on comprehension and recall. *Reading Research Quarterly, 17,* 367–388. A study involving vocabulary instruction.

Lopez, G. R., Scribner, J. D., & Mahitivanichcha, K. (2001). Redefining parental involvement: Lessons from high-performing migrant-impacted schools. *American Educational Research Journal, 38,* 253–388. A study of effective migrant-impacted school districts.

Nagy, W. E., García, G. E., Durgunoğlu, A., & Hancin-Bhatt, B. (1993). Spanish-English bilingual children's use and recognition of cognates in English reading. *Journal of Reading Behavior, 25,* 241–259. A study of bilinguals use of cognates.

Nagy, W. E., & Scott, J. A. (2000). Vocabulary processes. In M. L. Kamil, P. B. Mosenthal, P. D. Pearson, & R. Barr (Eds.), *Handbook of reading research, Vol. III* (pp. 269–284). Manwah, NJ: Lawrence Erlbaum.

National Reading Panel. (2000). *Report of the National Reading Panel: Teaching children to read.* Bethesda, MD: National Institute of Child Health and Human Development. An influential review of research on early reading.

Pressley, M. (2000). What should reading comprehension instruction be the instruction of? In M. Kamil, P. Mosenthal, P. D. Pearson, & R. Barr (Eds.), *Handbook of reading research* (Vol. 3, pp. 545–561). Mahwah, NJ: Lawrence Erlbaum. A review and commentary on the current state of reading comprehension instruction and needed future directions.

RAND Reading Study Group. (2002). *Reading for understanding: Toward an R&D program in reading comprehension.* Santa Monica, CA: RAND Education. Excellent research report representing current thinking on reading.

Rousseau, M. K., Tam, B. K. Y., & Ramnarain, R. (1993). Increasing reading proficiency of language-minority students with speech and language impairments. *Education and Treatments of Children, 16,* 254–271. Reports on ways to help improve the reading of English-language learners who have speech and language impairments.

Ryan, A. M., & Patrick, H. (2001). The classroom social environment and changes in adolescents' motivation and engagement during middle school. *American Educational Research Journal, 38,* 437–460. A study of middle-school students' perceptions of the social environments in their classrooms.

Saunders, W., O'Brien, G., Lennon, D., & McLean, J. (1998). Making the transition to English literacy successful: Effective strategies for studying literature with transition students. In R. Gersten & R. Jiménez (Eds.), *Effective strategies for teaching language minority students* (pp. 99–132). Belmont, CA: Wadsworth. A study on effective instruction with English-language learners.

Teachers of English to Speakers of Other Languages. (1997). *ESL standards for pre-K–12 students.* Alexandria, VA: Author. This international organization presents standards for English-language learners' education.

Thornburg, D. (1993). Intergenerational literacy learning with bilingual families: A context for the analysis of social mediation of thought. *Journal of Reading Behavior, 25,* 321–352. An analysis of literacy learning in bilingual families.

Vacca, R. T., & Vacca, J. A. L. (1993). *Content area reading* (4th ed.). New York: HarperCollins. Provides a clear and concise description of structured overviews with quite a few examples.

Verhallen, M., & Schoonen, R. (1993). Vocabulary knowledge of monolingual and bilingual children. *Applied Linguistics, 14,* 344–363. Examines aspects of vocabulary knowledge for monolingual and bilingual children.

Children's Literature Cited

Aamundsen, N. R. (1990). *Two short, one long.* Boston: Houghton Mifflin.

Adams, M. J. (2002). *SRE open court reading.* Columbus, OH: SRA/McGraw-Hill

Adler, D. A. (1989). *Jackie Robinson: He was the first.* New York: Holiday House.

Anacona. G. (1999). *Charo: The Mexican cowboy.* San Diego: Harcourt Brace.

Avi. (1990). *The true confessions of Charlotte Doyle.* New York: Orchard.

Blumberg, R. (1989). *The great American gold rush.* New York: Bradbury.

Brooks, B. (1990). *Everywhere.* New York: HarperCollins.

Carlson, J. (1989). *Harriet Tubman: Call to freedom.* New York: Fawcett Columbine.

Chin, C. (1993). *China's bravest girl: The legend of Hua Mu Lan.* San Francisco: Children's Press.

Cleary, B. (1984). *Ramona forever.* New York: William Morrow.

Clements, A. (1996). *Frindle.* New York: Simon & Schuster.

Collard, S. B., III. (2000). *Forest in the clouds.* Watertown, MA: Charlesbridge.

Conrad, P. (1991). *Pedro's journal.* Honesdale, PA: Boyds Mill Press.

Edwards, S. (1985). *George Midgett's war.* New York: Scribner.

Evans, L. (1988, November). Thomas Nast: Political cartoonist extraordinaire. *Cobblestone, 9,* 11–13.

Freedman, R. (1980). *Immigrant kids.* New York: E. P. Dutton.

Fritz, J. (1987). *Shh! We're writing the Constitution.* New York: G. P. Putnam's Sons.

Ganeri. A. (1994). *The oceans atlas.* New York: DK.

Gibbons, G. (1999). *Exploring the deep, dark sea.* Boston: Little, Brown.

Goble, P. (1988). *Her seven brothers.* New York: Bradbury.

Goodman, S. (1999). *The ultimate field trip 3: Wading into marine biology.* New York: Simon & Schuster.

González, J. (2000). *Harvest of the empire: A history of Latinos in America.* New York: Viking.

Graves, B. B. (1997). *Mystery of the tooth gremlin.* New York: Hyperion.

Grimes, N. (2000). Rainy season. In *Is it far to Zanzibar?* New York: Lothrop, Lee & Shepard.

Grolier (Publisher). (1997). *Vietnam.* Danbury, CT: Grolier.

Hamilton, V. (1990). *Cousins.* New York: Philomel.

Herrera, J. F. (2000). *The upside down boy: El niño de cabeza.* San Francisco: Children's Book Press/Libros Para Ninos.

Houston, J. (1977). *Frozen fire.* New York: Margaret K. McElderry.

Hurd, E. T. (2000). *Starfish.* New York: HarperCollins.

Karr, K. (2000). *The Boxer.* New York: Farrar.

Kimmel, E. A. (2000). *The two mountains: An Aztec legend.* New York: Holiday House.

Lord, S. (1993). *Garbage! The trashiest book you'll ever read.* New York: Scholastic.

Lowry, L. (1989). *Number the stars.* Boston: Houghton Mifflin.

MacLachlan, P. (1991). *Journey.* New York: Delacorte.

MacLachan, P. 1985). Sarah, plain and tall. New York: Harper & Row.

Markle, S. (1999). *Down, down, down in the ocean.* New York: Walker.

Marrin, A. (2000). *Sitting Bull and his world.* New York: Dutton Children's Books.

Meeks, L., & Heit, P. (1990). Your body systems and heath. In *Health: Focus on you.* Columbus, OH: Merrill.

Nava, Y. (2000). *It's all in the frijoles.* New York: Simon and Schuster.

Naylor, P. (1980–81). *The York Trilogy.* New York: Macmillan.

Paterson, K. (1977). *Bridge to Terabithia.* New York: Crowell.

Paterson, K. (1978). *The great Gilly Hopkins.* New York: Crowell.

Paulsen, G. (1987). *Hatchet.* New York: Bradbury.

Rogasky, B. (1988). *Smoke and ashes: The story of the Holocaust.* New York: Holiday House.

Russell, C. Y. (1994). *First apple.* Honesdale, PA: Boyds Mills.

Simon, S. (1991). *Earthquakes.* New York: Morrow.

Sorenson, V. (1956) *Miracles on Maple Hill.* New York: Harcourt.

Spinelli, J. (1990). *Maniac Magee.* Boston: Little Brown.

Thesman, J. (1990) *Rachel Chance.* Boston, MA: Houghton Mifflin.

Thomas, J. R. (1998). *Behind the mask: The life of Queen Elizabeth I.* New York: Clarion.

Wild, M. (1990). *The very best of friends.* San Diego: Harcourt Brace Jovanovich.

Winter, J. (2001). *¡Béisbol!: Latino baseball pioneers and legends.* New York: Lee & Low Books.

Yue, C., & Yue, D. (2000). *The wigwam and the longhouse.* Boston: Houghton Mifflin.

CHAPTER 6

DURING READING
ACTIVITIES

After you have motivated and prepared students to read with prereading activities, the next step is for students to *read*. Here students will meet and interact with the text. They will begin to extract and construct meaning from the text by reading or, occasionally, by being read to. During-reading activities include things that the students do as well as the things you might do to assist them in their reading. We have broken down the during-reading phase into five categories—silent reading, reading to students, supported reading, oral reading by students, and modifying the text.

DURING READING

1. Silent reading

2. Reading to students

3. Supported reading

4. Oral reading by students

5. Modifying the text

These categories, of course, reflect only one of many ways to organize and think about during-reading activities. Also, it's important to recognize that the activities themselves might also be used as pre- or postreading experiences. For example, reading to students could work as a prereading activity or oral reading by students as a postreading activity.

During-reading activities involve students with the text in a way that best suits the students, the text, and their purposes for reading it. Here are some questions you might ask before designing during-reading activities: How might the reading task best be accomplished? What might I do to actively involve students with the text? What can I do to help make this material come alive for students as they read? What would make this material more accessible to students? What might students do as they read that will make the text more understandable, or memorable, or enjoyable?

During-Reading Activities in Chapter 6

Silent reading

Reading to students   *The Appetizer*

Supported reading

    Journal writing   *Problem, Solution, Change*

    Letter writing   *Dear Diary*

    Reading Guides   *What Does It Mean?*

                        I Didn't Know That!

                        Group and Label

    Time line   *Who? What? When?*

Oral reading by students

    Choral reading   *Two Voices*

    Readers theatre   *On the Air!*

    Oral interactions   *Flag It*

Modifying the text   *Focusing*

                        Rewriting

Silent Reading

Silent reading will be the most frequent during-reading activity. Reading, obviously, is the primary activity of the scaffold—the *raison d'etre*. And most often students will be doing this reading by themselves silently. The other activities in the scaffold are designed to support students' *reading*—to prepare them for it, to guide them through it, and to take them beyond it.

Reading to Students

As previously mentioned, most of the time English-language learners will be reading a selection silently. Sometimes, however, it is appropriate to read aloud to them. If the material cries out to be heard, for whatever reasons—because the language is beautiful and inspiring, because students need a good send-off for a lengthy or challenging selection, because the concepts are new and need interpretation—then hearing the words, may help students grasp the material so that when, and if they do read it on their own, it will hold more meaning, pleasure, and interest for them.

Reading aloud to your English-language learners not only makes certain texts accessible to them, it also provides a model for expressive reading. By reading aloud, you can show your enthusiasm for the information, ideas, and language in the text. As storyteller and author Bill Martin, Jr. (1992), has said, "A blessed thing happened to me as a child. I had a teacher who read to me."

Because this book deals with helping English-language learners read specific selections, the reading to students we present here is done in conjunction with their doing some reading on their own. However, we do not want to miss this opportunity to emphasize the importance of reading to children as one critical component of a complete reading program. As Jim Trelease (2001) has pointed out so powerfully in *The New Read-Along Handbook*, "A large part of the educational research and practice of the last twenty years confirms conclusively that the best way to raise a reader is to read to that child—in the home and in the classroom." In fact, Trelease continues, "This simple, uncomplicated fifteen-minute-a-day exercise is not only one of the greatest intellectual gifts you can give a child; it is also the cheapest way to ensure the longevity of a culture." We most emphatically agree: Reading to English-language learners builds their vocabularies, their knowledge of the world, their knowledge of books and many of the conventions employed in books, and—probably most importantly—their interest in reading. Moreover, as Camille Blachowicz and Donna Ogle (2001) observe, reading aloud to children "can be one of the most enjoyable times of the day for both a teacher and a class." Reading to English-language learners might also help them to build their oral English facility. Additionally, reading to children in both native language and English will likely be of benefit because they will be maintaining and strengthening their native language understandings, and what they learn from listening in their native language might transfer to English.

Reading aloud to students is one way to demonstrate the beauty and power of language; and for students who struggle with reading on their own, have had little exposure to books, or are learning to read in a new language, it may be one of the most significant ways. The activity that follows demonstrates these functions.

READING TO STUDENTS Sample Activity: *The Appetizer*

In *The Appetizer,* you read the first chapter of a novel aloud in order to pique students' interest, engage them in the story, and motivate them to read the entire book.

Selection: *In the Year of the Boar and Jackie Robinson* by Bette Bao Lord. *In the Year of the Boar and Jackie Robinson* is a delightful and well-written novel that traces Chinese immigrant Shirley Temple Wong's first year in America. The year is 1947 and Shirley's engineer father, who lives in Brooklyn, New York, sends for Shirley and her mother. Shirley is hopeful and excited about venturing to a new and mysterious country as well as fearful and sad to leave her country and her family, the House of Wong. Once in America, Shirley is enrolled in P.S. 8 and her mother charges her with being "China's little ambassador." From March through December, Shirley is just that. She brings her modest yet invincible Chinese spirit to the tasks of learning the language and the customs, as well as to making friends. Shirley learns how to play stickball and becomes an avid Dodger fan, taking Jackie Robinson to be her personal hero. Throughout her growing assimilation into P.S. 8 and her Brooklyn neighborhood, Shirley manages to retain her loyalty and love for her people as well as claim the opportunities she discovers can be hers in America.

Students: Fourth or fifth graders of mixed reading abilities and from a variety of ethnic backgrounds. Two Vietnamese students in the class are recent arrivals to the United States and are in the beginning stages of learning English.

Reading Purpose: To understand and enjoy a well-written story and to gain insights into the perspective of a person with a Chinese background.

Goal of Activity: To introduce the characters, setting, and dilemma faced by the main character; to present terms and ideas that may be new to students; to pique students' interest and motivate them to read the novel on their own.

Rationale: Much of the appeal of this novel comes from the fact that Shirley stays very much Chinese while at the same time becoming a New Yorker. The first chapter titled "January—Chinese New Year" describes Shirley's home in China, her relatives, and their customs. Because the first chapter is filled with humor and colorful language, reading it aloud will both serve as an enticement for students to read the rest of the book on their own and help firmly establish in their minds the culture, country, and family Shirley is leaving behind—a people and way of life Shirley vows never to forget.

Procedure: Before reading the first chapter aloud, on the chalkboard write:

    China   The Year of the Dog   The Year of the Boar   1947

        Jackie Robinson   Brooklyn Dodgers

Explain that in the novel *In the Year of the Boar and Jackie Robinson,* the main character, Bandit, better known as Shirley Temple Wong, is from China. Locate

China on a map or globe. If there are any students in the class from China, the teacher can use these students or representatives from their families as reporters.

Tell students that the story begins in China on Chinese New Year's Eve. The Year of the Dog is just ending and The Year of the Boar just beginning. You might also want to explain that a boar is a wild pig and that the Chinese name their years after different animals. Tell students that the Year of the Boar is 1947, the year Jackie Robinson, the first Black major league baseball player, played with the Brooklyn Dodgers.

Ask students to speculate about why the title of the book might be *In the Year of the Boar and Jackie Robinson* and what a young Chinese girl and a Black baseball player might have in common. After students have given their responses, read the first chapter of the book aloud, which should take about 15 minutes. Then, invite students to continue reading this engaging story on their own. Match lower level readers with higher level readers, asking the higher level reader to read aloud while the other student follows along. Ask a Vietnamese student who has been in the class for some time to read aloud to the two newly arrived Vietnamese students.

Adapting the Activity: Reading the first chapter of a novel or informational book aloud is appropriate any time you want to motivate students to read the book on their own or to introduce a book that some students might have difficulty getting into. Because first chapters in novels must accomplish the tasks of establishing the setting and tone of a book, introducing the characters, and beginning the plot, they can frequently be more challenging than the rest of the book. Thus, they are natural places for giving students a helping hand. Other books for which you might offer your students an *appetizer* are *Canyons* by Gary Paulsen, *Maniac Magee* by Jerry Spinelli, and *Journey* by Patricia MacLachlan. Each of these books is somewhat more challenging than what some students might be used to.

Reading poetry aloud to students is also very appropriate to prepare them to read poems silently and as an introduction and preparation for performing poetry. A particularly beautiful collection of poetry written by Latinos and edited by Pat Mora and illustrated by Paula S. Barragán M. is *Love to Mamá: A Tribute to Mothers*. Another collection of poems by award-winning author Gary Soto is *Neighborhood Odes*, illustrated by David Diaz, a collection of poems that bring to life a Mexican-American neighborhood.

Reflection: *The* Appetizer *activity is a straightforward but very useful one. Your oral reading serves as an enticement for reading in general, because it demonstrates to students what written words are meant to do—inform, entertain, enlighten, and inspire. It's also a lot of fun for you. Indulge yourself and indulge your kids. Give them a running start by reading the beginning of a selection whenever the spirit moves you.*

Supported Reading

Much of the time, particularly with narratives, students will read the material from beginning to end without stopping to record or reflect on what they are reading. The interactions that take place are often personal ones between the reader and the text. As Louise Rosenblatt (1978, 1994) has explained, the primary concern with narratives is likely to be with what happens to students as they read rather than what they remember afterward. Responses to what they have read might be shared after they have read or perhaps not at all. Sometimes, however, it is appropriate to guide students' reading, to help them focus on, understand, and learn from certain aspects of the text.

Supported reading means just that—supporting the thought processes that accompany reading. Supported reading activities encourage generative learning that Merlin Wittrock (1990) sees as promoting real learning—they lead students to make connections among ideas in the text and between their existing experience and knowledge with what is presented in the text. They can be particularly helpful to English-language learners in the early and middle phases of learning English.

Although supported reading activities are most often used to help students read expository material, they can also be used for narratives. Perhaps you feel students would understand and enjoy a story more if they focused their attention on certain aspects of character, setting, plot, or theme. Or maybe you want them to be aware of colorful or unusual language. Maybe you would like for them to make personal responses to what they read, make predictions, or consider how they or the characters are feeling. These are all good reasons for designing supported reading activities. Some general kinds of supported reading activities for narratives might include these:

+ Informal writing that elicits personal responses such as journaling or writing letters,

+ Reading with a partner and pausing to reflect out loud, or

+ Using reading guides, which might include answering questions, or completing charts or outlines that focus on character, plot development, point of view, or various aspects of language or style.

As we mentioned earlier, supporting reading activities are most frequently used to help students understand and remember the information presented in expository materials. Some general kinds of supported reading activities for expository texts might include these:

+ Having students focus on various organizational patterns of text such as sequencing, cause and effect, or comparison/contrast;

♦ Encouraging critical thinking by having students note examples of fact and opinion, make inferences, draw conclusions, or predict outcomes;

♦ Leading students to manipulate the text in ways that will help them better understand and retain key concepts. For example, recording main ideas and their supporting details, outlining, summarizing, semantic mapping, and time lines; or

♦ Having students monitor their understanding of what they read.

Supported reading activities can be effective scaffolds for students while they read in any genre. Again, the value and effectiveness of any sort of activity will depend on your students, the material they are reading, and the purposes for reading it. When designing supported reading activities, you might ask, "What is it that students should be attending to as they read? Should they be looking for key concepts? Cause-and-effect issues? The author's biases or perspective? Colorful language? Motives of characters? Sequence of events?" Or you might design supported reading activities to encourage students to be metacognitive as they read. "What do I know about this topic?" is the type of question that you would like them to ask frequently as they approach an informational piece. Alternately, supported reading activities can lead students to consider particular points or questions that come up at various junctures in their reading. "Does what the author says about clouds make sense in terms of what I know about clouds, water vapor, rain, and so on?"

What supported reading does is get students thinking about and manipulating the ideas and concepts in the material in a way that will help them understand, enjoy, and remember it better. The six activities that follow are designed to do just that.

SUPPORTED READING Sample Activity 1: *Problem, Solution, Change*

In *Problem, Solution, Change* students record in journals what they think are *problems* the main character faces, *solutions* to those problems, and *changes* that took place in the main character because of the problem and solution.

Selection: *Yang the Youngest and His Terrible Ear* by Lensey Namioka. Nine-year old Yingtao Yang and his family have recently moved from China to Seattle, and he wants to learn English and make new friends at school. He has to help his father with an important family music recital, but Yintao has a "terrible ear" for music. He's afraid his bad violin playing will ruin the recital. He and his friend Matthew figure out a sure-fire plan to save the recital, certain that nothing will go wrong. Many issues are explored in this book, including language use, cultural differences, diversity, self-realization, friendship, courage, and duty, making it a rich resource for a wide variety of classroom discussions.

Students: Sixth graders with mixed English reading abilities. There are two English-language learners from China and one from Japan who have been in the United States since the beginning of fourth grade.

Reading Purpose: To read and enjoy a story by focusing on the basic plot elements of problem, solution, and change.

Goal of Activity: To focus students' attention on the elements of plot as they develop and unfold throughout the novel and to encourage students to make connections between ideas in the text and their own lives.

Rationale: Having students think about the problems a main character faces, how he or she solves that problem, and what sorts of changes take place within the character because of the problem and resolution can help students discover one of the most salient features of fiction—characters meet up with problems, find ways to solve them, and are changed in the process. Because Yingtao's problems are ones that are likely to resonate with both English-language learners and native-English speakers alike, *Yang the Youngest and His Terrible Ear* is an outstanding vehicle for the study of a problem–solution plot line.

Procedure: Ideally this activity would follow a *Common Threads* prereading activity in which students have recorded problems, solutions, and changes in their own lives. Begin by reading the back cover blurb, which provides a synopsis of Yingtau's introduction into the United States and of the family dilemma he faces.

If you have done the *Common Threads* prereading activity, remind students of some of their responses and then have them predict what sorts of problems a nine-year-old boy from China might have living in a family of talented musicians and what problems he might encounter when beginning schooling in the United States, how he might go about solving those problems, and how he might be changed because of them.

Explain that part of the pleasure and purpose of reading literature is to reflect on the actions and thoughts of the main characters in a story in order to better understand ourselves and others. In most fiction they read, students will find a character who is faced with a problem. *Yang the Youngest and His Terrible Ear* is no exception. This is a thought-provoking novel injected with dry humor in which Yingtao is faced with numerous and very difficult problems that he must solve. In the process of dealing with each of these dilemmas he is changed a bit, until by the end of the novel he is a more mature person.

Tell students that they will be keeping a journal as they read the novel. Their journal will focus on Yingtao's problems, solutions, and changes. Explain that keeping their own journal will help them keep track of the events and that in doing so they will be able to extend and enrich their own knowledge and explore new ideas along with the main character, Yingtau.

Next, provide students with several sheets of lined paper to serve as their journal. Have them fold the paper in thirds to form three columns. This will allow students to record their ideas regarding Yingtau's problems, solutions, and changes.

Problem   **Solution**   **How Changed?**

Next, bind the pages together—a simple staple would do or you might want students to create a front and back cover of construction paper, which they can later embellish.

Before students begin reading the novel and recording Yingtau's problems, solutions, and changes, you might want to read the first chapter aloud and then demonstrate how to make the journal entries. After reading the chapter aloud, have students suggest problems, solutions, and changes. Write these suggestions on the board.

Remind students that there are no right or wrong responses. Anything they feel constitutes a problem, solution, or change should be recorded. Also, sometimes a problem may not have an immediate solution or any change in Yingtau may not be recognizable at the moment. They may need to read further in the novel to discover solutions and changes, and they may identify some problems that aren't resolved in the novel.

When students are clear as to what they will be doing, have them begin reading the novel and recording problems, solutions, and changes in their journals. Tell them that when they finish they will have an opportunity to share and discuss what they discover about Yingtau's problems and solutions as well as how they relate to those problems and solutions.

Adapting the Activity: This type of activity is appropriate for almost any novel in which the main character is faced with numerous problems to solve or obstacles to overcome. Just a few examples include *Blanca's Feather* by Antonio Hernández Madrigal, illustrated by Gerardo Suzán; *The True Confessions of Charlotte Doyle* by Avi; *Cousins* by Virginia Hamilton; *Everywhere* by Bruce Brooks; the survival story, *Hatchet,* by Gary Paulsen; *Chato and the Party* Animals by Gary Soto, illustrated by Susan Guevara; *Dixie Storms* by Barbara Hall; *A Handful of Stars* by Rafik Schami; *Maniac Magee* by Jerry Spinelli; *Number the Stars* by Lois Lowry; and *Rachel Chance* by Jean Thesman. As a matter of fact, it is probably harder to find novels or short stories that do not lend themselves to such an analysis than to find those that do.

Reflection: Most students will probably have little trouble identifying the problems that come up in the novel. Native-English speakers may be surprised by some of the language and cultural problems Yingtau encounters, perhaps never having thought about these issues. Some students may find it difficult to identify some of Yang's solutions, such as how he used an inner strength to deal with his family's criticisms of his musical ability. Even more students may have a hard time finding the changes that took place in Yingtau. It's a good idea to encourage students not to become bogged down looking for precise answers. They should realize that not everyone will see Yingtaus problems, solutions, and changes in the same way and that some solutions may not come until the end of the novel, and some not at all. The idea of the activity is for them to see how problems cry out for solutions and that change is a big part of the problem-solving process. Because fiction mirrors life, it provides a rich resource for examining this process.

It is worth noting the general function this supported reading activity has served because it is a very useful function and one that supported reading activities can serve fairly frequently. We have focused students' attention on an aspect of the text that both helps them understand and appreciate this text, will aid them in appreciating a number of texts they read in the future, and will help them understand and appreciate themselves and each other. This certainly has not been a full-blown lesson in which we have attempted to give students a definite strategy for identifying problems, solutions, and changes that often occur in narratives; and you may at some time want to provide a more substantial strategy lesson on this topic—a matter considered at some length in Graves, Juel, and Graves (2001). But at the very least, the mini-lesson will give students a start in learning to look for such patterns in literature.

Also, this response activity is only one of many types that might be implemented for this selection. Another procedure, a two-column response journal described by Hilda Ollmann (1992), could be used for this novel, as well as for many other stories, poems, or expository pieces. When following this procedure, students write quotes from the text in one column and their personal responses to the quotes in another. For example, an entry for chapter 1 in Yang the Youngest and His Terrible Ear might look like this:

In the text	In My Head
p. 6. "Parents didn't want to bring their children to a music teacher who spoke so little English and had such a strong Chinese accent."	I know what that's about! My parents go to English school at night two times a week. I'm proud of them, but they are afraid to talk in English at the store because they think people will think they talk funny.

Response journals of this type are one way to actively involve readers with text and to encourage analytical, evaluative, and creative thinking.

SUPPORTED READING Sample Activity 2: *Dear Diary*

In *Dear Diary* students compose diary entries from the point of view of the protagonist.

Selection: *Harriet Tubman: Call to Freedom* by Judy Carlson. This biography chronicles the extraordinary life of Harriet Tubman, a black woman of invincible spirit and determination who worked unceasingly to bring freedom and justice to Black people. Harriet was born in Maryland in 1820 and died in Auburn, New York, in 1913. For almost a century Harriet fought for the ideals she believed in: human dignity, justice, and equality. Strong in body and spirit and empowered by an unshakable faith in God, Harriet led hundreds of slaves to freedom through the underground railroad, was an eloquent antislavery spokesperson, worked in the Union army as a nurse and a scout, established schools and homes for the poor, and supported the rights of Blacks and women to vote.

Students: Fifth graders of mixed reading abilities and from a variety of ethnic backgrounds.

Reading Purpose: To learn more about the plight of Blacks in the United States during the mid-1800s and to appreciate and be inspired by the courage, resourcefulness, and commitment of Harriet Tubman.

Goal of Activity: To help students become involved with the text at a personal and emotional level by identifying with the subject of the biography and to encourage use of the comprehension skills of summarizing and determining what is important.

Rationale: Writing diary entries reflecting historical events, as well as the thoughts and emotions of the protagonist, not only requires that the reader summarize important events, it also challenges the reader to experience these events through the senses of another person. Such role playing will encourage empathy and promote comprehension and recall.

Procedure: Read the first chapter of the biography aloud to the students. Then, ask them to tell what they learned about Harriet Tubman from this first chapter and to give a word or phase that describes her. Write their suggestions on the chalkboard. Some of their comments might include the following:

a slave   brave   spiritual or religious   strong   determined

Explain that the author chose to begin the biography by describing an incident that took place when Harriet Tubman was in her twenties. The next chapter begins with Harriet at age 6, and the chapters that follow proceed in chronological order. The last chapter ends with Harriet's death at 93. Tell the students that every chapter includes much action and vivid details and that these actions and details reveal the extraordinary person that Harriet Tubman was. Then, introduce writing diary entries with something like this: "Harriet couldn't read or write, but she had thoughts and strong opinions that she expressed in both words and actions. Let's pretend that Harriet could read and also express herself in writing. What would she write and to whom? Harriet had strong feelings about cruelty and injustice. She wanted to see wrongs righted. She wanted to move people to action. She wanted her voice heard. But of course at that time it was too dangerous to speak out. Let's say Harriet decided to pour out her thoughts and feelings in a diary." If students are unfamiliar with diary entries, read a few examples, perhaps from *The Diary of a Young Girl* by Anne Frank. You might also want to allude to Alice Walker's *The Color Purple*, in which the protagonist works through her pain by writing letters to God. Older students might be familiar with the novel or with the movie.

Ask the students if, after hearing the first chapter, the following letter is one Harriet might write to Dear Diary.

Dear Diary,

I have just completed a successful journey on the Underground Railroad. The trip wasn't easy, and I can tell you there were many times I thought I'd be caught or thrown off. But I made it with the help of a lot of kind folks and am now in Philadelphia—a free woman at last.

I am going to continue to fight for liberty for my people as long as my strength lasts. I think all people deserve to live in freedom. Do you think so too?

Your friend,

Harriet

Discuss the letter with the students. Focus on what Harriet chose to write about and why.

As a class, compose another Dear Diary letter for the chapter and write it on the chalkboard. Have students think about what else Harriet might choose to write in her diary and why.

Before students begin reading the biography on their own, tell them that as they read through the book, you want them to write a letter from Harriet Tubman to her diary after each chapter. For English-language learners who cannot yet fully participate by writing their own letters, match them with other learners who can write in English with ease and ask them to dictate their letters. Or if they can write in Spanish, ask them to write their letters in Spanish. The letter should reflect the incidents and concerns Harriet experiences in that chapter. The students should try to put themselves in Harriet's shoes, to try and write as she would write. They will have 10 diary entries by the end of the book.

To give you an idea of what students might write, we have included some sample letters:

From Chapter 3, "Nat Turner's Rebellion"

Dear Diary,

Things are bad. A man named Nat Turner tried to free my people but he got caught and they shot him. Now our masters won't let us meet for church on Sundays or read the Bible even, and yesterday the traders came and took my two sisters. I'm afraid I'll never see them again, and every night I have a horrible nightmare that the traders are going to come and take me. I am so afraid. What should I do?

Your Friend,

Harriet

From Chapter 4, "The Turning Point"

Dear Diary,

I'm thirteen, but I feel so old. I thought things couldn't get worse but they did. An overseer hit me in the head with a two-pound weight and I nearly died. And all the time I was sick Master tried to sell me. I prayed hard for the Lord to change his heart and make him a Christian. But then when I heard some of us was going to be sold to the chain gang I changed my prayer. I told the Lord that if he wasn't going to change that man's heart he should kill him so he won't do no more mischief. Then Master up and died! I felt it was me who had killed him. And since my head was hurt I have these sleeping spells and dreams that I think are telling me the future. Do you think I killed my master and that dreams can predict the future?

Your Friend,

Harriet

Adapting the Activity: One additional activity students could undertake here is to compile their letters and publish them in a booklet titled "The Diary of Harriet Tubman." Diary entries might be composed as a group activity, too. Students can get together after reading each chapter and decide what they will put in a letter and then compose one letter for the group.

This activity—writing diary entries from the point of view of the protagonist—can be done with any kind of material in which the main character is confronted with obstacles to overcome or problems to solve. For example, while reading *Samir and*

Yonatan, an International Reading Association 2001 Notable Book for a Global Society, written by Daniella Carmi and translated by Yael Lotan, students could be asked to put themselves in Samir's place. Samir is a Palestinian boy who finds himself wounded and in an Israeli hospital ward. While reading *The Glory Girl* by Betsy Byars, the students could write diary letters from the main character Anna's point of view as she struggles to find her own identity as the only nonsinger in a family of gospel singers. Another good book for this activity is Jerry Spinelli's *Fourth Grade Rats.* The protagonist Suds goes through some interesting inward struggles as he tries to please his friend Joey and make the transition from third-grade "angel" to fourth-grade "rat." Writing diary entries from Lily's point of view in Patricia Reilly Giff's *Lily's Crossing* would be a fun and worthwhile activity for fifth graders, especially while studying the World War II years. Diary entries for Gilly from Katherine Paterson's *The Great Gilly Hopkins*, or for Lyddie from Paterson's book by the same name, would also make for interesting writing and reading. A variation on this theme would be to have students write "Dear Abby" type letters instead of "Dear Diary" ones. In these letters, students would ask for advice as well as tell about the events, thoughts, and feelings as experienced through the story characters.

Reflection: *In addition to actively involving students in the life and thoughts of the protagonist, this activity provides an ideal opportunity to review the elements and formatting of an informal letter. To extend the activity, students might write letters to newspaper columnists in which they ask for advice or sound off on an issue in "letters to the editor." Letters could be reviewed and discussed by a panel of "experts" who then write responses to the letters. Letters and responses could be read aloud to the entire class or in small groups. Also, students might write letters to the characters in a novel. For instance, fifth graders might write to Cal in the novel C, My Name Is Cal by Norma Fox Mazer, or to the author, to discuss aspects of the story as they unfold. Or, they might write a letter to a friend or classmate telling about the events that take place in each chapter or their reactions to characters or events.*

SUPPORTED READING Sample Activity 3: *What Does It Mean?*

In *What Does It Mean?* students interpret colorful or figurative language in order to better understand the text as well as appreciate the subject of the text.

Selection: *I Have a Dream, The Story of Martin Luther King, Jr.,* by Margaret Davidson. This biography traces the emergence of Martin Luther King, Jr., as a powerful civil rights leader and pacifist, from his youth in Atlanta, Georgia, through his assassination at age 39 in Memphis, Tennessee. The biography stresses King's compassion, intelligence, and eloquence as well as his unquenchable spirit and commitment to justice, equality, and peace.

Students: Fifth to seventh graders of mixed reading abilities and from various ethnic backgrounds, including two English-language learners recently arrived from the Balkans.

Reading Purpose: To understand and appreciate Martin Luther King, Jr., as a person as well learning about his accomplishments as a civil rights leader. The purposes for the two English-language learners is for them to learn to read two English words and garner some information about Reverend King.

Goal of Activity: To introduce or reintroduce the concept of figurative language and to have students focus on this language in order to better understand Martin Luther King, Jr., and to understand the concept of civil rights. The purposes for the two English-language learners are for them to learn some very basic information about Martin Luther King, Jr., and what he accomplished in the United States, and to understand the concept of civil rights.

Rationale: Martin Luther King, Jr., was, of course, an eloquent speaker with a passion for words and ideas. King often spoke in colorful and figurative language, examples of which are sprinkled throughout the biography. Calling the reader's attention to these and interpreting their meaning will help the reader to better understand the text and to appreciate King as a person.

Preparation: Before the lesson—either on the chalkboard, a transparency, or handouts—write the following phrases and page numbers.

Page 54:	"My feet is tired, but my soul is at rest."
Page 59:	"Cold fingers of fear creeping up my soul."
Page 63:	"I want it to be known in the length and breadth of the land."
Page 66:	"The clock said it was noon, but it was midnight in my soul."
Page 67:	"We got our heads up now, and we won't ever bow down again."
Page 73:	"It's an idea whose time has come."
Page 74:	"The weapon that cuts without wounding. It is the sword that heals."
Page 77:	"We do not want freedom fed to us in teaspoons over another 150 years."
Page 80:	Find the figurative statement: *"God's companionship doesn't stop at the door of a jail cell."*
Page 87:	Find the figurative statement: *"We have started a fire in Birmingham that water can't put out."*

Procedure: At the beginning of the lesson write "I may *smell* like a mule, but I don't *think* like one" on the chalkboard. Ask a volunteer to read the sentence; then encourage students to explain what it means. Tell them that Martin Luther King, Jr., spoke those words to his friends when he was just about their age. (King was 10 at the time.) Show a picture of him, and write his name. For the English-language learners, point to the picture and to his name as you say it. Tell the class that King loved words and ideas and often spoke in colorful and figurative language. If students don't know what a figurative statement is, give them some examples and nonexamples.

Literal (nonexample)	**Figurative** (example)
I'm hot.	I'm burning up.
I'm cold.	I'm frozen.
I'm tired.	I'm dead.

Ask student to explain how figurative statements are different from literal ones. Then let them give examples of their own.

Show students a copy of the book *I Have a Dream.* Tell them that it is a biography of Martin Luther King, Jr., and that it is filled with King's language. Explain that in order to fully understand and appreciate the ideas in the book, it is helpful to understand the meaning of King's colorful and figurative statements.

Direct students' attention to the sentences on the chalkboard or worksheet. Ask volunteers to read these aloud. Explain that while they are reading the biography, they are to write in their own words what each of these sentences means. (For pages 80 and 87 only, they need to also identify the figurative statements. They should write down the statements and explain what each means.)

Tell students that language was one of King's most effective tools. By really thinking about the meaning behind King's words, they will better understand Martin Luther King, Jr., and what happened in his short but powerful life.

Write the words *civil rights* on the board. Ask the class what these words mean and to give examples. For the English-language learners, draw pictures that show an example or two of the concept. For instance, the teacher might draw a big bus with lots of children on it. She could show a "bully" trying to trip a Latino girl as she walks onto the bus. Then, she could put Martin Luther King's picture beside the bus and draw a "bubble" from his mouth, saying "No." Following this, she could then put a big "X" on the bus and draw a new picture with the same Latino girl getting on the bus and the bully keeping to himself. Over this picture, she can show King saying "Yes," and also write the words *civil rights.*

Adapting the Activity: This activity can be used with any text that contains colorful or figurative language: *Yoshi's Feast*, an International Reading Association 2001 Notable Book for a Global Society, written by Kimiko Kajikawa and illustrated by Yumi Heo; Cynthia Rylant's *A Couple of Kooks and Other Stories About* Love and *Appalachia: The Voices of Sleeping Birds;* Gregory Alexander's interpretation of Kipling's *The Jungle Book;* Richard Kennedy's *Amy's Eyes*, a fantasy-mystery rich in metaphor and colorful language; Patricia Pendergraft's *Miracle at Clement's Pond;* or Steve Sanfield's African American folktales, *The Adventures of High John the Conqueror* all contain language worthy of pondering and savoring. Another possibility is to have English-language learners tell about some of the figurative language that they know from their native languages.

Reflection: It is very likely that students will become so caught up in the drama of King's life that they may pass by the figurative phrases and have to backtrack to find them. Giving them 10 strips of colored construction paper to mark the pages on which the figurative language is found is one way to remind them. You might mention something about the colorful paper symbolizing the colorful language King used.

Obviously this is only one of many supported reading activities that could be implemented with this book, and ideally it would be used in conjunction with literature activities in which students are introduced to the concepts of SIMILE and META-PHOR. Also, as students are focusing on and pondering over the colorful language King used, they could at the same time take a look at the figurative language they hear on television or in music lyrics or even phrases they use themselves. Additionally, seeing a film or video of King's "I Have a Dream" speech is a powerful way to illustrate the effectiveness of language in general and King's rhetorical style in particular.

This activity prompts us to make three generalizations. One is that although the activities we have mentioned here all focus on figurative language that occurs through-out a selection, often it is appropriate to focus on just one use of figurative language in a selection, a particularly vivid or informative instance. Another general point is that the brief listing of examples and nonexamples of figurative language is another instance of a mini-lesson, a brief segment of instruction imbedded within an authentic reading experience. The third general point is that this focus on figurative language is just one example of our commitment to providing a variety of activities designed to get students interested in language. Other focuses—for example, focusing on the clarity or power with which an author makes a point—are frequently useful.

SUPPORTED READING Sample Activity 4: *I Didn't Know That!*

In *I Didn't Know That!* students record in their own words interesting facts from the topics and subtopics in a science chapter.

Selection: "Waves," from *Science in Your World.* This chapter from a science text discusses the physical phenomenon of waves as rhythmic disturbances that transfer energy—mechanical waves involve matter and electromagnetic waves involve electric and magnetic fields. Some of the topics covered are how waves transfer energy, the properties of waves, and electromagnetic waves, which include radio waves, infrared waves, light, ultraviolet waves, X-rays, and gamma rays.

Students: Fifth-grade students of mixed reading abilities in a suburban setting, including one English-language learner who just arrived from Southeast Asia a few months ago and is in the very beginning phase of learning English.

Reading Purpose: To build on existing knowledge and gain new information about the properties of mechanical and electronic waves and how they transfer energy.

Goal of Activity: To encourage students to focus on interesting information that is new to them in order to help them better understand and remember what they read. This will be an extremely difficult topic and lesson for the English-language learner. At this point in time, she cannot be expected to understand much. However, some goals such as the following could be set for her: first, to learn one main concept—there are physical waves and other waves; second, to learn two key vocabulary words in English—*waves* and *light*; and third, to try to participate in the class session in some way.

Rationale: This text is a not a particularly dense one, but it does have a number of concepts that will be new and possibly challenging for students. Having them interact with the text ideas as they are reading by thinking about what information is new or particularly interesting to them will increase students' understanding of the material and their memory of what they learn.

Procedure: Before the lesson, duplicate the following outline on a handout or the chalkboard. If a handout is used, be sure to leave enough space between topics and subtopics for students to write their information.

WAVES

How Do Waves Transfer Energy

Wave Properties

Electromagnetic Waves

Radio Waves

Higher Frequency Waves

Infrared Waves

Light

Ultraviolet Waves

X-Rays and Gamma Rays

Lasers

At the beginning of the lesson, say something like this: "When I first read this chapter on waves, I found out some really interesting things I didn't know before. For instance, in the section on 'How Do Waves Transfer Energy?' I learned that there are two kinds of waves—mechanical and electromagnetic—and that both types transfer energy." For the English-language learner, write the word *waves* and draw a picture of waves. Point to pictures from the book that help to define *waves.* Write *two kinds* beside the word. "With mechanical waves, the energy is transferred as the wave travels through matter. For example, in a wave created by a rock thrown in the water, the water moves up and down but isn't carried along with the wave." For the English-language learner, under the phrase *two kinds,* place a picture of ocean waves. Continuing, say something like "Electromagnetic waves don' t have to travel through matter. They can transfer energy through empty space." For the English-language learner, under the phrase *two kinds,* place a picture or two showing the abstraction of waves emanating from TV or radio.

Then, say to the class, "I know you will discover some information in this chapter that is new to you also. To help you better understand and remember the ideas in the chapter, write down one interesting piece of information from each topic and subtopic in the chapter. After everyone has finished reading the chapter and recording their facts, you can share the new pieces of information you have learned." Have the English-language learner sit with another student in the class while the other student writes. If the English-language learner understands well enough to be able to write something in her native language, encourage her to do so.

Before students begin reading, review the topics and subtopics for the chapter and ask if there are any questions. With some classes you may want to read the first and/or second topics and subtopics aloud before students tackle the chapter on their own. This chapter contains heady concepts, so be sure to offer students encouragement and praise their participation. Tell them that they are improving their reading and thinking skills all the time and they should be pleased with their progress.

While students are reading the chapter silently, be available to answer questions and give feedback or read the chapter yourself while students read, recording new or interesting information you discover. Have the English-language learner sit beside a student who is a good reader while the reader whispers the text.

Adapting the Activity: Having students record the interesting facts they encounter while reading can be done almost any time you want them to focus on new and interesting information. This activity would work well with texts in publishers' reading series such as the *Content Area Readers* series by Judith Irvin. This series includes *The United States: Change and Challenge, A World in Transition,* and *The Ancient World.* It would also work well with *informational* trade books such as Russell Freedman's *Immigrant Kids.* With this book, students could record new and interesting information they find in each of the five chapters in the book, writing down a few interesting facts about the immigrants' journey to America while reading the chapter titled "Coming Over," about their home life while reading "At Home," and about immigrants' school, work, and play experiences while reading "At School," "At Work," and "At Play." Also, while reading Lisa Westberg Peters' *Water's Way*, students could record three or four interesting facts they learn about the different forms that water can have. To turn this into a cooperative endeavor, as a postreading activity, students might meet in five different groups and make charts for each chapter. The charts would list all the interesting facts students from each group found in their particular chapter. Students could then use the chart information to develop skits, compose songs or poems, or paint murals.

Reflection: *For this to be a truly generative learning activity, the sort that Wittrock (1990) has shown to be effective in promoting learning and understanding, students will need to do more than just copy information verbatim from the text. They will need to think about what information is new to them and be encouraged to write that information in their own words. To learn to recognize when they have succeeded in recasting an author's thoughts—in paraphrasing—they are likely to need your feedback. Thus, at least when students are first learning to paraphrase, you will want to read their paraphrases and give them feedback on whether they have successfully captured the author's ideas and on whether they have done so in their own words. Of course, many English-language learners will find feedback particularly beneficial.*

SUPPORTED READING Sample Activity 5: *Group and Label*

In this semantic mapping activity (Heimlich & Pittelman, 1986; Pearson & Johnson, 1978), students, working in pairs or groups, read a selection and sort the information in it into various categories.

Selection: *Inside and Outside You* by Sandra Markle. In this 38-page informational book about the human body, the author begins by discussing the makeup and function of skin, then proceeds to give readers a close look at the inner workings of the human body.

Students: Third graders of mixed reading abilities, three of whom are English-language learners who have good oral English conversational abilities and have been in the school district since kindergarten.

Reading Purpose: To learn about, appreciate, and remember the various parts of the body and their functions.

Goal of Activity: To help students understand and remember the names and functions of various parts of the human body by identifying and categorizing those parts and writing them on a chart.

Rationale: Since this book contains a myriad of labels and concepts, having students organize these to show how they are related may be needed to help them understand the concepts and remember them.

Procedure: Give each student two sheets of paper and tell them you are going to conduct an experiment. Next, tell them to put their heads on their desks and close their eyes while you place several items on the table (a flower, a dish, a button, a fork, a chalk eraser, a hat, a ball, a small mirror, a comb, a pencil, a toothbrush).

Have students gather around the table and look at the objects, giving them 20 seconds to do so. Tell them to return to their seats while you scoop the items back in a paper bag. Then, tell students to write down on one of their sheets of paper as many items as they can remember, advising them not to worry about spelling at this time. It is fine if English-language learners use their native language. Give them a minute to record their answers, then collect the papers.

Tell students to once again close their eyes. Take several different items from another bag, but this time arrange them on the table in three groups: Group 1—a small paintbrush, a tin of paints, a pack of colored chalk, crayons; Group 2—a measuring cup, a cookbook, a spatula, a wooden spoon; Group 3—a piece of lined paper, a pencil, an eraser, a dictionary.

While students still have their eyes closed, tell students you have arranged the items into three groups: drawing and painting items, cooking items, and writing items. Tell them that they will have only half the time they did before to look at the items, but that they are still to try and remember as many items as they can.

Have students return to the table. Point to each group of items and say, "drawing and painting items, cooking items, and writing items." Again, give students 20 seconds to look at the items before you put them away. Then give them a minute to write down as many as they can remember—in English or in their native language—on their second sheet of paper. Collect the papers and tally the number of correct guesses for each set on the chalkboard.

Without Groups	With Groups

Barring some bizarre result, students will remember considerably more of the grouped items than the ungrouped ones. Encourage them to deduce why they remembered more of the grouped items. Explain to students that it is almost always easier to understand and remember information if you group it into sets of things that have common characteristics. For example, if they were reading a book about games to find some suitable ones to play at their birthday party, as they read they might group the games in their mind into these sorts of categories:

Games for four or more people

Games that use the equipment I have

Games that my mom would let us play in the house

Games you have to play outside

Games that sound the most fun to me

After they finished reading, they might add a final category: Games I want to play at my birthday party.

Show them the book *Inside and Outside You* by Sandra Markle, and explain that it is a good book with which to practice the grouping technique because it has lots of names of things in it. Tell them the names will be easier to remember if they group them.

Give students copies of the chart shown below and explain the categories to them.

Semantic Map for *Inside and Outside You*

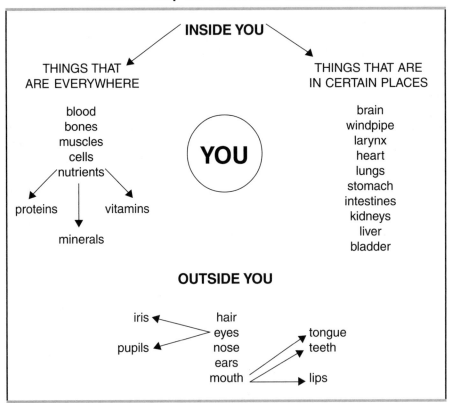

After explaining how to complete the chart, have students work in pairs or groups, taking turns reading the text aloud and completing the chart. After students have finished reading and completing their charts, bring the whole class together again. As a group complete the same chart, which you have drawn on the chalkboard.

Adapting the Activity: This activity can be used any time a text lends itself to grouping information. For example, this technique would work well with Janet S. Wong's *The Trip Back Home,* illustrated by Bo Jia, a delightful recounting of a visit made by a young girl and her mother to Korea to see their extended family. Another possibility is Joanna Cole's *The Magic School Bus* series. In these books, Ms. Cole provides a great deal of information on a variety of subjects (the human body, the solar system, inside the earth, at the waterworks) in a narrative style. Even though these books are packed with information, children love them because they are humorous and have plots and characters with whom youngsters can identify. Using semantic maps can help students organize the information to better understand and retain it.

Reflection: Obviously, semantic maps that are designed to serve as reading guides will vary from selection to selection since they will reflect the information contained in it. Also, while semantic mapping can sometimes be useful as a during-reading activity, it is also a worthwhile prereading or postreading activity. As a prereading activity, semantic mapping can be used to activate prior knowledge, and as a postreading activity to recall and organize information contained in the reading material. For example, before students read any number of books about pioneers— such as Pioneer Children of Appalachia, Spanish Pioneers of the Southwest, and Pioneer Settlers of New France, all by Joan Anderson—you might develop a semantic map for the concept PIONEERS. Write pioneer on the board along with categories such as People Who Were Pioneers, Pioneer Activities, Reasons for Being Pioneers, and Characteristics of Pioneers, and have students suggest words and phrases for each category. After students have read a specific book about pioneers, you could do this same activity. The word pioneers would still be the target word, but the categories you select and students' responses to those categories will reflect the information that was presented in the text. This postreading activity works well for any number of selections whose topics or themes might range from frogs to friendship.

Considered more generally, the matter of grouping items is frequently worth considering as you plan instruction. As George Miller (1956) pointed out in an article with the rather catchy title "The Magic Number Seven Plus or Minus Two," our mind's capacity to remember ungrouped items is severely limited. Specifically, we can generally remember only five to nine ungrouped items—seven-digit phone numbers are a good example. If, however, we group items into meaningful categories, each category functions more or less like a single item, and the total number of items we can remember is greatly increased. Thus, for example, if we head off to the supermarket with 20 ungrouped things to buy and no list, we are likely to be in trouble. If, on the other hand, we take those 20 things and group them as three vegetables, two fruits, two dairy products, and the like, we stand a good chance of remembering all 20 of them. It's exactly the same with students learning from text. To remember information, they need to group it in meaningful categories.

SUPPORTED READING Sample Activity 6: *Who? What? When?*

In this activity, students record on a time line the important names, events, and dates from a chapter in a trade book that chronicles the history of a scientific discovery.

Selection: *Neptune*, from the *How Did We Find Out About?* series by Isaac Asimov. *How Did We Find Out About Neptune?* chronicles the years of observation by astronomers that led to the discovery of Neptune's existence. It also describes many fascinating and unusual things about the eighth planet from the sun, including its rings, its giant moon, and a tornado called the Great Blue Spot. Asimov challenges his readers to think about the questions that astronomers asked prior to making their discoveries and to pose new questions that might lead to a more complete understanding of the planet.

Students: Sixth graders of average to high English reading ability. Three of the students are English-language learners who have been in the United States for at least three years and have good English conversational abilities.

Reading Purpose: To gain new knowledge about the discovery of Neptune and to understand and appreciate the people, times, and places involved in the discovery process.

Goal of Activity: To help students conceptualize important events that led up to Neptune's discovery by recording these events in chronological order.

Rationale: This text is filled with numerous dates, persons, and events that led to the discovery of the planet. Having students record these facts on a time line will help fix names and events in their minds.

Procedure: Before students begin reading, provide them with five 2- x 18-inch strips of paper, one for each chapter in the book.

At the end of whatever prereading activities you do, explain that *Neptune* contains many dates, persons, and events that led to the planet's discovery. Each of these in some way serves as a link or clue to the ultimate discovery of Neptune and our present-day knowledge of the planet. To help students visualize the path to Neptune's discovery, they will record these facts on time lines.

You may want to review the procedure for constructing a time line. One way would be to have students skim the first chapter, "Uranus," for names and dates while you record these on a time line you have made on the board or a strip of butcher paper.

1543	1608	1610	1665
Copernicus claimed planets revolved around sun	telescope invented	Galileo discovered 4 satellites that circled Jupiter	Huygens discovered a satellite that circled Saturn

__|_____|_____|_____|_____

Because some students might be tempted to skim the chapter for names and dates and not do a thorough reading, tell them that after they have read the chapter and recorded the persons, dates, and events on their time line, they should reread the chapter to make sure they have understood how these persons and events are related and how they are likely to influence what happens in subsequent chapters. At the same time, let your English-language learners know that if they do not have time to reread the chapter, that's fine. As students' time lines will reveal, the discovery of Neptune occurred because of the questions and discoveries of many different people over many years, and newer discoveries were built on older ones. Tell them that this process is not unlike one they go through every day—adding to and building on to their own storehouse of knowledge.

Adapting the Activity: Time lines can be used whenever the reading selection includes a number of persons, dates, and events that can be understood and recalled better if visually presented in chronological order. For example, time lines might be used with younger children for a book like *¡El Cucuy!: A Bogeyman Cuento in English and Spanish,* written by Joe Hayes and illustrated by Honorio Robledo, or for older students with any one of the books from Asimov's *How Did We Find Out About?* series and other informational selections such as Milton Meltzer's *Bill of Rights* and Olga Litowinsky's *The High Voyage: The Final Crossing of Christopher Columbus.* Since narratives also have a chronological structure, time lines can be used with them. However, most students will be able to follow the chronology of narratives without using a time line.

Reflection: How Did We Find Out About Neptune? *is a fairly dense text and to read it successfully many students may need various kinds of during-reading help—a time line being only one possibility. After reading the text yourself, you will discover the ideas and information that you want your students to focus on, to manipulate and retain. These then will determine the makeup of your reading guide.*

Rather than having students note sequence, as the time line does, perhaps you feel your students' purposes might be better served by having them focus on cause and effect—this event happened because of this, and as a result, this happened— your reading guide then will reflect this goal. Reading guides are scaffolds designed to help students reach reading goals. They are also, as we have pointed out, opportunities for mini-lessons; and one topic very appropriate for mini-lessons is that of organizational patterns. Thus, when the text students are going to read exemplifies a particular pattern—simple listing, sequence, cause and effect, compare and contrast, and the like—you have the teachable moment for a mini-lesson on that pattern.

Oral Reading by Students

Having students read aloud can achieve some of the same purposes that reading *to* students accomplishes—students experimenting with and enjoying the sound of language as well as focusing on meaning. Additionally, if done in a supportive, nonthreatening way, students' read-aloud activities can enhance their interest and enjoyment of reading, improve fluency, increase vocabulary, and add to their storehouse of knowledge and concepts.

However, when working with English-language learners who are learning to read in a new language, it is very important to consider the students' learning levels for the new language as well as their "comfort" level with the material to be read aloud. As we noted in chapter 4, many new English learners go through a "silent period" when they do not feel comfortable speaking the new language. It is almost certainly unwise to ask students to read aloud when they do not feel comfortable enough to speak aloud. Similarly, when students are in the early and middle phases of learning to read in English, they are often in classrooms where the texts are above their own instructional English reading level. In these cases, we advise that the students should not be asked to read aloud. Finally, a good rule of thumb to use is to always allow English-language learners the opportunity to read a selection silently before they have to read it aloud. In fact, this is generally a good practice with all students.

Two popular read-aloud activities are choral reading and Readers Theatre. In choral reading—by using contrasts such as high and low voices, different voice combinations and contrasts, sound effects, movements, gestures, or increasing or decreasing tempo—students combine their voices to convey and construct the meaning of a text. Choral reading can accomplish several purposes. It gives students the opportunity to hear printed language, and because choral reading requires repeated readings, the chances for adding words to their reading vocabularies and becoming increasingly fluent in reading also increases. Also, choral reading gives English-language learners who are unsure of their pronunciation an opportunity to hang back a bit and listen to their classmates before committing to a presentation. Choral reading has been traditionally used with poetry, but some narratives lend themselves to this activity as well. Primary-grade students might enjoy doing a choral presentation of Michael Rosen's *We're Going on a Bear Hunt*—a repetitive tale with wonderful rhythmic lines, imagery, and alliteration, and third or fourth graders studying Japan might enjoy making a choral presentation out of David Wisniewski's picture book, *The Warrior and the Wiseman*, a Japanese folktale.

Readers Theatre, in which students take turns or assume roles in reading portions of text aloud, can be used effectively with poetry, narratives, and has even been done successfully with expository materials (Young & Vardell, 1993). In Readers Theatre students present drama, prose, or poetry by "reading the text out loud using their voices, reading fast or slow, loudly or softly, emphasizing certain words or phrases to reading rate, intonation, and emphasis on the meaning-bearing cadences of language to make print come alive" (Hoyt, 1992). Fifth- or sixth-grade students studying U.S. history could turn Julius Lester's *To Be a Slave* into a powerful Readers Theatre presentation. In this book, Lester chronicles the tragedy of slavery through many eloquent and provocative voices—the slaves themselves and the comments from various newspaper editors of the times. With Readers Theatre, students could make this piece of history come to life.

Choral reading and Readers Theatre provide an entertaining, cooperative, nonthreatening atmosphere in which students can build meaning from text and learn more about language—its purpose, beauty, and power. It is an outlet for oral interpretation and an opportunity to perform and gain confidence in speaking and reading.

In addition to performance activities such as choral reading and Readers Theatre, reading text aloud can be used in conjunction with what

Linda Hoyt (1992) has described as "oral interactions"—dialogue that is stimulated in response to the ideas and information students discover as they read in various texts. As students read through material silently, they mark certain passages as "hot spots"—ideas they liked, didn't understand or disagreed with, or ones that answered a question they had, or another student had, or that the teacher posed. In pairs or groups students share their "hot spots" by reading the passages aloud and talking about them.

Choral reading, Readers Theatre, and oral interactions are only three of many kinds of oral reading activities you might use in your classroom. Here we describe how you might implement each of these.

ORAL READING BY STUDENTS Sample Activity 1: *Two Voices*

In *Two Voices* students are organized into two groups that alternately read and dramatize the lines of a poem, an activity adapted from McCauley and McCauley (1992).

Selection: "I'm Thankful," from *The New Kid on the Block* by Jack Prelutsky. This light-hearted poem lists the many things a young boy or girl might be thankful for, but with a humorous twist.

Students: Third and fourth graders, several of whom are English-language learners with different ethnicities and mixed English reading abilities.

Reading Purpose: To enjoy the humor and satire in a piece of light verse.

Goal of the Activity: To provide an entertaining, low-stress situation in which students can expand their reading vocabularies, improve fluency and diction, gain language proficiency, and gain confidence in reading aloud.

Rationale: Because much of the meaning and effect of poetry relies on auditory devices such as repetition of sounds, cadence, and rhythm, it needs to be heard to be truly appreciated. Jack Prelutsky's poems in this selection are ideal for choral presentation. Children will delight in Prelutsky's humor and love hearing and reciting poems that so succinctly express the topics and emotions of childhood. As we have noted, choral reading also provides a safe environment to help English learners grow in their understanding of English words and phrases.

Procedure: Briefly discuss with students some of the things they are thankful for. Then tell them you would like to share a poem with them titled "I'm Thankful" by Jack Prelutsky. Explain that the poet has a humorous way of looking at all the things he's thankful for. Ask students to listen for the funny lines in the poem, then read the poem aloud.

> I'm thankful for my baseball bat,
> *I cracked it yesterday.*
> I'm thankful for my checker set,
> *I haven't learned to play.*
> I'm thankful for my mittens,
> *one is missing in the snow.*

I'm thankful for my hamsters,
they escaped a month ago.

I'm thankful for my basketball,
it's sprung another leak.
I'm thankful for my parakeet,
it bit me twice last week.
I'm thankful for my bicycle,
I crashed into a tree.
I'm thankful for my roller skates,
I fell and scraped my knee.

I'm thankful for my model plane,
it's short a dozen parts.
I'm thankful for my target game,
I'm sure I'll find the darts.
I'm thankful for my bathing suit,
it came off in the river,
I'm thankful for so many things,
except, of course, for LIVER!

Read the poem again, this time holding up the object (or a picture of the object) the poet is writing about and dramatize the italicized lines. The italicized lines are asides, so you might cup one hand next to your mouth and lean toward the audience as if letting them in on a secret, then do a dramatization. For example, for the lines "I'm thankful for my baseball bat, *I cracked it yesterday,*" you might hold up a baseball bat, lower your voice when you say, "*I cracked it yesterday,*" then act out what might have happened to the bat by acting mad, sad, disgusted, surprised, whatever.

For the third reading, display the poem on a chart or overhead. Read the poem slowly, and have students read along with you. Let a volunteer hold up the items or pictures of them as they are read, while another volunteer acts out the asides and dramatizations.

Read the poem aloud a few more times, increasing the tempo a bit with each reading. With these readings have students stand and read along with you while they dramatize the italicized lines.

When you feel students are comfortable with the words and movements, divide the class into two groups (January–July birthdays and August–December birthdays, or curly hair and straight hair, or divide the class down the middle of the room). Have one group stand on one side of the room and read the lines that tell what they are thankful for and the other group stand on the opposite side and say the asides with gestures and dramatizations, with you as the audience. Let students practice reading the poem this way, then have students switch lines. However, continue only if students express interest. The purpose for the activity is not to achieve a polished performance, but for the students to read and have fun. Be sure to applaud your students' efforts.

While you do not want to do much of this if students aren't very interested, if students do show interest in the poem, you might want to have them prepare it to perform for another class.

Adapting the Activity: *Two Voices* may be done with any number of poems and even some prose material. Poems in editor Pat Mora's collection *Love to Mamá*, illustrated by Paula S. Barragán M., which contains some poems written in English and some in Spanish, could be read and even memorized by middle-grades students, with students reading or saying alternate stanzas. *The Whipping Boy* by Sid Fleischman, for example, lends itself to a two-part choral reading, with the two groups reading alternating paragraphs aloud, or one group taking the role of Jemmy and the other that of Prince Brat. *A Joyful Noise, Poems for Two Voices* by Paul Fleischman is particularly suited for a two-part choral reading activity.

For choral reading in general some good choices are *Hail to Mail* by Samuel Marshak and *Country Crossing* by Jim Aylesworth to use with primary students, *Where the Sidewalk Ends* by Shel Silverstein and *If I Were in Charge of the World and Other Worries* by Judith Viorst with middle graders, and Victoria Forrester's *A Latch Against the Wind* with older readers.

Reflection: Dividing students into two groups is only one way to implement a choral reading experience. Some selections lend themselves to solos, ensembles, or whole-group work. Because the lines in "I'm Thankful" are written as declarative statements followed by asides, it lends itself well to a two-part reading. We chose also to add dramatization to this piece, but the asides would work well with a simple gesture and a lowering of the voice.

Be cautious of trying to have students recite lengthy passages which may result in mottled production or expressionless sing-song. Successful and enjoyable experiences are often those in which students have only simple, single phrases to recite such as "except, of course, for LIVER!"

We have already noted that choral reading can be effective with English-language learners. We want to emphasize this point. Choral reading gives students repeated exposure to English words. When students are reading at instructional level, choral reading can assist them toward automaticity in recognizing English words. Choral reading also can give them practice with English structures and intonation patterns, and it gives an opportunity to participate and succeed in the same activity in which native speakers are engaged. Moreover, it does all of this in a nonthreatening environment.

ORAL READING BY STUDENTS Sample Activity 2: *On the Air!*

Students meet in small groups to prepare the story as a play. Then, they tape the story as they "act it out" by reading aloud.

Selection: *Tikki Tikki Tembo*, retold by Arlene Mosel, is a time-honored classic folktale of how the Chinese came to give all of their children short names. Mother's favorite son, Tikki Tikki Tembo-no sa rembo-chari bari ruchi-pip peri pembo, and her second son, Chang, fall into trouble and as the story unfolds, the problems associated with having a long name become clear.

Reading Purpose: To appreciate the language and intent of a classic piece of folklore.

Students: Third graders of average to high English reading ability. Half of the students are Anglo and Black of African descent and half are Latino. All of the students participated in bilingual education in first and second grade. At the beginning of third grade, they were placed in an all-English classroom setting.

Goal of the Activity: To help students interpret and appreciate a piece of literature by using oral language to help make print come alive.

Rationale: Performing this tale not only gives students a chance to practice and hone their interpretive reading skills, it also exposes them to the effective use of language and the insights we can gain about ourselves and others through literature.

Procedure: Background information: Students in this class have performed works in the Readers Theatre a number of times prior to this activity. They also have made a collection of story tapes they call "Radio Show" tapes for students to listen to in their spare time. The best of these have been duplicated and given to the media center for other students in the school to listen to.

Read the first two pages aloud to students, delivering the lines with the pizzazz you would like to inspire in students for their own oral readings. After you have finished reading, discuss with students whether or not they think this would be a good story to perform as a Readers Theatre activity and to add to their collection of "Radio Show" tapes. If they show interest, divide the class into groups of four students, with each group ready to prepare to read orally.

After students have prepared, beginning with the first group, make a tape recording of their reading, complete with sound effects or other embellishments they have come up with. All tapes can be donated to the school media center.

Adapting the Activity: Shelby Anne Wolf (1993) has used Readers Theatre successfully with this selection with English-language learners. For younger children, books like these two would work well: *The Boy Who Wouldn't Obey: A Mayan Legend*, told and illustrated by Anne Rockwell, and *Blanca's Feather*, written by Antonio Hernández Madrigal and illustrated by Gerardo Suzán. As mentioned earlier, Terrell Young and Sylvia Vardell (1993) have reported Readers Theatre success with nonfiction materials across the curriculum—in math using David M. Schwartz's *How Much Is a Million?* and in science using Joanna Cole's *The Magic School Bus Lost in the Solar System* and Billy Goodman's *A Kid's Guide to How to Save the Planet*. For the latter selection, a seventh-grade teacher turned the text into a Readers Theatre script by creating a radio call-in show hosted by Earthman Jack and other DJ's. Other possible nonfiction texts for creating Readers Theatre texts are Tomie dePaola's *The Popcorn Book*, Ina Chang's *A Separate Battle: Women and the Civil War*, and Russell Freedman's *Buffalo Hunt*.

Reflection: *Students typically enjoy performing and because a part can be made as brief as necessary for a particular student to succeed with it, every student— whatever his or her English reading proficiency—can experience success in reading a part. Still, if some students are reluctant to participate as readers, they can be assigned to create sound effects, or introduce the readers, or be in charge of production (operating and caring for equipment). In time, and with encouragement, these reluctant students might eventually risk taking a reading part, but until then they will learn about language by listening to others and gain confidence in their abilities by contributing to the group project.*

ORAL READING BY STUDENTS Sample Activity 3: *Flag It*

In *Flag It* students use self-stick notes to mark passages in the text. *Flag It* combines teacher oral reading, supported silent reading, and student oral reading to stimulate discussion on certain aspects of a text. This activity is based on one suggested by Hoyt (1992).

Selection: Selections from chapter 12, "Fortaleza," or "Fortitude," in *It's All in the Frijoles* by Yolanda Nava. The book is a unique compendium of inspiring recollections and stories by 100 well-known and beloved contemporary and historic Latino figures, from Jaime Escalante, the sensitive and courageous teacher in the movie *Stand and Deliver*, to actor Hector Elizondo, to Benito Juarez, president of Mexico in the mid-1800s, and many others. As the author says in the introduction to the book, her upbringing was filled to overflowing with a sense of values that contributed to her own character. Yolanda Nava has named and arranged these values in a way that transcends the personal and moves to broader human and cultural values.

Students: The students are in an eighth-grade all-English language arts class. About one-fourth of the students in the class are English-language learners of Latino descent, one-half are Anglo and Black of African descent, and one-fourth are English-language learners of Asian descent. The students' English reading levels are mixed, ranging from second-grade level to high school level. Some Latino students can read at or near grade level in Spanish.

Reading Purpose: To relate the students' personal lives and values to what is read and to consider how authors use writing for the purpose of teaching others.

Goal of Activity: To help students better understand cultural values that the author believes are woven into Latino existence, and to consider the extent to which the same or similar values exist in the cultures of students who are not Latino. Other goals are to give students an opportunity to practice oral reading and provide a forum for sharing ideas and listening to the ideas of others.

Rationale: Having students read about individuals' personal stories and memories related to cultural values can help students see the connection between what we do and who we are as well as how our families and cultural heritage influence us. Also, reading aloud gives students a chance to hear well-written material and practice their oral reading skills. Discussion gives students the opportunity to think more carefully about their responses, practice defending and justifying a viewpoint, and hear and learn from others' interpretations.

Procedure: Begin by reading and discussing the quotes at the beginning of the chapter:

> "Donde hay voluntad, hay modo." "Where there is a will, there is a way." (p. 239, no source cited)

> "There is no substitute for persistence. It overrides everything." (Andy García, actor, p. 239)

> "Roma no se construyó en un día." "Rome wasn't built in a day." (Cervantes, *Don Quixote*, p. 230)

> "La constancia hace milagros." "Consistency creates miracles." (p. 239, no source cited)

"Action is the antidote to despair." (Joan Baez, p. 240)

"Si, se puede." "Yes, you can." (César Chavez, president, UFW, p. 240)

Ask the class what they think these quotes are about and if they can think of some words that embody the meanings of the quotes. If the class does not use the word *fortitude,* say it and write it on the board. Explain that this book is a collection of stories, memories, anecdotes, quotes, and sayings by famous Latinos that the author has arranged into chapters representing values and beliefs. Ms. Nava personally interviewed many of the people who gave her stories and memories for the book. The class is going to read selections from the chapter called "Fortaleza," or "Fortitude."

Tell students they are going to read the selections using an activity called *Flag It.* In this activity they will use self-stick notes to keep track of the parts that they can identify with or that they feel are unusual or really different from their own beliefs or values. Then, after they have finished reading the novel, they will get the chance to read these portions aloud and discuss how they identify with them or how they are different from their own experiences.

Demonstrate how students will do this activity by reading Ms. Nava's introduction to the chapter aloud, pausing at those places that you can relate to or identify with, showing students how you would mark these passages with a self-stick note, and telling them what you might write on the note. For example, on page 241, at the following part, you place a sticky note: "Strength and tenacity were her middle name. And, through all the travails of her often painful and difficult life, she exhibited a courage and strength of character in the midst of pain, affliction, and hardship. It is a characteristic we often see manifested in the best of our women, la fortaleza." Your sticky note says, "My mother was a British war bride who left her close-knit family at the age of 28 to move to the United States, and she didn't get to see, or speak to, her family again for 10 years. She was courageous and strong and had fortaleza."

After you have modeled this procedure and students understand what they are to do, give students pads of self-stick notes and have them read the selections by Jesus Treviño (director and activist) on pages 243 and 244, Gloria Santiago (author) on pages 244 and 245, Suzanna Guzmán (mezzo-soprano) on pages 249 and 250, and Edward James Olmos (actor) on pages 254 and 255. They should read them on their own and flag those passages they identify with or find very different from their own experience.

When students have finished reading, have them get together in pairs or small groups to read their passages aloud and discuss how they identified with them or found them hard to relate to. Match pairs so that students are mixed by ethnicity and so that higher level readers are with lower level readers so that they can help them with the reading. Before you have students meet in pairs or groups, we recommend you lead a demonstration of the oral reading and discussion procedures students are to use. This might consist of calling on volunteers to read their flagged passages and their sticky notes. Doing this will allow you to clear up any misunderstandings before students work on their own. While students are meeting in pairs or small groups, you might sit in as a participant or circulate among the groups, giving support and encouragement.

The activity might conclude with a whole-group discussion focusing on particular themes in the class responses, such as that everyone could find something to identify with in the passages or that certain statements were difficult for some students to relate to. An evaluative discussion might also be in order, with students answering questions such as these:

- ✦ Was this a worthwhile activity? Why or why not?
- ✦ Did group work go smoothly? Why or why not?
- ✦ If we use this activity again, what might we do differently?

Adapting the Activity: *Flag It* can be used with any number of narrative or expository materials in which you want students to focus on a certain aspect of the text. For example, you might use *Flag It* to have students flag those incidents in Jerry Spinelli's *Fourth Grade Rats* in which Suds exhibits "rat-like" characteristics. In the discussion, students can tell how Suds feels about his rat-like behavior in each of these incidences. *Flag It* might also be used with an informational book such as *Inside and Outside You* by Sandra Markle for students to flag the five most interesting things they learned about their insides. Or, while students read the biography *I Have a Dream* by Margaret Davidson, they might flag the five most important events in the life of Martin Luther King, Jr. Their individual responses, which are likely to reflect some interesting differences, will make for lively discussions.

Reflection: *As you can see,* Flag It *is a supported reading activity with an oral reading component. Typically, an activity such as this is preceded by prereading components, which could include a number of different activities, but definitely should include some attention to the main theme of the reading. One prereading activity might be to have students write a paragraph on their own personal experience of the theme, such as writing to answer the question "Can you think of a particular instance in your life when you've exhibited great fortitude?"*

We presented this activity as if this were the students' first encounter with the book. However, you might introduce this activity after students have read through the selections once for pure pleasure. Also, you might have students read the whole chapter, rather than selections from it. This will depend on you and your students' preferences. Some students do better reading everything in a chapter or story, beginning to end, without having to stop and physically interact with it. Others would profit from stopping and considering matters from time to time.

Modifying the Text

The purpose of SREs is to ensure that English-language learners have success in reading—that they are able to engage in meaning making and will gain new knowledge, new insights, and a sense of accomplishment from a reading selection. For some students achieving success requires your presenting a selection in a format that is a variation of the original. Sometimes because of what is either required by your school district or what is available, or because the text is mismatched to your English-language learners' current English-reading levels, the material may be too challenging for some students. In these cases, modifying or shortening the selections is a viable option. This is especially true for English-language learners who are just beginning to read in English, but it can also apply even as they become more accomplished.

Let us say, for instance, you are a fifth-grade teacher and your school district requires that students learn the concepts presented in the state-adopted U.S. history text. The text is written at a fifth- to sixth-grade reading level, but the reading ability of the native-English speakers in your class ranges from second grade to twelfth grade, and for your English-language learners, it ranges from second- to fifth-grade level. If the material in this text is going to be made accessible to the students reading well below fifth grade, something may need to be done to the material. This might mean tape recording some sections, assigning only certain portions of the text to read, or writing (or having students write) simplified versions or summaries of the most important concepts. Also, some of the practices we mentioned in chapter 5 under the categories of "Using Students' Native Language" and "Involving English-Language Learner Communities, Parents, Siblings" would likely be useful here. For instance, where possible, translating the selection into the native language may also be helpful. You might pair your English-language learners with students who can read and write at, or above, grade level, and have these students help the English-language learners write books of their own on a subtopic in U.S. history. The more capable writers could write a simplified version of a subtopic in the text. The English-language learners will not be reading the same words as the other students, but the ideas will be similar, and they will be *reading*.

Sometimes it isn't feasible or even advisable for students to read an entire selection. When lack of time or other constraints make reading an entire selection impractical, shortening the reading assignment is one workable option. In doing this you have students read only selected portions of a chapter—the topics you feel are most important for them to understand. Of course, students will miss some of the information presented in the chapter, but assuming they cannot or will not read all of it, success in reading part of it is certainly preferable to failure in reading all of it. Moreover, as Walter Kintsch and Tuen van Dijk (1978) have emphasized, what readers typically remember after reading a text is its gist. By no means do they remember everything.

Some insights gleaned by Isabel Beck and her colleagues (Beck, McKeown, Hamilton, & Kucan, 1997, 1998) while working with Questioning the Author suggests another possibility for modifying text. Readers sometimes blame themselves for not understanding text, when in fact, the fault may lie with the text author. The author, perhaps, has assumed too much background knowledge on the part of his or her audience, or simply has not presented ideas clearly or with sufficient elaboration to make them understandable. When you run across texts like these, you might have the students themselves rewrite the text so that it makes sense to them. "How would you write this paragraph," you might ask them, "to make it more understandable?"

Students should acknowledge the author's expertise and knowledge, but not be intimidated by it or believe that printed text is beyond reproach. If they aren't building meaning with a text, the fault may not lie with them, but with the author. Grappling with the ideas—rewording, rearranging, and embellishing—may be the only way meaning building will take place. Students at all levels of reading ability can rewrite text in order to understand it. Students also might do this rewriting in groups or pairs, with their main task being to answer the question "How can we rewrite this—rephrase, reorganize, add, subtract—to make it more understandable?"

Two sample activities follow that demonstrate different ways of modifying texts to make them more accessible to your English-language learners.

MODIFYING THE TEXT Sample Activity 1: *Focusing*

In *Focusing*, instead of assigning an entire chapter or selection, you choose certain portions of the material for students to read.

Selection: "Electricity" in *Science in Your World*. In this science text chapter, static electricity, current electricity, and circuits are discussed. Other topics covered are electricity in the home, electric motors, and measuring electric usage. A special section on pacemakers is also included.

Students: A small group of fifth-grade English-language learners of various ethnicities, working in a Sheltered English instruction setting. The students' reading levels range from third- to fourth-grade level in English. The students have been in schools in the United States for two to three years, and their conversational English is good.

Reading Purpose: To expand student's knowledge of electricity—what it is and its uses.

Goal of Activity: To focus on certain key concepts in the text and to make these ideas more accessible to students by creating a reading assignment of a length that they can handle more successfully.

Rationale: In deciding what portions of this chapter on electricity the students would read, we took into account the students' English reading levels, their conversational English levels, what they already knew about the topic, the difficulty of the material, and how much time we could spend covering the chapter. Because they had studied static and current electricity previously, we decided to briefly review these topics in a group discussion and then have students read the sections on circuits, electricity in the home, electric motors, and measuring electric usage on their own.

Procedure: Prior to the lesson, write the following outline on the chalkboard:

Electricity

Static Electricity—Discussed/Review

Current Electricity—Discussed/Review

Circuits—Read pages 82–84

Electricity in Your Home — Read pages 86–89

Electric Motors—Read pages 90–91

Measuring Electric Usage—Discuss

Pacemakers—Page 96; optional

Draw students' attention to the outline on the chalkboard. Tell them that since you have discussed static and current electricity already, they are only to read the sections on circuits, electricity in the home, and electric motors, and that you will talk with them about measuring electric usage. The section on pacemakers is optional reading. Explain that after they have finished reading, the group as a whole will discuss the required sections, and volunteers can discuss the section on pacemakers.

Adapting the Activity: Shortening selections by assigning only certain portions of a piece works best for expository material that contains previously covered information, text that is too lengthy and just a little too challenging to be read in its entirety by your students, or material that contains information you feel your students don't need to deal with at the present time. If you wanted your students to get the information in Russell Freedman' book *Immigrant Kids,* for example, but didn't feel your students could handle the book alone in the time they had, you could assign reading specific chapters to groups of students who would be responsible for writing a summary of their chapter and make these available for other students to read. Or, instead of every student reading each of the folktales included in Virginia Hamilton's collection of African American folktales, *The People Could Fly*, groups of students could choose one of the tales to read and then present a dramatization of their chosen tale. In that way, although students read only one story, they are able to learn about and enjoy each of them.

Reflection: The purpose of students reading the chapter is to add to their knowledge of electricity. An activity such as this one reduces the amount of information students have to deal with, thereby increasing the chances of their successfully understanding and retaining the most crucial concepts they need for further understanding electricity and related topics. Reducing the amount of text students need to read is an extremely simple task, both conceptually and practically. However, it can pay dividends in terms of students successfully building meaning with those parts of the text you ask them to read.

MODIFYING THE TEXT Sample Activity 2: *Rewriting*

In *Rewriting*, older and more accomplished readers rewrite a text for younger students who are just beginning to learn to read in the text language.

Selection: *Blanca's Feather*, written by Antonio Hernández Madrigal and illustrated by Gerardo Suzán, an illustrator who has been designated a national treasure of Mexico. In *Blanca's Feather*, Rosalía wants to take her pet hen, Blanca, to the blessing on Saint Francis of Assisi's Day. The blessing protects animals from disease and predators. Saint Francis of Assisi's Day is celebrated in Mexico and many other countries, including the United States, each year on October 4. Readers learn about the rituals of the ceremony as they are engaged in the special friendship between a young girl and her pet. This text is written at a level that would probably be about what a typically developing native-language speaker might read at an early to late third-grade reading level.

Students: Two groups of students are involved in this activity. One group is fourth-grade Latino students who were in bilingual education classes in first through third grades and can read in English at fourth-grade level and above. The other group is second-grade Anglo, Black of African descent, and Latino students who have been in a bilingual education class since kindergarten.

Reading Purpose: For the fourth graders: To relate to the theme of loving and caring for pets, to identify main ideas and significant details, to consider the plot structure, to discriminate difficult syntax from easier syntax, and to consider nuances of word meanings. For the second graders: To relate the theme of loving and caring for pets to the children's own lives, to understand the blessing ritual, and to learn to read three new words.

Goal of Activity: For the fourth graders: To elaborate their understandings of what makes texts easier or more difficult in order to improve their comprehension of texts as well as their own writing. For the second graders: To offer them a text that is rich in concepts related to their own lives and which will help them to learn to read in English.

Rationale: Older students reading on a higher level can learn about texts, how authors work, what makes texts easier and harder by rewriting texts for younger beginning readers. Beginning readers can make progress in reading when they read texts that have "just right" difficulty levels.

Procedure: Phase One: First give copies of the book to a small group of fourth graders. Tell the students that although this is a picture book, the way it is written makes it hard for younger readers to read this book on their own. Explain that you would like them to rewrite the book so that some second graders—Latinos, Blacks of African descents, and Anglos who have been in bilingual classes since kindergarten—can read it pretty easily. Show the students a couple of examples of texts that are written at an early second-grade level. Tell them that in their revisions, there should be a few (three or four) hard words for the second graders, but no more. Ask them to read the book independently, and then meet with them as a group. In the group, review the book, asking what were the main ideas and what details were especially important to understanding the book. Ask them what they think might make this book hard to read for the group of second graders you mentioned earlier. Prompt the students to consider vocabulary difficulty—pointing to some of the words that would be hard for the second graders, the way the sentences are constructed, mismatch of some of the students' background knowledge with the ceremonial ritual in the book. Write "Hard" at the top of one side of a chart, and as the students mention items, list them on the chart. Ask the students how they will think about rewriting the text, and write "Easier" at the other side of the chart, and list ways the students mention. Then ask the students to work either independently or in pairs to rewrite the text, having them write the text on pages to match the pages for which they substitute. When the students are finished, bring them together for a group conference in which they read aloud their rewritten stories. After each one shares his or her story, the teacher asks the group, "What do you like about the way *(name of student)* rewrote his story?" "What do you think could be changed?" "How would *(name of student)* change that?" Then, have the students rewrite their texts as they choose. Finally, have the students type the new pages of texts on the computer, using a font size similar to that of the original book. Paste the new text onto large "sticky notes." Give them copies of the book and have them "stick" the new texts over the original texts. Finally, give each version to a different first- or second-grade teacher to use.

Phase Two: Give the copies to the second-grade children and do a shared reading with the book. Start by telling the title and telling about the author and illustrator. Show some of the pictures of the book and explain that the main character is Rosalía and that she has a pet hen. This may be an unusual concept for the children, so some time may be spent exploring the idea of having a farm animal as a pet. Ask if the children know about the ritual of blessing animals. If none know about the ritual, explain it. Ask the children what they think the book will be about. Next, read the book all the way through and ask the children to look at the words and pictures as you read. Discuss their predictions and other ideas in the book. Next, reread the book, asking the children to chime in wherever they want. At the end of the lesson, choose three "new" sight words from the story, hold them up and say them, asking the children to look at them and say them.

Various lessons could follow that involve activities such as the students in reading the book, writing hard words, discussing the book further, writing sentence strips from the story, cutting up the strips into words, scrambling them, reordering them, and reading them.

Finally, the teacher might read the original version of the book to the students and conduct a discussion comparing the two versions.

Adapting the Activity: This activity will work with most fiction and informational texts, but is likely to work best when the text reading level is not too much higher than the students' reading level. Trying to adapt text, especially informational text, that is three or more grades higher than your students' reading level is probably not advisable because too much content might be lost in the "translation."

One adaptation would be to give the older students a list of words that you want them to be sure to include in their rewrites. This way, you could be sure that certain concepts or new sight words that you wanted the younger students to learn would be included. Another adaptation would be to have the students doing the revising rewrite an easier text to make it a higher reading level. This would help them consider both the function of embellishment and how to do the embellishing. The revised text could be useful with English-language learners because it would offer them an enriched text with a deeper "web" of ideas to consider and potentially, to remember.

Reflection: *Rewriting texts can be time consuming and often unrealistic for teachers to do. Having older students revise texts can help both the older and the younger students. Older students can learn about how texts and authors work, understandings that will enhance their own reading and writing. Younger students can improve* *their own reading abilities by reading texts that are at a "just right" difficulty level. Rewriting texts, particularly relatively brief ones, is also a possible activity for English-language learners' parents and siblings and for other community volunteers.*

During Reading: A Final Word

How do you decide what sort of during-reading activities will benefit your English-language learners? First of all, as is the case with any of the three phases of SRE—prereading, during reading, or postreading—the kinds of activities your students engage in will depend on their needs, interests, and abilities; the material they are reading; and their purposes for reading. What is their English reading level? What is their native-language reading level? Are they reading for pleasure or information? What is it they need or want to get from the text? Which activity will be most helpful for each English-language learner in the class? If they are reading primarily to enjoy a well-told tale, then preparing a study guide for them would definitely be a waste of time. However, if the purpose is to understand the salient features of the industrial revolution as they are described in a social studies text, they might be able to benefit from a reading guide designed to help them focus on cause and effect.

As is the case with prereading, the purpose of during-reading activities is to provide a scaffold that will help ensure students achieve their reading goals. As is also the case with prereading, as well as with postreading, there is the matter of your time to consider. There simply is not enough time for you to create all of the activities you might like to, and thus you must focus on creating those that will best help your English-language learners to be as successful as possible in the reading they do.

References

Beck, I. L., McKeown, M. G., Hamilton, R. L., & Kucan, L. (1997). *Questioning the author: An approach to enhancing student engagement with text.* Newark, DE: International Reading Association. An entire monograph on the authors' QtA approach.

Beck, I. L., McKeown, M. G., Hamilton, R. L., & Kucan, L. (1998, Spring/ Summer). Getting the meaning: How to help students unpack difficult text. *American Educator, 22,* 66–71. Describes how to help students comprehend better.

Blachowicz, C., & Ogle, D. (2001). *Reading comprehension: Strategies for independent learners.* New York: Guilford Press. Contains a host of very practical ideas for creating readers who can read and learn on their own.

Graves, M. F., Juel, C., & Graves, B. B. (2001). *Teaching reading in the 21st century* (2nd ed). Needham Heights, MA: Allyn & Bacon. This comprehensive text contains a thorough discussion of how to teach comprehension strategies as well as information on how to teach most of the other components of an elementary reading program.

Heimlich, J. E., & Pittelman, S. D. (1986). *Semantic mapping: Classroom applications.* Newark, DE: International Reading Association. A very practical guide to using semantic mapping for a variety of purposes.

Hoyt, L. (1992). Many ways of knowing: Using drama, oral interactions, and the visual arts to enhance reading comprehension. *The Reading Teacher, 45*(8), 580–584. Practical ideas for expanding ways of teaching comprehension.

Kintsch, W., & van Dijk, T. (1978). Toward a model of text comprehension and production. *Psychological Review, 85,* 363–394. A technical and challenging yet very insightful discussion of how we understand and remember text.

Martin, B. (1992). Afterword. In B. E. Cullinan (Ed.), *Invitation to read: More children's literature in the classroom* (pp. 179–182). Newark, DE: International Reading Association. Well-known author tells about reading experiences.

McCauley, J. K., & McCauley, D. S. (1992) Using choral reading to promote language learning for ESL students. *The Reading Teacher, 45*(7), 526–533. Describes how to use choral reading with English-language learners.

Miller, G. A. (1956). The magical number seven, plus-or-minus two: Some limits on our capacity for processing information. *Psychological Review, 63,* 81–97. A true classic; significant for its contributions to both theory and practice.

Ollmann, H. E. (1992). Two-column response to literature. *Journal of Reading, 36,* pp. 58–59. A simple yet powerful use of journals.

Pearson, P. D., & Johnson, D. D. (1978). *Teaching reading comprehension.* New York: Holt, Rinehart and Winston. Probably the first text to present a view of teaching reading consistent with cognitive psychology, this book contains one of, if not *the,* earliest treatments of semantic mapping.

Rosenblatt, L. M. (1978). *The reader, the text, the poem: The transactional theory of the literary work.* Carbondale, IL: Southern Illinois Press. One of several presentations of Rosenblatt's very influential response theory.

Rosenblatt, L. M. (1994). The transactional theory of reading and writing. In R. B. Ruddell, M. R. Ruddell, & H. Singer (Eds.), *Theoretical models and processes of reading* (4th ed., pp. 1057–1092). Newark, DE: International Reading Association. Provides a revision of Rosenblatt's earlier theory.

Trelease, J. (2001). *The read-aloud handbook* (5th ed.). New York: Penguin. This bestseller contains a wealth of insights for both teachers and parents.

Wittrock, M. C. (1990). Generative processes of comprehension. *Educational Psychologist, 24,* 345–376. Another view of generative comprehension processes.

Wolf, S. A. (1993). What's in a name? Labels and literacy in Readers Theatre. *The Reading Teacher, 46*(7), 546–551. Describes techniques in Readers Theatre.

Young, T. A., & Vardell, S. (1993). Weaving Readers Theatre and nonfiction into the curriculum. *The Reading Teacher, 46*(5), 396–406. Describes how to incorporate nonfiction into Readers Theatre.

Children's Literature

Alexander, G. (1991). *The jungle book.* New York: Arcade.

Anderson, J. (1986). *Pioneer children of Appalachia.* New York: Lodestar.

Anderson, J. (1989). *Spanish pioneers of the Southwest.* New York: Lodestar.

Anderson, J. (1990). *Pioneer settlers of New France.* New York: Lodestar.

Asimov, I. (1990). *How did we find out about Neptune?* New York: Walker.

Avi. (1990). *The true confessions of Charlotte Doyle.* New York: Orchard.

Aylesworth, J. (1991). *Country crossing.* New York: Atheneum.

Brooks, B. (1990). *Everywhere.* New York: HarperCollins.

Byars, B. (1983). *The glory girl.* New York: Viking.

Carlson, J. (1989). *Harriet Tubman: Call to freedom.* New York: Fawcett Columbine.

Carmi, D. (2000). *Samir and Yonatan.* Trans. by Yael Lotan. New York: Arthur A. Levine Books. Original text copyright 1994, by Daniella Carmi.

Chang, I. (1991). *A separate battle: Women and the Civil War.* New York: Lodestar.

Cole, J. (1990). *The magic school bus lost in the solar system.* New York: Scholastic.

Davidson, M. (1986). *I have a dream, the story of Martin Luther King, Jr.* New York: Scholastic.

dePaola, T. (1978). *The popcorn book.* New York: Holiday House.

Fleischman, P. (1988). *A joyful noise: Poems for two voices.* New York: Harper & Row.

Fleischman, S. (1986). *The whipping boy.* New York: Greenwillow Books.

Forrester, V. (1985). *A latch against the wind.* New York: Atheneum.

Frank, A. (1978). *The diary of a young girl.* New York: Randon House.

Freedman, R. (1980). *Immigrant kids.* New York: E. P. Dutton.

Freedman, R. (1988). *Buffalo hunt.* New York: Holiday House.

Giff, P. R. (1997). *Lily's crossing.* New York: Delacorte.

Goodman, B. (1990). *A kid's guide to how to save the planet.* New York: Avon Books.

Hackett, J. K., & Moyer, R. H. (1991). Electricity. In *Science in your world.* New York: Macmillan/McGraw-Hill.

Hackett, J. K., & Moyer, R. H. (1991). Waves. In *Science in your world,* Level 6. New York: Macmillan/McGraw-Hill.

Hall, B. (1990). *Dixie storms.* San Diego: Harcourt Brace Jovanovich.

Hamilton, V. (1985). *The people could fly.* New York: Knopf.

Hamilton, V. (1990). *Cousins.* New York: Philomel.

Hayes, J. (2001). *¡El cucuy!: A bogeyman cuento in English and Spanish.* El Paso: Cinco Puntos.

Irvin, J. (2003). *The United States: Change and challenge, A world in transition,* and *The ancient world* (*Content Area Readers* series). Austin, TX: Holt, Rinehart and Winston.

Kajikawa, K. (2002). *Yoshi's feast.* New York: DK Publishing.

Kennedy, R. (1985). *Amy's eyes.* New York: Harper & Row.

Lester, L. (1968). *To be a slave.* New York: E. P. Dutton.

Litowinsky, O. (1991). *The high voyage: The final crossing of Christopher Columbus.* New York: Delacorte.

Lord, B. B. (1984). *In the year of the boar and Jackie Robinson.* New York: Harper & Row.

Lowry, L. (1989). *Number the stars.* New York: Dell.

MacLachlan, P. (1991). *Journey.* New York: Delacorte.

Madrigal, A. H. (2000). *Blanca's feather.* Flagstaff, AZ: Rising Moon.

Markle, S. (1991). *Inside and outside you.* New York: Bradbury.

Marshak, S. (1990). *Hail to mail.* New York: Henry Holt.

Mazer, N. F. (1990). *C, my name is Cal.* New York: Scholastic.

Meltzer, M. (1990). *Bill of Rights.* New York: HarperCollins.

Mora, P. (Ed.) (2001). *Love to mamá: A tribute to mothers.* New York: Lee & Low Books.

Mosel, A. (1968). *Tikki tikki tembo.* New York: Henry Holt.

Namioka, L. (1992). *Yang the youngest and his terrible ear.* New York: Dell.

Nava, Y. (2000). *It's all in the frijoles.* New York: Simon and Schuster.

Paterson, K. (1978). *The great Gilly Hopkins.* New York: Crowell.

Paterson, K. (1991). *Lyddie.* New York: E. P. Dutton.

Paulsen, G. (1990). *Canyons.* New York: Delacorte.

Paulsen, G. (1987). *Hatchet.* New York: Bradbury.

Pendergraft, P. (1987). *Miracle at Clement's Pond.* New York: Philomel.

Peters, L. W. (1991). *Water's way.* New York: Arcade.

Prelutsky, J. (1984). *The new kid on the block.* New York: William Morrow.

Rockwell, A. (2000). *The boy who wouldn't obey: A Mayan legend.* New York: Harper Collins.

Rosen, M. (1989). *We're going on a bear hunt.* New York: McElderry Books.

Rylant, C. (1990). *A couple of kooks and other stories about love.* New York: Orchard.

Rylant, C. (1991). *Appalachia: The voices of sleeping birds.* San Diego: Harcourt Brace Jovanovich.

Sanfield, S. (1989). *The adventures of high John the conqueror.* New York: Orchard.

Schami, R. (1990). *A hand full of stars.* New York: Dutton.

Schwartz, D. M. (1985). *How much is a million?* New York: Lothrop, Lee & Shepard.

Silverstein, S. (1974). *Where the sidewalk ends.* New York: Harper & Row.

Soto, G. (1992). *Neighborhood odes.* New York: Harcourt, Brace, Jovanovich.

Soto, G. (2000). *Chato and the party animals.* New York: G. P. Putnam's Sons.

Spinelli, J. (1990). *Maniac Magee.* Boston: Little Brown.

Spinelli, J. (1991). *Fourth grade rats.* New York: Scholastic.

Thesman, J. (1990). *Rachel Chance.* Boston: Houghton Mifflin.

Viorst, J. (1983). *If I were in charge of the world and other worries.* New York: Atheneum.

Walker, A. (1982). *The color purple.* San Diego: Harcourt Brace Jovanovich.

Wisniewski, D. (1989). *The warrior and the wiseman.* New York: Lothrop, Lee & Shepard.

Wong, J. S. (2000). *The trip back home.* New York: Harcourt.

CHAPTER 7

POSTREADING
ACTIVITIES

Postreading activities, the last set of optional activities in the Scaffolded Reading Experience, assist English-language learners in making a reading experience meaningful by engaging them in a variety of activities. Why engage English-language learners in postreading activities? What function do these sorts of activities serve in the scaffold?

As Francis Bacon observed, "Some books are to be tasted, others to be swallowed, and some few to be chewed and digested." Not every reading experience needs to be followed by some sort of activity. There will be times when students will read, reflect, and respond in their own personal way. When students are just "tasting" a selection, their reflection and response may be quite brief. Sometimes, however, it is appropriate to provide activities that encourage students to do something with the information and ideas in a selection after they have read it—to chew and digest. To determine the appropriateness and the type of activity called for, we turn once again to our model and think about the students, the selection, and the purposes for reading.

Postreading activities encourage English-language learners to *do* something with the material they have just read, to think—critically, logically, and creatively—about the information and ideas that emerge from their reading, and sometimes to transform their thinking into action. When doing recreational reading, we often create meaning with a text without much of an effort or involvement, and that is fine—for recreational reading. But for a lot of reading that our English-language learner students do in school, it isn't fine. As we explained in chapter 4, until English-language learners do something with what they have read, they are a long way from getting the most they can from a text. In many cases, in order to really own a text, English-language learners will use a process like this:

Read   —>   Think and Elaborate   <—>   Respond

As the model illustrates, in some cases they read, think and elaborate, and then respond; and that response may foster further thought and elaboration, which may in turn foster further response. Response can take a variety of forms: speaking, writing, dramatics, creative arts, construction, or application and outreach activities. In postreading activities students recall what they've read and demonstrate understanding, but they also do much more than this. They apply, analyze, synthesize, evaluate, and elaborate the information and ideas created through reading the text and connect the information and ideas to their prior knowledge, to other things they've read, to information and ideas they already have, and to the world in which they live. Postreading activities also provide opportunities for students to extend ideas, to explore new ways of thinking, doing, and seeing—to invent and create, to ponder the question "What if?"

In chapter 2, we described the eight categories of postreading activities:

Postreading

1. Questioning

2. Discussion

3. Writing

4. Drama

5. Artistic, graphic, and nonverbal activities

6. Application and outreach activities

7. Building connections

8. Reteaching

The activities in the first seven categories encourage students to think in the ways we just suggested—to recall, understand, apply, analyze, synthesize, evaluate, and elaborate information and ideas, to make logical connections between and among ideas, and to go beyond given information or ideas to explore new ways of thinking and of expressing themselves.

To these we add an eighth category, reteaching. Reteaching is the safety net in the reading scaffold. You don't want students leaving a reading selection without some sense of accomplishment, of a job well done. Sometimes if that goal hasn't been achieved, it means retracing steps to find out what didn't work and why, and then perhaps trying a different approach. You and your students are jointly accountable for a successful reading experience.

This list is not the only way postreading activities might be described or categorized. As with pre- and during-reading categories, our postreading categories are options. Although not all reading selections are meant to be "digested," some sort of postreading experience is often appropriate. Not engaging in postreading activities is a bit like taking a trip and promptly forgetting about it. If you want to keep that vacation memory alive, you need to do something further with it—perhaps put together a scrapbook, or organize your slides, videos, and photographs and share these with friends. Postreading activities allow students to relive the reading experience and to discover new insights to take from it, explore ways to act on those discoveries, and build bridges to other experiences, whether those experiences take place in their lives or in other texts.

Postreading Activities in Chapter 7

Questioning	*What Do YOU Think?*
	The Yellow Brick Road Story Map
Discussion	*Paideia Seminar*
	Three's a Charm!
	Both Sides
	The Virtual Field Trip
Writing	*Compare/Contrast*
	Fanciful Writing
Drama	*History Comes to Life*
Artistic, graphic, and nonverbal activities	*Worth a Thousand Words*
Application and outreach activities	*Getting to Know You*
Building connections	*Problems & Solutions*
Reteaching	*Play It Again, Sam*

Questioning

Questioning activities encourage English-language learners to think about and react—either orally or in writing—to the information and ideas in the material they have read. Questions might be designed to have students recall what they have read, show that they understand what was read, apply, analyze, synthesize, or elaborate information and ideas. Questions might also encourage creative, interpretive, or metacognitive thinking. As an example of these various levels of thinking, here are some questions students might be asked to answer after reading *Shh! We're Writing the Constitution* by Jean Fritz. These and other sorts of questions are considered at length in the new version of Bloom's Taxonomy (Anderson & Krathwohl, 2001).

> *Recalling:* How many delegates were supposed to attend the grand convention in 1787?
>
> *Understanding:* How did the delegates keep the proceedings a secret?
>
> *Applying:* What are some things you might do to keep a secret meeting secret?
>
> *Analyzing:* Why did the delegates decide to keep the proceedings a secret?
>
> *Synthesizing:* What do you think might have happened if the public had found out what was going on in the meetings?
>
> *Evaluating:* Do you think it was a good idea to keep the meetings a secret? Why or why not?
>
> *Elaborating:* What do you think were the most effective features of the delegates' plan to keep the proceedings secret?
>
> *Creating:* What if the delegates had decided there should be three presidents presiding over the nation instead of one? What might have happened?
>
> *Interpreting:* How do you think Benjamin Franklin felt being the oldest delegate at the convention?
>
> *Thinking metacognitively:* Did you understand the author's description of the three branches of government on page 14? If you didn't, what might you do to make this explanation more clear to yourself?

Questions that stimulate these various kinds and levels of thinking are appropriate for narrative and informational materials. After reading narratives, questions also can be developed that prompt students to focus on elements of theme, plot, setting, or character traits, motives and development. In Jerry Spinelli's *Fourth Grade Rats*, in order to please his best friend, the protagonist Suds tries hard to make the transition from being a third-grade "angel" to a fourth grade "rat." In doing so, he acquires some pretty obnoxious behavior. Questions such as "At first, why didn't Suds want to become a rat?" "What happened to make him change his mind?" and "What did he finally decide about being a rat and why?" can help lead students to discover the story's theme.

Questions that involve feelings are also appropriate for narratives. English-language learners can be guided to examine the feelings of the characters in the story and their own emotional reactions as well. "How do you think Suds felt when he started saying 'no' to his Mom?" "Why do you think he felt this way?" "How do you think Suds' Mom felt when he said 'no' to her?" "Why do you think she felt this way?" and "How did you feel about Suds' behavior toward his mother?"

Questions that lead learners to think about universal themes and feelings help them make the connection between literature and real life. If English-language learners can see themselves and their situations in the stories they read in school, they are likely to feel a bit more comfortable in school and more a part of what goes on in school.

Questions can also guide students toward becoming metacognitive readers. "Were there parts of the text you didn't understand? Why didn't you understand these? What might you do to better understand the ideas?" "Should you reread parts of the text, take some notes, draw a map, do some background reading, ask a friend for assistance?" These kinds of questions encourage students to monitor their own understanding and focus their attention on considering and implementing fix-up strategies.

In responding to questions, English-language learners should generally be aware of their audience. For whom are they answering? Themselves? Their teacher? Other students? The author? In the questions listed earlier for *Shh! We're Writing the Constitution*, the audience was a teacher. However, questions might also be constructed from the point of view of the author, as if the author himself were asking questions of his readers. For example, for the novel *The Star Fisher* by Lawrence Yep, author-asked questions might include these: "What do you like best about the character Emily?" "What is your favorite scene in the story and why do you like it?" "Did Emily say or do anything that helped or inspired you? If she did, what was it?" Students would answer these questions as if they were writing to Lawrence Yep himself. Or for the informational book *Touch, Taste, and Smell* by Steve Parker, author-asked questions might be "What did you find most interesting about how you perceive a smell?" "Why did you find this part interesting?" "When you came across a word you didn't understand, what did you do?" and "How could I have helped you better understand what the word meant?"

Also, English-language learners might ask and answer their own questions. For example, after reading a chapter on California missions in their social studies text, they might write five questions they still have about the issues or topics in the chapter. To answer the questions, they might refer back to the text or look for the answers in other sources. Another possibility is to have students develop a set of questions for the books they read that other students will answer. These questions can be written on a sheet of paper and placed in the book. Whoever reads the book next would write answers to the questions and give them to the student author. Together the two students could discuss the questions and answers.

Another line of questioning has been suggested by Isabel Beck and colleagues (Beck, McKeown, Hamilton, & Kucan, 1997, 1998) that they have labeled *Questioning the Author*. As we mentioned in Chapter 6 when talking about modifying text, students are often under the impression that if they do not understand what they read, the fault lies with them and certainly not with the author. This may or may not be the case. English-language learners need to realize that authors are not infallible—they are not always the lucid communicators they attempt to be. Asking questions such as "What was the author trying to tell you?" "How could the author have expressed the ideas in a clearer way?" and "What would you want to say instead?" can prompt students to actively participate in building meaning from text.

Although postreading questioning activities sometimes serve to assess students' reading comprehension and their ability to think at various levels, the primary purpose of the postreading questioning we have described is to allow and encourage English-language learners to delve more deeply into the texts they read. Questioning activities tap into students' innate curiosity about the world and provide opportunities for them to think about and respond to information and ideas on a variety of levels.

It is important to think about matching types of questions to the English-language learner's current knowledge. Sometimes you may want to ask all of the children in a class to think about a certain set of questions. Other times, you may want to have some students work with questions that may be more difficult while other students work with ones that are less difficult. Our point here is reminiscent of the concept of finding the zone of proximal development that we discussed in chapter 4. English-language learners are likely to make the most progress if they work in that zone. Questions that target students' zones of proximal development will be the ones most likely to help them learn and grow. For example, if you have a class in which there are a few students who are in the early phases of learning English, you may want to ask them to think about *part* of a question that is given to the rest of the students in the class. If you ask the class as a whole, "What happened to change Suds' mind about becoming a rat?" you might ask the new English learners in the group "What does 'being a rat' mean in this book?" Another way to lessen the cognitive load for the new English learners or native-English speakers who are less skilled readers is to ask them questions that involve their own feelings and opinions. These sorts of answers are less "risky," and while the students have to have some understandings that come from reading the story, they aren't required to engage in complexities that may require a struggle on their part. Also, all students can participate in the group discussions.

While "matching" questions to students is important, equally important is the idea that *all* students should be challenged to grow. We want to be clear here that we are not advocating that English-language learners and less skilled readers *only* be asked certain kinds of questions forever. Rather, we are suggesting that by lightening their cognitive load where you can, you make it easier for them to participate and to learn. When teachers "shoulder" students in these ways, they should always keep the goal in mind of having the students at some point be able to answer the questions asked of others in the class as well.

On the following pages, we present two examples of questioning activities, the first of which is *What Do YOU Think?*

QUESTIONING Sample Activity 1: *What Do YOU Think?*

In *What Do YOU Think?* students write their personal responses to the question "Is there anything in this story that you can relate to?" These responses are then displayed on a reader response chart.

Selection: *Me Llamo María Isabel,* by Alma Flor Ada, recounts the emotions María Isabel confronts when she arrives at a new school and, because there are two other children named María in the class, the teacher changes her name to Mary. When the teacher calls her "Mary," María doesn't respond because she doesn't recognize the name. This leads to a number of misunderstandings and complications, including excluding María from the school's Winter Pageant. María finds solace in a library book, *Charlotte's Web*, and also seemingly unconsciously uses the book to work through her own problems. The teacher's writing assignment, "My Greatest Wish," gives María an opportunity to help the teacher understand her better. Not only does the book address a challenge that many youngsters face in U.S. classrooms—having others change their names—it also illustrates how children can use literature and writing to think through problems and to talk with others. Fortunately, *Me Llamo María Isabel* is available in Spanish and English, so you can choose which version or versions to use with your students.

Students: Third-grade students in a bilingual education class. About half the students are Latino, one-fourth Anglo, and one-fourth Black of African descent. The students have been in bilingual education since kindergarten. The text is written in Spanish, and the teacher conducts the entire lesson in Spanish. Their Spanish reading levels range from slightly below to slightly above grade level. We write about the lesson here in English even though the lesson is conducted in Spanish.

Reading Purpose: To enjoy a sensitive well-crafted piece of literature and to make connections between the ideas developed in the story and the reader's own life.

Goal of the Activity: To help students feel secure in their responses to a particular work and not be dependent on someone else's response, to encourage respect for the responses of others, and to help students recognize the common and diverse elements in different readers' responses to the same piece of literature.

Rationale: *Me Llamo María Isabel* is one of those well-crafted stories that deserves to be "chewed and digested." It also invites personal response because of the unique way it portrays themes surrounding the meanings of names as they relate to personal heritage. By asking students if they relate to anything in the story, they are invited to connect their own understandings and lives with characters and events in the book. By noting how others respond to the same question, they will discover similarities and differences among responses.

Procedure: After students have finished reading the book, tell them that you're all going to talk about the story together, but first, you want them to write answers to the question "Is there anything in this story that you can relate to?" Display a reader response chart showing the question at the top. Explain that their written responses might be as short as a sentence or as long as a paragraph.

After students have written responses, post these on the reader response chart. After the responses have been posted on the chart, let each student read his or her response, and then discuss the similarities and differences among them. If groups of types of responses emerge, have the class help you sort the responses into groups. For instance, some children may identify most directly with having someone else change their name. Another group of children may have written about how they were left out of a school event. Still others may have written about how they like to read to escape their problems or to help them think about their problems.

Adapting the Activity: This type of activity can be used with any number of expository works, novels, short stories, or poems—simply change the title, author, and question. For example, after reading Isaac Asimov's *How Did We Find Out About Our Genes?* advanced fifth and sixth graders might answer the question "Why do you think people want to know what effect heredity has on our personality and intelligence?" Or, after reading *The Happiest Ending* by Yoshiko Uchida, upper elementary students could answer the question "Why do you think Rinko was opposed to the Japanese custom of arranged marriages?" Also, reader responses can be recorded in a class journal as well as on a chart. Simply write the book title, author, and question on the top of a page (a scrapbook size book works well) and have students write their responses on individual strips of paper and glue these to the appropriate page.

Reflection: Questions that elicit personal responses to a selection can help students understand the importance and significance of the schemata each individual brings to a selection—how the meaning one person constructs from a text might be somewhat different from the meaning another person constructs. If responses are made public, students will also be able to see that there are also common responses. However, when constructing personal response questions, teachers need to be careful not to invade students' privacy. "How did you feel when . . ." questions might be appropriate if students are writing responses in personal journals, but they may not be in situations where there is an audience.

Also, there are many other ways in which you might approach personal response questions. In some instances, these questions might be preceded by factual and inferential questions designed to ensure that students understand the selection before they give personal responses to it. For example, "Why didn't María Isabel answer the teacher?" or "Why do you think the teacher was angry with María Isabel?" Students might discuss these questions in groups or answer them personally in a journal. After they have answered these questions, they can then answer the question "Is there anything you relate to in the story?" for the reader response chart, or you can record their responses in the class journal.

Personal response questions could also be followed by application questions: "How could you use something you've learned from reading this story in your own life?" A question of this sort might best be answered in a personal journal rather than on a chart or class journal, since it applies to the student personally and she may want to refer to it at a later date in order to actually act on it.

QUESTIONING Sample Activity 2: *The Yellow Brick Road* Story Map

In *The Yellow Brick Road Story Map,* questions are developed that follow in sequential order the information that is central to understanding the selection. These questions create what Isabel Beck and Margaret McKeown (1981) call a story map, a set of questions that, when answered, constitute the essence of the story.

Selection: *How the Ox Star Fell from Heaven* by Lily Toy Hong. In this ancient Chinese folktale, Oxen used to live in luxury in the heavens and not on earth. When the Emperor of All the Heavens sent an Ox Star to earth by mistake, the Ox Star makes a mistake that causes all of the oxen to be banished from heaven and sent to earth. A celestial error becomes earth's blessing.

Students: Second graders of mixed English reading abilities with five English-language learners with different ethnic backgrounds, including one child whose parents immigrated to the United States from China before she was born. Four of the English-language learners have been in the school district since kindergarten, and one recently arrived from Japan. All of the English-language learners except the student from Japan have reasonably good conversational English, and read English at about mid-first-grade level.

Reading Goal: To enjoy a traditional folktale and to understand the story events in the sequence they occur.

Goal of Activity: To focus students' attention on the important events of the story in the order in which they take place in order to give students a basic understanding of the story.

Rationale: As do most folktales, *How the Ox Star Fell from Heaven* has a number of events that follow a predictable order. Having students answer questions about important story events in the sequence in which they occur can help promote comprehension of this particular story as well as help develop a general schema for story sequence.

Procedure: Before meeting with the students, list briefly the major events that reveal the essence of the story in the order in which they occur. Write a question for each event. Here we list the major events and matching questions for *How the Ox Star Fell from Heaven*.

> Setting 1: In the beginning, all oxen lived in heaven in luxury. Their life was easy. *Question: What was it like for the oxen when they all lived in heaven?*
>
> Setting 2: Life on earth without oxen was hard. People worked all day and were tired. They couldn't grow and harvest enough food to eat. Sometimes they went for days without eating. *Question: What was life on earth like when there were no oxen there?*
>
> Event 3: The Emperor of All the Heavens was kind and generous to the poor peasants on earth. He declared that the people on earth should eat at least once every three days. *Question: What did the Emperor decide?*
>
> Event 4: The Emperor sent his most trusted messenger, the Ox Star, to deliver his message. When the Ox Star arrived on earth, he gave them the wrong message, saying that the emperor declared they should eat three times a day. *Question: What did the Ox Star tell the people on earth?*
>
> Event 5: The Emperor heard the Ox Star's mistake and was angry. He banished all of the oxen from heaven. *Question: What did the Emperor do then?*
>
> Event 6: The oxen worked for the farmers, helping them in the fields. *Question: What did the oxen do on earth?*
>
> Event 7: The people ate warm rice, tender vegetables, and Chinese sweet cakes three times a day, every day. *Question: How did the story end?*

After constructing the questions, write a number for each on the "yellow brick" spaces as shown on the illustration below. Have students work in pairs of differing English oral and reading abilities to write the answers to the questions on a separate sheet of paper, or put the questions on transparencies for small groups of students of mixed English reading abilities and have students answer them in small groups, making notes about their answers. Then bring everyone together as a whole class and ask pair or group representatives to tell answers. Call on English-language learners according to their oral English abilities to respond.

Adapting the Activity: This activity can be used for any story in which the events proceed in chronological order. Simply identify the events of the story that reveal its basic meaning and write a question for each. *The Yellow Brick Road Story Map* might be used with *Vasilisa the Beautiful* by T. P. Whitney; the Zimbabwean folk tale, *Mufaro's Beautiful Daughters*, written and illustrated by John Steptoe; Aesop's fable

The Yellow Brick Road Story Map

1. What was it like for the oxen when they all lived in heaven?

2. What was life on earth like when there were no oxen there?

3. What did the Emperor decide?

4. What did Ox Star tell the people?

5. What did the Emperor do then?

6. What did the oxen do on earth?

7. How did the story end?

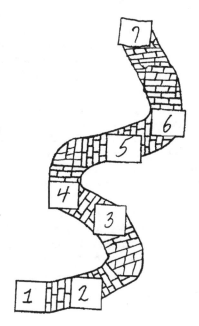

Androcles and the Lion, retold and illustrated by Janet Steven; and many other folktales, fables, and fairy tales.

Another way to use *The Yellow Brick Road Story Map* is to laminate the yellow brick road (without the questions on it) to a manila file folder to use as a game board for the folktales and fairy tales students read. This game is for students who will be able to read and speak English at least not too far below grade level. Write two questions for each event in the individual stories on separate index cards. Number one set of cards 1A, 2A, 3A, and so on, and the other set 1B, 2B, 3B, and put possible answers on the back of each card. Players take turns answering from either set A or B in chronological order. If a player answers to her partner's satisfaction, she can move up to the next space. The other player then has the chance to move forward by answering the other question correctly. The first person to reach "The End" is the "winner." The story board game and folder can be used for many different selections, simply change the questions to coincide with the story. The answers for open-ended questions such as "Do you think it was fair that people had to work so hard on earth when there were no oxen?" will have no right or wrong answer. Some rules will need to be established beforehand to determine acceptable answers.

Reflection: *Story maps are only one approach to formulating questions. As you probably noticed, most of the questions were literal ones. Although Beck and McKeown (1981) note that story maps include both literal and inferential questions, because they concentrate on providing students with a basic understanding of the story, they often consist largely of literal questions. However, as Beck and McKeown also note, these are not the only type of questions to ask on reading selections. As students understand the basic events of the story, including interpretive, analytical, and creative questions is appropriate.*

For informational material, questions can often coincide with the organizational approach taken by the author. For example, questions for text material described with details and concrete examples can reflect that organization: "What are three words that describe the Vietnam Memorial?" Cause-and-effect questions can be developed for text that presents issues by using that format, "What were the effects of the Boston Tea party?" or compare and contrast, "In what three ways are lizards and snakes alike? In what three ways are they different?" Whatever organizational scheme the author has chosen to develop his or her topic can be used and underscored by posing questions that parallel that organization.

Also, students themselves can be taught how to develop questions for selections for other students to answer. As a during-reading activity, students can compose questions while they read a selection that a partner or group members will answer as a postreading activity. Before students develop questions, however, they will need instruction on how to develop questions and the various kinds of questions they might ask.

Questioning activities encourage students to think about what they have read and to probe more deeply. By asking may different types and levels of questions students' thinking can be directed to help improve comprehension and recall, as well as foster critical and creative thinking.

Discussion

Almost every classroom reading experience will include some sort of discussion—exchanging ideas out loud (Alvermann, Dillon, & O'Brien, 1987). The key word here is *exchanging*. The intent of discussion is to freely explore ideas, to learn something new or gain a different perspective because of the information or insights more than one person has to give. Discussion is an active exchange of ideas, ideally one in which everyone has the opportunity to participate equally. Discussion provides an opportunity to solidify, clarify, or modify knowledge. Discussion activities give students a forum in which to talk about the meaning *they* constructed from texts, listen to the insights of *others*, and weigh their responses in light of those of their classmates. Here they can think about, ponder, consider, analyze, evaluate, and make connections between the text and their own lives and among the text, their personal experiences, and the thoughts and experiences of their classmates.

Although little research has been done on the use and effects of discussions with English-language learners (Gersten & Baker, 2000), several authorities on reading with English-language learners suggest discussions as ways to help English-language learners with, for instance, language fluency and/or reading comprehension, whether they are speaking in their native language or in a new language (Chamot & O'Malley, 1996; Echevarria, 1995; Goldenberg, 1992–1993). Also, discussion is a key feature in both cooperative learning and in peer tutoring, and a few studies support the potential of both of these with English-language learners (Gersten & Baker, 2000; Klingner & Vaughn, 1996; Muñiz-Swicegood, 1994).

One popular discussion format used with English-language learners is *instructional conversations* in which students learn to discuss texts in order to enhance their conversations. If you are interested in learning more about the format, you can find details in Claude Goldenberg's (1992–1993) article, "Instructional conversations: Promoting Comprehension Through Discussion" and in Echevarria's (1995) article, "Interactive Reading Instruction: A Comparison of Proximal and Distal Effects of Instructional Conversations." You might also be interested in reading more about the Cognitive Academic Language Learning Approach (CALLA), which places strong emphasis on student dialogue for English-language learners (Chamot & O'Malley, 1996).

When doing classroom discussions, it is good to keep in mind that new English-language learners may feel very shy about attempting to speak and that, for them, participating in discussion can be risky. Their contributions must be fully accepted and other students and teachers alike should make them feel supported.

Discussion groups can be teacher led or student led. They can involve the entire class, small groups, or pairs. But whatever format is used, here are a few guidelines for implementing discussions:

✦ Develop a clear purpose or purposes. What is it the discussion is to accomplish? Are students examining two or more sides of an issue? Are they looking to discover a book's theme? Are they trying to solve a problem? Master the content of a text? Discussion should not be rigidly structured, but without clear purpose or focus it runs the risk of deteriorating into meaningless chit-chat.

✦ Discussion leaders (as well as participants) should be supportive, noncritical, and open-minded. Leaders should encourage response from all members of the group and be sparing with their own comments and suggestions.

✦ Discussion prompts might include or begin with literal-level questioning but should go beyond these to stimulate critical and creative thinking as well. Discussions should incorporate a number of levels of thinking—recalling, applying, analyzing, synthesizing, evaluating, and interpreting.

✦ When differences of opinions arise concerning literal or recall questions, the text should be consulted in order to verify or refute.

✦ Encourage group members to evaluate discussions. Was the purpose achieved? Did everyone get a chance to participate equally? What were the strengths of the discussion? Weaknesses? What might be done differently in the future?

Because discussion is such a powerful and frequently used postreading activity, we give four sample discussion activities.

DISCUSSION Sample Activity 1: *Paideia Seminar*

A Paideia Seminar, first described and advocated by Mortimer Adler (1982, 1983, 1984), is a form of discussion that has recently seen resurgence in many schools across the nation (Billings & Fitzgerald, 2003; Roberts, 1999), probably because of renewed interest in reader response groups. The word *Paideia* is Greek, referring to the upbringing of a child. In a Paideia Seminar, student understanding is developed and enriched by having students talk to one another about ideas, concepts, and values involved in a text they have read. A major tenet of the seminar is that individuals' thinking abilities are nurtured through social interaction. The teacher's primary roles are to ask open-ended questions to prompt students to examine text concepts through conversation with one another.

Selection: *Tiger's Fall* by Molly Bang. This chapter book is based on true events and real people the author met while spending time at PROJIMO, Project of Rehabilitation Organized by Disabled Youth of Western Mexico, located in the village of Ajoya, about 80 miles north of Mazatlán, Mexico. Eleven-year-old Lupe loves riding her father's horse, and her fearlessness earned her the nickname "Tigrilla," or "Little Tiger." She has a terrible fall, and is paralyzed from the waist down. Filled with anger, Lupe is taken to the center in town which is run by and for people with disabilities. Slowly, she comes to terms with her disability. The book is written at a level that might easily be read by typically developing fourth-grade students reading in their native language.

Students: A small group of eight sixth graders, five Latino and three Anglo, in a bilingual education class in an inner-city magnet school focused on the arts with Spanish and English maintenance and development. The students in this group read in English at late third- through fifth-grade levels.

Reading Purpose: To understand the concept of DISABILITY, to relate to the theme of perseverance, and to review how using cognates across languages can help in reading.

Goal of Activity: To stimulate the students' thinking through dialogic discussion amongst themselves.

Rationale: Dialogic discussion that happens in Paideia Seminars can foster students' awareness of their own views, help them to compare their own positions to that of others, and enhance their critical thinking abilities.

Procedure: Over a period of several days, the students read the entire book. In advance of reading, the teacher prepared the students by providing some background knowledge and teaching new key vocabulary. She quickly reviewed the importance of using cognates between Spanish and English by asking students to find three cognates on the first page of the text (*plastic/plástico, November/noviembre, veranda/veranda*). She emphasized that looking for cognates is a good way to help your own reading in either English or Spanish. She also told the students that they would read the book through, one chapter each day, on their own, reading silently, and that after they had read the book, they would meet to do a discussion called a *seminar*—something they had not done before. For the seminar, the teacher prearranges desks into a circle so that all participants are seated at eye level. The teacher begins by explaining that a Seminar is a little different from other ways they've talked about books. Everyone should think, speak, listen, refer to the text, and treat others with respect. The idea is for the students to talk about what they think is most important and meaningful in the book. Importantly, the students should talk to each other, and ask each other questions. The teacher says that she will start their discussion with a prompt and that she may periodically prompt them or make a statement, but that she is going to try to stay out of the discussion. She also says that she has made a little seating chart, and she'll be making marks on it to keep track of who's talking. The idea is for everyone to participate equally. She asks if there are questions and then opens with "Please take a few minutes and write down a brief statement to answer this question: Was there anything in this book that struck a chord with you?" She then allows a few minutes for students to think and asks them to begin. If no student begins, she asks each student to read what he wrote, moving around the circle. She also has other open-ended prompt statements or questions prepared in case the students do not discuss the book easily or well.

Adapting the Activity: Paideia Seminars can be used with students in grades as low as kindergarten and as high as graduate school. They have a fairly set organization and purpose, but can be used with almost any text that is thought provoking. For a seminar to work well, usually the text must have a moral, portray an extreme view that others can oppose, portray two sides of an issue, provide a metaphor for something of interest to the readers, or elicit a sense of "kinship" with one or more characters. In short, there must be something about the book that provokes discussion and dialogue. Many books meet this requirement. A few examples for upper grades are Elizabeth King's *Quinceañera: Celebrating Fifteen*, in which Cindy Chávez's quinceañera ritual is portrayed in flowing language and gorgeous color photographs; Lulu Delacre's *Salsa Stories,* in which Carmen Teresa collects stories from her loved ones, stories which float through Latin American holidays and customs; and Daniella Carmi's *Samir and Yonatan*, the tale of a young Palestinian boy's recovery in an Israeli hospital.

Reflection: Paideia Seminars can be wonderfully rich and rewarding for English-language learners. At the same time, it can be hard for both teachers and students to learn how to do them. We teachers are often so used to talking and asking questions, and we have our own agendas about what is important in texts. Sometimes it is difficult for us to let go of complete control and support students in finding and making their own critiques and themes. We can say this about our own experiences in doing seminars, both with young children and with college students. Likewise, most students are used to trying to give teachers the answers they think the teacher wants, and they are not used to exploring ideas with each other. Consequently, it can take some time to develop rich seminars. Some tips for tips for creating really effective seminars include the following: (1) Try to choose texts that have ideas that can be controversial or that can have an alternative "side" or that the students can really relate to. (2) Limit your prompts and questions to three or four and carefully prepare them in advance of the seminar, making them open ended. If you make up a prompt or question that is a "real" one to you—something you really do want to find out about from the students—it will more likely be successful. Avoid questions that simply ask for affirmation that students understood something in the text. (3) Make sure to keep track of who is talking and intervene to ask quiet students what they think, so that everyone has a chance to talk. (4) Use "wait time" of up to about 10 seconds or so, and avoid eye contact with the students, indicating by your actions that you expect them to talk to each other. (5) Position yourself in the circle so that you are part of the circle, but not the "prominent" point of the circle. (6) Avoid making evaluative statements. (7) Most of all, try to understand that the purpose of the seminar is for the students to talk about points that interest them from the text.

DISCUSSION Sample Activity 2: *Three's a Charm*

In *Three's a Charm,* three groups of students find specific examples of three important concepts in the text and report their findings to the class.

Selection: *I Have a Dream, The Story of Martin Luther King, Jr.,* by Margaret Davidson. This biography traces the emergence of Martin Luther King, Jr., as a powerful civil rights leader and pacifist from his youth in Atlanta, Georgia, through his assassination at age 39 in Memphis, Tennessee. The biography stresses King's compassion, intelligence, and eloquence, as well as his unquenchable spirit and commitment to justice, equality, and peace.

Students: Fifth to seventh graders of middle to high reading abilities and from various ethnic backgrounds, including two English-language learners recently arrived from the Balkans.

Reading Purpose: To understand and appreciate the purpose and results of Martin Luther King, Jr.'s efforts to promote civil rights. To understand civil rights as a general concept. To draw attention to the concept in contemporary society in the Balkans.

Goal of Activity: To stimulate students' use of recall and critical thinking skills and to provide an opportunity for students to work together in order to come to a consensus.

Rationale: This text is rich in examples of King's methods and strategies to peacefully bring about change in policies and attitudes toward African Americans. To single out just three of these methods as particularly noteworthy requires that students recall the significant strategies and evaluate the effectiveness of each. To reach consensus on the three most effective tools, students must substantiate their choices with sound reasoning as well as exercise such skills as persuasiveness and diplomacy.

Procedure: Tell students that Martin Luther King, Jr., and others in the civil rights movement used a number of different strategies to achieve their ends, but that probably there were three that were used most often and most effectively. Explain that they will get the chance to talk about what three they think were most effective, listen to what others think, and come to a common agreement.

Divide the class into three groups and appoint a leader and three recorders for each. Put both of the English-language learners in one of the three groups so they can help each other in their native language. Explain that the groups are to meet and decide what they think were the three main tools of the civil rights movement. (Boycotts, sit-ins, and protest marches were the principal three, but students may find others.) Instruct students to bring their copy of King's biography with them when their group meets. Each group should review the biography to identify the three methods and be ready to give specific examples of each from the text. Encourage students in each group to take turns telling about a strategy and locating examples of it in the text. (You may want to model this procedure before students meet in their groups.) Explain to the students that after the groups have decided which they think were the three most effective strategies, the three recorders will write the specific examples of each of the three strategies from the text. Give the groups about 15 or 20 minutes discussion time, while you circulate among the groups giving help, encouragement, and praise where needed. Help to make sure that the two English-language learners are able to participate at least a little. If they are not participating, ask the rest of the group to briefly act out one of the three strategies for the two English learners in a way that they can better understand at least one of the main ideas. After the discussions are completed, let the three recorders for each group report their group's findings and then compare and contrast each group's answers. Was there a consistency among the three choices? If so, what was the reason for this consistency? Was there discrepancy? If so, can group members defend their choices?

Also, as a class, evaluate how the discussion groups went, considering such matters as whether all group members contributed, if students listened to each other, if they supported and encouraged each other's contributions. As David Johnson and his colleagues (Johnson, Johnson, & Holubec, 1994) have noted and as we discuss further in Chapter 8, this sort of group processing is crucial to students' learning to work in groups effectively.

Adapting the Activity: This activity can be used for almost any reading selection. Simply choose concepts that coincide with that particular selection. For example, after reading *Cuban Kids* by George Ancona, you could ask the students to consider three important things they learned about student life in Cuba. Another example could be after reading Seymour Simon's *Oceans*, the prompt for the *Three's a Charm* activity could be "If you were going to tell a visitor from another planet (assuming that visitor could understand your language) three of the most important facts about the earth's oceans, what three things would you choose?" Or after reading Beverly Cleary's *Strider*, which is written in a diary format, the prompt might be "What were the three most important days in Leigh Bott's year?" Of course, even though three is often considered a magic number, this activity might have other numbers of items. Anything from two to six often works well.

Reflection*: Ideally, students will have been given the focusing question before they read so they can be looking for the three "big" or "most important" ideas, perhaps* *using book markers or jotting down notes in their journals. Again, as this activity so clearly illustrates, pre-, during-, and postreading activities are linked. Students' attention is focused before they read. While they read, they are looking for the "big ideas" as they construct meaning with the text. For many English-language learners, focusing on "big ideas" rather than a lot of details is a good way to reduce cognitive overload (Fitzgerald, 1993; Nurss & Hough, 1992).*

After students read, they check their responses against those of others and evaluate and make decisions based on their ideas, the text, and their group members' ideas. The discussion that follows is always lively as well as illuminating because students tend to have strong ideas about what they perceive as "most important."

This activity serves as a useful background against which to consider two related questions: To what extent should we take the position that there are right answers, and to what extent should students be expected to come to consensus when engaged in group activities? These are huge questions, which may not have "right" answers. To the extent that they do have answers, those answers are deserving of a book rather than a brief comment such as we are including here. Nevertheless, we feel obligated to give brief, personal responses to each of them.

With respect to there being right answers, we would note as we did in chapter 4, that we agree with current constructivist thinking, which stresses that much of the meaning a reader constructs from a text is constructed by the reader himself or herself. However, this does not mean that all meaning is constructed by the reader, it does not mean that all texts are equally open to the reader's interpretation, and it does not mean that there are no wrong answers. Children are growing up in a world in which they need to consider the evidence and make important decisions. We need to guide them in becoming critical readers, readers who consider the text and other information and arrive at defensible interpretations.

With respect to groups needing to come to a consensus, we would stress that in everyday life this is often the most desirable outcome. Children, adults, and societies need to work toward consensus. However, we do not believe that students should be forced into consensus. If, after their best efforts at agreement, students in a group still disagree on some matters, then all sides need to be heard, and the reality that such disagreements will occur needs be acknowledged and accepted. In fact, because different outlooks are a normal part of life, it can be very healthy for students to learn to be able to state their own views and accept others' views as divergent. Being able to accept diverse outlooks, including those that are opposed to your own, without malice and frustration, is an important lesson that can be carried outside of school life. Doing so is, of course, a sort of higher level thinking. It is also something that all too few adults learn to do.

DISCUSSION Sample Activity 3: *Both Sides*

Both Sides is a discussion web activity (Alvermann, 1991) in which students use a graphic aid to help them look at both sides of an issue before drawing conclusions. In this activity, students meet in pairs and then as groups of four to reach a consensus about a question raised by their reading.

Selection: *Frozen Fire* by James Houston. *Frozen Fire* is the story of Matthew Morgan and his Eskimo friend Kayak, who battle to stay alive in the harsh Canadian wilderness close to the Arctic circle while attempting to rescue Matthew's father and a helicopter pilot.

Students: Fourth and fifth graders of average to high English reading ability, including advanced English-language learners.

Reading Goal: To understand and enjoy an exciting survival story.

Goal of the Activity: To help students understand how literature can be a medium for learning about the various ways people have of responding to similar situations and issues, and to provide *all* students with the opportunity to voice their opinions and work toward coming to a group consensus.

Rationale: *Frozen Fire* poses a number of questions worth pondering. One in particular arises from an incident in which Matthew discovers gold nuggets at a frozen waterfall. The boys have given up their search for Matthew's dad and are desperately trying to make their way back to Frobisar. Their food supply is nearly gone and death is imminent if they don't reach Frobisar soon. However, overjoyed at the fortune within his grasp, Matthew loads his pockets and backpack with the precious metal against Kayak's warning that the gold will be only a hindrance to their struggle to get home. Since most students this age are intrigued by the idea of instant fortune, the question "Should Matthew have taken the gold nuggets?" should make for a lively discussion.

Procedure: On the chalkboard, a transparency, or individual worksheets, duplicate the following chart.

Both Sides Chart

Reasons

_____		_____
_____		_____
_____	**NO** *Should Matthew have taken* **YES**	_____
	the gold nuggets?	
_____		_____
_____		_____

Conclusions

Pair students and explain that they are to discuss the pros and cons of Matthew's taking the gold nuggets. Mix English-language learners with native-English speakers. Encourage them to come up with good reasons for both sides of the issue and to write these down on a sheet of paper. Stress that initially the goal is to get down all possible reasons for and against taking the gold, *not* to support one position for the other. Explain that they might want to refer to their books but need only write key words or phrases in the appropriate column. They should to try and give an equal number of reasons in each column. Below are some sample responses.

Both Sides Chart with Sample Responses

Reasons

Didn't belong to him   *Didn't belong to anybody*

Were worthless in Arctic   *Would make him rich*

Kayak told him not to   *Would have made his dad happy*

NO   *Should Matthew have taken*   **YES**
the gold nuggets?

Would slow Matthew down   *Could buy things for Kayak's family*

Could cost him his life   *If he took only a few*

Would have been a little richer

Conclusions

After the partners have had a chance to jot down their reasons, pair one set of partners with another set. Ask the new groups of four students to compare their reasons why Matthew should or shouldn't have taken the gold nuggets. Explain to students that while the goal is to work toward a consensus, it is perfectly acceptable for members to disagree with that conclusion. Tell them that you will have a large group discussion at the end of the period in which dissenting views will be heard.

When the groups of four have reached their conclusions, select a spokesperson for each group or have them select their own. Give each group about three minutes to choose the one reason that best supports the group's conclusion, and have the spokesperson jot it down. When each group has chosen its reason, call on the different spokespersons to report their group's decision. At this time ask the spokesperson to also give any dissenting viewpoints and the support for these positions.

As a follow-up activity to the discussion web, you might want to have students write their individual answers to the question "Should Matthew have taken the gold nuggets?" and post these in the classroom for others to read.

Adapting the Activity: The *Both Sides* activity can be used any time students read material that raises a question that might evoke dissenting viewpoints. For example, in *In the Year of the Boar and Jackie Robinson* by Bette Bao Lord, Emily, the sixth-grade class president, is supposed to present Jackie Robinson with the key to P.S. 8, but lets Shirley Wong, the protagonist in the story, give the key instead. Students might use the discussion web to decide the answer to the question "Should Shirley have allowed Emily to give her the honor of making the presentation to Jackie Robinson?" Or after reading *The Kids from Kennedy Middle School: Choosing Sides* by Ilene Cooper, students might discuss the question "Should Jon have quit the basketball team?" Also, the discussion web can be modified to use across the curriculum. Suppose students have read a selection on the Civil War that discusses Stephen A. Douglas and Abraham Lincoln and their opposing views on the slavery issue. As a postreading activity, you might substitute the names DOUGLAS and LINCOLN for the YES and NO columns of the discussion web, write *slavery* in the box where the question usually goes, and have students discuss the two men's differing views on the issue.

Reflection: *Although the primary purpose of this activity is to discuss the pros and cons of an issue before drawing conclusions, in many cases this activity could generate further discussion, leading to a consideration of a story's theme. Such a discussion might be prompted by a question such as "Why did the author include this episode?" This in turn might lead to these considerations: "Was he trying to show the contrast between what has value in a wilderness survival situation contrasted to the values of civilization?' or "Was he making a statement about the cost of individual greed on collective survival?"*

Quality literature and nonfiction serve the purpose of generating and communicating ideas—ideas humans need to survive, to make strides personally and collectively. Discussion provides not only a forum to make ideas accessible to students but a way to take sparks and create flames.

DISCUSSION Sample Activity 4: *The Virtual Field Trip*

In this activity, adapted from one used by Cheri Cooke (2002), the teacher shows the students pictures from websites in order to provide a fuller sense of the cultural features in the topic being studied. She involves the students in small-group discussion using material from websites to engage the students in thinking about the text they are reading. The teacher structures the discussion in segments so as to make the activity easier and more "doable," providing one discussion prompt at a time. While in small groups, a recorder writes notes about the main ideas the students talk about. Finally, in a large group, reporters from each small group tell the main ideas they discussed, and the teacher invites the students to talk about any remaining questions they have about the reading.

Selection: In *"Jijan,"* by Rebecca Hanma, a young girl of Japanese heritage portrays the loss of her grandfather and of how the loss affected her life. Her grandfather died when she was 13, and she is the narrator, telling us the story 25 years later, after she has grown up. The author skillfully represents her "blended" faith—her understandings from church Sunday school and from the Buddhist faith.

Students: The students are seventh, eighth, and ninth graders in a Sheltered English classroom for two periods of the school day. The students are of different ethnic backgrounds, including Latino, South East Asian, Pacific Islanders, and Asian. All of the students have been in the United States for one year, beginning public school fully in Sheltered English instruction and gradually increasing the amount of instruction done in all-English settings. The students' conversational English is reasonably good, and their English-reading levels range from third to early high school level. Peers are studying religions of the world in their social studies classes and one of the books they are reading is *"Jijan."*

Reading Goal: The main goals of the reading are for students to learn about features of a religion that may not be familiar to them, Buddhism, and to better understand how some individuals, especially immigrants, often mix or blend aspects of their homeland cultures with those in their "new land" culture. Another goal is for the students to consider the idea that individuals, such as the author of this story, sometimes use writing to explain and explore aspects of their own lives.

Goal of the Activity: A main goal of this activity is for the students to realize that the Internet can help them to better understand other lands and cultures and that it can enrich their understandings from reading texts.

Rationale: English-language learners often feel "caught" between many cultures. Reading about how one individual maintained spiritual beliefs from two different cultures can provide fertile material for students to better examine their own beliefs and dilemmas in resolving, or not resolving, differences in outlooks and beliefs that can occur in their own lives. Also, raising their awareness of how to use the Internet to connect to their understandings from texts they read can provide them with a tool for reflection on, and comprehension of, future reading.

Procedure: The teacher did several prereading activities before the students read the book. She introduced the book by telling the students a little about the author and about the Japanese American theme of the book. She mentioned that the girl in the book took something of her grandfather's after he died so that she would be able to remember him well. The teacher also said that the girl is religious and that some of what she says about religion would be familiar, while other things would be unfamiliar to at least some of the students in the class. Part of the girl's learnings are in the traditions of the Buddhist faith, a faith that many Japanese adhere to. The teacher explained that Buddhists believe that dead ancestors look after their living relatives and guide and protect them, while the living pay tribute to them, honor them, and provide food for them.

Next, the teacher asked the class to consider whether they have any similar beliefs in their own cultures. One student referred to "All Saints Day" in his church, a day devoted to remembrance of the dead. Another student mentioned Memorial Day, when at the end of May, there is a U.S. holiday to honor people who died in wars. Another student talked about the TV show *Touched by An Angel,* referring to how angels help people at times of trouble.

The teacher then pretaught some of the vocabulary by showing the words and a sentence for each, asking the students to figure out the meanings of the words from the sentences. The words she taught were *exploits, premonitions, ritual, mangoes,* and *escalated.*

The students read the story silently, using a discussion guide provided by the teacher.

The teacher began postreading discussion by taking the students on a virtual field trip to Japan. She projected from the computer onto the wall screen and logged onto the site *http://web.missouri.edu/~c563382/P_Pages/Pictures.html.* She shows pictures of houses, bridges, Buddha, baths, castles, pagodas, and temples, and said something like "You can see from these pictures that an important part of the life of the Japanese includes their religion. As you learned before, one of the main religions practiced in Japan is Buddhism. Let's look at another website. We will read from a Japanese website and look at one of the religious handbooks. This handbook presents guidelines for many Buddhists living in Japan." The teacher moves to the website at *http://www.terakoya.com/index_e.htm.* She links to "ABC of Buddhist Practice, the Jodo Shinshu Handbook" and then to "Memorial Rites and Ancestor Worship." She scrolls to the following parts and reads:

Are Buddhist memorial rites acts of ancestor worship? Ancestor worship has two aspects. First, the rites are conducted as expressions of respect and gratitude to the deceased for the blessings and traditions left to us. In this sense it is not strictly a worship. As followers of the Buddha's teachings, of course, we must cherish this feeling.

When are memorial rites held? A memorial rite marking the death of the deceased not only calls for the adornment of the altar and the reading of the sutra but also is a precious occasion for recalling the cherished memories of the beloved and most of all to realize the blessings of the Light of Wisdom which embraces us all.

Traditionally, memorial rites are held from the afternoon for a period of a whole day and night on the day previous to that of the actual decease. Monthly rites are held on the memorial day each month and the annual rites are held on the day and month of decease. Besides these there are special rites held on designated years and these will vary according to local customs but usually the pattern that was set in China seems most prevalent. These are: 49th day rites (Expiration of probationary period); 100th day rites (100 days from death); 1st annual memorial (dated from death), 3rd, 7th, 13th, 25th, 33rd, 50th anniversary memorials (dated from death) and every 50th year thereafter. (The preceding sentence has been paraphrased from the original at the website.) Unless we keep the deceased committed to heart we are apt to forget, and a rite performed only when reminded loses its meaning.

The teacher asks the students to look back at pages 203 and 208 in the story and see if they now have a better understanding of why the time periods of 49 days and 25 years are important. She then reads the following quote and tells the class that the author is Buddhist:

My father and mother have taught me that it is important to honor our ancestors. Ancestors are the relatives who have lived before us, such as our grandparents and great-grandparents. On special days, we light incense in front of a picture of my grandparents. We leave treats of rice cakes in front of the picture. We also sing special songs and pray. (Quinn, 1996, p. 21)

The teacher asks the students to compare this quote from a Buddhist to the author's beliefs in the story, helping them to understand the author's "blended" religious beliefs.

The teacher places the students in small groups of three or four students. Once the students are in their small groups, the teacher asks them to choose a recorder and a reporter. The teacher then leads the students to discuss the following four questions in their small groups. She poses one question (sometimes reading aloud first), allows time for discussion, and then poses the next question, and so on. After stating each question, she also tells the groups that the recorder should write down the main ideas discussed in the group to bring back to the whole group.

Question 1

The teacher reads the following two quotes aloud:

> A stone for a pillow. It sounds odd to us, until we remember that very few people on this planet go to bed at night on soft pillows. In Japan the head-rest is often made of wood. In some countries it is simply the ground. I've tried a stone, not in bed, but late on a hot afternoon, when I call the dogs, and walk across the fields to the woods. Placed under the neck in just the right way, a stone can help me relax after a morning of typing—though I wouldn't want it for a whole night. But for a time to rest, to think, to let go and be, a warm, rounded stone can be a good pillow. (L'Engle, 1986)

> Sleeping with a wooden pillow is something the Buddha [a religious leader] himself recommended as a way to train ourselves in not oversleeping. *Mära* has no chance to take over the person who doesn't indulge in sleep, who is strong and active both physically and mentally. . . . Both wanderers and warriors slept with wooden pillows. (http://www.suanmokkh.org/archive/asiti/let2.htm)

Then the teacher asks, "How might these quotes help you better understand the grandfather in the story?"

Question 2

The teacher shows a chart with the following words and meanings and says, *Jiisan* means grandfather or male senior citizen. *Baka* means a fool or an idiot or a trivial matter or folly. *Denki* means electricity or light. Compare and contrast the words in the list above with the words as the narrator used them in the story."

Question 3

On the last page of the story, we read, "But Jijan, tell me, is it true? Was I stupid for taking your pillow? Is that why you don't talk to me?" Write a statement responding to the narrator's question. What would you say to her?

Question 4

The teacher refers to the last line of the story—"Jozu jozu—Jijan, that's all I have. Won't you tell me more?" What do you think the narrator means?

When the students have finished discussing all four questions, the teacher then calls them back into a whole group and asks the reporters to tell the main ideas from each group. She also asks the students if there is any part of it that they still find puzzling, and the whole group talks about those parts.

Adapting the Activity: "The Virtual Field Trip" could easily be modified to be used as a prereading activity by using pictures and quotes from websites to set up central ideas in the text. For advanced learners, either before or after reading a text, the teacher might ask the students to locate certain kinds of information on the web and write down answers to her prompt questions. The students could then bring their written notes about the prompts to small-group or whole-group discussions in class.

Reflection: *The more students can learn to connect ideas—between texts and between their lives and texts—the more their capacity to have broader and richer understandings. By connecting texts and pictures from the Internet with material they read in books as well as with their own personal experiences, English-language learners acquire sound means of building never-ending networks of outlooks and knowledge. Showing students how to extend their thinking about a text through using the Internet models use of a valuable tool for English-language learners.*

Writing

E. M. Forster said, "I don't know what I think until I see what I said." For many of us, that adage rings true. Writing is the twin sister of reading (Fitzgerald & Shanahan, 2000; Vacca & Linek, 1992)—a powerful way to integrate what you know and what you've learned as well as to find out what you really understand and what you don't. Writing is powerful because it requires a reader to actively manipulate information and ideas. Also, writing can be a terrific way for English-language learners to work out their own ideas without the additional demands of saying it orally.

Writing does not lie exclusively in the domain of postreading activities. Writing has its place as both a prereading activity—a tool for motivating, for activating background knowledge, for relating a selection to students' lives—and as a during-reading activity—a device for guiding students' thought processes as they build meaning from a text. As a postreading activity, writing can serve all the purposes we listed at the beginning of the chapter: demonstrating understanding of the information and ideas presented in a text; applying, analyzing, synthesizing, evaluating, and elaborating text information and ideas; and connecting information and ideas in a logical way. Writing also provides opportunities for students to extend ideas, to explore new ways of thinking, doing, seeing—to invent, evaluate, create, and ponder.

In discussing writing activities, we focus on two issues that really go hand in hand: purpose and audience. Why are we encouraging English-language learners to write; what purpose does the writing serve? For whom is the student writing—himself or herself or someone else?

Breaking down writing purpose into two broad categories—writing to learn and writing to learn about communicating with others—can help you identify the kinds of writing you might encourage students to do after they read a selection, as well as determine the appropriate audience for their writing. However, it is important to keep in mind that, whether students are writing to learn, to explore, or to communicate, they are actively manipulating ideas and language. Thus, learning is always taking place.

Shown below are writing activities appropriate for each of these purposes. The two sample writing activities described next illustrate just a few of the many types of writing that can be fruitfully incorporated into reading experiences.

Writing Activities for Learning About Oneself or the World

Audience: Self

Informational Writing

  Personal journals
  Diaries of daily events
  Free writing
  Learning logs
  Charts and diagrams
  Notes, summaries, time lines,
    and outlining

Aesthetic Writing

  Stories
  Poems
  Free writing

Writing Activities for Learning About Communicating With Others

Audiences: Teachers, other students, authors, family members, perspective employers, and the greater community of readers

Informational Writing
  Letters
  Reports
  Charts and diagrams
  Dialogue journals
  Essays

Aesthetic Writing
  Poetry
  Stories
  Plays
  Nonfiction
  Memoirs
  Biographies
  Essays

WRITING Sample Activity 1:
Informational Writing to Learn—*Compare/Contrast*

In *Compare/Contrast*, after completing a Venn diagram, students write three paragraphs to compare and contrast two topics.

Selection: The chapter "Members of Our Solar System" in *Science in Your World*. The last section of this chapter, "Other Members of Our Solar System," explains how comets and meteoroids are both members of our solar system. Comets, which come from the far outer edges of the solar system, have very large orbits, and are composed of ice mixed with dust particles. Meteoroids are small pieces of metal or rock that are scattered in different orbits around the sun.

Students: A small group of sixth-grade English-language learners working with the teacher of English-language learners. The students have been at the school for two years and have good conversational English. Their English reading levels are about one year below grade level. The reading selection is being used in their classrooms, and the teacher of English-language learners decides to supplement their regular classroom instruction and to help the boys to understand the passage better through this writing activity.

Reading Goal: To understand the concepts of comets and meteoroids, what part they play in the solar system, the differences they have, and the similarities they share in order to appreciate the intricacies and diversity of the universe as well as the laws that govern it.

Goal of Activity: To help students organize the textual information on comets and meteoroids showing similarities and differences in order to better understand what comets and meteoroids are and how they function as members of our solar system.

Rationale: Although they may have heard the terms, most students will probably not have a good understanding of exactly what comets and meteoroids are—in fact, they may well lump the two together. Some English-language learners may have the concept of comets and/or meteoroids, but not have their labels, either in Spanish or English. After having read the first part of the chapter, they will have learned about the planets, their differing orbits, and how the planets themselves share differences as well as similarities. Having students organize the textual information on comets and meteoroids by using a graphic aid such as a Venn diagram will aid them in understanding, remembering, and appreciating these two concepts. Completing a Venn diagram requires that students classify information to highlight differences and similarities. They then use the completed diagram to write three paragraphs, one describing the unique qualities of comets, one the unique qualities of meteoroids, and one the qualities they have in common.

Procedure: After students have finished reading the chapter on the solar system, briefly discuss some of the similarities and differences they found among the planets. Next, tell them that there is a good device—the Venn diagram—they can use for looking at the similarities and differences between things. Draw a sample Venn diagram such as that shown below on the board. Show students how they can use it in comparing and contrasting Venus and Earth, and have them refer to their texts as you complete the diagram together.

Next, explain that the Venn diagram is also useful in organizing their thoughts for writing an essay or writing to get a better understanding of a subject. Together write a short composition on Venus and the Earth, using the information recorded on the Venn diagram. Tell students that the audience for this composition is themselves— they are writing to get a better understanding of the two planets, not to communicate this information to anyone else. Also tell them this is just a draft, so they should "go for" ideas first and worry about spelling and mechanics second. This will help to alleviate some of the many cognitive demands the English learners are burdened with. Explain that in another draft they could go back and work on mechanical issues. As they write, they should add anything that connects the information they have written in the diagram with something they already know. An example of what these paragraphs might look like follows:

> *Venus is not a planet I want to live on. It's very hot and smells. There are clouds of sulfur.*
>
> *But Earth has great air. One reason is that it has water—water in river and sea and water in the air (clouds). Also Earth has life on it. There is life because there is water and a temperature that's not too hot or cold for people and animals. Earth also has a satellite called the moon.*
>
> *Venus has been called Earth's twin. They are nearly the same size. I can't see too much the same about these two planets. Oh, I guess they both go around the sun!*

Use the Venn diagram to compare and contrast as many other planets as you feel appropriate, composing three-paragraph expositions that use the information from the diagram. When students sufficiently understand the activity, have them develop a Venn diagram for comets and meteoroids and write three paragraphs using the information they have recorded on the diagram. Remind them that the audience for the composition is themselves—the purpose of writing is for a better understanding of comets and meteoroids.

Adapting the Activity: Venn diagrams are particularly useful for writing-to-learn with expository texts in which the author has presented material that can be compared and contrasted, but they can also be used with narratives. Students can use them to analyze differences and similarities between characters in the same story or to compare and contrast characters in different stories. For example, you might have students select two opposite types of women after reading *Fiesta Femenina: Celebrating Women in Mexican Folktale*, retold by Mary-Joan Gerson and illustrated by Maya Christina Gonzalez. The students could then use a Venn diagram to illustrate their differences and similarities. You might have students use a Venn diagram in writing about the two protagonists, Prince Brat and Jemmy, in Sid Fleishman's *The Whipping Boy*. The appropriate audience for this composition might be the teacher or classmates. Or students might use a Venn diagram in writing an essay comparing and contrasting Patricia MacLachlan's *Sarah, Plain and Tall* and *Prairie Songs* by Pam Conrad. The audience for this composition might be the authors of these two works. The students are attempting to communicate to the authors what he or she perceived as the similarities and differences in the two books. This will give students' writing a slightly different flavor compared to the writing they might do for themselves, their teacher, or their classmates.

Reflection: *This activity, in which a Venn diagram is used to facilitate learning and writing, is only one of many graphic approaches that might be used in dealing with information material. Instead of using a Venn diagram, students might record information in outline form using each of the members of the solar system as a subtitle and recording two or three important details about each member under the title. As they compose, students would then use the notes to write a paragraph on each topic. Or students might use a tree structure to show the hierarchical organization of a topic, producing a structure such as that below. Then they could use the tree to organize their writing.*

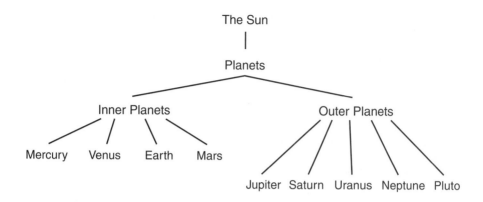

One matter to consider as you plan what sorts of graphic aids you might suggest students use for organizing their writing is how many different kinds of graphics you want to present. On the one hand, different graphics accomplish somewhat different purposes, and students appreciate variety. On the other hand, it takes time for students to learn to use different graphics, and introducing too many of them may take too much time or even be confusing for some students.

Whatever sorts of graphics students use, the audiences can be the students themselves, students in other classes, parents, and any number of others. With any writing activity, students should be aware of its purpose as well as the audience for whom the writing is intended, and writing that is intended for an audience other than the students themselves will require that the students revise their initial drafts.

WRITING Sample Activity 2:
Writing to Learn About Authors' Devices and Style—*Fanciful Writing*

In *Fanciful Writing*, after students read a selection that has some fanciful elements in it, the teachers asks the students to note some of the parts of the text that seem to be fantasy. She asks the class what effect these parts of the text have on them as readers and then leads a discussion of author's purposes in incorporating fanciful events and language into their texts. Finally, she asks the class to consider some other fanciful situations the author could have written for *The Upside Down Boy, El Niño de Cabeza* and to individually write some down.

Selection: *The Upside Down Boy, El Niño de Cabeza*, written by award-winning poet Juan Felipe Herrera and illustrated by Elizabeth Gomez, is written so that both English and Spanish appear practically side by side across pages. The story is a recounting of the year the author's migrant family settled down so that he could go to school for the first time. Juanito is confused by the new school and misses the solace of country life. Everything makes him feel out of sync—upside down. A sensitive teacher and a loving family help him to find a place in the life of his new world. The language of the book is playful and poetic, and the author builds a fanciful metaphor for Juanito's experiences in his topsy turvy world.

Students: The school is in a state where "special" instruction in a foreign language is mandated in kindergarten through 12th grades. In this school, Spanish is taught in pullout classes in kindergarten through 5th grade, twice weekly for periods of 30 to 50 minutes. Over the years, the Spanish teacher has typically taught a lesson using a book in Spanish about once a month. The students in this scenario are fifth graders. Most of them are native-English speakers, Anglos and Blacks of African descent. The remaining students are primarily native-Spanish speakers who have lived in the United States for varying numbers of years—some were born in the United States, some went to school in the United States for one or two years, and a few are recent arrivals to the United States. There are two Southeast Asian students who have been at the school for three years. The students' reading levels in English are diverse, ranging from first-grade level to fifth-grade level. Their Spanish reading levels from kindergarten level to second-grade level. None of the children in the room could read this text in Spanish on their own.

Reading Goal: The main reading goal is for students to relate to what it feels like to be in a new and strange situation and how difficult it is to adapt.

Goal of the Activity: The main activity goals are to help students understand both the concept of how authors incorporate fantasy into their writing and why they might do so. Another goal is to help students to understand the emotions involved for immigrants to the United States.

Rationale: Fantasy and incorporation of fanciful situations are common forms of writing in Latino culture, including writings for adults, and they are often used by authors in many other cultures. Students should be familiar with writing styles and forms that are common to their own and to other cultures. The role of fantasy in revealing emotions is often not well understood by many students. Similarly, the devices authors use to create fanciful situations and reveal emotions often are not apparent to students. Discussing the roles of fantasy in books and ways of using fanciful situations can help raise students' level of awareness as they read, and therefore help them to create deeper meanings.

Procedure: Speaking in Spanish, show the cover of the book and read the title. Ask the students what they think the book might be about, and write their ideas in notation form on the board in Spanish, speaking slowly and saying the word. Some students can only say a word or two in Spanish. Others speak entirely in Spanish. Tell the students to listen and look at the pictures as you read. Tell them that after you finish reading, they'll talk about which of their ideas were right. Read the book in Spanish, showing all of the pictures, and then have the class discuss their earlier ideas in relation to what they now know. On the board, cross out ideas that were wrong, and add to the board as necessary to fill in important points in the story. Next, create a chart with the following:

"Normal"	"Fanciful"
(street lamp) el poste del alumbrado	(golden cornstalk with a dusty gray coat) una espiga dorada de maíz con un saco gris polvoriento

| (cars) | (fancy melting cars) |
| coches | flamantes coches que se derriten |

| (tongue) | ("Will my tongue turn into a rock?") |
| la lengua | "¿Se me hará la lengua una piedra?" |

(clock clicks)	("clock…clicks and aims its strange
reloj marca el tiempo	arrows at me")
	"reloj…marca el tiempo y apunta sus
	extrañas flechas hacia mi."

Read the entries on the chart, pointing out what would be considered "normal" and how the author has turned the "normal" situation into a fanciful one. Ask the class to help you add to the list. Divide them into pairs and write down one or two examples. It might be helpful to read aloud, starting on page 10 and stopping at the end of each page, so that the pairs can hear the language again. As you read this time, you might read in English, so that the Spanish learners might have an opportunity to hear the words in their native language. After reading a few more pages and allowing ample time for the pairs to write down some of the fanciful situations, ask the class to help you add to the list on the chart.

Next, ask the students to look at the first few entries on the chart and ask why the author might have written the fanciful situations into the story. Lead the class to see that by choosing something "real" like a car passing by or a clock on the wall, and by shifting the reality a little, like making the car blur into something "melting," or making the clock demonically pointing to Juanito, the author creates a physical representation of Juanito's emotions, in this case, of feeling "displaced," "out of sync," and "on the spot."

Finally, the teacher asks the students to consider some other fanciful situations the author could have written for the book. For instance, as Juanito sits at his desk in his new classroom, perhaps the legs of his desk become animated and start to move and hop like a horse. Or as he watches his classmates play baseball, a ball is hit over the mountains. After the students have written some ideas, ask a few students to read what they wrote to the whole group. Close the lesson by summarizing the idea that authors sometimes take real physical situations and "twist" them so that they become "unreal," and that this can be called "fanciful" writing. Fanciful writing can be used as a metaphor for some emotion or feeling the author wants us to understand better. Also tell the students that they can use this device in their own compositions.

Adapting the Activity: *Fanciful Writing* could be used after reading just about any story that contains devices to elicit readers' understandings of a character's emotions. Stories could include fantasy and science fiction. You could ask students to extend their understanding of the devices by having them write a complete story in parallel to the one just read. For instance, after reading *The Upside Down Boy, El Niño do Cabeza*, students might write *The Upside Down Girl, El Niña de Cabeza*, about a girl from Kansas of African descent who moved to Guatemala.

Reflection: *Helping students to understand authors' devices can help them become better readers. By bringing authors' devices to light, you help students to become more metacognitive readers, and this in turn can help them to be more* *thoughtful and more analytical readers who create deeper and richer meanings for the texts they read. This postreading activity can also be a terrific transition into a set of new activities for helping students to develop their composing skills.*

Drama

Drama is a natural part of childhood. As soon as their language and social skills begin to develop, many children act out scenarios and routines from their everyday life, taking on the roles of adults and other children in those scenes. Depending on their cultural background, some play "house," "my family," "doctor," or "school" with their playmates. Some use props and enact dramas with their dolls, trucks, cars, or plastic figures of their favorite cartoon, movie, and TV characters. Others act out stories using drawings that detail the scene. Not only are children participants in these playtime dramas, but also their creators. Through drama, the child is translating what he or she knows about the world into oral and body language (Collins, 1992).

Drama as a postreading activity encourages English-language learners to extend existing meanings and generate new ones. And it is fun—a highly motivating way to involve students in all of the cognitive tasks we listed at the beginning of the chapter: recalling, applying, analyzing, synthesizing, evaluating, and creating. Drama can also be a boon to English-language learners who are just beginning to learn English because they can learn ideas through watching them being enacted, and they can also learn through their own dramatic participation. Be careful, however, to remember that some new English learners will be shy about participating. These students can be encouraged to participate and supported if they do so, but they should not be forced to engage in the activity.

In postreading dramatic activities, students create settings, characters, dialogue, action, and props by combining the meaning they have constructed with the text, the resources available to them, and their own ideas to produce a "play," using their bodies and voices to communicate. This play might consist of a 1-minute pantomime involving just one "actor" or a 50-minute production of *The Best Christmas Pageant Ever* involving the entire class, props, costumes, and lighting.

Dramatic activities can emerge from fiction, nonfiction, or poetry. Two fifth graders might play the parts of Gilly and Miss Ellis, Gilly's caseworker, and dramatize the opening scene from Katherine Paterson's *The Great Gilly Hopkins*; an entire class of second graders might dramatize Indian tigers after reading or listening to Ted Lewin's informational picture book

Tiger Trek; and small groups of first- through third-grade students might gather to dramatize their favorite poems in Jack Prelutsky's *Tyrannosaurus Was a Beast*.

As English-language learners dramatize informally, they are involved in all sorts of decision making. What will I say? How will I say it? What actions and facial expressions will I use? What costumes or props will I need? Will I need to play more than one part? To illustrate that last question, let us say two first graders are dramatizing "The Kite" from Arnold Lobel's *Days with Frog and Toad*, which has two main characters, Frog and Toad, and a choir of minor characters, the Robins. One student might take the part of Frog and the other Toad and both might assume the roles of the Robins. Problem solving, which requires their using the resources available to them to devise their own unique interpretations of a selection, is part of the creative process.

Although an audience is sometimes appropriate, dramatizations don't require one. The audience may consist of only the students who are enacting the drama. After reading a chapter in a history or social studies text, students might pair up, choosing two historical figures to portray. After reading a chapter that discusses the sixties, for example, two fifth or sixth graders might decide to portray Martin Luther King, Jr., and Lyndon B. Johnson. First they need to collect data on these individuals—policies, actions, attitudes, style of speech—and then select a topic or topics to discuss. What would Martin Luther King, Jr., and Lyndon B. Johnson talk to each other about? For the dramatization, students carry on a conversation posing as these individuals. This dramatization could end here, or students might choose to perform it for other students, or an even greater audience such as another class or parents. Drama doesn't need to, but it can move beyond the school walls to places such as day care centers or nursing homes.

With dramatic activities you will play a variety of roles, again depending on the students, the selection, and the purpose the activity. Occasionally you might need to assume the role of director/producer, but more often your job will be that of facilitator/encourager. In that capacity, you might find yourself stepping in to fill the role of the Troll in *Three Billy Goats Gruff*, reading passages from *The Magic School Bus* series by Joanna Cole, helping build a puppet stage or sew puppets, or showing students how to make "princess" hats for Ruth Sanderson's version of *The Twelve Dancing Princesses*.

Drama has great potential for showing English-language learners that language can be transformed, and ideas can be seen, heard, and felt, as the next sample activity demonstrates.

DRAMA Sample Activity: *History Comes to Life*

In *History Comes to Life*, groups of students dramatize scenes from a biography.

Selection: *Harriet Tubman: Call to Freedom* by Judy Carlson. This biography chronicles the extraordinary life of Harriet Tubman, a woman of African heritage who had been enslaved herself. She was a person of invincible spirit and determination who worked unceasingly to bring freedom and justice to slaves. Harriet was born in Maryland in 1820 or 1821 and died in Auburn, New York, in 1913. For almost a century, Harriet fought for the ideals she believed in: human dignity, justice, and equality. Strong in body and spirit and empowered by an unshakable faith in God, Harriet led hundreds of slaves to freedom through the underground railroad, was an eloquent antislavery spokesperson, worked in the Union army as a nurse and a scout, established schools and homes for the poor, and supported the rights of people who had been enslaved and women to vote.

Students: Sixth graders of low to average English reading ability. Four of the students are English-language learners who have been in the school system for two years and have excellent conversational English.

Reading Purpose: To learn more about the plight of slaves during the mid-1800s and to appreciate and be inspired by the courage, resourcefulness, and commitment of Harriet Tubman.

Goal of Activity: To provide students with an opportunity to practice their problem-solving and decision-making skills, to come to a better understanding of Harriet Tubman and the times and conditions in which she lived.

Rationale: To successfully dramatize a scene from the biography, students must combine their knowledge of what they know about dramatizing events and portraying characters generally with the specific information in the text. They need to make decisions about what events to portray, what characters to include, who will play these characters, what action will take place, what will be said, which props, if any, will be used, and a number of smaller matters. These are the sorts of cognitive tasks students are continually involved in both in and out of school. Providing a supportive setting in which children can succeed at these tasks is one way to increase their confidence and encourage risk tasking—certainly a desirable goal since children's willingness to take risks is crucial to their growth in skill and knowledge.

Procedure: After the students have read the biography and you have spent some time discussing its main themes and issues, explain that students are going to form small groups and dramatize various events in the book. Have them suggest incidents from the biography that might work as dramatizations and write these on the chalkboard. Along with these incidents write the number of actors required for each. Some of these incidents could include the following:

> Harriet being sent off at age 6 to work for the Cooks, getting the measles, and being brought home sick. *Roles needed:* Mr. and Mrs. Cook, Harriet, Harriet's mom.

> Harriet working for Miss Susan, trying to dust and take care of the baby, stealing the sugar cube, running away. *Roles needed:* Miss Susan, Miss Emily, Harriet.

Harriet's family life—eating together, singing, talking, listening to Bible stories. *Roles needed:* Harriet, Old Rit, Ben, brothers and sisters.

Harriet trying to help the slave escape and getting hit with the two-pound weight. *Roles needed:* Harriet, slave, overseer, Old Rit, Ben.

Harriet leading her brother James and two friends to freedom. *Roles needed:* Harriet, James, two friends, search party, Thomas Garrett.

As a class, discuss why these incidents would or wouldn't work as dramatizations *(interesting action to portray; too much action; not enough action; good speaking parts; not enough dialogue; too much dialog; reasonable number of characters in scene; too many characters; not enough characters; workable setting or settings; too many changes of scenes).*

Divide the class into groups of two to six students to work on a dramatization of their choice. Remind students that they will need to cooperate in assigning roles. Explain that for a successful dramatization they will need to be thoroughly familiar with the incident they are dramatizing and that each person will need to know what he or she is to say and do. They may want to write scripts that detail the dialogue and summarize the action. Help the English-language learners to take on roles with which they will be comfortable. Some may not feel comfortable in roles that require considerable speaking, while others may relish the chance.

Be available as the groups are working to encourage creative thinking, praise cooperative behavior, and supply resources. Use one or two class periods for students to prepare the dramatization and another to present them.

Adapting the Activity: This kind of activity in which students are recreating through drama events from a specific selection can be used with any number of expository or narrative works that contain memorable characters and vivid, portrayable scenes: biographies, history texts, contemporary stories, folktales and fairy tales. For older students, selected passages such as the opening from Albert Marrin's *Sitting Bull and His World* would make for meaty dramatic renditions. Folklore also lends itself well to dramatic representation. For instance, selections from *Fiesta Femenina: Celebrating Women in Mexican Folktale*, retold by Mary-Joan Gerson and illustrated by Maya Christina Gonzalez, might work well for dramatic rendition. Some of the scenes from *Fourth Grade Rats* by Jerry Spinelli might be fun for third or fourth graders to enact because they will be able to identify so well with the protagonist Suds and his need for peer approval, his desire to "grow up," to have some status, and his feelings of self-doubt. Fourth to sixth graders might enjoy dramatizing scenes from the action-packed fantasy novel *Amy's Eyes* by Richard Kennedy, and first graders might enjoy dramatizing *The Five Silly Fishermen* by Roberta Edwards. Finally, if you have enough native-language speakers of a language other than English in your class, have those students act out the piece in their native language. If the piece has quite a bit of action and involves considerable facial expression and gesturing, the students could perform it for another class. Even if students in the other class do not understand the language, they should be able to glean the main meanings from the acting.

Reflection: *Prerequisite to dramatizing scenes is spending some time discussing character and theme as well as pinpointing those events and scenes that work best for dramatizing. Also, students are bound to get frustrated if they don't know or can't* *do what is expected of them. Thus, giving them clear explanations of what it is they are to do and how they are to do it before they form their groups is imperative for success. You can help the English-language learners to participate by supporting and encouraging participation and enabling those who are uncomfortable with speaking English to participate in nonspeaking roles or to help with props. Additionally, students need to know the purpose of these dramatizations. Are they to work out a scene that can be presented to other students, or are they simply doing it for the enjoyment and understanding it will bring to them?*

The chance of a successful experience can also be enhanced by putting students into heterogeneous groups. Dispersing your leaders, more competent readers, most creative thinkers, diplomats, and good followers among the groups can help ensure that groups achieve their goals. Sometimes you may want to disperse English-language learners into various groups so that each can find a unique place. Other times you may want to place two or more English-language learners who speak the same native language in the same group so that they can help each other out. Each student should be aware of the unique contribution he or she is able to make to the group effort and that his or her contribution is both necessary and appreciated. Adam may not be "the best reader," but he has a heck of a voice and can be a model of "good voice projection" for the rest of the group. Adam's gift should be recognized and encouraged. Cudos should not be handed exclusively to those who "know the most" or "read the best." If throughout the year students are encouraged to discover what their particular talents are and given opportunities to hone and polish these talents, when it comes time for group work they will be ready to put these talents to work in achieving the group goal. Working toward achieving a common goal with their peers helps students realize that each person's contribution is important toward achieving that goal; in this case, putting together a dramatization that makes sense in terms of its faithful rendition to the text and students' expectations of what drama should achieve.

Also, dramatizing scenes from historical pieces immerses students in a powerful context for understanding unique times and unique people. In putting themselves in the roles of historical characters, students can discover some common threads that weave through different ages, stories, and characters—humans' desire for respect, love, freedom, justice. We hope they will also discover the attributes that allow individuals to achieve these goals—courage, diligence, concern for others—and also identify those attributes that work against achieving them—greed, self-interest, ignorance, hatred.

Having students act out pieces in their native language benefits the students by enabling them to use their full range of understandings as they dramatize the piece. It also helps them and their audiences who do not speak the language to better understand how language communication involves more than just hearing and speaking words. Also, members of an audience who do not speak the language can experience at least a little of what it feels like to be in a circumstance where you want to understand but can not speak the language yet. Such empathy building can have an impact on social and political relations in a school.

Artistic, Graphic, and Nonverbal Activities

In this category, we include the visual arts, music, and dance—each a specialized language that can be used in response to printed and spoken communication. Visuals, in particular, have been emphasized as especially important by professionals who work with English-language learners (Gersten & Baker, 2000). Also, a few studies have supported the contention that visuals increase learning (Rousseau, Tam, & Ramnarain, 1993; Saunders, O'Brien, Lennon, & McLean, 1998). In this section, we include response activities that involve the creation of media productions such as audiotapes; videos; slide shows; visual displays such as bulletin boards, artifacts, and specimens; and visual representations of information such as graphs, maps, and charts. Each of these varied forms of expression provides students with a special way to deepen and broaden their understanding of the ideas and information found in the texts they read. Just as dramatization can be a great way to help English-language learners understand new concepts and enrich known concepts, so too might these varied forms of expression also support their learning. The varied forms of expression might serve as extra supports for learning through new modalities, and they can also provide ways in which English-language learners can learn, participate, and make contributions to the classroom community without the burdens that can be attached to speaking aloud or writing.

To illustrate how the languages of art, music, and dance can be connected to written and spoken language, we present the following example. Suppose that your third-grade class has just finished a unit on animals. Over a four-week period, they have read numerous fiction and nonfiction trade books, and you have read *The Story of Dr. Doolittle* by Hugh Lofting aloud to them as well. As a culminating activity, you read William Jay Smith's book of poems called *Birds and Beasts*. Next, you divide the class into three heterogeneous groups and assign them one of the three non-verbal expressive languages: art, music, or dance. Each group then decides which animal it will portray in their appointed "language" and brainstorms about what materials and approach they might take. For example, the art group might suggest watercolor painting, collages, scratch boards, paper sculpture, clay modeling, papier-mâché, or wood sculpture. After the students have brainstormed together and decided on their animal and some possibilities for depicting this animal in a visual way with the resources available, they then work individually, in subgroups, or pairs to create their animals using whatever medium they feel will best capture the essence of their animal.

The music group's goal is to create an instrumental piece to depict their animal. During their brainstorming session, students think about the musical resources available to them as well as the characteristics of their particular animal. They consider rhythm and percussion instruments and those that produce melody. Some of their suggestions might include drums, cymbals, sticks, sandpaper blocks, recorders, song flutes, xylophone, bells, piano, and keyboard. After they think about what animal they are going to depict and how they might depict this animal through music, they begin working in pairs or small groups to recreate their animal through music.

The dance group's goal is to depict their chosen animal through movement. During their brainstorming session, students offer suggestions about what body movements represent this animal. Their discussion involves both showing and telling, with these sorts of words describing the characteristics and movements of their chosen animal: slow, steady, heavy, swinging, head moving, tail swishing, clomp, clomp, clomp. The group might decide to work together to create one dance that represents their animal, or they might choose to work in pairs or subgroups.

After their brainstorming sessions, students spend an hour or so over two or three days to come up with nonverbal expressions of their chosen animals. On the fourth day they present their work; their animals come to life in visual art, in music, and in dance, and other students guess the animals they are depicting.

A similar approach might be used for any number of subjects or selections. A few possibilities for connecting art, music, and dance to reading are as follows:

✦   After reading several books on Native American culture, read the *Dancing Teepees* by Virginia Driving Hawk Sneve and have students choose a tribe or nation to depict in art, music, and dance.

✦   After reading folktales from many cultures, read the poem *Lord of the Dance: An African Retelling* by Veronique Tadjo and choose one culture to illustrate in art, music, and dance.

✦   After a unit on seasons, read Myra Cohn Livingston's *A Circle of Seasons* and have students choose one of the four seasons to illustrate in art, music, and dance.

✦   After a unit on feelings with middle-grade students, read Cynthia Rylant's *Waiting to Waltz: A Childhood* and have students choose one of the emotions of growing up to depict in art, music, and dance.

Books, journals, and periodicals abound with suggestions for artistic and nonverbal activities that students can do in your classroom. Because it is impossible to even begin suggesting all the possibilities or to describe the ones that might work best for you in your particular situation, with your particular students, we can only offer a sampling of ideas. Undoubtedly, you can think of many more immediately and will discover even more as time goes on.

On the next several pages, we have jotted down some of our ideas for implementing visual art, music, dance, and audiovisual presentations and displays. Think of these pages as formative. Use them to write down your own ideas as you read through the categories and examples. When you run across another idea someplace else, you might want to jot it down here also.

Potpourri of Visual Arts Activities

Learning Activities

After reading about art or an artist:
Invite a guest artist to demonstrate a technique a children's book illustrator uses.
See a film about an artist you have read about.
Visit an art museum or gallery.
Borrow paintings from the library.

Creating Activities

Kinds of activities
sculpting
origami
weaving
painting
drawing
carving
etching
macramé

What to Use
fingerpaints
watercolors
chalk, crayons
clay
wood
paper
magazines
objects from nature
material scraps
yarn, straw

What to Make
masks
murals
dioramas
collages
mats
quilts
posters
baskets
totem poles
pottery
puppets
costumes
props
scenery
jewelry

Potpourri of Musical Activities

Learning Activities

Learn
to sing or play a song—period songs after historical fiction
to play an instrument
about the instruments—go to hear an orchestra play, listen to recordings, invite a musician to class
about composers—listen to recording of their works, do research on a composer
about the kinds of music—contemporary, classical, jazz, rock, rap, country, gospel — go to a concert, listen to recordings

Creating Activities

Experiment
with rhythm and tempo
with percussion
with melody and harmony
with instruments, voices, and computer synthesizers

Create a song or poem about
horses (after reading *Misty of Chincoteague* by Marguerite Henry)
a famous person (after reading about Abe Lincoln or Michael Jordan)
a time in history (after reading about the expansion of the West)
a place (after reading about Japan)
a story character (after reading about Pippi Longstocking or Huckleberry Finn)
a feeling or mood (after reading poetry)

Create different kinds of songs about story characters: a jingle, a ballad, a funny song, a sad song, a happy song

Potpourri of Dance Activities

Learning Activities

See a dance:
Invite a person from an ethnic group to perform a dance.
Watch a film or video of a dance.
Go to a dance production—notice dance titles.
Invite a dancer to talk about "dance language."

Learn a dance
ethnic dances—Native American, Russian, Scottish, Polish, Hawaiian (invite a person from an ethnic group to teach a dance)
kinds of dances—square dance, period American dances from the 20s, 30s, 40s, 50s, 60s, 70s, 80s, and 90s.

Creating Activities

Invent a dance to show:
   a scene from a story
   a poem
   a character from a story
   a culture you have read about
   a subject you have read about: wind, turtles, exploration, dinosaurs, robots
   an abstract idea from a story you have read about love, friendship, courage, per-
      sonal growth

Potpourri of Audio Visual Displays

Create
   Videotapes
   Audiotapes
   Filmstrips
   Bulletin boards
   Charts
   Maps
   Graphs
   Diagrams
   Models
   Displays
   Scrapbooks
   Photo albums
   Board games
   Posters
   Time lines

ARTISTIC, GRAPHIC, AND NONVERBAL Sample Activity:
Worth a Thousand Words

In *Worth a Thousand Words,* students create a collage by cutting pictures from magazines that illustrate the concepts in *From Seed to Plant.*

Selection: *From Seed to Plant* by Gail Gibbons. *From Seed to Plant* is an outstanding informational book. The author does an exceptional job of conveying the concept of plant reproduction with simple straightforward prose and colorful illustrations. Parts of a flower are described, as well as the processes of pollination, seed dispersal, and germination.

Students: Second graders of average reading ability. One student is an English-language learner, recently arrived in the United States, who is just learning English. The student speaks a native Indian language, and has learned some Spanish. She sporadically attended a small school in a pueblo in Central America and has no prior experience with reading in any language.

Reading Goal: To learn how plants reproduce and to gain an appreciation for the creative processes at work in nature. A goal for the English-language learner is to learn to read two key words in the selection.

Goal of the Activity: To reinforce and expand on the concepts presented in the text and to encourage creative thinking and responding. A goal for the English-language learner is to understand one of the less complex ideas in the text—that plants can grow from seeds.

Rationale: Making a collage that represents concepts found in a text encourages critical thinking, since it requires students to make decisions about what to include and what not to include based on what they have learned from reading the text. In selecting pictures for a plant reproduction collage, students must think about all the elements that go into producing new plants and flowers. Making a collage also gives students an opportunity to express themselves creatively—something they may not have the opportunity to do as often as we would like.

Procedure: After students have finished reading the book, write these words on the board: *seeds, flowers, pollen, stamen, pistil, stigma, animals, birds, fruit, pods, streams, ponds, rivers, rain, soil, buds.*

Taking a word at a time, have students briefly tell what part each of these plays in growing a new plant. Put the words *birds* and *rain* on two index cards with pictures of each on their backs. Give the English-language learner the cards and point to each word as you say it, showing the picture on the back for each word, and ask her to point to each word and say it.

After students have had a chance to think about the role of each word, tell them they are going to make a collage that represents the "from seed to plant" idea that Gail Gibbons illustrates in her book. Explain that in creating their collages they will cut out pictures from magazines. In choosing which pictures they will include in their collage, they will need to decide if it represents a part in the "seed to plant" idea in Gail Gibbons' book. Tell them that doing this kind of thinking and decision making will help them understand better and appreciate how plants are produced. It will also give them a chance to think about how to use color, shape, and design to create something that is pleasing to look at. It is unlikely that the English-language learner will understand much from this explanation, but she will be able to participate in the group work. Be sure that one student in her group makes sure that she gets included and learns as much as possible.

If students haven't made collages before, show them an example (such as those in author/illustrator Eric Carle's picture books) and explain that a collage is made by pasting different items onto a piece of board or paper in a way that pleases the eye. Explain that for their collages, they will be cutting pictures out of magazines that illustrate things that are involved in making a new plant. They might create collages that are abstract—don't represent any particular object—or they might want to arrange their cut-outs in such a way that they represent something—some sort of flower or plant, or perhaps a scene depicting a landscape or garden. (If you have Eric Carle's books you could show how he creates scenes and objects using collages.)

Next, hold up a few magazine illustrations and ask students to suggest what they might cut from these pictures for their collage. Cut these out and demonstrate how they might arrange them.

Supply students with ample magazines, scissors, paste, and sheets of construction paper or tagboard on which to paste their pictures. After they have completed their collages, display them on a bulletin board. Keep a copy of Gail Gibbons' *From Seed to Plant* on display nearby also. Finally, show the English-language learner the two index cards with the words *birds* and *rain* on them and ask her if she can read the words.

Adapting the Activity: Collages of this type are an appropriate postreading activity for any selection that contains several concepts for which illustrations can be found. For example, after reading a chapter on medicines and drugs in a science text, sixth-grade students could make a collage by cutting out pictures in magazines as well as using real labels and parts of the packaging from these items. Students might, for instance, paste part of an Alka Seltzer package or the label from an aspirin box on a collage of common over-the-counter medicines. After reading *The Senses* by John Gaskin, third graders might make a collage representing each of the five senses. Magazines abound with pictures depicting some aspect of sensory experience. After reading Alice Provensen's *The Buck Stops Here: The Presidents of the United States,* in which the author illustrates the contributions of the presidents with a collage surrounding each, students might make a collage of artifacts and symbols that represent their own lives or perhaps someone whom they admire.

Reflection: Because we assumed that the second graders in this example had created collages before, very little was said about the techniques for creating an aesthetically pleasing composition. If students have had little instruction on what makes for a pleasing two-dimensional design—balance, color, and repetition, for example—then these ideas will need to be discussed. To help students develop an understanding of the difference between designs that "work" and those that "don't work," you can show them examples and nonexamples of eye-pleasing designs (shapes pasted haphazardly onto the paper, no repetition in shape or color, no unifying point of interest). Providing students with plenty of exposure to the quality art that abounds in children's literature is one way to provide students with excellent models, and of course working with illustrations rather than a second language gives English-language learners a chance to excel. (This is one good reason why picture books should be made accessible to students of all ages.) Another way is to display art work in your classroom. Reprints of well-known works are of course available at a relatively low cost at most discount stores and also through loan programs at many libraries. Wall calendars and appointment calendars are another good source for art reprints. Around December you might want to encourage students to check with their parents to see if they have any of these types of calendars and ask them to bring them to school in January. Display the calendar art around the room or create a bulletin board. Collecting old calendars is a wonderful way to build your own reprint library. Not only can these prints be used as examples of good art, but often their subject matter is appropriate to use for other reading activities.

Application and Outreach Activities

Books open doors. They invite us to step out, to go beyond what the text says to see for ourselves, to act on our newfound knowledge, and to apply

it in a unique way. In this sense, all of the previously mentioned categories in one way or another reflect the idea of going beyond the text to
explore other realms and other applications of information and ideas.

Activities that we are labeling specifically as "application and outreach"
endeavors are those in which students take the ideas and information
from a text and deliberately test, use, or explore it further. Students might
read an article on how to make friends, but the information has little
value unless students try out the author's ideas to see if they work. Students might read a story about making ice cream or an article describing
several science experiments, but it's not quite as much fun as actually
following the steps and eating the ice cream or doing the experiments in
Sandra Markle's *Science Mini-Mysteries* to see if they actually work. The
logical next step after reading about something is to try it out in the real
world.

It is not just "how to" books that invite real-world applications, however. A chapter on the environment in a science text may inspire students
to do something themselves to better care for the Earth. Or, after finishing a novel in which the main character has a disability, a reader might
change his or her attitude about persons with disabilities and begin to act
differently toward them. Application activities invite and encourage many
different kinds of personal and social action.

The fiction, nonfiction, and poetry that students read can open doors
to the wider world. Mary Ann Hoberman's poem "Cricket" from her book
Bugs might send them into summer fields to find out for themselves if a
cricket's wing can really "sing a song" or to the science museum to explore the entomology exhibit to find out if "a cricket's ear is in its leg."
Or, after reading Jane Yolen's *Owl Moon*, seven- and eight-year-olds might
beg their parents or grandparents to take them "owling" in the night
woods.

Outreach activities not only take children beyond the school walls to
explore a topic or idea further or to discover more, but also can inspire
them to social action. After reading Chris Van Allsburg's *Just a Dream*, in
which a child dreams of a future wasted due to poor management of the
environment, students might decide to write letters to state and local
representatives encouraging them to support environmental legislation
or develop an environmental ad campaign for their school or neighborhood. The letters and some of the ad campaign material could be in English-
language learners' native languages. Barbara Huff's *Greening the City Streets:
The Story of Community Gardens* might inspire urban readers to plan and
develop community gardens in their neighborhood. Or from reading Mem
Fox's touching picture book *Wilfrid Gordon McDonald Partridge*—in which
a young boy discovers a unique way to help the forgetful Miss Nancy
recapture her memories—students might be inspired to share the story

with residents in a nursing home or to try this memory-recapturing approach with an elderly relative or friend.

English-language learners will not always make the connections necessary to transfer ideas from the text to the real world on their own. By providing activities that demonstrate this connection, you can drive home a critical aspect of the nature of text—we should not be the same after we have read it. We are a little more than we were before. Our new selves contain new information and ideas that we can now use. The following activity shows one way students might apply what they have discovered in a text by reaching out to others.

APPLICATION AND OUTREACH Sample Activity: *Getting to Know You*

In *Getting to Know You,* students think about ways to get to know senior citizens better and plan ways to achieve this.

Selection: *China: A Portrait of the Country Through Its Festivals and Traditions* is from a series by Grolier, with each book focusing on a country. The selection the teacher has chosen from this book is about the Chinese New Year. The book tells of traditions, festivals, and songs from China. Colorful photographs and illustrations add appeal. It is the beginning of the new year in the United States, and the teacher has chosen this piece to show one example of how people of different cultures celebrate the new year. She also has chosen the selection to help all the students in her class understand the rich heritage of her English-language learners who moved to the United States from China.

Students: Fourth graders of mixed reading abilities. Two of the students are English-language learners who have been in the school district since second grade. The English-language learners' native country is China. They have good conversational English, are doing well academically, and read in English slightly above grade level.

Reading Purpose: To understand and enjoy an engaging selection and to learn about one way of celebrating the new year.

Goal of the Activity: To encourage students' understanding and appreciation of people who are a number of years older than themselves and to encourage students to understand and appreciate different cultural customs.

Rationale: Enlarging students' horizons about different cultural traditions is one way to help multicultural communities to learn about their own similarities and differences. Ideally, after reading this book and participating in this activity, students will come up with their own ideas of ways to reach out to others, in addition to having some of their stereotypes dispelled.

Procedure: After students have read the selection, talk about the ideas in the text, such as that the Chinese New Year takes place at a different time than the U.S. New Year, why kitchens have to be cleaned and debts paid, and that certain foods dominate the celebration. Ask the students to compare different features of the Chinese

New Year to the celebrations of the New Year that they have in their own homes and communities. If the idea doesn't come up, lead the students to the idea that the Chinese New Year is now celebrated in some parts of the United States, especially in big cities like New York and San Francisco where there are large communities of people with Chinese heritage. Then ask the students how they might interview older people in their own neighborhoods, at places where they worship, or in their families about how they celebrate the New Year.

Talk about what students might do as a group or as individuals to bring together seniors and young people in order to better understand celebrations from different cultures. Record their suggestions on the chalkboard or a chart. (You may need to remind students that they will need their parents' permission to do things like visiting or giving gifts.) If having a party for seniors is one of the students' suggestions, you may want to do this as a class activity. Students could invite seniors from their neighborhood, places of worship, families, or from a nearby nursing home. Together, students could plan a time and a place for their party, refreshments, activities, and decorations, as well as a list of questions to ask the seniors about how they celebrated the New Year in their family when they were little children.

Adapting the Activity: This type of activity can be used after reading any story that has content that can vary by culture. Postreading discussion could focus on similarities and differences across selected cultures in ways of celebrating and possible reasons for differences. The discussion could then move to why it matters that we learn about the ways other cultures celebrate, leading to an appreciation of how our lives our enriched by seeing through others' eyes and understanding them better. However, parties and other outreach activities such as letters, gifts, and visits should come out of a sincere spontaneous desire by the students, not as a teacher assignment. Outreach activities that focus on an elaborated perspective or attitude about other people or cultures might include having third or fourth graders invite a class of younger students (or older) to a "Getting to Know You" party after reading *Fourth Grade Rats* by Jerry Spinelli or inviting a guest from the Native American community to come to talk about Native American rites and traditions to a class of second graders after they have read the mystical story *Bring Back the Deer* by Jeffrey Prusski.

Reflection: Outreach activities can be preplanned, but often the best ones are generated from the students themselves as they respond to a selection. This is the ultimate goal of this kind of activity: to get students to make their own connections, to see how a text can build bridges to other ideas and other places. Still, the central theme here is scaffolding, and many students will require scaffolding to move from passive to active modes of responding to what they read—to reaching outward as a result of the inward effect reading has had on them.

Building Connections

The category of activities just discussed, application and outreach activities, offers English-language learners many opportunities to build connections. So why, you might ask, do we also include this section on building connections? We do so because a huge amount of what we have learned during the past 30 years about students' learning—from David Rumelhart's early work (1980) on schema theory to contemporary reports on teaching and learning by the National Research Council (Bransford, Brown, & Cocking, 2000; National Research Council, 1999), Snow, Burns, and Griffin (1998), the National Reading Panel (2000), and the RAND Reading Study Group (2002)—highlights the huge importance of children's store of organized knowledge to their learning and success in and out of school. Many authorities see a similar importance for English-language learners (Gersten & Baker, 2000). Building connections—establishing links among the vast array of schemas that English-language learners internalize—is important whether students are involved in reading narratives or exposition, factual material or fiction, or history, science, or any other subject.

Moreover, we want English-language learners to build connections in several directions. First, we want them to realize that what they bring to school—the wealth of out-of-school experiences that they bring when they enter first grade and that are constantly enriched each year—is relevant to their understanding and making sense of what they are learning in school; that, for example, the pride they felt when they were first allowed to go to the market alone can provide insight into a story characters' feelings when she successfully meets some challenge and may be a useful experience that they can use in their writing. Second, we want English-language learners to realize that the various subjects they deal with in school are interrelated in many ways. That, for example, the understanding of the American revolutionary period they gained in social studies can be used in understanding some of the motives of Johnny in Esther Forbes' *Johnny Tremain*. Third, we want students to realize that ideas and concepts learned in school are relevant to their lives outside of school; that, for example, a character's finding that persistence paid off in meeting her goal suggests that similar persistence may pay off for students in doing their homework and achieving their goal of graduating from high school, going to college, or attending a trade school.

We believe that very little of what we do as teachers is more important than helping students build these sorts of connections. The following activity provides one example of how we can do so.

BUILDING CONNECTIONS Sample Activity: *Problems and Solutions*

In *Problems and Solutions*, students identify the problems and solutions of a story's protagonist and compare and contrast those with problems and solutions from their own lives.

Selection: *Taking Care of Trouble* by Bonnie Graves. In this humorous chapter book, 11-year-old Joel is coerced by his best friend's older sister into watching her babysitting charge Tucker, AKA *Trouble*, while she goes to the mall to hear her favorite rock group perform. Joel, the only kid in Junior Adventurers (JAs) who hasn't earned his Emergency Preparedness badge because he panics in emergency situations, is sure there's going to be some sort of emergency he can't handle—just what he doesn't need the day before he's to take the Emergency Preparedness test for the umpteenth time. And pass it he must in order to go on the JA's mountain-biking adventure in the Rockies later that summer. Joel's worst fears, of course, come true. Tucker's toddler antics challenge him with a minor emergency at every turn. However, surprising himself, Joel rises to each challenge, proving to himself he is capable of handling emergency situations and giving him the confidence he needs for the upcoming test.

Students: Fourth graders of average English and Spanish reading ability in a bilingual class. The students have been in bilingual education since first grade. This lesson is conducted in English.

Reading Goal: To enjoy a lighthearted piece of literature and to make personal connections with the text.

Goal of the Activity: To help students better understand the connections between literature and life and more specifically connect the problems and solutions in a story with the problems and solutions that occur in their own lives.

Rationale: One of the characteristics of literature is that it allows readers to vicariously experience life's challenges and the rewards of meeting those challenges along with a story's protagonist. Taking students through an activity such as *Problems and Solutions* in which they compare and contrast the character's problems and strategies for solving them with their own problems and problem-solving strategies can help make students feel they are not alone in the kinds of challenges they face and also, perhaps, give them insights as to how they might go about solving similar problems that occur in their own lives.

Procedure: After students have finished reading this short chapter book, say something like "Joel, the main character in this story, sure had his share of problems in this story. Didn't he? How many of you have found yourselves in situations that caused *you* problems?" Your typical group of fourth graders will certainly answer affirmatively.

Ask, "What is a problem anyway?" Have students discuss what constitutes a problem. (*A situation that requires a solution.*) Have students give examples of problems that have come up in their own lives.

"Let's look at some of the problems Joel faced in the story *Taking Care of Trouble.*" Tell students you are going to read the first part of the story aloud, and as soon as they hear what they think constitutes a problem for the main character Joel they are to raise their hands. Read a page or so aloud until several students have identified a problem and have raised their hands. Ask students to share what they thought Joel's first problem was and why it was a problem. (*For example, it was a problem for Joel when he heard the girl next door scream because he thought it was an emergency of some sort and that he might be required to do something and Joel always freaked out in emergency situations.*)

Next ask, "What did Joel do about the problem?" (*Tried to duck out of sight.*) And, "Did Joel's solution solve his problem? Why or why not?" (*He didn't solve it by trying to hide, because the girl saw him, called to him, and asked him for help.*)

Put Problems and Solutions Chart 1 on an overhead projector and fill in the first row of blanks with students responses for the first problem encountered in the story.

Problems and Solutions Chart 1

Character's Problem	Why was it a problem?	How did the character try to solve the problem?	Was the problem solved? Why or why not?
He hears a girl scream.	He's afraid he'll be asked to help.	He ducks out of sight.	No, because the girl sees him and asks for help.

Ask students if they've ever found themselves in problem situations, what they did to try and solve the problem, and whether or not their actions were successful in solving the problem. Briefly discuss. Put Problems and Solutions Chart 2 on the overhead and write their responses in the blanks.

Problems and Solutions Chart 2

Character's Problem	Why was it a problem?	How did the character try to solve the problem?	Was the problem solved? Why or why not?
Mom asked me to go to the store for her.	I wanted to watch my favorite TV show.	I asked if I could go latert.	No, because she needed tortillas right away so she could fix our supper.

Read the next page or so in *Taking Care of Trouble* aloud and have students raise their hands when they hear what they think is the next problem the main character encounters. Continue filling in Problems and Solutions Chart 1.

Explain that literature often shows people dealing with problems similar to ones readers encounter. In *Taking Care of Trouble,* although Joel had lots of problems to deal with throughout the story, one problem was larger than the others, one he finally solved in the end. What was it? Discuss. (*Not being able to handle emergency situations, or lacking the confidence that he could.*) How did Joel solve the problem? (*By using his head and the resources at hand, by not giving up, and by taking his baby-sitting job seriously. In doing those things he proved to himself he was capable of handling emergency situations.*) Explain that one of the things literature does sometimes is show us people dealing with situations similar to ones we find ourselves in. Sometimes seeing the hero of a story solve his or her problems can inspire us to try and solve our problems in a similar way.

Ask students what were some of the things Joel did to solve his main problem. Write their suggestions on the board.

Didn't give up. Worked hard. Used his head. Used the resources he had. Tried to solve problem on own.

"Think of a problem in your own life you are trying to solve. Would any of the things Joel did be helpful in solving your problem?" Briefly discuss.

Adapting the Activity: Because most literature portrays a character faced with at least one main problem and several smaller problems to overcome as they try to solve the big one, this activity can be used with almost any piece of fiction. This activity could be modified to use with primary-grade children after reading the picture book *Lilly's Purple Plastic Purse* by Kevin Henkes. In this delightful tale, Lilly causes problems for herself when she brings her purple plastic purse to school and can't resist showing it off to everyone. Another good choice for primary students is *Circus Family Dog* by Andrew Clements and illustrated by Sue Truesdell. Here, Old Grumps the circus dog's cushy life is turned upside down when a younger dog, Sparks, bursts onto the circus scene. In adapting the activity for younger students, you may want to pare the problems listed on the chart to three, the one major one and two others that the protagonist faces in trying to solve the big one. For upper-grade students, a good choice for the *Problems and Solutions* activity is Will Hobbs' gripping survival story *Far North*, a 226-page novel in which two Native American boys struggle to survive in the Canadian wilderness after their plane crashes and the pilot dies.

Biographies for any grade level are also excellent choices for this activity since the subjects of most biographies are prime examples of problem solvers, people who have overcome numerous challenging obstacles in their noteworthy lives. For upper-grade students, this activity could be adapted to use after reading *Ida B. Wells: Mother of the Civil Rights Movement* by Dennis and Judith Fradin and for younger students reading Robert Coles' *The Story of Ruby Bridges,* illustrated by George Ford, a picture book that recounts the hostilities faced by 6-year-old Ruby Bridges, the first African-American girl to attend the Frantz Elementary School in New Orleans in 1960.

Reflection: *Because students don't always make the connection between their lives and the literature they read, it is helpful to provide an activity such as* Problems and Solutions *that will help them make these connections. During the discussion portion of the activity when students are talking about themselves and their own problems and solutions, sometimes they will forget the relevance to the story, will not, in fact, see how their problems and solutions are connected to the story characters' at all. Because this is often the case, we have found it necessary to help students make these connections by asking questions such as "How is the problem you just told us about similar to the one faced by our story character? How is it different? What did you do to solve your problem that was similar to the character's? Was there anything the character did that might have helped you in solving your problem?" Questions such as these help connect students' lives to the literature and to school more generally, a particularly important goal for English-language learners, who may find school a rather distant place.*

Because some students may be reluctant to share their own problems, we have also found it helpful to invite students to suggest problems and solutions from people they know—anonymous family members or friends. They don't need to identify these people, just the problems and solutions.

Reteaching

One of the advantages of categorizing ideas is that it allows us to focus our thoughts, to structure and order them so that we can see relationships among ideas. Through this mental effort, logical patterns of organization will often emerge and with them a workable framework—a structure that will help us move ideas from the abstract to the concrete and suggest ways of implementing them in real-life situations, in this case, the classroom. The disadvantage is that categorizing can sometimes lure us into thinking ideas can be pigeonholed. They cannot. When dealing with such a complex and organic process as teaching, we need to search for models that will help guide our thinking and suggest ways for effectively designing and implementing instruction in the classroom. But because teaching is so complex and organic, any kind of order, structure, or model can only serve as a guide, a beginning, a framework. Coming at last to the final category of our postreading activities—reteaching—we are reminded of that truth.

In our ordering of activities, we have placed reteaching in the postreading category. However, as anyone who has spent even an hour in the classroom knows, reteaching is an ongoing process. Teachers, as the artists they are, are constantly assessing the efficacy of their instruction. "Are the students understanding what I'm saying and doing? Do I need to try another approach?" Teachers are continually using the feedback they receive from students to modify their approaches *as they teach*. Sometimes, however, after the entire lesson has been completed, and even though the teacher has tried her best to ensure that all students succeed, some still fall short of their goals. When this happens, reteaching is called for.

In general, reteaching might be necessary when students, after reading a selection and engaging in various activities, have not reached their reading goals. If the goal was for them to recall the organs of the human body and understand their functions, and discussion, questioning, or writing activities indicate that students did not achieve this goal, then reteaching is in order.

For English-language learners, the decision to reteach is often dependent on their English reading level and the amount of time they have been learning English. As we've said before, new English learners cannot be expected to learn everything all at once. So, especially in the beginning, for them, the teacher may focus on subsets of goals, not the entire set that is expected for the rest of the class. There will be times when you think a student can meet one of your goals, but he doesn't, and you will want to reteach for that concept. At other times, you may decide after a lesson that you set the subset of goals too high for certain English-language learners. In this case, you won't want to reteach. As we've said often before in this book, it may boil down to your ability to find the student's zone of proximal development. If you think you set the right goals—that is, if the goals were in the "zone"—then you probably will want to reteach.

Reteaching will often focus on encouraging students to self-evaluate, to become metacognitive readers. After all, while the teacher is there to encourage and assist, it is the student who is ultimately responsible for his or her own learning. Activities that encourage English-language learners to ask questions for themselves can help nudge them in the direction of being responsible, active readers. Here are some of the questions students might be asked to consider after not understanding the information in a text about the organs of the body.

+ Why didn't I understand what the author said about the way the heart functions? Were there too many words I didn't know? Was I reading too fast? What might I do to understand the information?

+ Was I concentrating on what the author was saying or was my mind wandering? What might I do to help me concentrate?

Help English-language learners see the importance of asking these sorts of questions and suggest possible strategies for students to use:

+ Adjust your reading speed to reflect difficulty of material.

+ Write down key words or phrases.

+ Draw a map to show the relationship among the ideas in the chapter.

+ Tell the teacher the book is too hard.

Such assistance will foster the development of readers who know how to construct meaning from text—how to be co-partners with the authors and with the teacher. Let students know their job is just as important as the author's and the teacher's. Without their own effort, no communication takes place, no meaning is born, no idea comes to life. The words exist as mere marks on a page.

In addition to encouraging metacognitive thinking in English-language learners, reteaching activities might include your retracing the steps of a specific activity with students to see what went wrong and where. Perhaps students had difficulty completing a reading guide or answering postreading questions. In these cases, reteaching might include discussing with students the problems they had, why they had them, and then reviewing the purposes and steps involved in completing the guide or answering the questions. During this review process, you might decide to alter the approach of the original activity to reflect the new insights the discussion revealed or to create a totally different activity. Alternately, you might have students simply repeat the original activity with their new level of understanding. The purpose of this approach—discussing the problem and then modifying the activity, creating a new activity, or repeating the original one—is to give students another opportunity to succeed.

RETEACHING Sample Activity: *Play It Again, Sam*

In *Play It Again, Sam,* a previous lesson is repeated with those students who didn't achieve the goals of the activity.

Selection: *Frozen Fire* by James Houston. *Frozen Fire* is the story of Matthew Morgan and his Eskimo friend Kayak, who battle to stay alive in the harsh Canadian wilderness close to the Arctic circle while attempting to rescue Matthew's father and a helicopter pilot who are lost.

Students: Fourth and fifth graders of average to high English reading ability, including advanced English-language learners.

Reading Goal: To understand and enjoy an exciting survival adventure story.

Goal of the Original Activity: To help students understand how literature can be a medium for understanding the various ways people have of responding to similar situations and issues, and to provide *all* students with the opportunity to voice their opinions and reach their own conclusions.

Goal of Reteaching Activity: To make sure all students have the opportunity to successfully draw their own conclusions about ideas presented in the text.

Rationale: In the *Both Sides* postreading discussion a handful of students had problems coming up with more than one or two reasons to support their responses to the question "Should Matthew have taken the gold nuggets?" By repeating this activity in a supportive setting, students have the opportunity to review procedures or concepts not grasped in a previous lesson and to achieve success.

Procedure: On the chalkboard, overhead, or a handout, provide students with a copy of the original discussion web. Then read the section from the novel aloud in which Matthew finds the gold nuggets. After each page or so, pause and let students think about the question "Should Matthew have taken the gold nuggets?" and have them suggest reasons why Matthew should have taken the nuggets or why he shouldn't have. Write these on the chart or have students record them.

For example, below is an excerpt from the text that might support the position that Matthew *shouldn't* have taken the nuggets and therefore belongs in the NO column.

> Matthew pushed up the right sleeve of his parka shirt and sweater as far as he could and, lying on the ice, reached down into the water.
>
> "Wahh! You're acting crazy," whispered Kayak. "You'll freeze your arm off, freeze yourself to death."

Write a word or phrase in the NO column that supports the position that Matthew should not have taken the nuggets, as shown below.

Reteaching the Both Sides Activity

Reasons

<u>freeze yourself to death</u>   _____

_____

_____   **NO**   *Should Matthew have taken*   **YES**   _____
                                   the gold nuggets?

_____   _____

_____   _____

Conclusions

Proceed similarly with the remaining pages, encouraging each student to partici- pate in giving his or her responses. After you have finished reading aloud and stu- dents have provided several responses for each column, have each student write his or her own conclusion based on the chart you have constructed together. Then have each student choose the reason that best supports his or her answer. Let students tell what reason they have chosen and why, and be sure to commend them for their efforts.

Adapting the Activity: *Play it Again Sam* can be used whenever students haven't achieved their reading goals and repeating that activity with assistance from you will help ensure a successful experience. For example, let us say some students had problems answering some of the questions in the *Yellow Brick Road* postreading questions. Meet with those students, find out which questions posed problems, and read aloud parts of the story that might provide the answers, lead students to dis- cover the answers. Alternately, if some students had difficulty writing paragraphs using the Venn diagram in the *Compare/Contrast* activity, meet with them and re- view the procedures for gathering information on the diagram and the procedures for using that information in their writing.

Reflection: *A reteaching activity of this sort in which you are primarily repeating the original procedure with students is helpful when they are likely to profit from addi- tional exposure and practice of a particular activity. Sometimes, however, a reteach- ing activity will involve trying a whole new approach. In this case, you will toss out your original activity and return to your primary reading goal. For the folktale* The Runaway Rice Cake, *the purpose might be "To understand and enjoy a story in the folktale tradition and to learn some of the customs and events surrounding the Chi- nese New Year."*

Postreading: A Final Word

Many of the postreading activities described in this section have been traditionally thought of as "enrichment" activities. And indeed they are, for they do "enrich" the reader. But we need to be careful when we use this label that we are being *inclusive* and not *exclusive* in selecting stu- dents who will be enriched. If we think of *all* students who read as *rich*— those who soar as well as those who flounder, those who are experienced with the language and those who are new to it—then we need to be certain to provide activities that will enrich them all. Sometimes, English- language learners who face the many challenges associated with learning a new language, native-English speakers who struggle with the basics, and students who have not acquired "grade-level" skills have been left out of these activities and thus not been allowed the opportunities for growth that enrichment activities can provide. We believe that all stu- dents deserve and will benefit from a variety of postreading activities and should be given opportunities to explore as many of them possible. Activities that students engage in after reading drive home the fact that reading has purpose—they can actually *do* something with the ideas in books. They can make connections between what they know and what they discover in texts and apply that new knowledge so that their lives become more enjoyable, more productive, and more meaningful—*enriched*, if you will.

References

Adler, M. J. (1982). *The Paideia proposal.* New York: Macmillan. The seminal work on the Paideia instruction.

Adler, M. J. (1983). *Paideia, problems, and possibilities.* New York: Macmillan.

Adler, M. J. (1984). *The Paideia program.* New York: Macmillan.

Alvermann, D. E. (1991). The discussion web: A graphic aid for learning across the curriculum. *The Reading Teacher, 45,* 92–99. A complete description of this very useful graphic aid and the teaching procedures that accompany it.

Alvermann, D. E., Dillon, D. R., & O'Brien, D. G. (1987). *Using discussion to promote reading comprehension.* Newark, DE: International Reading Association. Although some of this is most appropriate for high school students, much of it applies to younger students. It is particularly useful for discussion of informational texts

Anderson, L. W., & Krathwohl, D. R. (2001). *A taxonomy for learning, teaching, and assessing.* New York: Longman. A substantially revised and much enlarged version of Bloom's *Taxonomy of Educational Objectives.*

Beck, I. L., & McKeown, M. G. (1981). Developing questions that promote comprehension: The story map. *Language Arts, 58,* 913–918. Discusses problematic approaches to selecting and sequencing and offers a valuable alternative.

Beck, I. L., McKeown, M. G., Hamilton, R. L., & Kucan, L. (1997). *Questioning the author: An approach for enhancing student engagement with text.* Newark, DE: International Reading Association. An in-depth description of the Questioning the Author approach to fostering a deep and thorough understanding of text.

Beck, I. L., McKeown, M. G., Hamilton, R. L., & Kucan, L. (1998). Getting the meaning. *American Educator, 22,* 66–71, 85. Describes a specific approach, questioning the author to fostering deep and thorough understanding of text.

Billings, L., & Fitzgerald, J. (2003). Dialogic discussion and the Paideia Seminar. *American Educational Research Journal, 39,* 907–941.

Bransford, J. D., Brown, A. L., & Cocking, R. R. (2000). *How people learn: Brain, mind, experience, and school* (expanded ed.). Washington, DC: National Academy Press. A panel report on issues in learning.

Chamot, A. U., & O'Malley, J. M. (1996). The Cognitive Academic Language Learning Approach (CALLA): A model for linguistically diverse classrooms. *Elementary School Journal, 96,* 259–274. Describes a popular approach for teaching English-language learners in which discussions play a significant role.

Collins, P. M. (1992). Before, during and after: Using drama to read deeply. In C. Temple & P. Collins (Eds.), *Stories and readers: New perspectives on literature in the elementary classroom* (pp. 141–155). Norwood, MA: Christopher-Gordon. Excellent discussion of ways in which dramatic activities can help children explore literature deeply.

Cooke, C. L. (2002). *The effects of scaffolding multicultural short stories on students' comprehension, response, and attitudes.* Unpublished doctoral dissertation, University of Minnesota, Minneapolis. Shows very positive effects of using SREs with multicultural stories.

Echevarria, J. (1995). Interactive reading instruction: A comparison of proximal and distal effects of instructional conversations. *Exceptional Children, 61,* 536–552. A study of the effectiveness of the instructional conversation format.

Fitzgerald, J. (1993). Literacy and students who are learning English as a second language. *The Reading Teacher, 46,* 638–647. Addresses questions commonly asked by teachers; provides research-based guidelines and instructional practices for helping English-language learners' reading.

Fitzgerald, J., & Shanahan, T. (2000). Reading and writing relations and their development. *Educational Psychologist, 35,* 39–50. Reviews research on reading and writing connections and their development.

Gersten, R., & Baker, S. (2000). What we know about effective instructional practices for English-language learners. *Exceptional Children, 66,* 454–470. A synthesis of research and professional views on effective instructional practices with English-language learners.

Goldenberg, C. (1992–1993). Instructional conversations: Promoting comprehension through discussion. *The Reading Teacher, 46,* 316–326. Describes a format for doing discussions.

Johnson, D. W., Johnson, R. T., & Holubec, E. J. (1994). *The new circles of learning: Cooperation in the classroom and school.* Alexandria, VA: Association for Supervision and Curriculum Development. Although this book deals specifically with cooperative learning, it contains a great deal of useful information on group work more generally.

Klingner, J. K., & Vaughn, S. (1996). Reciprocal teaching of reading comprehension strategies for students with learning disabilities who use English as a second language. *Elementary School Journal, 96,* 275–293. A study of the effectiveness of instructional strategies with English-language learners.

L'Engle, M. (1986). *A stone for a pillow.* Wheaton, IL: H. Shaw. Spiritual reflections by the world famous children's author.

Muñiz-Swicegood, M. (1994). The effects of metacognitive reading strategy training on the reading performance and student reading analysis strategies of third grade bilingual students. *Bilingual Research Journal, 18,* 83–97. A study of instructional effects on English-language learners' reading.

National Reading Panel. (2000). *Report of the National Reading Panel: Teaching children to read.* Bethesda, MD: National Institute of Child Health and Human Development. A major review of research on teaching reading.

National Research Council. (1999). *Improving student learning.* Washington, DC: National Academy Press. A plan for research that would, as the title indicates, improve student learning.

Nurss, J. R., & Hough, R. A. (1992). Reading and the ESL student. In S. J. Samuels & A. E. Farstrup (Eds.), *What research has to say about reading instruction* (2nd ed., pp. 277–313). Newark, DE: International Reading Association. Provides practical, research-based ideas about reading instruction for English-language learners.

Quinn, D. P. (1996). *Religions of the world: I am Buddhist.* New York: Rosen. Describes the Buddhist religion.

RAND Reading Study Group. (2002). *Reading for understanding: Toward an R&D program in reading comprehension.* Santa Monica, CA: Rand Education. Available at http://www.rand.org/multi/achievementforall/reading/. A plan for research on reading comprehension.

Roberts, T. (1999). *The Paideia classroom: Teaching for understanding.* Larchmont, NY: Eye on Education. Explains and examines various aspects of doing a Paideia approach, including the Paideia Seminar.

Rousseau, M. K., Tam, B. K. Y., & Ramnarain, R. (1993). Increasing reading proficiency of language-minority students with speech and language impairments. *Education and Treatments of Children, 16,* 254–271. A study of different methods of vocabulary instruction with English-language learners.

Rumelhart, D. E. (1980). Schemata: The building blocks of cognition. In R. J. Spiro, B. C. Bruce, & W. F. Brewer (Eds.), *Theoretical issues in reading comprehension* (pp. 33–58). Hillsdale, NJ: Lawrence Erlbaum. One of the earliest descriptions of concept of the schemata, detailed and revealing.

Saunders, W., O'Brien, G., Lennon, D., & McLean, J. (1998). Making the transition to English literacy successful: Effective strategies for studying literature with transition students. In R. Gersten & R. Jimenez (Eds.), *Effective strategies for teaching language minority students* (pp. 99–132). Belmont, CA: Wadsworth. Describes literacy instructional strategies for students in transitional programs.

Snow, C. E., Burns, M. S., & Griffin, P. (Eds.). (1998). *Preventing reading difficulties in young children.* Washington, DC: National Academy Press. Seminal review of research on what makes early reading instruction and experiences effective.

Vacca, R. T., & Linek, W. M. (1992). Writing to learn. In J. W. Irwin & M. A. Doyle (Eds.), *Reading/writing connections: Learning from research* (pp. 145–159). Newark, DE: International Reading Association. Another good source on using writing to promote learning.

Children's Literature Cited

Ada, A. F. (1993). *Me llamo María Isabel.* New York: Atheneum. (English title is *My name is María Isabel.*)

Ancona, G. (2000). *Cuban kids.* New York: Marshall Cavendish.

Asimov, I. (1983). *How did we find out about genes?* New York: Walker.

Bang, M. (2001). *Tiger's fall.* New York: Henry Holt and Company.

Carlson, J. (1989). *Harriet Tubman: Call to freedom.* New York: Fawcett Columbine.

Carmi, D. (2000). *Samir and Yonatan.* Transl. by Yael Lotan. New York: Arthur A. Levine Books.

Cleary, B. (1991). *Strider.* New York: William Morrow.

Clements, A. (2000). *Circus family dog.* New York: Clarion.

Cole, J. (1990). *The magic school bus: Lost in the solar system.* New York: Scholastic.

Coles, R. (1995). *The story of Ruby Bridges.* New York: Scholastic.

Conrad, P. (1985). *Prairie songs.* New York: Harper & Row.

Cooper, I. (1990). *The kids from Kennedy Middle School: Choosing sides.* New York: William Morrow.

Davidson, M. (1986). *I have a dream, the story of Martin Luther King, Jr.* New York: Scholastic.

Delacre, L. (2000). *Salsa stories.* New York: Scholastic.

Edwards, R. (1989). *The five silly fishermen.* New York: Random House.

Fleischman, S. (1986). *The whipping boy.* New York: Greenwillow.

Forbes, E. (1971). *Johnny Tremain.* New York: Dell.

Fox, M. (1985). *Wilfrid Gordon McDonald Partridge.* New York: Kane/Miller.

Fradin, D. B., & Fradin, J. B. (2000). *Ida B. Wells: Mother of the civil rights movement.* New York: Clarion.

Fritz, J. (1987). *Shh! We're writing the Constitution.* New York: Scholastic.

Gaskin, J. (1985). *The senses.* New York: Franklin Watts.

Gerson, M. J. (retold by). (2001). *Fiesta femenina: Celebrating women in Mexican folktale.* New York: Barefoot Books.

Gibbons, G. (1991). *From seed to plant.* New York: Holiday House.

Graves, B. (2001). *Taking care of trouble.* New York: Dutton.

Grolier (Publisher). (1997). *China: A portrait of the country through its festivals and traditions.* Danbury, CT: Author.

Hackett, J. K., & Moyer, R. H. (1991). Members of our solar system. In *Science in your world.* New York: Macmillan/McGraw-Hill.

Hanma, R. (1993). "Jijan." In L. Yep. *American dragons: Twenty-five Asian American voices.* New York: HarperCollins.

Henkes, K. (1996). *Lilly's purple plastic purse.* New York: Greenwillow.

Henry, M. (1947). *Misty of Chincoteague.* New York: Macmillan.

Herrera, J. F. (2000). *The upside down boy, El niño de cabeza.* San Francisco: Children's Book Press/Libros Para Niños.

Hobbs, W. (1996). *Far north.* New York: Morrow.

Hoberman, M. A. (1976). *Bugs.* New York: Viking.

Hong, L. T. (1991). *How the Ox Star fell from heaven.* Chicago: Albert Whitman.

Houston, J. (1977). *Frozen fire.* New York: Margaret K. McElderry.

Huff, B. A. (1990). *Greening the city streets: The story of community gardens.* New York: Clarion.

Kennedy, R. (1985). *Amy's eyes.* New York: Harper & Row.

King, E. (1998). *Quinceañera: Celebrating fifteen.* New York: Dutton Children's Books.

Lewin, T. (1990). *Tiger trek*. New York: Macmillan.

Livingston, M.C. (1982). *A circle of seasons*. New York: Holiday House.

Lobel, A. (1979). *Days with frog and toad*. New York: Scholastic.

Lofting, H. (1988). *The story of Doctor Doolittle*. New York: Delacorte.

Lord, B. B. (1984). *In the year of the boar and Jackie Robinson*. New York: Harper & Row.

MacLachlan, P. (1985). *Sarah, plain and tall*. New York: Harper & Row.

Marrin, A. (2000). *Sitting Bull and his world*. New York: Dutton Children's Books.

Markle, S. (1988). *Science mini-mysteries*. New York: Atheneum.

Parker, S. (1989). *Touch, taste, and smell*. New York: Franklin Watts.

Paterson, K. (1977). *The great Gilly Hopkins*. New York: Crowell.

Prelutsky, J. (1988). *Tyrannosaurus was a beast*. New York: Greenwillow.

Provensen, A. *The buck stops here: The presidents of the United States*. New York: Harper.

Prusski, J. (1988). *Bring back the deer*. San Diego: Harcourt Brace Jovanovich.

Rylant, C. (1984). *Waiting to waltz: A childhood*. New York: Bradbury.

Sanderson, R. (1990). *The twelve dancing princesses*. Boston: Little Brown.

Simon, S. (1990). *Oceans*. New York: William Morrow.

Smith, W. J. (1990). *Birds and beasts*. New York: Godine.

Sneve, V. D. H. (1989). *Dancing teepees*. New York: Holiday House.

Spinelli, J. (1991). *Fourth grade rats*. New York: Scholastic.

Steptoe, J. (1987). *Mufaro's beautiful daughters*. New York: Lothrop, Lee & Shepard.

Steven, J. (1989). *Androcles and the lion*. New York: Holiday House.

Tadjo, V. (1989). *Lord of the dance: An African retelling*. New York: Lippincott.

Uchida, Y. (1985). *The happiest ending*. New York: Atheneum.

Van Allsburg, C. (1990). *Just a dream*. Boston: Houghton Mifflin.

Whitney, T. P. (1970) *Vasilisa the beautiful*. New York: Macmillan.

Yep, L. (1991). *The star fisher*. New York: Penguin.

Yolen, J. (1987). *Owl moon*. New York: Philomel.

CHAPTER 8

COMPREHENSIVE SCAFFOLDED READING EXPERIENCES FOR ENGLISH-LANGUAGE LEARNERS

In each of the preceding three chapters, we focused on a single segment of the SRE framework for English-language learners: prereading, during reading, or postreading. This was convenient because it allowed us to take an in-depth look at each segment. However, it did not allow us to discuss or demonstrate one essential feature of the SRE framework. An SRE is a carefully coordinated, integrated, and sequenced set of prereading, during-reading, and postreading activities. What you do in any segment of an SRE is very strongly influenced by what you do in the other segments. In fact, this point should be made more strongly: What you do in any segment of an SRE really makes sense only in terms of what you do in the other segments. Moreover, the prereading, during-reading, and postreading activities in an SRE are strongly influenced by the factors that you consider during the planning phase—the students, the text, and the purpose or purposes for which students are reading.

In this chapter, we provide examples of complete SREs for classrooms that include English-language learners, illustrating how prereading, during-reading, and postreading activities are interrelated and influenced by the students, the text, and the purposes of the reading. Here again is the basic SRE framework.

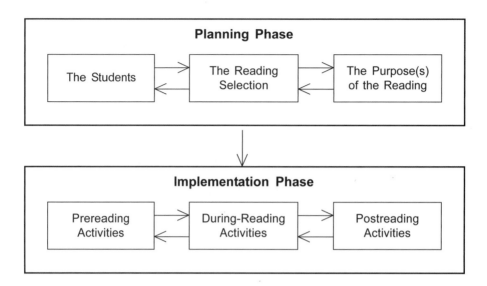

Consider two SREs you might use with *The Girl Who Struck Out Babe Ruth*, a biography by Joan L. S. Patrick. It's about Jackie Mitchell, a 17-year-old pitcher and the first female member of a minor league team called the Lookouts. In 1931, Jackie struck out New York Yankee legends Babe Ruth and Lou Gehrig. While many English-language learners might be familiar with the game of baseball, others might not. With some English-language learners, a fairly healthy scaffold would be appropriate. Here is one for a small group of second graders.

SRE for *The Girl Who Struck Out Babe Ruth*

Students	Selection	Purpose
Second-graders (three English-language learners and one academically challenged student)	*The Girl Who Struck Out Babe Ruth* by Joan L. S. Patrick	To understand and enjoy an inspiring biography

Prereading	During Reading	Postreading
• Motivating • Preteaching Vocabulary • Building Background Knowledge • Suggesting Strategies	• Supported Reading • Reading to Students • Silent Reading	• Discussion • Drama • Artistic Activity • Reteaching (This became part of the SRE when it became apparent that students were having problems using the strategy suggested during prereading.)

Now here is another SRE for the same selection but with a different group of students. These are above average and gifted third-grade native-English speakers and English-language learners who have been in dual-language classes since kindergarten, and they are unlikely to need as much scaffolding as the second-grade group.

AN ALTERNATIVE SRE FOR *The Girl Who Struck Out Babe Ruth*

Students	Selection	Purpose
Third graders (above average and gifted), native-English speakers and English-language learners who have been in dual-language immersion classes since kindergarten	*The Girl Who Struck Out Babe Ruth* by Joan L. S. Patrick	To understand and enjoy an inspiring biography

Prereading	During Reading	Postreading
• Building Background Knowledge (which combines motivation and purpose setting)	• Supported Reading • Silent Reading	• Discussion • Artistic Activity

---

You can see from this brief example the effects that students, the texts being read, and the purposes of the reading have on the types and numbers of activities you create. At this point, we want to again note that the purpose of the SRE is not to fill up precious reading time with a lot of activities, no matter how engaging or purposeful they might be in their own right, but rather to provide a scaffold for students to successfully comprehend and learn from what they read

Some activities in the SRE may be quite brief, taking a only a few minutes, while others will take much longer. For example, a motivational activity might include no more than your saying, "I learned more about the United States Civil War by reading this article than from anything I've read before." Whereas, a concept-building activity that includes demonstrations of Newton's laws of gravity may take 20 minutes or more. What you need to consider is the cost effectiveness of each activity: How much scaffolding do students need to successfully comprehend and respond to this selection? How much help will they need to understand and enjoy a folktale? To write a mathematical sentence for a story problem? To recall and respond to the major events that led up to the Civil War?

Another point to keep in mind is that what is important is the function or functions an activity serves, not what it's labeled. For instance, if you know from past experience that you really have to motivate your fourth graders before they read any kind of expository material, then when planning an SRE for an informational trade book on Japan, you know you must include motivation. As you are creating the motivational activity, you discover that it is accomplishing several purposes simultaneously. It serves to relate the reading to the students' lives, activate their prior knowledge, and introduce vocabulary. You sought motivation and ended up with additional aids in the scaffold. This overlapping of functions will cause no problems. You know what your activity is accomplishing, and that should be enough—unless you also want to tell your students, which we recommend you do frequently.

Although your motivational activity may include activating prior knowledge and introducing vocabulary, you may still choose to build a sturdier prereading scaffold by including a separate preteaching vocabulary activity. Overlap between activities is to be expected.

The length of an entire SRE can range from minutes to days, depending again on the students, selection, and purpose. If the reading selection is a short story to be read by an average group of fourth-grade English-language learners and native-English speakers for the purpose of understanding the story's theme and reviewing the concept of theme, the SRE might be broken down this way:

SRE for a Short Story

Students	Selection	Purpose
Fourth graders, including some English-language learners, reading in English at third/fourth-grade level	Short Story: *Thanksgiving Gumbo* by Janet Graber	To enjoy the story and identify its theme

Prereading	During Reading	Postreading
• Activating Background Knowledge, which includes preteaching the concept of theme (15 min.) • Direction Setting: Identifying the story's theme (5 min.)	• Silent Reading (10 min.)	• Discussion: Small-group discussions on the story's theme (15 min.) • Discussion: Large-group discussion on the story's theme and the general concept of theme (10 min.)

You might be asking, "Isn't that a lot of activity time for 10 minutes of reading?" Maybe, but theme is a challenging concept and an important one, so it deserves some time. Moreover, for a change of pace, the next day students can read self-selected books and magazine stories independently.

While the SRE for *Thanksgiving Gumbo* took about an hour, an SRE could also take several weeks. Let us suppose, you are going to have your fifth-grade students in a bilingual education class read biographies of people they have been studying about in history. Here's an brief look at a 20-day SRE in a bilingual education classroom, with the lessons conducted in Spanish, in English, or both.

Twenty-Day SRE for Various Biographies of Historical Figures

Students	Selection	Purpose
Fifth graders in a bilingual education class with mixed English- and Spanish-reading levels	Various biographies of historical figures—men and women who have influenced history	To understand and appreciate the lives of the men and women who have influenced history

Week 1:

Day 1

Prereading	During Reading	Postreading
• Motivating Activity, which may include a visit from a person in the community who has written or been the subject of a biography (15 min.)	• Reading to Students by teacher or guest author (20 min.)	• Discussion focusing on biographical writing, comparing and contrasting it with other genres (15 min.)

Day 2

Prereading	During Reading	Postreading
• Provide Text-Specific Knowledge: Give previews and information about biographies from which students will be selecting (20 min.)	• Reading to Students: Read excerpts from bios (20 min.) • Silent Reading: Have students read selected bios (20 min.)	• Discussion: Return to ideas raised in the Day One discussion and how they apply to biographies students will read (15 min.)

Day 3

Prereading	During Reading	Postreading
• Prequestioning: Have students develop a set of questions they would like to have answered in bios along with a set of teacher-developed questions (10 min.) • Direction Setting: Focus students' attention on the questions they raised and the teacher developed ones (5 min.)	• Silent Reading (30 min.)	None

Day 4

Prereading	During Reading	Postreading
• Direction Setting: Review previous day's questions (10 min.)	• Silent Reading (35 min.)	None

Day 5

Prereading	During Reading	Postreading
• Preteaching Concepts: semantic map for *perseverance* (10 min.)	• Supported Reading: Students look for examples of perseverance in their biographies and flag these. • Silent Reading (20 min.) • Oral Reading by Students: Students read passages that exemplify perseverance (15 min.)	• Discussion: Discuss perseverance of historical figures using concrete examples. (10 min.)

Week 2 (further abbreviated):

Prereading	During Reading	Postreading
• Suggesting a Strategy: surveying • Building Background Knowledge: Preview several more biographies	• Use survey strategy to select additional biographies to read • Silent Reading • Reading to Students	• Writing: Construct a Venn diagram to use in writing an essay comparing and contrasting two historical figures.

Weeks 3 & 4 (still further abbreviated):

Prereading	During Reading	Postreading
• Preteaching Concepts: *commitment, vision* • Relating the Reading to Students' Lives: Where are attributes of historical figures represented in lives of students?	• Reading to Students • Silent Reading • Supported Reading: Find examples of key concepts discussed • Modifying the Text: Put bios on audiotapes from biographies	• Writing: Biographies of people the students know • Artistic and Nonverbal: Compose songs; make a bulleting board or mural • Drama: Dramatize events • Outreach: Take dramas to senior citizens' center; visit history museum

In the remainder of the chapter, we give samples of three complete scaffolded reading experiences with English-language learners. In each sample, we include an overview of the entire SRE, a detailed day-by-day description of possible prereading, during-reading, and postreading activities, and a brief reflection on the entire SRE.

Guide to Complete SREs in Chapter 8

Sample 1: *Earthquakes* (p. 274)

   Students: Fourth-grade students with low to average English reading ability in an ethnically diverse classroom in California, including several English-language learners.

   Selection: *Earthquakes* by Seymour Simon.

   Purpose: To learn about earthquakes, what causes them, and what effect they have on life and property.

Sample 2: A Theme-Based SRE on *Real Life Heroes* (p. 282)

   Students: Third-grade students reflecting a variety of English reading levels and ethnic backgrounds, including some English-language learners.

Selections: Self-selected books reflecting the theme "real-life heroes."

Purpose: To understand how real-life heroes are made, how they have met challenges and achieved their goals, what makes them "heroes."

Sample 3: *Black Powder* (p. 292)

Students: Seventh through ninth graders in a Sheltered English class. Native languages of the students are Spanish, Chinese, Vietnamese, and Hmong. The students' English reading levels range from fourth- to sixth-grade level.

Selection: *Black Powder* by William Wu.

Purpose: To learn about aspects of living in outer space, about ancient Chinese memorial ceremonies and rituals for the dead, and to consider how the past, present, and future intersect in the students' own lives.

Sample 1: A Complete SRE for English-Language Learners on *Earthquakes*

This SRE uses the K–W–L procedure recommended by Donna Ogle (1986). K–W–L includes pre-, during-, and postreading activities in which students actively consider what they know, *what* they *want* to know, and what they *learn.*

Students: Fourth-grade students with low to average English reading ability in an ethnically diverse classroom in California, including several English-language learners.

Selection: *Earthquakes* by Seymour Simon. This informational book gives a dramatic photographic account of the causes and effects of earthquakes around the globe.

Reading Purpose: To learn about earthquakes, what causes them, what effects they have on people and property, and what might be done to prepare for them.

Earthquakes Overview

Students	Selection	Purpose
Fourth graders, average to low English reading levels, including several English-language learners	*Earthquakes* by Seymour Simon	To learn more about earthquakes

Day 1

Prereading	During Reading	Postreading
Motivating and Relating Reading to Students' Lives (10 min.)	Supported Reading (5 min.)	Discussion (20 min)

(Continued on next page)

Day 1 *(Continued from previous page)*

Prereading	During Reading	Postreading
Activating Background Knowledge (10 min.)	Reading to Students (5 min.)	None
Prequestioning and Direction Setting (5 min.)		

Day 2

Prereading	During Reading	Postreading
Prequestioning and Direction Setting (5 min.)	Modifying the Text (30 min.)	Discussion (10 min)
		Application: jigsaw groups (10 min)

Prereading for Day 1

MOTIVATING and RELATING READING TO STUDENTS' LIVES: *What's Your Story?*

In this activity, an event relating to the topic of the text is described and then students relate their own similar experiences.

Goal of the Activity: To pique students' interest in a topic and activate their background knowledge.

Rationale: Describing an event in a way that requires students to infer what is happening can be an effective way to stimulate interest and introduce a topic at the same time. Having students then discuss their own experiences requires that they access relevant knowledge, which will help them build meaning from the text.

Procedure: Begin by describing a scenario similar to the following: "Imagine yourself in this situation. You are asleep in bed. Suddenly, the bed begins to move back and forth. Half awake, you say to the sibling in the bed next to yours, 'Stop shaking the bed.'" Ask students to explain what is going on. Tell students this was an experience you had with earthquakes and encourage them to talk about their own experiences.

ACTIVATING BACKGROUND KNOWLEDGE: *What I Know*

In this activity, students brainstorm to find out what they know about a topic and then generate categories of information that are likely to be found in the text they will read.

Goal of the Activity: To have students activate their prior knowledge about a topic and consider what information on that topic might be included in a specific text.

Rationale: Students who have been in California for some time are likely to have some knowledge of earthquakes. Activating this knowledge before reading can help establish a framework to aid them in understanding and remembering. If some of the English-language learners are new to California and unfamiliar with earthquakes, they can learn from their classmates.

Procedure: On the chalkboard, write the title *Earthquakes.* Underneath that title and to the left, write the heading *What I Know*. Ask students to give some of the facts they know about earthquakes. Jot their responses under the heading *What I Know*.

EARTHQUAKES

What I Know

Can cause damage

Are unpredictable

Are scary

Happen in California

Not all are the same

Shake the earth

Don't happen at night

Are getting worse

As you will notice, not all of the students' responses are accurate. During this brainstorming session, you might ask students various questions such as "How did you learn that?" or "How could you prove that?" Later, during the postreading discussion, you can clear up any remaining misconceptions.

After students have given a variety of responses, show them the cover illustration on the book *Earthquakes*. Ask them to think about the kind of information that might be included in the book and write their suggestions on the board to the left of their initial responses. Some of their suggestions might include how earthquakes happen, where they happen, what we can do about them, how much damage they do, why they happen, and descriptions of some of the worst quakes.

PREQUESTIONING and DIRECTION SETTING: *What I Would Like to Know*

In this activity, students consider what they would like to know about a topic that might be discussed in a specific text.

Goal of the Activity: To turn students' interest in earthquakes into a desire to read about them.

Rationale: Having learners think about what they would like to know about a topic sets up a purpose for reading. If students have questions in mind, they will be looking for answers to those questions as they read and comprehension will be facilitated.

Procedure: Explain that informational books such as *Earthquakes* are written to give us information that we might need or want. Ask students to think about what they would like to know about earthquakes—things they don't already know or aren't quite sure of. Write their responses on the board in a column to the right of the *What I Know* column.

EARTHQUAKES

What I Would Like to Know?

What causes earthquakes?

How are earthquakes measured?

What places have earthquakes?

What was the worst earthquake?

Where are most earthquakes?

What we can do about earthquakes?

During Reading for Day 1

GUIDED READING: *What I Find Out*

In this activity, students write down answers to the questions they posed prior to reading that are given in the text, and then they consider which of their questions still need answering.

Goal of the Activity: To have students transform questions into answers and thoughts into writing.

Rationale: Having students search for answers to their questions requires active reading on their part. Transforming what they learn into writing requires and promotes even deeper understanding. Having students go a step further and check what questions still need answering lets them know that the information an author chooses is selective and they may need to check other sources to get their answers.

Procedure: On the chalkboard to the right of the previous two headings, write *What I Found Out*. Explain to students that this will be the last part of the K–W–L procedure—a procedure they can use when they read informational books and articles. They have already completed the first two steps—thinking about and writing down what they know about earthquakes and what they would like to know. The last step is to record what information they do learn.

Direct students' attention to the information they wanted to know. Explain that as they read they will look for the answers to these questions.

READING TO STUDENTS: *The Appetizer*

In this activity, you read the first few pages of an informational book aloud to students.

Goal of the Activity: To interest students further in the topic of the book and motivate them to read it on their own.

Rationale: Reading aloud can help ease many students into the material. A good enthusiastic rendition can also be an enticement for students to read on their own. At the same time, some of your English-language learners may be stronger readers than listeners, so be sure to allow any students who want to follow along in the text. In addition to getting students off to a good start, this shared experience allows you to complete the third step of the K–W–L procedure as a group and provide clarification of the task before students read and record answers on their own.

Ask students to listen carefully as you read the first five pages in the book aloud. They should be thinking about the questions they had listed on the board and decide whether or not they are answered in these pages.

Postreading for Day 1

DISCUSSION: *Questions Answered?*

In this activity, students decide which questions were answered in the text.

Goal of the Activity: To have students realize that, although a specific text may answer some of their questions, it may not answer all of them and they will need to seek other sources for some questions.

Rationale: To become critical thinkers and readers, students need to realize that, while our questions about a topic might be answered in a text, they also might not be. Authors have to be selective in what they include. What we may wish to know may not be in the scope of the text and, therefore, we need to consult others.

Procedure: Draw students attention to the questions asked in the prereading activity.

EARTHQUAKES

What I Would Like to Know?

What causes earthquakes?

How are earthquakes measured?

What places have earthquakes?

What was the worst earthquake?

Where are most earthquakes?

What we can do about earthquakes?

Begin by asking students, "Was the first question, *'What causes earthquakes?'* answered in the first five pages of the book?" If students answer "yes," ask them to tell you if they can what the answer is and write that answer in the column *What I Found Out.* Proceed in a similar manner with each of the questions. If questions aren't answered, tell students that these questions still might be answered in the remainder of the text or that they may not be answered in this particular text at all and they will need to consult other sources for the answers.

Prereading for Day 2

PREQUESTIONING and DIRECTION SETTING: *K–W–L*

In this activity, students record what they know about a topic, what they would like to know, and what they learned from reading a text.

Goal of the Activity: To have students access their knowledge on a topic, think about what more they would like to learn about that topic, and better understand and remember the information that interests them most.

Rationale: Having students access appropriate knowledge before reading a text, posing their own questions, and writing down the answers to those questions can help them better understand and remember text material.

Procedure: Hand out the *What I KNOW—What I WANT to Know —What I LEARNED* chart shown below.

What I KNOW—What I WANT to Know—What I LEARNED

When students have their charts, review the three types of information they will record. First they will think about and record what they **know** about earthquakes, then write down what they **want** to know in the second column. As they read the book, they will write the answers to their questions or what they **learned** in the third column. Remind students of what they had done as a group the day before and explain that today they will have the opportunity to focus on their individual knowledge and interest in earthquakes or perhaps work with one other student as they read. Quietly invite each of your English-language learners to team up with a native-English speaker who is a good reader if they like.

Remind students that not all of their questions will be answered in the text. This might be a good opportunity to talk about other resources for finding answers if this particular text doesn't provide them.

Explain that when they finish they will get a change to share what they learned about earthquakes.

During Reading for Day 2

MODIFYING THE TEXT: *Tape It*

In this activity, an audiotape recording is made available for students to listen to as they follow along in the text.

Goal of the Activity: To make the concepts in the text accessible to readers who might have difficulty reading the text on their own.

Rationale: Although this text is richly illustrated and not particularly dense, some English-language learners may have difficulty with it. Having an audiotape available will help make the concepts accessible for those students whose oral skills are more developed than their reading skills.

Procedure: Make a recording of the story on an audiotape or have an older or more competent student do it. Make as many copies as necessary or hook up one tape player to several receivers.

Postreading for Day 2

DISCUSSION 1: *What Did You Learn?*

Students meet in small groups to discuss what they learned from the text.

Goal of the Activity: To give students the opportunity to express their ideas to an audience and hear other students' ideas as well.

Rationale: Expressing themselves in an informal small-group setting gives students the opportunity to clarify their thoughts and also receive new information and insights from their classmates.

Procedure: After students have finished reading the text and have completed their K–W–L charts, have them meet in groups of three to six, with no more than one or two English-language learners in any one group. Appoint a facilitator—perhaps an English-language learner—and a recorder for each group. In the groups, students take turns telling what their questions were, which ones were answered, and what the answers were. The facilitator's job is to make sure everyone gets a chance to speak and the recorder keeps an account of the questions that were *not* answered in the text.

DISCUSSION 2: *Research It*

The recorders from each small-group discussion session report to the class what questions are still left to be answered, and then each group takes a question to research.

Goal of the Activity: To have students work in small groups to check multiple sources in order to find answers to a question.

Rationale: As previously mentioned, students need to realize that finding the information they want sometimes requires searching in one or more additional sources. Working in heterogeneous groups to locate these sources and answers requires that group members support one another in their efforts. Learning to work cooperatively is a skill that is not only necessary in school but in many aspects of life.

Procedure: After the groups have met to discuss what they learned in *Earthquakes*, have the recorders report to the entire class what questions their group members still have. Write these questions on the chalkboard. Have each group choose one question to research. That group is then responsible for finding the answer and reporting their findings to the entire class.

This may also be a good time to compare the statements students listed in the *What I Know* activity with what they actually did learn from the text. For example, one student had said, "They are getting worse." Ask students if the idea that earthquakes are getting worse was validated by the text. If the consensus is "no," the student who offered this initial comment may concur or perhaps decide to pursue independent research to try to confirm his statement.

Since this class is familiar with library research techniques, students need only be reminded at this time on how to proceed. This may require only a brief discussion to activate students' prior knowledge and review guidelines they might follow.

APPLICATION AND OUTREACH: *Let's Jigsaw*

Students form cooperative Jigsaw groups (Aronson & Patnoe, 1997) and take a topic that emerged from their readings to make posters that will be displayed in the school cafeteria, library, or other public places.

Goal of the Activity: To help reinforce the concepts students learned in their reading and to provide an opportunity for students to apply their knowledge in a practical, helpful way.

Rationale: Having groups of students—again with no more than one or two English-language learners—work together to create posters designed to communicate information they learned from reading about earthquakes can provide students with practice in working cooperatively, recalling, analyzing, and summarizing information, and thinking creatively. They learn how to present information in a clear, concise, yet eye-catching way. It also demonstrates that information garnered from reading can be shared with others and can be important and useful.

Procedure: After students have met in their discussion groups, bring the entire class together again. Discuss some of the major points of interest in their reading about earthquakes and ask students to think about what information might be of interest to other students in the school. Have students offer their suggestions and write these on the board. Some of their suggestions might include these:

> How earthquakes are measured
>
> What you should do to prepare for an earthquake
>
> What you should do when an earthquake happens
>
> How earthquakes happen
>
> Where earthquakes happen

Assign (or let each group choose) one of the topics to make a poster of. If sample posters are available, show these to students. Or you can clip appropriate advertisements from magazines and discuss what makes these informative and eye catching. Be aware that some of your English-language learners may be able to do a particularly good job with this nonverbal activity and be prepared to fully support their efforts.

Each group will then meet to decide what information, graphics, and illustrations will go onto their poster. Next, they will use the resources available to them to produce a poster that will communicate information on their topic in the most interesting way possible. Finally, they will publicly display their poster.

Adapting the Activity: The K–W–L activity can be used any time students' purpose for reading is to learn information. Students might use this procedure while reading content-areas textbooks, magazine articles, or any number of informational trade books. For example, students might use a K–W–L chart to help them learn more about Benjamin Franklin while reading *The Many Lives of Benjamin Franklin* by Mary Pope Osborne, to learn more about space exploration in *Can You Hear a Shout in Space?* by Melvin and Gilda Berger, or to discover what it means to be president when reading the Caldecott-winning picture book *So You Want to be President?* by Judith St. George and illustrated by David Small, or to learn more about the California condor and the efforts to save this very endangered species when reading *California Condor: Flying Free* by Bonnie Graves.

Reflection: This SRE is based primarily on the K–W–L teaching model developed by Donna Ogle (1986). Although it is not the only procedure that might be used with Earthquakes, it's a good one. The prereading and postreading activities, of course, will reflect the material students are reading and their purposes for reading it. The essence of the model, however, includes three phases: brainstorming, purpose setting through asking questions, and finding answers to those questions. The procedure provides a scaffold that helps support students' own interests and inquiries. According to Ogle, K–W–L "helps students keep control of their own inquiry, extending the pursuit of knowledge beyond just the one article. The teacher is making clear that learning shouldn't be framed around just what an author chooses to include, but that it involves the identification of the learner's questions and the search for authors or articles dealing with those questions."

Sample 2: A Complete SRE
on the Theme "Real-Life Heroes"

This is a different type of SRE from the previous one in that it is built to support not a single selection, but many different selections that have been chosen to reflect a specific theme. In this SRE, the theme is real-life heroes. In the following example, we show how a theme-based SRE might be developed.

Students: Third graders reflecting a variety of English reading levels and ethnic backgrounds, including some English-language learners.

Selections: Some of the possibilities are listed below. Following this list, we present a sample SRE for Robert Coles' *The Story of Ruby Bridges*, the story of the first black student to attend Frantz Elementary School in New Orleans.

> *Stone Girl, Bone Girl: The Story of Mary Anning* by Laurence Anholt. Set in England at the beginning of the 19th century, this picture book tells the story of Mary Anning's beginnings as one of history's most celebrated fossil finders.

> *Through My Eyes* by Ruby Bridges. Ruby Bridges tells of her experiences as the first black student to attend Frantz Elementary, an all-white school in New Orleans.

> *Journey for Peace: The Story of Rigoberta Menchú,* by Marlene Targ Brill, depicts the difficult journey of Menchú, who won the Nobel Peace Prize in 1992, as she struggled to free her native Mayans in Guatemala and all native cultures from oppression.

> *Uncommon Traveler: Mary Kingsley in Africa* by Don Brown. This picture book tells of Kingsley's adventures on her two trips to West Africa in 1893 and 1894.

> *A Journey: The Autobiography of Apolo Anton Ohno* by Apolo Anton Ohno and Nancy Ann Richardson. This is a first-person account of the life of this Olympic champion.

> *The Story of Ruby Bridges,* by Robert Coles, is a picture book depicting the first black student, first-grader Ruby Bridges, to attend Frantz Elementary School in New Orleans, Louisiana in 1960.

> *Mandela: From the Life of the South African Statesman* by Floyd Cooper. This picture book depicts the extraordinary life of Nelson Mandela from childhood until his election to presidency of the new government in South Africa in 1994.

> *Women Pioneers in Science,* by Louis Harber, provides biographical sketches of inspiring women in science.

> *Heroes: Great Men Through the Ages* by Rebecca Hazell. By presenting the extraordinary lives of 12 heroes, beginning with Socrates and ending with Martin Luther King, Jr., the author depicts real people—replete with strengths and weaknesses—who, with courage and determination, were able to change the world or the way in which we view it.

Farewell to Manzanar, by Jeanne Wakatsuki Houston and James D. Houston, is a first-person account of a Japanese American family's internment in the California desert during World War II.

Maria's Comet, by Deborah Hopkinson, is a fictionalized account of America's first woman astronomer and her childhood yearning for adventure.

Wilma Unlimited: How Wilma Rudolf Became the World's Fastest Woman, by Kathleen Krull, tells of Rudolf's inspiring journey from a child stricken with polio to an Olympic legend.

Tomas and the Library Lady, by Pat Mora, is a fictionalized account of the migrant worker, Tomas Rivera, who eventually became a university chancellor and the librarian who aided him.

Mount Everest and Beyond: Sir Edmund Hillary, by Sue Muller Hacking, tells of Hillary's assent of Mt. Everest in 1953 and his subsequent good will efforts and challenges.

Starry Messenger: Galileo Galilei, by Peter Sis, is a picture book detailing the triumphs and tragedies of this early astronomer.

Danger Marches to the Palace: Queen Lili'uokalani by Margo Sorenson. This is a fictionalized account of the bravery of Hawaii's Queen *Lili'uokalani* in overcoming would-be traitors.

Flight, written by Robert Burleigh and illustrated by Mike Wimmer, is a picture book telling of the determined Charles Lindberg's exciting solo flight across the Atlantic Ocean.

Reading Purpose: To read a text or number of texts for the pleasure of seeing how they can help us understand how real people have dealt with and solved various kinds of issues, challenges, and problems. Here is an overview of this SRE.

Real-Life Heroes Overview

Students	Selection	Purpose
Third graders with mixed English reading levels, including some English-language learners	*Ruby Bridges* by Robert Coles A variety of selections reflecting the theme "real-life heroes"	Enjoyment and new insights into what makes for a hero

Day 1

Prereading	During Reading	Postreading
• Motivating (10 min.) • Relating Reading to Students' Lives (10 min.)	• Reading to Students: *Ruby Bridges* by Robert Coles (20 min.)	• Discussion and Questioning (10 min.)

Day 2

Prereading	During Reading	Postreading
• Direction Setting (10 min.) • Providing Text-Specific Knowledge (15 min.)	• Silent and Oral Reading (20 min.) • Modifying the Text: audio recordings available (15 min.)	• Writing: graffiti board and journal entries (20 min.) • Artistic and Nonverbal Activities: illustrations (20 min.)

Day 3 to End of Unit

Prereading	During Reading	Postreading
None	None	• Discussion: small group (20 min.) • Drama; Artistic, Graphic, and Nonverbal; music, dance (30 min.) • Writing (30 min.)

Note: Times will vary with individual students and what they are reading.

Prereading for Day 1

MOTIVATING: *Let's Talk About You!*

In this activity, students talk about the challenges they've faced and the problems they've encountered and how they dealt with these.

Goal of the Activity: To encourage students to think about problems and challenges and what can be done about them.

Rationale: Because youngsters at this age are still quite egocentric, they always enjoy thinking and talking about themselves. And getting them to ponder and discuss their own life experiences is the first step in leading them to make connections between themselves and the real-life heroes in the biographies they will read.

Procedure: Encourage students to talk about what problems or challenges they have encountered, and how they solved them. For example, students might talk about something that was hard for them to do but they were able to do it. Also, try to get them to talk about how they felt about themselves as they tried to solve the problem. What were some of the obstacles they encountered? What made them keep going? How did they feel when things went wrong? What did they do to correct things that went wrong? Did they learn anything new about themselves? Elicit the problem-solving strategies they used and feelings they had.

RELATING READING TO STUDENTS' LIVES: *They Did It! Real-Life Heroes*

In this activity, students discuss stories they have read in which the people triumphed over difficult situations.

Goal of the Activity: To move students' thinking from themselves to story characters and to help them make the connection between real life and literature.

Rationale: Students need to know that they are not alone in what they think, feel, and experience. People everywhere, in other times and other places, no matter what sex, religion, or ethnic background, have similar needs, emotions, and thoughts and similar ways of dealing with difficult situations. These common characteristics are expressed through literature. Biographies provide particularly good examples of people who have overcome difficulties or achieved important goals.

Procedure: Ask students to think about books they have read in which the characters faced a situation they thought was difficult or impossible but were able to triumph in the end.

Explain that there have been many stories written over the years that show the kind of situation in which a character has a problem to solve or goal to achieve. Ask students to think about why this is so. (Because it is a situation that most people face many times in their lives. Life, it seems, is always presenting us with challenges—problems to solve, goals we want to achieve.) Some of the best of these kinds of stories are about real-life heroes, or biographies. Ask students to name books in which the main characters were real-life heroes who were able to solve a problem or achieve a special goal. Ask students if they thought these people learned anything about themselves while they were working so hard or when they achieved (or didn't achieve) their goals. List students' suggestions on the board with the challenges they faced.

Ask students if they like to read about real people and their struggles, and if so why. Keep the discussion lively and brief. Show students an assortment of biographies that represent real-life heroes. Discuss with students what they think makes a hero a hero and write their responses on the board.

During Reading for Day 1

READING TO STUDENTS: *A Shared Experience*

In this activity, a selection that represents a real-life hero is read aloud. We have chosen *Ruby Bridges* by Robert Coles.

Selection: *Ruby Bridges* by Robert Coles. For months, six-year-old Ruby Bridges must confront the hostility of white segregationists when she becomes the first African American girl to integrate Frantz Elementary School in New Orleans, Louisiana, in 1960.

Goal of the Activity: To give students the opportunity to hear noteworthy literature and to provide all students with a common literary experience.

Rationale: Since each student will be reading different texts for this SRE, providing one shared experience establishes a common source of background information on which future discussions might be based. It also gives students the opportunity to hear quality literature read aloud and is a way to focus their attention on the theme of real-life heroes.

Procedure: Tell students that *Ruby Bridges* by Robert Coles tells the true story of six-year-old Ruby Bridges, who was the first black person to go to a school in New Orleans that had only white students. Explain that schools in the South at that time, 1960, were segregated—the blacks went to their schools and the whites went to theirs. The story takes place in New Orleans, Louisiana, in 1960. Ask students to listen carefully and to see if they think Ruby was a hero or not on that day she went to school. Read *Ruby Bridges* aloud.

Postreading for Day 1

DISCUSSION AND QUESTIONING: *Do You Agree?*

In this activity, the teacher suggests a story's theme, and students discuss whether or not they agree.

Selection: *Ruby Bridges* by Robert Coles. For months, six-year-old Ruby Bridges must confront the hostility of white segregationists when she becomes the first African American girl to integrate Frantz Elementary School in New Orleans, Louisiana, in 1960.

Goal of the Activity: To encourage students to think about themes and how themes are portrayed through the words and actions of the story's protagonist.

Rationale: Getting students to consider what a story says to them can help them appreciate their role as a reader and understand how the elements of character and theme are intertwined.

Procedure: After reading the story, discuss whether or not students think Ruby Bridges was a hero and why they think as they do. After students have given their opinions, have them consider the following questions:

> Did Ruby have a problem or problems? What was that problem or problems?
>
> What did Ruby do about the problems she faced? Did he solve her problems? How? In what way?
>
> Was Ruby different at the end of the story from what she was at the beginning? If so, in what ways was she different?
>
> Did anyone else in the story change? Who? In what ways did they change and why?
>
> What did Ruby discover about herself? Do you think she thought of herself as a hero? Do you? Why or why not?

Prereading for Day 2

DIRECTION SETTING: *Graffiti Board: Self-Discovery and Personal Triumph*

In *Graffiti Board,* students write their personal responses to texts on a large sheet of butcher paper.

Goal of the Activity: To encourage students to think about and respond to what they read and to communicate those responses to others.

Rationale: Students need to know what they think has value. An activity of this sort can give students confidence in their ability to consider ideas and respond to them. It also provides an opportunity to learn how others respond to literature and to become aware of common issues and themes.

Procedure: Prior to beginning the SRE activities for the day, tack up a large sheet of butcher paper on one section of a wall. At the top of the sheet in bold letters write "Real-Life Heroes." Nearby, provide several colored felt tip pens for students to write their "graffiti." Display the biographies you have selected for students on a table or chalkboard ledge.

Begin your prereading discussion by reminding students of Ruby Bridges' special accomplishments and your previous discussions about how heroes solve problems or find ways to achieve their goals. Indicate the books on display and explain that each of them in one way or another expresses the theme of real-life heroes. Write "Hero" on the chalkboard and discuss what it means, drawing on the previous day's discussion and Ruby Bridges as examples. (How did Ruby triumph? What did she learn about herself? Others? Do you think Ruby is a hero. Why or why not?)

After the discussion, draw students' attention to the butcher paper on the wall. Tell them this is a "graffiti board," and ask them to speculate on what it might be for. Call on someone to read the heading and hold up the colored pens. Tell them the graffiti board has something to do with the books they will be reading and the theme "Real-Life Heroes."

Next, explain that graffiti are sayings written on walls in public places. The graffiti they will write on the wall will be about the stories they read and the theme. Tell them about a book you have recently read, *Impressionist* by Joan King, explaining that the book is about the famous impressionist painter Mary Cassatt and that Mary began painting at a time when few women did. To achieve her goal of becoming a painter, she had many obstacles to overcome—first convincing her very obstinate and domineering father to send her to art school, then proving her competence to the world in an area dominated by men.

Tell students that while you were reading the story, there were many thoughts that you had that you wanted to share with someone else, but no one else was around. If you had had a graffiti board nearby, you might have written on it. That's what gave you the idea of a graffiti board in class. On the chalkboard, model the activity by writing down the kinds of thoughts you might want to express on the graffiti board.

> *Impressionist* by Joan King. I can't believe how persevering Mary Cassatt was, how determined she was to become a painter even though there were very few women painters at the time. Nothing came easy for her yet she persisted. Her small successes and her intense love for the art must have kept her going. She learned she did have what it takes to be an artist among men. Mrs. G.

Tell students they can use the graffiti board to write anything they choose, but ideally it will relate to the theme of real-life heroes. Students should write the title of the biography they're responding to, the author, their "graffiti" and their name. Copy your graffiti onto the graffiti board to serve as your contribution as well as a sample for the students. Ask students to suggest any graffiti they might create for *Ruby Bridges,* and let volunteers write it on the board.

PROVIDING TEXT-SPECIFIC KNOWLEDGE: *The Coming Attraction*

In *The Coming Attraction,* a preview of a selection is provided in which some of the most salient and interesting details of the selection are revealed. Previews of this sort have been described by Graves, Prenn, and Cooke (1985).

Goal of the Activity: To pique students' interest in various selections and give them background information on what the books contain.

Rationale: Using previews to introduce books can help students decide which books to select. These brief sketches can also serve as enticements to read as well as schemata builders.

Procedure: Give a thumbnail description of each of the biographies—something about the person being written about and the setting. Explain that each in a different way shows a different kind of hero, but each of these heroes tries to solve a problem or achieve a goal. Let students peruse and select a biography to read.

During Reading for Day 2

SILENT AND ORAL READING: *To Each His Own*

In this activity, students have the option to read their chosen selections in a variety of ways: alone silently, orally with partners or in small groups, or silently while listening to a tape recording of the story.

Goal of the Activity: To provide students with the opportunity to read books that interest them and that they can handle successfully.

Rationale: Providing students with a variety of texts both in content and readability and a variety of ways to build meaning from the text gives them many supports for an enjoyable and worthwhile reading experience.

Procedure: Tell students they may read their books alone or with a partner and that a few of the books are available on tape, so that is also an option. You may want to make some specific recommendations to individual students—books that will have some special meaning for that student and are at his or her reading level—to ensure a successful experience. For instance, in a class of third graders you might enthusiastically suggest *Stone Girl, Bone Girl: The Story of Mary Anning* to Amanda, a rather shy student with adequate but not superior reading skills, and *Journey for Peace: The Story of Rigoberta Menchú* to Manuella, a good reader whose family has roots in Guatemala, and *Mount Everest and Beyond: Sir Edmund Hillary* to Michael, who is an average reader but who is always up to a challenge. You might recommend that two friends, Josh and B. J. read *Flight* together. You might also suggest that superior readers Emily, Monika, and Summer read *Women Pioneers in Science* and have a three-way discussion after each chapter, reading aloud some of their favorite scenes. And you might let Natasha, an English-language learner who is struggling with reading, know that you have made an audio recording of *Maria's Comet,* which she is welcome to listen to as she follows along in the text.

Before they begin reading, remind students that their purposes for reading the biographies are first to just enjoy the books and second to see how biographies reveal ways in which heroes from different times and places are similar in important ways. They also might want to think about what the central figure hoped to achieve or what problem he or she tried to solve. While they read, they are free to write on the graffiti board, and journal writing is always an option. After they finish reading, they will have a chance to talk about their ideas in small discussion groups.

The time it takes students to read will vary tremendously. You will want to provide adequate time for the chapter book readers and encourage the picture book and easy-to-read book readers to choose additional books to read, or respond to the stories by drawing pictures or writing responses on the graffiti board or in their journals. Tell students approximately the amount of class time they will have (three days, two weeks, or whatever you decide is appropriate) to read books dealing with real-life heroes. Also, at this time or some time during the SRE, you will want to prepare students for their self-selected postreading activities, which are described in *Express Yourself!* at the end of this SRE example.

Postreading for Day 2

WRITING: ARTISTIC, GRAPHIC, AND NONVERBAL ACTIVITIES: *Now You Respond*

After students finish reading one of their selected texts, they respond to it by writing in their journals, writing on the graffiti board, or creating illustrations that communicate some aspect of self-discovery and personal triumph as illustrated in the story.

Goal of the Activity: To provide students with the opportunity to respond to the theme of a text in a personal way.

Rationale: In order to respond, students will need to have understood what they read, reflect on it, synthesize events and ideas, and decide how these events and ideas relate to the idea of self-discovery and personal triumph. This kind of reflective thinking and responding gives students an opportunity to grow in their ability to ponder, analyze, and draw thoughtful conclusions about the meaning of text.

Procedure: Explain to students that after they finish reading a story, they can write or create with a drawing, painting, collage, and so forth, something that communicates the theme of self-discovery and personal triumph in that particular story. They can write or draw on the graffiti board or in their journals or both. Explain that they will have a chance to share their ideas in small group discussion.

Postreading Culminating Activities: Day 3 to End of Unit

DISCUSSION: *Let's Talk About Heroes: Self-Discovery and Personal Triumph*

In this activity, students gather in small groups to discuss the theme of "real-life heroes: self-discovery and personal triumph" as expressed through the subjects of the biographies they have read.

Goal of the Activity: To give students the opportunity to think about what makes for a hero, to discuss what they have discovered through literature, and to listen to the responses of their classmates.

Rationale: Discussion provides an excellent forum for students to express, clarify, and expand their thinking. Hearing other's ideas also can give them new insights and perspectives. Also, discussing the problems real-life heroes grapple with and how they resolve these issues can help students realize that problems have various faces, are common to everyone, and can be solved in numerous different ways.

Procedure: After students have finished reading their selections, have them meet in groups of three to six to discuss the problems their heroes faced or the goals they were trying to achieve, what they did about these problems and goals, whether or not they triumphed in the end, and what these characters learned about themselves. If you think your students need extra support in focusing their discussion, you might provide the discussion leaders with questions similar to the ones you raised for *Ruby Bridges*.

Did the hero have a problem or problems? What was that problem or problems?

What did the hero do about the problems he or she faced? Did he or she solve the problems? How? In what way?

Was the hero different at the end of the story from the beginning? If so, in what ways was he/she different?

Did anyone else in the story change? Who? In what ways did they change and why?

What did the hero discover about himself/herself? In what way did he/she triumph?

After the discussion, students might like to write their responses on the graffiti board. Also, after the small groups have had an opportunity to meet, you might want to conduct a whole-class discussion in which students can share the discoveries they made about their story characters with the whole class.

DRAMA; ARTISTIC, GRAPHIC, and NONVERBAL ACTIVITIES; and WRITING: *Express Yourself!*

In the *Express Yourself!* activity, students select the way or ways in which they would like to respond to a story.

Goal of the Activity: To give students the opportunity to express themselves in a way that best suits them and the biography they read.

Rationale: Providing students with a number of options for expression can increase their chances for creating a response or application that is meaningful to them.

Procedure: Sometime during the SRE, encourage students to think about how they might like to respond to the story or stories they are reading. Would they like to dramatize a scene with a partner or partners, or dress like the hero and do a pantomime or monologue?

Would they like to take a chapter book they have read and turn it into a picture book, diorama, or mural? Would they like to make a poster to advertise the book or the hero? Would a sculpture or collage be the best way to express their heroes?

Would they like to create a dance that would show how the hero developed from the beginning of the story to the end? Or a dance that expressed the mood of the biography?

Would an instrumental piece or a jingle or ballad express their hero? Could they compose a score to accompany the reading or dramatization of one of the scenes from the story?

Perhaps they would like to write something in response to their biography—a letter to the author or hero, or perhaps write a biography of a hero in their lives or their autobiography.

Ideally, the activities should allow for as much freedom to explore as possible with the only restriction being that students base their responses on the subject of their biographies and its themes or their stories using the resources they and you are able to supply.

Adapting the SRE: Instead of, or in addition to, focusing on biographies, you might have students read other types of expository selections that express the idea of solving a problem and that also provide the resources and the steps that are taken (or that might be taken) to solve it or fictional pieces where the main character turns out to be a hero.

Nonfiction

Kids' Computer Capers: Investigations for Beginners by Sandra Markle. History and workings of computers and computer programming. Info book.

Robotics by Stuart and Donna Paltorwitz. How robots work and ways in which they are useful. Info book.

How to Think Like a Scientist by Stephen P. Kramer. Clear presentation of using the scientific method to solve several of life's everyday questions. Info book.

Science Mini-Mysteries by Sandra Markle. Twenty-nine short mysteries to be solved with science experiments. Info book.

Before the Wright Brothers by Don Berliner. Chronicles history of flight beginning in 400 B.C.

Totem Pole by Diane Hoyt-Goldsmith. Photos and text show techniques for creating a totem pole, their traditional designs, and the meanings of these designs.

Greening the City Streets: The Story of Community Gardens by Barbara A. Huff and Peter Ziebel. Photo essay showing how Manhattan families and individuals develop and maintain urban garden plots.

Round Buildings, Square Buildings, & Buildings That Wiggle Like a Fish by Phillip M. Isaacson. Photographs and lyrical text describe elements that go into architectural planning and building.

Model Buildings and How to Make Them by Harvey Weiss. Text, photos, and drawings show just how to make them.

The Furry News: How to Make a Newspaper by Loreen Leedy. Lighthearted picture book story illustrating through the character Big Bear how to start a newspaper.

Explorers and Mapmakers by Peter Ryan. Traces world exploration and the need for maps.

The President Builds a House by Tom Shachtman. Photo essay on Habitat for Humanity featuring the contributions of former President Carter and Mrs. Carter.

Thinking Big by Susan Kuklin. Describes through photographs how an eight-year-old girl copes with the challenges of being a dwarf.

Mrs. Armitage on Wheels by Quentin Blake. A engaging picture book that illustrates in a comical way how inventions are precipitated by need.

Fiction

Cracker Jackon by Betsy Byars. Cracker takes responsibility for helping a babysitter who is a victim of physical abuse.

Stone Soup by John Warren Stewig. A young girl figures out a way to get stingy people to share. Picture book.

The Fourth Question: A Chinese Tale by Rosalind C. Wang. Yee-Lee figures out a way to solve his family's poverty as well as the dilemmas of many others. Picture book.

The True Confessions of Charlotte Doyle by Avi. Prim 13-year-old school girl turns seasoned sailor in this historical novel of adventure and intrigue.

Hatchet by Gary Paulsen. Through his courage and ingenuity, 13-year-old Brian is able to survive for 54 days in the Canadian wilderness.

Amazing Grace, written by Mary Hoffman and illustrated by Caroline Binch. Plucky Grace overcomes obstacles and earns the role of Peter Pan in the school play. Picture book.

. . . and Now Miguel by Joseph Krumgold. Set in the Sangre de Christo mountains of New Mexico, a young boy learns the joys and struggles of being a sheepherder.

Yossi Asks the Angels for Help by Miriam Chaiken. Yossi looks to angels for help in buying Hanukkah gifts after he loses his gift money.

How Sweetly Sings the Donkey by Vera Cleaver. Determined and resourceful teen Lily Snow works to improve her family's life.

The Sky Is Falling by Barbara Corcoran. Set during the Depression, Annah learns about growing up by accepting change.

Reflection: *What we have suggested here is only one of many possible variations for a theme-based Scaffolded Reading Experience. Although a good deal of effort and skill are involved in orchestrating a theme-based SRE, there are great rewards: making discoveries along with your students and seeing all of them—whether they are fully proficient in English or just beginning to gain proficiency—find in literature some new and special connections with their own lives and some insights that will stay with them long after they leave your classroom.*

Sample 3: A Complete SRE for *Black Powder*

This SRE is modified from one that Cheri Cooke (2002) has used with fifth-grade students. It is yet another type of SRE in that the prereading, during-reading, and postreading activities are not done in every lesson. Rather, prereading is done on one day, during reading on another, and postreading and yet another day.

Students: Students are seventh through ninth graders in a sheltered English class. Native languages of the students are Spanish, Chinese, Vietnamese, and Hmong. The students' English reading levels range from fourth- to sixth-grade level.

Selection: *Black Powder,* by William Wu, is set in the year 2017, on Star Hector Space Station. Tom Leong, a 17-year-old high school student, has spent his whole life on the space station. As the family makes plans for Tom's father's funeral, young Tom's grandfather tells him of burial ceremonies and rituals from China. Cultures of the present and past, and of future possibilities, are artfully woven into *Black Powder*. The students' peers are learning about outer space in their science class and about Eastern cultures in their social studies classes. The teacher has chosen this selection because those two topics intersect in this story and because the story provides fertile ground for the English-language learners in her class to explore their own "places" in her school vis-à-vis the cultures in which they are rooted and the possibilities for their futures.

Reading Purpose: To learn about aspects of living in outer space, to learn about ancient Chinese memorial ceremonies and rituals for the dead, and to consider how the past, present, and future intersect in the students' own lives.

BLACK POWDER Overview

Students	Selection	Purpose
Seventh through ninth graders, Sheltered English class, mixed native-language backgrounds, fourth- to sixth-grade English reading levels	*Black Powder* by William Wu	To learn about living in space, about ancient Chinese burial customs, and to consider intersections of past and present cultures in the students' own lives

Day 1

Prereading	During Reading	Postreading
Motivating, Relating Reading to Students' Lives, and Building Background Knowledge (25 min.)		
Preteaching Vocabulary (20 min.)		

Day 2

Prereading	During Reading	Postreading
	Direction Setting (2 min.)	
	Reading to Students, Guided Reading, and Silent Reading (45 min.)	

Day 3

Prereading	During Reading	Postreading
		Discussion (50 min.)

Prereading for Day 1

MOTIVATING, RELATING READING TO STUDENTS' LIVES, and BUILDING BACKGROUND KNOWLEDGE: *The Virtual Field Trip*

The teacher leads students through a virtual field trip to the International Space Station by projecting documents and pictures from the Internet. She then asks students to imagine that they lived in a community on a space station in the year 2017 and leads them to consider what life might be like.

Goal of the Activity: To help students to consider a situation that may seem very strange to them and to try to connect themselves to it.

Rationale: Understanding the concept of outer space and living in outer space might be difficult for many English-language learners. The *Virtual Field Trip* makes many of the potentially unknown concepts vivid. Asking students to connect what they see on the *Virtual Field Trip* to their own lives can help them to understand the content of the text they are about to read.

Procedure: Throughout the lesson, speak slowly, use the simplest vocabulary and syntax possible, and try to augment concepts by showing words and pictures as much as possible. Begin by telling students that you're going to read a story called *Black Powder*, and show the book so the students can see the title as you say it. Tell the students that the story is about living on a space station, and write the words space station on the board. Explain that the story takes place in 2017—in the future, but that there are space stations now. Ask the students if they know what a space station is. If some students know about space stations, invite them to tell what they know about them. Tell the students that before we read the story, we are going on a "virtual field trip" so that we can better understand the story. Tell them we're going to imagine that we're going to one of the space stations that we have now. Explain that good readers often try to think about everything they know about a topic before they start the reading, and that's why you're starting this way. Project pictures from NASA's Johnson Space Center (*http://www.jsc.nasa.gov/*) downloaded from the Internet into a computer file. Give a brief description of the station and the countries involved in building the station. (This site contains literally thousands of photos from which to choose.) Explain that the space station isn't finished, and that you will now show some pictures of what the space station will look like as it is added on to more and more over the next few years. Project pictures from the NASA site (*http://www.spaceflight.nasa.gov/*) downloaded into a computer file, and explore them with students.

Ask the students what they think living on a space station permanently would be like. How would they breathe? How would they eat? What if someone got sick? What if a child were born? Would it be hard to raise a child there? What if someone died there?

Now ask the students to imagine that many of the problems of living on a space station have been solved, and the year now is 2017, a number of years into the future. Ask the students to imagine what it would be like if they were actually born on that space station. How would they know what their parents lives were like on Earth? How would they learn of the "old" world their parents left? Should they learn of it? Why?

PRETEACHING VOCABULARY: *Using the Context*

The teacher presents key vocabulary words as they occur in the story, showing either a sentence or several sentences. She also shows objects and pictures that illustrate the meaning of the words.

Goal of the Activity: To learn vocabulary that is central to the meaning of the story, and to learn a strategy for figuring out what new words means, namely, using the context to help define a word. Also, you will see in the procedures for this lesson that we suggest that the teacher call on Latino students to use their knowledge of cognates in Spanish to help them gain a better understanding of some of the word meanings in English.

Rationale: Many of the key concepts in the story are likely to be unfamiliar to most of the students in the class. Learning central concepts before reading will help the students to set up some background knowledge to make the reading more comprehensible and memorable. Using excerpts from the story will help the students to see that they can sometimes figure out some word meanings by strategically thinking about the context. Using objects and pictures will help make the concepts easier to grasp and more vivid. Students with Chinese backgrounds may know some of the concepts you present, such as WOK and STIR-FRY, though they may not know the pronunciations of the words in English. Having these students help to define the words for others in the class can reinforce for all of the class that everyone has important understandings from which we can all learn. Helping students to use their knowledge of "look-alike" words in their native language also helps them acquire a strategy they can use when reading independently.

Procedure: Tell the students that in *Black Powder*, the main character is Tom Leong, a 17-year-old high school student, who has spent his whole life on a space station called "Star Hector Space Station." The story is set in 2017, and there are some words that are central to the meanings of the story which you want to make sure they know. Show the following words, and in most cases, sentences from the story, each on a separate overhead transparency, speaking slowly and pointing to the word you're defining:

> *wok:* "This is a zero-gravity wok. A wok is a large, thin metal pan with a round bottom, used for cooking." (Show a wok at the same time.)

> *stir-fry:* "You stir-fry in it." (Mime the following as you say it.) "You cut food into little pieces, put a little fat in the wok, and fry at a very hot temperature. It's very fast. This definition applies to here on earth. It's different in space! You'll see how when you read."

> *Chinatown:* "Maybe somebody ought to start selling these down in Chinatown. Make a fortune. Do we have a Chinatown in our town/ city? Chinese immigrants often live together in North American cities. Their neighborhoods are often called Chinatowns. In our story, Alvin Kwok, young Tom's grandfather, grew up in Chicago's Chinatown."

> *concentric:* "The wheels are concentric." (Show a picture of several concentric circles.) Ask the class if the sentence gives a clue to the meaning. If it's not stated, tell the students that *concentric* means having the same center. A number of wheels that are concentric all have the same center. Ask the Latino students in the class if there are words they know in Spanish that help them to figure out the meaning of this word (*con* means "with," and *central* means "center").

> *centrifugal force:* "The faster they go, the more centrifugal force creates artificial gravity against the far inside wall, which is the floor here." Ask the class if they can tell what it feels like when they are in a car that goes fast around a curve. Explain that they are actually being held in by gravity—a force that draws us all "down" or "to the center." When we feel like we're being thrown outward, away from the "center," we are experiencing centrifugal force.

> *Episcopalians:* Explain that this is a Christian religion. Tell the class that Tom is an Episcopalian.

> *incense:* Show a stick of incense, and explain that when it is lit, it makes a sweet smell. Explain that incense is often used in ceremonies of many religions and ask if any of the students have seen it used and smelled it at their places of worship.

contraband: Ask the Latino students if they can think of a word in Spanish that looks or sounds like this word. A student is likely to say, *contrabandear.* Ask the student if he can tell what it means in English and, if needed, say, "In English, it means 'to smuggle.'" Explain that *contraband* refers to something smuggled or against the law to have.

Tell students that in the next class they'll read the story called *Black Powder* and find out about Tom's life and about his family.

During Reading for Day 2

DIRECTION SETTING: *Informing and Purpose Setting*

The teacher provides information about the story theme, gives an overview of the during-reading activities, and sets a purpose for reading the story.

Goal of the Activity: To provide students with a context for reading, to let them know what activities will be done, and give them a main purpose for reading.

Rationale: When students have an overview of activities during a lesson, they tend to be better able to participate and understand the reasons for the activities. Creating a context for reading and establishing a main purpose for reading also facilitate comprehension and remembering. In addition, setting a context for reading and purpose setting also model for students what we would like them to do as independent readers.

Procedure: Remind the students that the main character in the story is Tom Leong, a 17-year-old high school student who was born on Star Hector Space Station. The year is still 2017. Tom's father, known as the "elder" Tom Leong, recently died in an accident. Tom's father is buried with an Episcopal funeral service. Tom decides that his father should also have a funeral service which commemorates his Chinese ancestry. So he plans a memorial service based on what his grandfather tells him of ceremonies and rituals from China.

Give an overview of the day's activities, explaining that now the teacher will begin the reading by reading out loud as the students follow along, and then they'll read on their own. When they read on their own, they'll have a reading guide to fill out. They should read to find out how Tom becomes more understanding of his family's heritage.

READING TO STUDENTS, GUIDED READING, and SILENT READING: *Reading Guide*

The teacher introduces the reading guide, sets a general purpose for reading, reads aloud to the students, and asks the students to read silently and fill out the reading guide.

Goal of the Activity: The main goals are for students to understand the concepts involved in living in outer space, and to understand and relate to young Tom's desire to honor his father's memory by anchoring his memorial in his Chinese heritage.

Rationale: Some English-language learners will likely have difficulty with the concepts and vocabulary in this story. By reading aloud in the beginning, the teacher can ease students' potential difficulties in reading, helping to "shoulder" some of the burden of juggling many facets of reading. By providing a reading guide, she can point them to specific kinds of important information in the story. By having the students read silently, she gives them an opportunity to reread, skim, and read ahead as necessary in order to help themselves understand the material better.

Procedure: The teacher begins by introducing the reading guide, shown below The teacher explains that the guide points them to important information in the story and that they should write some notes on the spaces provided to answer each question. The students can fill in the notes as they are reading. She reminds them that the main purpose for reading is to see how Tom becomes more understanding of his family's heritage. She begins by reading the first four pages aloud while students follow along in their books. She then stops and gives time for the students to write some notes on their reading guides. Next, she asks them to continue reading on their own and to continue making notes on the guide.

Reading Guide for *Black Powder*

The purpose of this guide is to help you understand the story by keeping track of details and events as you read. Please answer the questions. They are written in the order they appear in the story and are included so that you stop to think as you read.

1. List the names of the characters you meet in the story. Next to each name, write down one important detail about his or her life.

_____

_____

_____

_____

_____

_____

_____

_____

2. **Page 219–220**: Summarize what Alvin explains to young Tom about the "Chinese folk religion." Based on what he has learned, what does young Tom decide to do?

_____

_____

_____

_____

_____

_____

_____

_____

3. **Pages 223–229**: List the supplies young Tom needs to perform the memorial ceremony. Then, state how he found or made each one.

_____

_____

_____

_____

_____

_____

4. **Page 229**: Briefly describe the arrangements Alvin and Ellen set up by the back wall of the living room.

_____
_____
_____
_____
_____
_____
_____

5. **Page 230–233**: List the actions or steps that took place during the memorial ceremony. As you list each action or step, state who performed it.

_____
_____
_____
_____
_____
_____
_____

6. **Page 233–234**: How did Alvin feel after the ceremony?

_____
_____
_____

7. **Page 234**: How does young Tom feel at the end of the story?

_____
_____
_____

8. Can you relate anything in the story to your own life?

_____
_____
_____
_____
_____
_____
_____

Postreading Day 3

DISCUSSION: *Me, Then You, Then Us*

Students meet in pairs to talk about their notes for each question on the discussion guide. Then the whole group talks about the last question on their guide.

Goal of the Activity: To give students an opportunity to share the information they learned from the text and to use their written notes along with oral language for the purpose of broadening their understandings of the text as well as their English learning.

Rationale: Some English-language learners will likely have limited notes from their reading, while others may have more copious notes. Meeting in pairs enables the students to learn from one another and to enrich their understandings of the story. Also, the guide provides a framework for their talk, helping them to stay "on topic."

Procedure: The teacher asks the students to meet in pairs. She can fashion the pairs so that more able English readers and writers are with those who are not as proficient in English literacy. In pairs, students look at the questions on their guides; and for each question, they tell what they noted. Then, the teacher brings the whole class together to discuss how Tom became more aware of his heritage and whether the students found anything in the story that they could relate to in their own lives.

Adapting the SRE: The activities in this SRE could be used for a wide variety of types of texts, both informational and narrative. For the prereading activities, if access to the Internet is problematic in your classroom, you could substitute a short film for the *Virtual Field Trip* activity or show pictures from books to make similar points. For the during-reading activities, if some students' English reading levels are below the instructional level of the text, you could pair students so that more able English readers could whisper as they read.

Reflection: In this SRE we showed how a Sheltered English teacher could help her students to learn about content that is taught in science and/or social studies classrooms for same-age native-English-speaking peers. Helping the students to relate the ideas in the text to their own personal experiences as immigrants or children of immigrants is an added feature of this lesson. By incorporating reading material and activities that are sensitive to the students' own situations and experiences, the teacher in our example shows sensitivity to the ways in which cultural backgrounds can be tied up in learning. The teacher in our example also helped some of the children to use their native language as they read in English, specifically in helping them to see cognate words. She also modeled for the students the importance of thinking about the topic and setting a context and purpose for reading—activities we would want all students to do for themselves when reading independently. Finally, she helped the students to develop the strategy of reading the context to help figure out word meanings.

Comprehensive Scaffolding Reading Experiences: A Final Word

The chapter illustrating comprehensive SREs for English-language learners gives us an opportunity to make a point we have made before but one we think deserves repeating. We want to again emphasize the very important distinction between two goals for English-language learners (Gersten & Baker, 2000). One goal is to help English-language learners to understand and remember new subject matter. The other is to help them learn to read in English and their native language. SREs are designed to address the first of these goals. While students will learn many things about reading and using reading as a tool for learning from working with SREs, SREs are by no means a comprehensive program of reading instruction. English-language learners deserve teachers who scaffold their reading and learning, and SREs serve these purposes. However, English-language learners also deserve a comprehensive and multifaceted program of reading instruction, one that directly assists them in learning the skills and strategies necessary to become an accomplished reader. In "The Place of SREs in a Comprehensive Literacy Program" section in chapter 9, we outline such a program.

References

Aronson, E., & Patnoe, S. (1997). *The jigsaw classroom: Building cooperation in the classroom* (2nd ed.). New York: Longman. A concise yet complete description of the powerful learning procedure.

Cooke, C. L. (2002). *The effects of scaffolding multicultural short stories on students' comprehension, response, and attitudes.* Unpublished doctoral dissertation, University of Minnesota, Minneapolis. Shows very positive effects of using SREs with multicultural stories.

Gersten, R., & Baker, S. (2000). What we know about effective instructional practices for English-language learners. *Exceptional Children, 66,* 454–470. A study of the knowledge base of effective instruction for English-language learners in elementary and middle school grades.

Graves, M. F., Prenn, M. C., & Cooke, C. L. (1985). The coming attraction: Previewing short stories to increase comprehension. *Journal of Reading, 28,* 549–598. A clear description of how to write previews and a summary of much of the research on previewing.

Ogle, D. (1986). K–W–L: A teaching model that develops active reading of expository text. *The Reading Teacher, 39,* 564–570. Describes a prereading, during-reading, and postreading lesson structure.

Children's Literature Cited

Anholt, L. (1999). *Stone girl, bone girl: The story of Mary Anning.* New York: Orchard.

Avi. (1990). *The true confessions of Charlotte Doyle.* New York: Orchard.

Berger, M., & Berger, G. (2001). *Can you hear a shout in space?* New York: Scholastic.

Berliner, D. (1990). *Before the Wright brothers.* Minneapolis, MN: Lerner.

Blake, Q. (1988). *Mrs. Armitage on wheels.* New York: Knopf.

Bridges, R. (1999). *Through my eyes.* New York: Scholastic.

Brill, M. T. (1996). *Journey for peace: The story of Rigoberta Menchú.* New York: Lodestar.

Brown, D. (2000). *Uncommon traveler: Mary Kingsley in Africa.* Boston: Houghton Mifflin.

Burleigh, R. (1991). *Flight: The journey of Charles Lindbergh.* Illus. by Mike Wimmer. New York: Philomel.

Byars, B. (1985). *Cracker Jackson.* New York: Viking Kestrel.

Chaiken, M. (1985). *Yossi asks the angels for help.* New York: Harper & Row.

Cleaver, V. (1985). *How sweetly sings the donkey.* New York: Lippincott.

Coles, R. (1995). *The story of Ruby Bridges.* Illus. by George Ford. New York: Scholastic.

Cooper, F. (1996). *Mandela: From the life of the South African statesman.* New York: Philomel.

Corcoran, B. (1988). *The sky is falling.* New York: Atheneum.

Graber, J. (2000, November). *Thanksgiving gumbo.* Peru, IL: Cricket Magazine.

Graves, B. (2002). *California condor: Flying free.* Des Moines, IA: Perfection Learning Corporation.

Hacking, S. M. (1997). *Mount Everest and beyond: Sir Edmund Hillary.* New York: Marshall Cavendish.

Harber, L. (1979). *Women pioneers in science.* San Diego: Harcourt Brace Jovanovich.

Hazell, R. (1997). *Heroes: Great men through the ages.* New York: Abbeyville.

Hoffman, M. (1991). *Amazing Grace.* New York: Dial.

Hopkinson, D. (1999). *Maria's comet.* New York: Atheneum.

Houston, J. W., & Houston, J. D. (2002). *Farewell to Manzanar.* Boston: Houghton Mifflin.

Hoyt-Goldsmith, D. (1990). *Totem pole.* New York: Holiday House.

Huff, B. A. (1990). *Greening the city streets: The story of community gardens.* New York: Clarion.

Isaacson, P. M. (1988). *Round buildings, square buildings, & buildings that wiggle like a fish.* New York: Knopf.

King, J. (1993). *Impressionist: A novel of Mary Cassatt.* New York: Beaufort Books.

Kramer, S. P. (1987). *How to think like a scientist.* New York: Crowell.

Krull, K. (1996). *Wilma unlimited: How Wilma Rudolf became the world's fastest woman.* San Diego: Harcourt Brace Jovanovich.

Krumgold, J. (1953). *. . . and now Miguel.* New York: Crowell.

Kuklin, S. (1986). *Thinking big.* New York: Lothrop, Lee & Shepard.

Leedy, L. (1990). *The furry news: How to make a newspaper.* New York: Holiday House.

Markle, S. (1983). *Kids' computer capers: Investigations for beginners.* New York: Lothrop, Lee & Shepard.

Markle, S. (1988). *Science mini-mysteries.* New York: Atheneum.

Mora, P. (1997). *Tomas and the library lady.* New York: Random House.

Ohno, A. A., & Richardson, N. A. (2002). *A journey: The autobiography of Apolo Anton Ohno.* New York: Simon & Schuster Children's Books.

Osborne, M. P. (1990). *The many lives of Benjamin Franklin.* New York: Dial Press.

Paltorwitz, S., & Paltorwitz, D. (1983). *Robotics.* New York: Jem Books.

Patrick, J. L. S. (2000). *The girl who struck out Babe Ruth.* Minneapolis, MN: Lerner Publishing Group.

Paulsen, G. (1987). *Hatchet.* New York: Bradbury.

Ryan, P. (1990). *Explorers and mapmakers.* New York: Lodestar.

Shachtman, T. (1989). *The president builds a house.* New York: Simon and Schuster.

Simon, S. (1991). *Earthquakes.* New York: Morrow Junior Books.

Sis, P. (2000). *Starry messenger: Galileo Galilei.* New York: Farrar, Straus & Giroux.

Sorenson, M. (1998). *Danger marches to the palace: Queen Lili'uokalani.* Des Moines, IA: Perfection Learning Corporation.

St. George, J. (2000). *So you want to be president?* Illus. by David Small. New York: Philomel.

Stewig, J. W. (1991). *Stone soup.* New York: Holiday House.

Wang, R. C. (1991). *The fourth question: A Chinese tale.* New York: Holiday House.

Weiss, H. (1979). *Model buildings and how to make them.* New York: Crowell.

Wu, W. F. (1993). Black powder. In L. Yep (Ed.), *American dragons: Twenty-five Asian American voices.* New York: HarperCollins.

CHAPTER 9

INCORPORATING SCAFFOLDED READING EXPERIENCES IN YOUR CLASSROOM WITH ENGLISH-LANGUAGE LEARNERS

In this chapter, we focus on three sets of broad issues that we believe are important in effectively using SREs with English-language learners. Each issue is considered in a separate section. In the first section, we discuss some of the principal decisions and challenges you face as you move to implement SREs in your setting with English-language learners. In the second section, we consider assessing students, texts, and the effects of SREs. Finally, in the third section, we consider the place of SREs in a comprehensive literacy program for English-language learners and again stress that SREs are only one component of a comprehensive program.

Decisions and Challenges in Implementing SREs for English-Language Learners

Here we consider the frequency of SREs for English-language learners, how much scaffolding to provide, how often to differentiate activities for different students, the importance of providing a balance between challenging and easier reading material, adjusting and differentiating postreading tasks to ensure student success, preparing English-language learners for cooperative learning, and involving students in constructing SREs.

Frequency of SREs

How frequently should SREs be used in classrooms with English-language learners? Of course, the answer to this question varies for different students, different teachers, different goals, different times of the year, and different grade levels, to name just a few of the myriad of factors affecting what does and should go on in any classroom. Nevertheless, we can suggest some considerations and guidelines to use as you consider the matter.

To begin, we believe that SREs ought to be used frequently with English-language learners, especially students in the early and middle phases of learning English, primarily because they offer a structure and support that is often necessary to help students learn and grow. SREs provide some of your best opportunities for extending students' zones of proximal development by scaffolding their efforts—helping them succeed in their reading and giving them some common experiences to talk about, write about, and know that they share. In this sense, SREs have an intrinsic value that would lead us to use them quite frequently for their own sake for the stretching, success, and shared experiences they can provide. To take advantage of these benefits, we would generally include at least one SRE for English-language learners as a part of reading instruction during most school weeks.

From another perspective, SREs are useful for the extrinsic reason that they facilitate students' reading and learning in various content areas. Because students need to do a good deal of reading in social studies, science, health, and the like—and because some of this reading is challenging for many English-language learners—SREs are often called for in content reading. Although SREs used in the content areas will sometimes be quite brief, we suggest that they be used much of the time that English-language learners are reading content-area material.

Finally, the question of how the frequency of SREs should differ at different grade levels, ages, and proficiency levels is worth considering. Two somewhat opposing lines of reasoning come into play. On the one hand, English-language learners obviously need to become increasingly independent and self-sufficient as they move toward adulthood. This of course argues for SREs becoming less frequent over time. On the other hand, remember that one purpose of SREs is to stretch students, enabling them to read material that would be too challenging without the assistance of an SRE. Certainly, we do not want to stretch students any less in later grades than in earlier ones.

The situation, then, appears to be this: Over time, English-language learners become increasingly competent. Over that same time, however, the materials students read and the tasks they complete with those materials become increasingly challenging. Thus, there continues to be a place for SREs throughout English-language learners' school lives. In fact, in our judgment, giving reading assignments without any scaffolding—the proverbial, "Read chapters 4 and 5 and come to class on Tuesday prepared to discuss them"—is almost always inappropriate. Consequently, although SREs will often be different for older students, they continue to be an important component of a complete and balanced instructional program throughout the school years.

Another important consideration is the English reading level of the English-language learner. This may be even more important than the age or grade level of the student. As we have said before, whenever English-language learners are in the early or even not-so-early phases of learning English and learning to read in English, the language demands are plentiful, and these demands can make learning extremely difficult. This is true regardless of whether the student is a 1st grader or a 12th grader. In fact, typically older novice English learners may face even more difficult learning situations than very young novice English learners. Older novices are confronted with learning very advanced concepts and deeply technical language immediately. Their classroom teachers may be used to teaching about reading or content areas for readers at advanced reading levels. The older novice English learner must acquire some low-level reading competencies (for example, learning word meanings and pronunciations) that teachers of older students are not typically teaching in their classes. So there are mismatches between the kinds of things that are normally taught about reading at the upper-grade levels and what novice English learners need, at least temporarily. Consequently, we suggest that SREs are extremely important, not just for younger English-language learners, but also for middle grades and high school students who are novice English learners. We would even go so far as to say that novice English learners in the middle and upper grades should experience SREs as often as teachers can possibly offer them, and for beginning English learners, with every lesson if at all possible.

How Much Scaffolding to Provide

We have already alluded to the matter of how much scaffolding to provide, but the topic is worth addressing directly. Our main point is that it is not always a case of the more the merrier. We should keep in mind that the main goal is for English-language learners to become independent as readers and learners. With that in mind, a general rule of thumb is to provide just enough scaffolding for students to be confident and successful in their reading, but not so much that they are not sufficiently challenged, feel that they are being spoon fed, or become bored. In general, then, the suggestion is to provide enough but not too much. Further reinforcing the notion that you do not want to do more scaffolding than is needed is the fact that constructing scaffolds takes your valuable time, time that is always at a premium.

How Often to Differentiate Activities

Two sorts of differentiation are worth considering. On the one hand, you will sometimes want to differentiate SREs based on students' interests. For example, students can read different books while pursuing a common topic or theme. Thus, in exploring the theme of cultural identity, some students might read Jane Kurtz's 2001 Notable Books for a Global Society selection, *Faraway Home*, about Desta's worries that her father's trip back to Ethiopia might make him struggle with where he really belongs; others might read another 2001 Notable Books for a Global Society selection, Janet S. Wong's *The Trip Back Home*, about a young girl's trip to Korea with her mother to visit her relatives; while yet others read An Na's two-time International Reading Association Children's Book Award for Fiction for Older Readers, *A Step from Heaven* about a young Korean girl's struggles to learn a new culture and a new language in the immigrant experience. Similarly, some students may choose to respond to a reading selection in writing, others with some sort of artwork, others with an oral presentation, and others by going to the library to pursue the topic further. The constraints on differentiation of this type are your time, ingenuity, and ability to orchestrate diverse activities. Additionally, you need to keep in mind that the more different activities students are involved in, the less time you have to assist them with each activity. At the extreme, if 30 students are each involved in a different activity, you can give each of them less than two minutes of your time each hour. Thus, there are a number of practical limits on differentiating on the basis of student interest. However, if these limits are kept in mind, differentiation based on interest is very often desirable.

The other sort of differentiation to consider is differentiation based on students' English skills. Here, the same limits that influence differentiation based on interest apply. That is, constraints include your time, ingenuity, ability to orchestrate diverse activities, and ability to assist students when many activities are going on at once. Beyond these considerations, however, is the matter of the effect that results from being repeatedly placed in a group that receives more assistance. It is important to ensure heterogeneous grouping often, especially for English-language learners in the initial and middle stages of learning English. However, differentiation can make the difference between success and failure. From time to time, it will be important to differentiate instruction to ensure English-language learners' success.

Providing a Balance of Challenging and Easy Reading

Consideration of differentiating SREs leads directly to the matter of providing a balance of challenging and easy reading. Every student needs and deserves opportunities to read easy material that can be understood and enjoyed without effort and "just right" challenging material that he or she needs to grapple with (Graves, Juel, & Graves, 2004). By "just right" challenging material, we mean material that is at the student's instructional, not frustrational level, the level at which the student can pronounce about 95% of the words with ease and can understand most of the material relatively well. Some new concepts and ideas are present in "just right" material, but not a huge number. Reading easy material fosters automaticity, builds confidence, creates interest in reading, and provides students with practice in a task they will face frequently in their everyday lives. Reading "just right" challenging materials builds students' knowledge bases, their vocabularies, and their critical thinking skills; it also provides students with practice in a task they will face frequently in school and college, in their work outside of school, and in becoming knowledgeable and responsible members of a democratic society. Reading "just right" challenging materials also builds students' confidence in their ability to deal with difficult reading selections—if you ensure that they are successful with the material.

The point that needs to be stressed here is that each student—more able, more skilled, and more knowledgeable students as well as less able, less skilled, and less knowledgeable students—needs both "just right" challenging and easy reading. This condition cannot be met by providing only material that is of average difficulty for the average student. Assuming classrooms are made up of students with varying skills, knowledge, abilities, and proficiency in English, a description that fits most classrooms, then routinely providing only material of average difficulty ensures that some students will repeatedly receive material that is difficult for them, others will repeatedly receive material that is of average difficulty for them, and still others will repeatedly receive material that is easy for them.

In many situations, such as when English-language learners are in classroom settings where only English is spoken, beginning and middle-phase English learners are constantly faced with frustration-level reading materials, that is, materials written in English that they cannot easily read. In some cases, you can find ways to provide necessary low-level reading materials. However, in many other cases, you simply cannot find enough time in a 24-hour day to hunt down or prepare those beginning reading materials. Regardless of the extent to which you can make materials available to English-language learners at their English instructional reading level, SREs can be terrific ways to help English-language learners in the most challenging reading and learning situations.

Tailoring Postreading Tasks to Ensure Success

In constructing and using SREs ourselves and in talking to teachers who have done so, we have found that sometimes—even after considering the students, the text, and the learning task, and arranging a series of prereading, during-reading, and postreading tasks—some students are still not likely to have a successful reading experience unless something more is done. Often these students are English-language learners who are in all-English classrooms. In such cases, a most feasible avenue is to simplify postreading tasks. Having been faced with this situation from time to time, we have identified five general ways to simplify them:

1. Ask students to do less rather than more.
2. Require recognition rather than recall.
3. Require assembly rather than creation.
4. Cue students to the place where answers can be found.
5. Precede production tasks with explicit instruction.

Almost certainly the most straightforward approach to simplifying postreading tasks is to ask students to do less rather than more. We have given several examples of this in preceding chapters. Everything else being equal, tasks in which students answer fewer questions, construct less involved models, or write shorter pieces are distinctly easier. For example, rather than asking newly arrived English-language learners to read *The Island of the Blue Dolphins* by Scott O'Dell, you could have a few other students plan a way to act out the story for the English-language learners. Or if you have English-language learners who can read English relatively well, but very slowly, after the class reads the book, you might ask English-language learners to identify *two* instances of courage and explain why these were courageous rather than having them deal with *four* instances.

Requiring recognition rather than recall is another straightforward approach to simplifying postreading tasks. Any time you allow students to return to the text to find answers or present them with alternatives from which to choose rather than requiring them to construct answers, their task is simplified. In the case of *The Island of the Blue Dolphins* just described, for example, letting students return to the text to find instances of courage is likely to make the task markedly easier.

Requiring assembly rather than creation is quite similar to requiring recognition rather than recall. For example, some students might find it difficult to construct a time line of major events after reading a history chapter on the origins of the Vietnam War. However, these students would be greatly aided if you gave them a list of those events and a list of dates out of order and asked them to reorder the events and dates to construct a time line.

Cueing students to the places where answers can be found is an easily implemented approach and a particularly powerful one to use when students are dealing with lengthy and challenging selections. This approach was first suggested by Harold Herber (1970) for use with secondary students, but we believe it is equally or more applicable with elementary and middle-school students. Depending on the difficulty students face, you can cue them to the chapter, page, or even paragraph in which the information needed to answer a question is found. For example, suppose some of your third-grade English-language learners have had a difficult time reading *Manatee on Location* by Kathy Darling, yet you want them to remember some of the ways in which manatees have become endangered. Giving them the pages on which the factors that have adversely affected the manatees are discussed when you ask them to review these factors will increase the likelihood that they will successfully complete the review.

Our final suggestion here is to precede challenging production tasks with explicit instruction (Graves et al., 2004). If you are going to ask English-language learners to summarize information, synthesize information, make inferences, and complete other activities that require them to construct new information, you may need to explicitly teach them how to do these tasks before asking them to complete them. Of course, some students will already have been taught the needed procedures. However, even when students have been taught a procedure, it will sometimes be a good idea to review it. For example, suppose the students' task is to compare and contrast Hector and Mando in Gary Soto's *Crazy Weekend*. In this case you might briefly review the notion of a comparison and contrast essay, suggest some of the characteristics on which students might compare and contrast these two boys, and suggest some order for their essay, perhaps that of first listing the ways in which the two were the same and then listing the way in which the two differed.

At this point, you may be thinking that we have suggested a great deal of simplification and that what we are recommending seems like spoon feeding and thus robs students of the opportunity to grapple with difficult tasks. We want to stress that this is not our message. We are not recommending that postreading tasks always be simplified, and we are certainly not recommending that some students routinely be given simplified postreading tasks. On the contrary, the simplifications suggested here are fix-up strategies to be used only in a case in which students might otherwise fail. For many English-language learners, this means using the simplifications quite a lot. The essence of the SRE approach is to choose selections wisely and involve students in prereading and during-reading activities that will enable them to succeed with the postreading activities in which they engage. Occasionally, however, even with everything you have done to accomplish this, you will look at some students and some postreading activities and say to yourself, "Some of these kids aren't going to be able to do this." This is the point at which simplifying postreading tasks becomes both appropriate and advisable.

Preparing English-Language Learners for Cooperative Learning

Cooperative learning is another approach to maximizing the likelihood of success for English-language learners (Gersten & Baker, 2000). As David and Roger Johnson (Johnson, Johnson, & Holubec, 1994), two of the principal architects of cooperative learning, have repeatedly said, "None of us is as smart as all of us." Groups of students working together have the potential to achieve well beyond the achievement of an individual working alone. Moreover, as the Johnsons and others convincingly argue, working in cooperative groups can produce multiple benefits. Cooperative learning can improve English-language learners' language facility, their achievement, their effort to succeed, their critical thinking, their attitudes toward the subjects studied, their psychological adjustment, and their self-esteem. Cooperative learning can also foster students' interpersonal relationships, improve their ability to work with others, and build interrelations among diverse racial, ethnic, and social groups. Because of its great potential for English-language learners, we have suggested group activities throughout the book. Although the groups we have suggested have not been formal cooperative groups—a concept we define next— many of them could be. Additionally, any sort of group is likely to work better if students are prepared to work in groups, and the sort of preparation students need for cooperative learning groups will help them achieve more in all sorts of groups. For these reasons, here we define cooperative learning, describe three of the most frequently used types of cooperative learning, and consider the skills students need to work cooperatively in groups.

What Is Cooperative Learning?   Johnson, Johnson, and Holubec (1994) define cooperative learning as "the instructional use of small groups so that students work together to maximize their own and each other's learning." Robert Slavin (1987), another leading advocate of cooperative learning, defines it as "instructional methods in which students of all performance levels work together toward a group goal." It is important to realize that not every situation in which students work together is an effective cooperative learning situation. As Johnson and his colleagues point out, effective cooperative groups have five characteristics, as discussed next.

Effective cooperative groups are positively interdependent. In positively interdependent groups, students are dependent on each other. Each student must accomplish the assigned task, and each student must ensure that other students in his or her group accomplish it.

Effective cooperative groups include face-to-face interaction. That is, in effective cooperative groups, students engage in face-to-face interchanges in which they prompt, assist, support, encourage, praise, and challenge each other as all work toward completing the common task.

In effective cooperative groups, each student is individually accountable for his or her work. It is not enough for students to be accountable for some shared product. Each individual is evaluated, and the results of the evaluation are reported to the individual and to the other members of the group.

In effective cooperative groups, students are given specific training in interpersonal and small-group skills. Simply putting students together and telling them to cooperate is not enough. Students need specific preparation in getting to know and trust each other, accurately communicating with each other, accepting and supporting each other and each others' contributions, and resolving conflicts when they occur.

Finally, for cooperative groups to be most effective, students need to spend some of their time discussing how they functioned as a group, how effective they were in achieving the goals they worked on, and how effectively they worked together in achieving those goals. Effective groups reflect back on their work and consider what they did that worked, what they did that did not work, and what they can do to improve their work as a group in the future. Note that this is an excellent time for English-language learners and native-English speakers to engage in very meaningful discussions.

Three Types of Cooperative Learning.   Three of the most frequently used types of cooperative learning are formal cooperative learning groups, student teams-achievement divisions, and jigsaw. Formal cooperative groups (Johnson et al., 1994) are heterogeneous groups of three or four students, typically students differing in ability, ethnicity, social class, and gender. These groups incorporate the five defining characteristics of cooperative learning we just described, and they generally involve students working together for several class sessions. Tasks for such groups include problem solving and decision making, reviewing homework, answering questions or completing postreading activities, writing and editing assignments, and making class presentations. This sort of cooperative learning is particularly effective in fostering creativity, promoting problem solving, and building critical thinking skills.

Student teams-achievement divisions (abbreviated STAD) is a stylized approach in which groups of four students differing in ability, ethnicity, social class, and gender work together (Slavin, 1987). In STAD groups, the teacher initially presents the lesson, students in the group work together to ensure that each student in the group masters the material, and students are then quizzed individually and receive points based on the extent to which each exceeds his or her previous performance. Individual scores are recorded and then totaled to form a team score, and students are rewarded for both their individual score and their team score. STAD groups generally work on a project for three to five class periods. The procedure is most appropriate for learning well-defined objectives with single right answers. This makes it particularly well suited for learning vocabulary, learning the main points of a selection, and learning central concepts in subject-matter areas. Thus, while formal cooperative learning is most appropriate for higher level tasks, STAD is more appropriate for basic learning tasks.

Jigsaw (Aronson & Patnoe, 1997) is another stylized approach, but it is quite different from STAD. In the jigsaw approach, a class of 30 or so students work in five heterogeneous groups of six or so students on material that the teacher has broken into subsections. To begin, each student in a group learns one part of the material being studied. For example, in studying a particular country, one student in each group might investigate its origins, another in each group its people, another its geography, and so on. After studying his or her subpart individually, the member of each group who has studied a particular subpart of the topic gets together with the four members from other teams who have studied the same subpart. The five students in each of these groups discuss their subtopic and become experts in it, and these experts then return to their own groups and teach their classmates about their specialty. Finally, students take individual exams on all of the material. Jigsaw can only be used in situations in which a subject can be broken into subparts, but many subjects lend themselves to such an approach.

Skills Needed to Work Cooperatively.   Johnson and his colleagues (1994) divide the sorts of skills needed to work cooperatively into three categories: forming skills, functioning skills, and formulating skills. Forming skills are a prerequisite to effective group functioning. Important skills include such basics as moving into groups without bothering others, staying with the group, talking in quiet voices, and encouraging everyone in the group to participate. Functioning skills are the specific skills that students use as they participate in group work. These include giving directions, expressing support and acceptance of others' ideas, asking for help or clarification when needed, and paraphrasing others' responses as a means of checking understanding. Finally, formulating skills are the skills needed to perform the roles that group members often assume. Some of the roles that cooperative group members perform are those of the summarizer, who summarizes the group's leaning, the elaborator, who elicits further information and explanation from group members, and the checker, who prompts the group to make the reasoning behind their thinking explicit.

This has been a very brief treatment of cooperative learning. For those of you who are not familiar with the approach, we hope it will serve as a prereading activity and that you will go on to read and learn more about cooperative learning. Of the books cited, Johnson and colleagues' (1994) *The New Circles of Learning* is probably the most informative and a book we would consider required reading for teachers who want to develop effective cooperative groups. Slavin's *Cooperative Learning: Student Teams* (1987) and Aronson and Patnoe's *The Jigsaw Classroom* (1997) also contain many useful ideas and some approaches not included in Johnson et al.'s book. Additionally, Johnson, Johnson, and Holubec's (1987) *Structuring Cooperative Learning: Lesson Plans for Teachers* includes excellent and detailed lesson plans illustrating cooperative activities.

Involving Students and Volunteers in Constructing SREs

One of the central themes of current thinking about instruction and learning, and a theme that we have repeatedly emphasized throughout the book, is that in order to really learn something students need to be actively involved in their learning. One approach to getting English-language learners actively involved in their learning is the one we just discussed, cooperative learning. Another approach to getting students actively involved in their learning is cross-age tutoring, involving older students and volunteers in the instruction of younger students.

Our experience as teachers, a substantial body of research (Block & Dellamura, 2000–2001; Cohen, Kulik, & Kulik, 1982; Juel, 1996), and common sense suggest that volunteer and cross-age tutoring can be extremely effective. We very much agree with the sentiments expressed by Wilbert McKeachie (McKeachie & Hofer, 2002), a person who has spent more than 50 years studying instruction, in this statement: "The best answer to the question, 'What is the most efficient method of teaching?' is that it depends on the goal, the student, the content, and the teacher. But the next best answer is, 'Students teaching other students.' There is a wealth of evidence that peer teaching is extremely effective for a wide range of goals, content, and students of different levels and personalities." These claims are likely to be especially true for English-language learners.

One way in which older students can assist in teaching younger students, or in which more proficient English-language learners (or simply more proficient English speakers regardless of their native language) can help novice English learners—and in doing so become actively involved in their learning—is by preparing SRE materials for other students. Consider what the student who is going to prepare a preview, a set of discussion questions, or a map of a short story needs to do in order to construct first-rate materials. He or she needs to read the story, understand it, pick out what is important, pick out what is likely to be of interest to the other students, decide what sort of language to use in addressing the younger student, and then prepare materials that will be interesting, informative, attractive, and engaging for the younger students. In other words, he or she needs to understand and appreciate the story fully, to use his or her creative and problem-solving skills to create material, and to use his or her linguistic skills to communicate with a genuine audience.

It is hard to imagine a task that presents more opportunities for learning, for doing something useful, and for feeling a sense of accomplishment. Moreover, the possibilities are certainly not limited to previewing, mapping, or writing discussion questions. Many prereading, during-reading, and postreading activities require some sorts of materials; with your help, older students are quite capable of constructing those materials. Selecting and teaching vocabulary and concepts, identifying the organization of a selection, recording parts of a selection on tape, developing a writing assignment, and many other scaffolded reading activities are within the older, or more proficient, English speakers' range. Finally, not only will students learn more from creating SRE activities, but having students participate in constructing SRE materials will free teachers' time to work with students individually, prepare other interesting and enriching activities, or perhaps even take an evening off once in a while.

Volunteers, including parent volunteers, can also help English-language learners by preparing SREs. Having volunteers watch a few lessons in which you are doing SREs can provide a start for their understanding of what an SRE is. Once a volunteer has seen an SRE, she could then be given a new text and asked to create an SRE like the one she just saw, preparing an outline and materials to be used during the lesson. If parents who are themselves English-language learners are the volunteers, they too can benefit from the preparation in the same way that older students in our previous example could.

In general, we tend to agree with the adage that if something seems too good to be true it probably is. However, we feel compelled to believe that students or volunteers assisting teachers in constructing SRE activities is absolutely a win–win situation.

Assessing Students, Texts, and the Effects of SREs

Both matching English-language learners to texts and assessing the effects of SREs are extremely important parts of working with SREs in ways that lead English-language learners to successful reading experiences and long-term success at reading. However, we do not believe that assessment should occupy anywhere near the amount of time and attention given to instruction or the amount it is currently receiving due to state and federal mandates in many schools. Moreover, assessment for English-language learners is especially complicated because of the dual-language and culturally specific nature of their understandings (Hurley & Tinajero, 2001). It is also difficult because there are few valid and reliable measures for students acquiring English as a second language (Lapp, Fisher, Flood, & Cabello, 2001; Valdes & Figueroa, 1994).

In this chapter, we cannot possibly cover all there is to say about assessment issues for English-language learners. Instead, we treat assessment very briefly, considering only the sorts of assessment that are necessary to match students and texts and to assess the effects of SREs.

Matching Students and Texts

To match English-language learners with appropriate texts, it is necessary to get some indication of the students' reading level in the language of the texts to be read and to get some indication of the texts' difficulty. Sometimes, when English-language learners are in the early phases of learning English and they are in all-English classrooms, it is pretty obvious that they cannot read the texts. At the other end of the continuum, you might have English-language learners who are very advanced in their English proficiency; and it is obvious that they can handle the English texts in your classroom. But there can also be many situations in which it is very hard to know about an English-language learners' ability to read your texts, whether in English or in students' native language.

When students are reading in their native language or when they are reading in English as a new language but have had ample time to develop proficiency, you might find it appropriate to use standardized or state reading tests, which are often given at the end or beginning of a grade.

However, for students who do not perform well on such tests, it is wise to be extremely cautious in using results, especially for students tested in English as a second language and students tested in their native language when they have not had ample opportunity for reading instruction in their native language.

Evaluations done by your students' previous teachers can be tremendously valuable, if available. Further, as the year progresses, it makes good sense to do some of your own informal assessments. Probably one of the best forms of informal assessments is to pay close attention to how your English-language learners individually do when you use an SRE in your classroom. Lorraine Valdez Pierce (2001) strongly supports informal assessment for English-language learners using prereading, during-reading, and postreading activities such as the ones we describe in this book.

You might also choose to do an informal reading inventory in either the student's native language or English. Informal reading inventories need to be done individually, and they can be time consuming; so if you have a reading teacher in your school, you might ask her to do one for you. An informal reading inventory can tell you a student's instructional reading level. The inventory is made up of a set of passages and questions representing a range of difficulty. There are published inventories (Burns & Roe, 2002), but you can also construct one yourself (Graves, Watts-Taffe, & Graves, 1999). Basically, you create an inventory by simply taking a short passage—perhaps 100 to 250 words or so depending on students' proficiency—out of a selection you are planning to read, constructing a short set of comprehension questions on the passage, and having students you want to know more about read the passages orally and answer the questions.

In general, in considering the results of such inventories, we would follow the traditional standards and consider the selection at students' instructional level when they correctly pronounce about 95% of the words and answer at least 75% of the comprehension questions correctly. However, if you have students somewhat below these broad guidelines, you may be able to use the selection with them if you construct a sturdy SRE to support their reading.

We suggest that you begin using these informal measures with students who you suspect may be challenged by the selections you are using. Over time, however, you could also gather information on your stronger readers, paying particular attention to the need to challenge and stretch able readers with more challenging tasks. As you begin to accumulate information on students' performance with different selections, you can better and better predict how they will do on other selections on which you have not tested them. This is particularly the case if you keep anecdotal records on their performance with the passages, making notes on such matters as their fluency as they read, their reading rates, and their interest in various topics. Measuring rate in words per minute is particularly helpful, since it gives you an idea of how much class time you need to allot to various selections or to how much homework you are demanding if you assign a selection to be read at home. Measuring students' interest in various topics is of course critical to discovering what engages students. Bill Harp's (2000) handbook on assessment contains useful suggestion on informal assessments on attitudes toward reading and informal interest inventories that you may find helpful.

To effectively match students with texts, you also need information on the texts, of course. Here, we recommend two things. As one step, if the text is in English, you can use a readability formula. To date, we are unaware of readability formulas for other languages. Although readability formulas have received a good deal of criticism and certainly deserve some criticism, they serve one extremely useful purpose. They are very useful in avoiding mismatches in which the text is markedly too difficult for the students. For English texts, we currently use the New Dale-Chall Readability Formula (Chall & Dale, 1995) for this purpose. It has several features to recommend it. It has been revised fairly recently, it has better than average instructions and explanations, it is as accurate as any formulas, and it is easy to use. We recommend that if you assess a text and find that it is two grade levels or more above the reading level of some of your students, you seriously consider if it is the right text for those students. If after such reflection you decide that it is, or if you have no alternative, then you will once again have to count on presenting a particularly sturdy SRE to these students.

In matching students and texts, we recommend that you also consider 10 factors that research and theory have shown to influence both the difficulty of text and its accessibility. In Chapter 10, "Text Difficulty and Accessibility for English-Language Learners," we describe these factors and how to use them in some detail, so we will say just a word about them here. They fall into two groups. In the first group are six factors that are fairly easily defined, fairly easily identified, and largely inherent in the text itself. These six factors are vocabulary, sentence structure, length, elaboration, coherence and unity, and text structure. In the second group are four factors that are less easily defined, less easily identified, and very definitely involve both the reader and the text. These are familiarity of content and background knowledge required, audience appropriateness, quality and verve of the writing, and interestingness. We should emphasize that these factors do not constitute a readability formula or yield a tidy grade level for a text. However, in the hands of skillful teachers they can be enormously informative.

Assessing the Effects of SREs

The second factor we consider in this section is assessing the effects of SREs on English-language learners' understanding and learning from the selections they read. For this, we offer a single tool, but we believe it is an enormously valuable tool: a story map as described by Isabel Beck and Margaret McKeown (1981). A story map is a listing of the major events and ideas in a selection in the order in which they occur. To create a story map, you first identify the major elements, both explicit and implicit, of a selection. Then, you generate a question for each major element for the students to answer. These questions elicit information that is central to understanding the selection, and the answers to the questions constitute the essence of the meaning of the selection. The chart below shows the major elements of a Russian folktale, *Baba Yaga*, in the left-hand column and the corresponding questions for students in the right-hand column.

Story Map and Extension Questions for *Baba Yaga*

Event	Corresponding Question
Event 1: Katrina's father warns her not to go into the woods where the witch Saba Yaga lives.	Why did Katrina's father warn her not to go into the woods?
Event 2: The cruel housemaid sends Katrina into the woods to take food to a sick aunt.	What did the cruel housemaid ask Katrina to do?
Event 3: Katrina finds a dying dog in the woods and revives it with milk from her jug.	What did Katrina do to help the dog she found in the woods?
Event 4: A bit farther, Katrina stops to grease the squeaky hinges of a rusted gate.	Why did Katrina stop to grease the gate?
Event 5: Deep in the forest, Katrina comes upon Saba Yaga's hut, not the sick aunt's, and realizes the housemaid has betrayed her.	Whose hut did Katrina reach deep in the woods?
Event 6: Saba Yaga takes Katrina as a prisoner and slave.	What did Saba Yaga do to Katrina?
Event 7: Katrina shows kindness to Saba Yaga's cat by combing its matted fur, and the cat tells her to flee from Saba Yaga at midnight.	Why did Saba Yaga's cat tell Katrina she should escape?

(Continued on next page)

Story Map and Extension Questions for *Baba Yaga* (*Continued*)

Event	Corresponding Question
Event 8: Katrina flees with Saba Yaga pursuing her but is able to escape with the aid and magic of those she was kind to—the cat, the gate, and the dog.	Who helped Katrina escape from Saba Yaga and why?
Event 9: Katrina throws the rag she had greased the gate with at Baba Yaga; it turns into a lake, and Baba Yaga drowns.	What happened when Katrina threw the rag at Saba Yaga?
Event 10: Katrina returns home and her father sends the evil housemaid packing.	Why did Katrina's father "send the housemaid packing"?

Extension Questions
Question 11: One frequent component of folktales such as Baba Yaba is magic. Note some instances of magic in Baba Yaba and some instances in other folktales.
Question 12: Another frequent component of folktales is characters who are distinctly evil. Think of some other folktales with evil characters. Why do you think folktales often contain such evil characters?

The answers to the story map questions are one important part of what we would expect students to know after reading a selection. As Beck and McKeown (1981) note, however, these are not the only questions to ask on a reading selection. Once students understand the essence of the selection, then interpretive, analytical, and creative questions are appropriate and important to pursue. For example, with Baba Yaga, you might add extension questions such as these: "Have you ever been warned not to do something as Katrina was? What were you warned not to do? What happened?" Typically, we would include two or three questions of this sort.

Once you have created the story map and extension questions, they can be used in several ways to assess English-language learners' comprehension and learning following an SRE. One is to have students study and answer the story map and extension questions individually and then have them or some of them come up and discuss their responses with you. Another is to have students write the answers to the questions and turn them in to you. And still a third is to have students discuss their responses in small groups as you listen in and consider the contributions of individual students.

What you are trying to find out is if students understood and learned from reading the selection and participating in the SRE activities you created, and if they can make valid inferences and generalizations based on the selection. If they can, terrific. Your SREs are assisting students in effectively dealing with texts. If they cannot, then it is important that you do not automatically assume that the English-language learners did not actually understand the material well. Their language proficiency in the text language must always be taken into account. Some English-language learners can, for example, understand a fair amount of English text but are *not* able to express themselves well enough in either oral or written English to demonstrate their full understanding. In these cases, it is very important that you make every effort to provide the utmost opportunities for the students to show what they know as fully as they can. Some students can do this better in writing, some do better by answering questions orally. Still, there will be times when you just cannot tell whether you've completely tapped the full extent of a student's knowledge.

Many times, your student assessments will lead you to make modifications in your teaching—creating stronger SREs, using different texts, giving students more time with the selections, or whatever it takes to lead your students to successfully reading and learning from what they read.

For additional assessments directly relevant to reading comprehension assessment and content-area assessment for English-language learners, we highly recommend chapters by Lorraine Valdez Pierce (2001), Sandra Rollins Hurley and Sally Blake (2001), and Jim Cummins (2001).

The Place of SREs in a Comprehensive Literacy Program

In chapter 2, we specifically pointed out that a Scaffolded Reading Experience is not a complete plan for a reading program. Here, as we approach the end of this book, we want to amplify on that point, saying a bit more about what we believe a comprehensive reading program should include. In the remainder of this chapter, we describe each of nine components, which together constitute a program we believe would serve students well. For those who want more information on these components, we suggest reading *Teaching Reading in the 21st Century* (Graves et al., 2004).

Building Positive Perceptions and Attitudes about Reading

We list building positive perceptions and attitudes about reading first because unless English-language learners learn to love reading and the enjoyment and knowledge it can give them, no amount of expertise in reading can be considered adequate learning. As Linda Fielding and her colleagues (1986) point out in introducing their study of children's reading of trade books, in most cases "the problem is not that students cannot read, but that on most days they do not choose to do so." This, they go on to say, is a real pity because they found that "among all the ways that children can spend their leisure time, average minutes per day reading books was the best and most consistent predictor of standardized comprehension test performance, size of vocabulary, and gains in reading achievement." We must do everything possible to encourage English-language learners to truly love and value reading, because only by loving and valuing reading—and therefore choosing to read frequently—will they reach their full potential as readers.

Building Knowledge About Print and Sounds

Although *Scaffolding Reading Experiences for English-Language Learners* does not deal with the very beginnings of reading instruction, a comprehensive literacy program must do so. Also, many older beginning English-language learners in the upper grades also need to learn about basic phonology and print relationships. As part of learning to read, whether in native language or in English, students need to internalize a substantial body of knowledge about the sounds of the language, about print, and about the relationships between print and speech. That knowledge includes such matters as becoming aware of distinct speech sounds and recognizing how symbols form patterns and relate to sounds in speech (National Reading Panel, 2000; Snow, Burns, & Griffin,1998).

Instruction in Word Identification Strategies

As they read, children often encounter words they do not immediately recognize, and at least some of the time they need to apply strategies to identify these words. Readers of the English language need to learn how to figure out a word by using analogous known words and orthographic rules for word pronunciations. Another word identification strategy they need to learn is structural analysis, which includes using roots, prefixes, and suffixes in arriving at the pronunciation and meaning of words. Still another strategy is how to use context to figure out a word. As we have noted several times, students need to respond automatically to most words they encounter; and thus they will not be constantly using their word identification strategies, but they do need to have the strategies available when needed.

English-language learners beginning to read in English may already have many, or all, of these strategies in their repertoires when reading in their native language. Even so, they still must work through a period where they learn to apply them in English. Others may not have acquired all, or any, of these strategies. They will need to learn about them.

Dolores Durkin's *Teaching Them to Read* (1993) and Cunningham, Moore, Cunningham, and Moore (1995) provide detailed descriptions of word identification strategies and procedures for teaching them, and Stephen Stahl's "Saying the 'P' Word" (1992) presents what we believe is a balanced view of phonics.

Systematic Vocabulary Instruction

Most native-English-speaking children enter school with very small reading vocabularies, perhaps numbering only a few dozen words. Each year, however, the average native-English-speaking student's reading vocabulary grows by something like 3000 to 4000 words (White, Graves, & Slater, 1990), and by the sixth grade the average native-English-speaking student is likely to have a vocabulary of approximately 20,000 that he or she can both read and understand (Nagy & Herman, 1987).

Learning English labels, as well as particular constructs, is one of the most important acquisitions for English-language learners. Clearly, all students need help with this monumental learning task (Biemiller, 2001), and English-language learners need even more help. Such help should include direct teaching of individual words, primarily the important words and concepts in materials students are reading, and instruction in learning words on their own, for example, using context, using word parts, using the dictionary and thesaurus, and the like. "The Elementary Vocabulary Curriculum: What Should It Be" (Graves, 1992) lays out a comprehensive curriculum for native speakers, and "The Place of English Reading Vocabulary Instruction in Multilingual Classrooms" (Graves, 2002) describes how to augment this curriculum for English-language learners.

Instruction That Fosters
Comprehension of Specific Selections

This, of course, is the part of a comprehensive literacy program that this book does cover. The Scaffolded Reading Experience is our approach to fostering comprehension of specific selections. The RAND Reading Study Group (2002) has recently analyzed our current knowledge about instruction that fosters comprehension of specific selections and teaching comprehension strategies, the next topic we discuss here.

Instruction in Reading Strategies

In addition to receiving assistance via SREs with individual selections, students need to become adept at independently using reading comprehension strategies. As David Pearson and his colleagues (1992) note, reading comprehension strategies are "conscious and flexible plans that readers apply and adapt to a variety of texts and tasks." They are deliberate processes that readers use in order to understand and remember what they read. Among the strategies that Pearson and his colleagues have identified as particularly important are using prior knowledge, asking and answering questions, determining what is important, summarizing, making inferences, dealing with graphic information, imaging, and monitoring comprehension. One approach to teaching these strategies, the approach we tend to favor, is to systematically provide focused, explicit instruction in each of them (Duffy, 2002; Graves et al., 2004). Another approach, one advocated by Michael Pressley and his colleagues (Pressley, 2000; Pressley, El-Dinary, Wharton-McDonald, & Brown, 1998) is to embed instruction in these strategies within the normal reading activities students undertake from day to day. Whichever approach is used, what is vital is that the strategies are taught and learned.

Fostering Deep Understanding, Higher Order Thinking, and Creative Thinking

Too often, we believe, schools concentrate on one sort of learning at the expense of others. Usually, the charge leveled against teachers of English-language learners is that too much attention is paid to factual information and too little to higher level thinking, and this may well be the case. Whether or not it is, our very strong belief is that, while all students need factual information, all students also need to engage in and receive instruction in a rich variety of thinking and reasoning activities: deep understanding, higher order thinking, and creative thinking. We have found the work of Anderson and Krathwohl (2002), Perkins (1992), Resnick (1987), and Sternberg and Spear-Swerling (1996) particularly insightful on these topics. Various sorts of learning—and thinking, and doing, and feeling—are important if English-language learners are to become independent, competent, productive, caring, fulfilled, and happy members of our adult society.

Integration of Reading, Writing, Speaking, and Listening

We have addressed directly the matter of the close relationship between reading and writing, the fact that instruction in reading and writing ought frequently to be coupled, and the fact that instruction and practice in one of these modalities reinforces learning in the other. Here, we simply add that this close and reciprocal relationship holds among all four language modalities. This is why English reading and writing also help English-language learners' oral language to develop as well. Experiences in reading, writing, speaking, and listening go hand in hand, reinforce each other, occur together in the world outside of school, and ought to be frequently integrated in the classroom as well. We have attempted to take advantage of these interrelationships and highlight them in the sample SRE activities we have presented. Judith Irwin's and Mary Anne Doyle's *Reading/Writing Connections* (1992), Timothy Shanahan's *Reading and Writing Together* (1990), and Jill Fitzgerald and Timothy Shanahan's article (2000) on the development of reading and writing describe theory, research, and practice on the matter.

Independent Reading

When using Scaffolded Reading Experiences, you are generally working with the whole of the class or relatively large groups of students in order to ensure understanding and success on the part of all students. SREs can also be used with small groups, and their use with such groups is frequently appropriate. Obviously, we believe that such experiences play a crucial part in students' developing literacy. So too, however, does independent reading. Eventually, if English-language learners are to continue reading, they need to become independent readers. You can play a major role in helping them on the road to independence by allowing and encouraging them to do a lot of independent reading.

Incorporating SREs: A Final Word

In this chapter, we have attempted to provide practical advice and some closure to the book by discussing some of the principal decisions you will need to make in implementing SREs when you have English-language learners as students. We have examined principal decisions and challenges to implementing SREs; considered assessing students, texts, and the effects of SREs; and placed SREs in the context of a comprehensive literacy program.

Becoming literate has grown increasingly important to every individual in our society over each decade of this century. Today, literacy is more important than ever. Effective communication throughout our society and with other societies is, quite simply, a requisite of survival. At the same time, the challenge of attaining literacy, for English-language learners in both native language and in English, has never been greater.

The diversity of cultures, languages, and values makes it so. SREs can, of course, play only a small role in meeting this challenge. But we believe that they can play a significant role. By considering your students, the selections they are reading, and the outcomes that you and they seek, and then constructing SREs specifically designed to allow your English-language learners to use those texts to achieve those outcomes, you will make those experiences successful ones—experiences that build English-language learners' sense of accomplishment, their competence, and their ability to communicate. By using SREs, you become an advocate for English-language learners' ongoing growth and well-being.

References

Anderson, L. W., & Krathwohl, D. R. (2001). *A taxonomy for learning, teaching, and assessing: A revision of Bloom's taxonomy of educational objectives.* New York: Longman. An updated and greatly expanded version of Bloom's classic work.

Aronson, E., & Patnoe, S. (1997). *The jigsaw classroom* (2nd ed.). New York: HarperCollins. A recently released update of Aronson's work on the jigsaw approach.

Beck, I. L., & McKeown, M. G. (1981). Developing questions that promote comprehension: The story map. *Language Arts, 58,* 913–918. A brief description of Beck and McKeown's plan for choosing questions to ask on reading selections.

Biemiller, A. (2001, Spring). Teaching vocabulary: Early, direct, and sequential. *American Educator,* 24–28, 47. An argument for direct instruction in vocabulary, particularly in the early grades.

Block, C. C , & Dellamura, R. J. (2000–2001). Better book buddies. *The Reading Teacher, 54,* 364–370. Some very useful advice on children helping other children in their reading.

Burns, P. C, & Roe, B. D. (2002). *Informal reading inventory, preprimer to twelfth grade* (6th ed.). Boston: Houghton Mifflin. Probably the best known commercial informal reading inventory.

Chall, J. S., & Dale, E. (1995). *Readability revisited: The new Dale-Chall readability formula.* Cambridge, MA: Brookline Books. Explanation and instructions for using the new Dale-Chall readability formula.

Cohen, P. A., Kulik, J. A., & Kulik, C. C. (1982). Educational outcomes of tutoring: A meta-analysis of findings. *American Educational Research Journal, 19,* 237–248. A comprehensive and sophisticated analysis of the findings on tutoring.

Cummins, J. (2001). Assessment and intervention with culturally and linguistically diverse learners. In S. R. Hurley and J. V. Tinajero (Eds.), *Literacy assessment of second language learners* (pp. 115–129). Boston: Allyn & Bacon.

Cunningham, P. M., Moore, S. A, Cunningham, J. W., & Moore, D. W. (1995). *Reading and writing in elementary classrooms: Strategies and observations.* New York: Longman. A widely used and teacher-friendly text for teaching reading and writing in the elementary grades.

Duffy, G. G. (2002). The case for direct explanation of strategies. In C. C. Block & M. Pressley (Eds.), *Comprehension instruction: Research-based best practices* (pp. 28–41). New York: Guilford. Explains, defends, and notes the limits of the direct explanation approach.

Durkin, D. (1993). *Teaching them to read* (6th ed.). Boston: Allyn & Bacon. This widely used methods text provides a detailed description of word recognition strategies and procedures for teaching them.

Fielding, L. G., Wilson, P. T., & Anderson, R. C. (1986). A new focus on free reading: The role of trade books in reading instruction. In T. E. Raphael (Ed.), *The contexts of school-based literacy.* New York: Random House. A forceful plea for using trade books.

Fitzgerald, J., & Shanahan, T. (2000). Reading and writing relations and their development. *Educational Psychologist, 35,* 39–50. Reviews research on reading and writing connections and their development.

Gersten, R., & Baker, S. (2000). What we know about effective instructional practices for English-language learners. *Exceptional Children, 66,* 454–470. A study of the knowledge base of effective instruction for English-language learners in elementary and middle-school grades.

Graves, M. F. (1992). The elementary vocabulary curriculum: What should it be? In M. J. Dreher & W. H. Slater (Eds.), *Elementary school literacy: Critical issues* (pp. 101–131). Norwood, MA: Christopher-Gordon. A discussion of the various elements that should go into a vocabulary program.

Graves, M. F. (2002, May). *English reading vocabulary instruction in multilingual classrooms.* Paper presented as part of the Literacy Instruction for English-Language Learners Symposium at the 47th Annual Convention of the International Reading Association. San Francisco.

Graves, M. F., Juel, C., & Graves, B. B. (2004). *Teaching reading in the 21st century* (3rd ed.). Boston: Allyn & Bacon. Second edition of a comprehensive elementary reading methods text focusing on research-based teaching practices.

Graves, M. F., Watts-Taffe, S. M., & Graves, B. B. (1999). *Essentials of elementary reading* (2nd ed.). Boston: Allyn & Bacon. A compact reading methods text. We include it because it includes a description of informal reading inventories.

Harp, B. (2000). *The handbook of literacy assessment and evaluation* (2nd ed.). Norwood, MA: Christopher-Gordon. A compendium of teacher-made and published assessment and evaluation tools.

Herber, H. L. (1970). *Teaching reading in content areas.* Englewood Cliffs, NJ: Prentice Hall. One of the first content-area reading texts and still a source of many ideas.

Hurley, S. R., & Blake, S. (2001). Assessment in the content areas for students acquiring English. In S. R. Hurley and J. V. Tinajero (Eds.), *Literacy assessment of second language learners* (pp. 84–103). Boston: Allyn & Bacon. Provides ideas for how to assess English-language learners' content-area knowledge.

Hurley, S. R., & Tinajero, J. V. (Eds.) (2001). *Literacy assessment of second language learners.* Boston: Allyn & Bacon. An up-to-date compendium of recommended practices in second-language learner assessment.

Irwin, J. W., & Doyle, M. A. (Eds.). (1992). *Reading/writing connections: Learning from research.* Newark, DE: International Reading Association. A variety of researched-based insights on the relationships between reading and writing.

Johnson, D. W., Johnson, R. T., & Holubec, E. J. (Eds.). (1987). *Structuring cooperative learning: Lesson plans for teachers.* Edina, MN: Interaction Book Company. Several dozen detailed lesson plans illustrating applications of cooperative learning.

Johnson, D. W., Johnson, R. T., & Holubec, E. J. (1994). *The new circles of learning: Cooperation in the classroom.* Alexandria, VA: Association for Supervision and Curriculum Development. A brief, informative, and extremely readable description of the Johnsons' approach. Highly recommended.

Juel, C. (1996). What makes literacy tutoring effective? *Reading Research Quarterly, 31,* 268–289. Careful examination of factors making tutoring effective.

Lapp, D., Fisher, D., Flood, J., & Cabello, A. (2001). An integrated approach to the teaching and assessment of language arts. In S. R. Hurley and J. V. Tinajero (Eds.), *Literacy assessment of second language learners* (pp. 1–26). Boston: Allyn and Bacon.

McKeachie, W. J., & Hofer, B. K. (2002). *McKeachie's teaching tips: Strategies, research, and theory for college and university teachers* (11th ed.). Boston: Houghton Mifflin.

Nagy, W. E., & Herman, P. A. (1987). Breadth and depth of vocabulary knowledge: Implications for acquisition and instruction. In M. G. McKeown & M. E. Curtis (Eds.), *The nature of vocabulary acquisition*. Hillsdale, NJ: Lawrence Erlbaum. Provides an accurate estimate of vocabulary size and growth.

National Reading Panel. (2000). *Report of the National Reading Panel: Teaching children to read*. Bethesda, MD: National Institute of Child Health and Human Development. Influential review and synthesis of research on reading.

Pearson, P. D., Roehler, L. R., Dole, J. A., & Duffy, G. G. (1992). Developing expertise in reading comprehension. In S. J. Samuels & A. E. Farstrup (Eds.), *What research has to say about reading instruction* (2nd ed., pp. 145–199). Newark, DE: International Reading Association. Presents a contemporary view of reading comprehension instruction, with particular emphasis on teaching comprehension strategies.

Perkins, D. (1992). *Smart schools: From training memories to educating minds.* New York: The Free Press. A powerful analysis of teaching for understanding.

Pierce, L. V. (2001). Assessment of reading comprehension strategies for intermediate bilingual learners. In S. R. Hurley and J. V. Tinajero (Eds.), *Literacy assessment of second language learners* (pp. 64–83). Boston: Allyn & Bacon.

Pressley, M. (2000). What should reading comprehension instruction be the instruction of. In M. Kamil, P. Mosenthal, P. D. Pearson, & R. Barr (Eds.), *Handbook of reading research* (Vol. 3, pp. 545–561). Mahwah, NJ: Lawrence Erlbaum. Consideration of a variety of component parts that constitute a comprehensive instructional program aimed at developing reading comprehension.

Pressley, M., El-Dinary, P. B., Wharton-McDonald, R., & Brown, R. (1998). Transactional instruction of comprehension strategies in the elementary grades. In D. H. Schunk & B. J. Zimmerman (Eds.), *Self-regulated learning: From teaching to self-reflective practice* (pp. 42–56). New York: Guilford Press. A concise summary of Pressley and his colleague's work on transactional strategies instruction.

RAND Reading Study Group. (2002). *Reading for understanding: Toward an R&D program in reading comprehension.* Santa Monica, CA: RAND Education. A comprehensive and balanced assessment of what we know about comprehension instruction.

Resnick, L. G. (1987). *Education and learning to think.* Washington, DC: National Academy Press. A concise and insightful view of higher order thinking.

Shanahan, T. (Ed.). (1990). *Reading and writing together: New perspectives for the classroom.* Norwood, MA: Christopher-Gordon. Diverse, scholarly perspectives on the reading/writing relationship.

Slavin, R. E. (1987). *Cooperative learning: Student teams* (2nd ed.). Washington, DC: National Education Association. A brief introduction to several types of cooperative learning Slavin works with.

Snow, C. E., Burns, S. M., & Griffin, P. (1998). *Preventing reading difficulties in young children.* Washington, DC: National Academy Press. Influential review of research on beginning reading instruction.

Stahl, S. A. (1992). Saying the "p" word: Nine guidelines for exemplary phonics instruction. *The Reading Teacher, 45,* 618–625. Well-conceived guidelines for a phonics program that does not overshadow other aspects of the reading program.

Sternberg, R. J., & Spear-Swerling, L. S. (1996). *Teaching for thinking.* Washington, DC: American Psychological Association. Describes Sternberg's triadic theory of intelligence, which includes analytic, practical, and creative thinking.

Valdes, G., & Figueroa, R. A. (1994). *Bilingualism and testing: A special case of bias.* Norwood, NJ: Ablex.

White, T. G., Graves, M. F., & Slater, W. H. (1990). Growth of reading vocabulary in diverse elementary schools: Decoding and word meaning. *Journal of Educational Psychology, 82*(2), 281–290. Details on the size of first- through fourth-grade students' vocabularies.

Children's Literature

Darling, K. (1991). *Manatee on location.* New York: Lothrop, Lee, & Shepard.

Kurtz, V. (2000). *Faraway home.* New York: Harcourt.

Na, A. (2001). *A step from heaven.* Asheville, NC: Front Street.

O'Dell, S. (1960). *The island of the blue dolphins.* Boston: Houghton Mifflin.

Phinney, M. Y. (1995). *Baba Yaga: A Russian folk tale.* Greenvale, NY: Mondo.

Soto, G. (2002). *Crazy weekend.* New York: Persea Books.

Wong, J. S. (2000). *The trip back home.* San Diego, New York, London: Harcourt.

Chapter 10

Text Difficulty and Accessibility for English-Language Learners

One of the factors taken into account in planning a Scaffolded Reading Experience for English-language learners is of course the text itself. You need to assess the difficulty of the texts you consider using in relation to your students' reading levels in the language of the text, as well as the likelihood that students will be motivated to read them. As we have said previously, both of these matters are very important when you are working with English-language learners. While matching texts to learners' reading levels is difficult and achieving a perfect match is an illusive goal, we need to do our best to achieve the best possible match, and we need to do it without watering down the text (Gersten & Baker, 2000).

Here, we provide you with a reasonably comprehensive yet manageable set of factors to consider when selecting reading materials. We describe and discuss the factors for you to consider carefully, along with, of course, considering the students who will be reading the selection, their reading abilities for the language of the text, your purposes and their purposes for reading it, and the assistance you will give them in dealing with it. Rather than giving you a checklist of things that should or should not be there or a "recipe" that indicates just how much of this or that a text needs, we simply suggest a list of factors to consider, along with your best overall judgment, as you match students with texts. If you would like to read more about these and other factors, you may want to consult some of the following sources: Anderson and Armbruster (1984); Beck and McKeown (1989); Beck, McKeown, and Gromoll (1989); Beck, McKeown, and Worthy, (1995); Chambliss and Calfee (1998); Everson (2002); Linderholm et al., (2000); McKeown, Beck, Sinatra, and Loxterman (1992); and Otero, Leon, and Graesser (2002).

In all, we discuss 10 factors, divided into two groups. In the first group are 6 factors that are fairly easily defined, fairly easily identified, and largely inherent in the text itself. Of course, because reading is an interactive process that involves both the reader and the text, no text factors are fully independent of the reader. The second group includes 4 factors that are less easily defined, less easily identified, and very definitely involve both the reader and the text. All 10 factors are shown in the following chart.

Factors Influencing Text Difficulty and Accessibility

Vocabulary

Sentence Structure

Length

Elaboration

Coherence and Unity

Text Structure

Familiarity of Content and Background Knowledge Required

Audience Appropriateness

Quality and Verve of the Writing

Interestingness

Factors Influencing Text Difficulty and Accessibility

We derived the list of factors from our reading of the research and instructional literature on English-language learners and on reading comprehension and from our experiences as teachers of English-language learners and other students and as researchers at both the elementary school and college levels. As our title suggests, text difficulty and accessibility reflect either the ease or difficulty English-language learners may have in comprehending a text and how interesting and accessible the material will be for them. Of course, the more interesting and accessible the material is, the better the chance that students will pursue it, understand it, learn from it, and enjoy it.

You may be familiar with readability formulas, which are mathematical equations that typically take into account vocabulary difficulty and sentence complexity and assign a grade level to a text. You may also know that readability formulas have been criticized, primarily because they over-simplify the factors that make a text difficult (Alexander & Jetton, 2000; Britton & Black, 1985; Chall, Bissex, Conard, & Harris-Sharples, 1996; Chambliss & Calfee,1998; Cullinan & Fitzgerald, 1984–1985; Goldman & Rakestraw, 2000; Linderholm et al., 2000; Muth, 1989; Rouet, Vidal-Abarca, Erboul, & Millogo, 2001; Sawyer, 1991). We agree with the criticisms of the formulas, and believe that teachers should consider an array of factors in determining a text's readability in relation to particular students. That is why we discuss a variety of factors that are important when determining a text's difficulty relative to a particular learner.

However, we also think that, for beginning teachers, and for teachers who are not familiar with a wide range of text levels, sometimes a readability formula offers a quick way to get a ball park estimate of the potential difficulty level of a text. For these purposes and for English texts, we suggest Fry's readability graph (Fry, 1968) or the Dale-Chall formula (Chall & Dale, 1995). If you do use a readability formula on occasion, however, we suggest that you always consider the difficulty level you obtain from it as supplemental information, and that you consider the factors we suggest in this chapter as primary information for your decision making.

Factors Largely Inherent in the Text Itself

Linguistic complexity of a text can certainly impede English-language learners' performance, even on culturally relevant texts (Droop & Verhoeven, 1998). The six linguistic complexity factors considered here are vocabulary, sentence structure, length, elaboration, coherence and unity, and text structure. The first two, vocabulary and sentence structure, are ones you may be familiar with because they are the two factors most often considered in readability formulas. However, we want to stress that, although these two factors deserve consideration, they should not be relied on too heavily or to the exclusion of a number of other factors.

Vocabulary

We list vocabulary as the first matter to consider because, as we have said earlier in this book, understanding vocabulary meanings—both the concepts underlying word labels and the labels themselves—is one of the significant keys for English-language learners as they are learning to read in a new language (Garcia, 1991; Nagy, 1997; Nation, 2001; Schmidt, 2000; Verhoeven, 1990). We also place it first because vocabulary complexity can be one of the easiest characteristics to identify in a text.

Research suggests that texts containing a lot of difficult words are likely to be texts that are harder for English-language learners (Garcia, 1991;

Gersten & Baker, 2000). Also, results of some studies suggest that limited vocabulary meaning knowledge can be a major determinant of poor reading comprehension for Latino students (Garcia, 1991) and that acquiring "depth" of word knowledge can be difficult for second-language learners (Verhallen & Schoonen, 1993).

We want to stress, however, that a *few* difficult words are unlikely to pose serious barriers to comprehension. The rule of thumb for native speakers is that for independent reading no more than 5% of the words should be unfamiliar. While we do not know for sure if this percentage holds for English-language learners, we believe that too many difficult vocabulary words can indeed be problematic for English-language learners' efforts and understandings. We would not want to routinely require English-language learners to read texts where many words were unknown. However, it is also well known that individuals in general can learn new vocabulary through reading, with one study reporting 0.15 probability of learning an unknown word through incidental reading (Swanborn & deGlopper, 1999). Again, we do not know if this statistic also applies to English-language learners, but it does seem likely that if English-language learners read only texts in which all the words are familiar, they will be denied a major opportunity for enlarging their vocabularies.

However, for English-language learners we always need to be mindful of at least two more issues with regard to the vocabulary in texts. First, when English-language learners are in the early and middle stages of learning English, very few of the language and reading subprocesses are automatic. Vocabulary "overloads" can really strain and constrain an English-language learners' thinking. Still, key vocabulary meanings take on a central place in making a text comprehensible. Readers who "miss" the key meanings will have trouble making sense of the piece. So finding a good match between new vocabulary load in a text and an English-language learner's vocabulary knowledge is essential to helping the student reduce cognitive demands and enable learning (Echevarria, Vogt, & Short, 2000).

Second, many English-language learners can seem to have reasonably good conversational English but much less developed academic English. Sometimes it is easy for us, as teachers, to assume from their conversational English that they can handle more difficult content-area texts, but such an assumption is not always a safe one. Instead, we are better off if we keep in mind the distinction between word meanings used in everyday conversation and those used in academic texts, especially technical or content-area texts. It is a good idea to continually "check on" an English-language learner's understanding of key word meanings as new texts are presented.

Sentence Structure

Sentence structure, another text characteristic that is fairly easy to assess, is a second factor that reflects difficulty. Very long, very complex, and certainly very convoluted sentences make texts more difficult to read. However, for students in general, sentence structure does not have nearly as strong an effect as vocabulary (Coleman, 1971). Moreover, the sentences in a text need to be complex enough to clearly convey the meaning of the text (Pearson, 1974–1975). If the intended meaning is something like "Ted failed to win the award because neither his test scores nor his grades were high enough," breaking that sentence up into something like "Ted failed to win the award. His test scores were not high enough. His grades were not high enough" is not likely to result in more comprehensible text for many readers. Texts that lack logical connectives require students to infer relationships that could have been stated explicitly, and inferring relationships may cause problems for some students.

On the other hand, some sentences are clearly likely to be difficult for most readers. Here is one from "Shooting an Elephant" by George Orwell: "Its mahout, the only person who could manage it when it was in that state, had set out in pursuit, but had taken the wrong direction and was now twelve hour's journey away, and in the morning the elephant had suddenly reappeared in the town." Materials that contain a very large percentage of complex sentences are likely to present special difficulties for beginning and middle-level English-language learners and for younger and less able readers reading in their native language or in a new language.

At the same time, texts that employ artificially short sentences, the sort sometimes written for beginning or remedial readers, do not have the sound of real language. Here is a paragraph from a high interest–easy reading book. To our ears, at least, it sounds unnatural; and we suspect the author used this series of short sentences to keep the readability score down.

Payton's training paid off. He rushed for 1,421 yards in 1983. He caught passes for 607 yards. That was the most passes (53) of any Bear. He passed for 95 yards. He gained a total of more than 2,000 yards for the second time in his career. His yardage was thirty-six percent of the Bear's total yardage. He was almost a one man team.

Many readers, even remedial ones, would do better with a more natural sounding text, and at least one study with native-English speakers (Green & Olsen, 1988) has shown that readers, particularly less able ones, comprehend original texts just as well as simplified ones and actually prefer original texts to simplified ones.

It can also be argued that the more "natural" sounding texts are good for English-language learners because the connections to the natural sounding oral language patterns they are learning can make the reading easier for them. Also, reading the natural sounding texts may strengthen their oral English learning.

Still, we are back to the consideration we have mentioned frequently in this book. Teachers should help ease the often-times "overload" the English-language learner must bear for quite some time in learning a new language. As a result, teachers should examine the natural sounding text and evaluate it against the degree of complexity involved. Most likely, sometimes he will decide the natural sounding text is preferable, and at other times, he will think that reducing the complexity is more important.

Length

An obvious but sometimes overlooked factor influencing the difficulty of a selection, and the likelihood that a new or middle-level English-language learner or a less avid reader will make a real stab at finishing it, is its length. Particularly for beginning or middle-level English-language learners and students who do not read fluently, length alone can be a very formidable obstacle (Grobe, 1970). Additionally, in some cases shorter texts—summaries or much reduced versions of complete texts—can actually produce better comprehension and memory than longer ones (Carroll, 1990; Reder, 1982). If the intent of a reading assignment is to have students retain key information, then short summaries specifically designed to convey that key information may well be more effective than longer, less focused selections.

Fortunately, how much material and what parts of the material we ask students to read is usually directly under our control as teachers. When you think your English-language learners will learn more and more deeply from reading a shortened version, such as a summary, or even a subsection of a longer text, then by all means you should not hesitate to ask them to do less reading.

Elaboration

Texts can be written so that they present concepts without much explanation, or so that they present concepts along with a good deal of explanatory material, examples, analogies, and links of various sorts. *Elaboration* refers to a certain sort of explanatory material. Elaborative information is information that explains the reasons behind the bare bones information presented. Elaboration makes information more meaningful and understandable, and information that is more understandable is more memorable. The concept is an important one and worth some examples. Here are two examples, one from a psychological experiment on elaboration with native-English speakers (Bransford & Johnson, 1972) and one from an elementary social studies text.

In the experiment, some students were given unelaborated statements such as "The tall man bought the crackers," "The bald man read the newspaper," and "The funny man liked the ring," and other students were given elaborated statements such as "The tall man purchased the crackers that had been lying on the top shelf," "The bald man read the newspaper in order to look for a hat sale," and "The funny man liked the ring that squirted water." Then, both groups were given questions such as "Who bought the crackers?" "Who read the newspaper?" and "Who liked the ring?" Students who read the unelaborated statements could answer almost no questions, while those who read the elaborated text could answer nearly all of them.

The passage from a social studies textbook concerned American Indian houses. It consisted of statements such as "The Indians of the Northwest Coast lived in slant-roofed houses made of cedar planks," "Some California Indian tribes lived in simple, earth-covered or brush shelters," and "The Plains Indians lived mainly in tepees." But the textbook contained nothing to explain these facts and make them something other than arbitrary pieces of information. For example, it said nothing about the relationships between the types of houses and the climates of the areas, the types of building materials available in the area, or the lifestyles of the various groups. Unelaborated information is difficult to remember and not very interesting.

It makes good sense that elaborations facilitate comprehension and recall, and the facilitative effects of elaborated text have been empirically documented (Bransford & Johnson, 1972; Reder, Charney, & Morgan, 1986). However, as we noted earlier, shorter texts sometimes produce better comprehension and memory than longer ones. The matter of just when elaborations help and when they hinder is not yet resolved. It appears to be the case for learners in general, though, that shorter texts may be more effective if the goal is simply to remember material, while elaborated texts may be more effective if one needs to thoroughly understand material, for example, to write about what he or she has read or apply it in some real-world context such as operating computer software (Charney & Reder, 1988).

As you consider texts in relation to your English-language learners, it is likely that sometimes you will decide elaboration will be helpful. At other times, especially when your students are just beginning to learn English, you may feel that the elaboration is part of "overload," and that the students will be better served by an unelaborated text.

Coherence and Unity

Coherence refers to the integration of material, to how each topic and subtopic is defined and to how well the parts relate to each other (Anderson & Armbruster, 1984; Beck & McKeown, 1989). Two types of coherence have been identified: local coherence and global coherence. Local coherence comes when the reader can establish a connection between the sentence he or she is reading and the sentence immediately preceding it. Global coherence comes when the reader "is able to form connections between the sentence currently being read and either (a) information that occurs much earlier in the text or (b) the overall theme of the text" (Everson, 2002). Both sorts are important.

Unity refers to oneness of purpose. Good texts are directed toward particular topics, particular points, particular themes, and particular concepts. After reading a selection, the reader should be able to summarize the content of the text and explain its purpose fairly succinctly because the text has not dealt with a myriad of topics. In general, texts that wander, or those that contain pockets of irrelevant material, are difficult to read, to summarize, and to remember.

Beck and McKeown (1989) give a number of specific examples of elementary texts in which coherence and unity have been obscured. Here are three of them. In one fourth-grade text, an 800-word expository selection on subways is introduced with a 100-word anecdote in which the reader is asked to imagine that he or she is at home alone and needs to get someplace quickly: "It is Saturday morning. You are alone in the house when the phone rings. A friend of yours needs help." In this case, the reader may well be riveted, but unfortunately he or she is likely to be riveted on the wrong topic. The reader is focused on an adventure, while the text is intended to provide information about subways. In another fourth-grade text, in a 950-word selection about volcanoes, a description of the volcano Mt. Fuji is interrupted with a 60-word digression about Mt. Fuji as a summer resort. It may be interesting to know that Mt. Fuji is a popular vacation spot, but the digression does nothing to further the reader's knowledge about volcanoes, the topic the passage is intended to present. As a third example, Beck and McKeown cite a 900-word, third-grade selection on the brain, which attempts to describe diverse functions such as "neural impulse, memory and dreaming in addition to the brain's physical appearance." Such an attempt at presenting a huge and diverse body of information in so few words, Beck and McKeown note, "absolutely prohibits both supportive elaboration. . . . and development of logical connections necessary for coherent presentation."

With English-language learners and with material that is unfamiliar to students, it is particularly important that authors be explicit about how each piece of information fits with the other information in the text and about how each piece of information helps explain the event or idea the text presents. When a text lacks coherence or unity, you can help the students by pointing out the problem in the way the text is written, requiring students to read only parts of the text, and using SREs, such as supplying an outline in advance of reading.

Text Structure

Text structure refers to the organization of a text. The majority of texts students encounter in school can be placed into one of two broad categories, narratives or exposition/information, and these two types of texts are organized very differently (Drum, 1984; Everson, 2002; RAND Reading Study Group, 2002). Typical narratives reflect real-life events in which motives, actions, results, and reactions occur in sequence, and episodes in the main character's life are integrated by goals and subgoals. Time thus provides a natural structure for remembering episodic information. Most children's books are narratives, most of the material parents read to children are narratives, and most of the selections in primary-grade basal readers are narratives.

Exposition is another matter. Expository text, even well-written expository texts, can have a wider variety of organizations, and different authors have created different lists of the organizational patterns of expository writing. Anderson and Armbruster (1984), for example, list description, temporal sequences, explanation, compare/contrast, definition/examples, and problem/solution as typical organizational patterns. Chambliss and Calfee (1998), on the other hand, identify description and sequence as the two major rhetorical patterns and then further divide each of these categories. In addition to these rhetorical patterns, Calfee and Chambliss identify several functional devices—introductions, transitions, and conclusions—that serve to link the various parts of a text. Unfortunately, in surveying social studies texts, Calfee and Chambliss found that authors frequently employed weak rhetorical patterns such as lists or simply presented material without any apparent pattern. Additionally, the texts employed few effective functional devices to aid the reader. What is needed is expository texts that are clearly organized and that make that organization apparent to the reader (Chambliss & Calfee, 1998), and it appears that many of the expository texts used in schools fail to meet these criteria.

Moreover, since there is no single prototypic structure for exposition, previous reading of exposition—even well-written exposition—does not provide the clues to the structure of upcoming expositions that previous reading of narratives provides to the structure of upcoming narratives. Additionally, although on the rise, very little children's literature is exposition, parents read little if any expository material to preschoolers, and primary-grade basal readers and even some intermediate-grade basals contain little exposition. For these reasons, many students find expository text difficult.

As we have mentioned before, English-language learners may not be familiar with many of the structures in texts written in English. This is true even for narrative materials; many English-language learners may be acquainted with narrative organizations in their native-language culture, which can be quite different from those used in English. In many cases, teachers may not know the extent to which the text structures used in their classrooms are different from ones known by their English-language learners in native-language cultures. However, it is always important for teachers to think about the text structures of new materials for their English-language learners, and it is always good for teachers to find ways of strengthening knowledge of the structures used in the texts their students will read.

Factors Involving the Reader and the Text

The factors considered here are familiarity of content and background knowledge required, audience appropriateness, the verve and quality of the writing, and interestingness. As we have already noted, each of these factors definitely involves both the reader and the text; for example, one reader may find the content of a particular text quite familiar while another might find it largely unfamiliar. Additionally, you need to recognize that assessing texts along these dimensions is very much a subjective task.

Familiarity of Content and Background Knowledge Required

Reading a selection on a topic for which we have little familiarity is difficult for both native-English speakers and English-language learners alike. Reading a selection on a topic that is totally unfamiliar to us is simply impossible (Adams & Bruce, 1982). Younger English-language learners tend to read more narrative than expository material, and much of this material contains familiar content. A descriptive piece about a zoo will contain a good deal of content familiar to students who have visited zoos. Similarly, a narrative set in a suburban community and focusing on the adventures and misadventures of a Cub Scout will contain a lot of material familiar to a Cub Scout from the suburbs. However, the same narrative may contain much less material familiar to a young Latino living in

Los Angeles. Still, even when placed in unfamiliar settings, narratives are likely to contain familiar themes. Most children are raised by adults who become their parents; and situations that arise between adults and children, between authority figures and youngsters, occur everywhere. Children have peers with whom they play, fight, and engage in a host of other pleasant and unpleasant human interactions. They go to school, shop at the store, and sleep at night. These commonalties result in a good deal of familiar content in most short stories and novels. In contrast, expository text content is less likely to be familiar to readers.

Not only must the reader have some familiarity with the contents of a selection, he or she must also have the background knowledge assumed by the author (Adams & Bruce, 1982; Anderson, 1984). In some cases, the general knowledge that one picks up from day-to-day living is sufficient. This, as we just noted, is true of many short stories and novels. In other cases, much more specific knowledge is required to understand the text. This is particularly the case in technical and scientific areas. Many of us could deal with a calculus text about as well with the cover closed as with it opened. However, many humanities and social science texts also require extensive background knowledge for comprehension and thus pose problems for some students.

An example from a television serial, an example in which the content is not difficult but for which those of you not familiar with the serial will lack relevant background knowledge, will perhaps illustrate the point. The serial is *Dr. Who*, a fantasy series that was popular with many pre-teens and teens some years ago. Imagine that you are watching the beginning of the show and see a barren, desert-like scene, obviously hot and evidentially devoid of life. Suddenly, a red British phone booth appears in the desert. The camera zooms in to what should be the inside of the phone booth, but what you see is the cabin of some sort of a space ship, and it is much larger than the inside of a phone booth. In the cabin are a tall, lanky man wearing a long coat and a wool muffler reaching nearly to the floor and a young woman in contemporary clothes. The camera zooms out and you are again looking at the British phone booth in the desert, yet out of it walk the tall man and the young woman. The man then turns to the woman and says in a very solemn voice, "As the fourth Doctor, the tardis is of course my responsibility." The woman nods, showing her full understanding of the fourth Doctor's evidently poignant message.

But what are the uninitiated to think? What is a phone booth doing in the middle of the desert? Is the large cabin supposed to be inside that little phone booth? Why does the man wear a long coat and an even longer muffler in the middle of a desert? In what sense is he the *fourth* Doctor? Is there a third Doctor? A fifth? What is a *tardis*?

The answers to these questions and a host of others are readily available to *Dr. Who* fans, but totally unavailable to those who know nothing of the show; and while in this case one could acquire the background knowledge rather readily, in many cases a reader must know a myriad of facts, concepts, and relationships in order to approach a particular text.

As we have said before, English-language learners' background knowledge in relation to a particular text is a critical variable to consider. The knowledge of topics quite familiar to native-English speakers may, for example, be as thin as your knowledge of *Dr. Who*. It is always a good idea for teachers to wonder about the match between their English-language learners' background knowledge and texts they are asked to read and also to check their students' background knowledge in relation to texts.

Audience Appropriateness

Obviously, the topic of a selection and the sophistication with which the topic is treated need to be appropriate for the students reading the selection (Spiro & Taylor, 1987). Consider, for example, two human interest pieces, both out of periodicals and both written for adults, but both readily interpretable by many fifth or sixth graders. The first is by William Geist, a columnist for the *New York Times*. It is titled "The Friends of Trees" and begins like this:

> Marianne Holden could not restrain herself any longer. She whipped out her trusty 12 inch folding saw and attacked a Japanese pagoda tree.
>
> "It feels sooo good," she said, standing on her tiptoes while she removed a limb the tree did not need. A wise guy walking by yelled "Timberrrr!" when the little branch dropped to the ground.

The sketch goes on to describe a group of New Yorkers who help the city in caring for boulevard trees. It is well written, and we like it because it shows people doing something positive and caring. But how appropriate is it for fifth or sixth graders? Will they appreciate it, relate to it, be interested in it? We are not sure, but it seems likely that many students will not find it engaging.

Now consider another human interest piece. This one is by Charles Kuralt, the CBS journalist. It is titled "The Butterfly Mystery," and it begins like this:

Monarch butterflies spend the winter in Pacific Grove, California. In early spring, the monarchs migrate north. This fact is part of a mystery that suggests all kinds of troubling questions.

In the first place, the monarchs are confused by radio, television, and radar waves. And they are destroyed by fertilizer, insect sprays, and air pollution. So how do they survive at all?

In the second place, after they leave Pacific Grove, they fly as far as 2,000 miles into Canada. They fly through storms and across mountains and deserts, even though they are as fragile as feathers. How do they do it?

The sketch goes on to describe some of the other mysteries of the butterflies' annual visit to Pacific Grove, never really explaining them but describing some of the folktales about the monarchs' visits and all in all presenting the visits as a rather magical and wonderful annual event. It too is well written, and we like it because we find the phenomenon an interesting one. But is it appropriate for fifth and sixth graders? Will they appreciate it, relate to it, and be interested in it? It seems likely that they will. It seems likely that of the two pieces, both about the same length, both about the same difficulty, and both well written, "The Butterfly Mystery" will be more appropriate for many fifth and sixth graders.

Similarly, English-language learners are often very interested in reading about people, customs, challenges, and problems when texts are about their native lands and people. Moreover, native-English speakers can benefit from reading the same books as one way to come to appreciate and understand English-language learners. Books such as *Fiesta Fireworks*, by George Ancona, which portrays the role of fireworks in a Mexican pueblo, can not only readily engage readers, but also enable comparison to the use of fireworks in U.S. celebrations.

As you get to know your students better over the course of a year, and from year to year, you will be better and better able to gauge the appropriateness of various texts for your English-language learners. Of course, in general, materials that seem directly relevant to pressing issues in their own lives are highly likely to be appropriate for them, as are texts that prize their own heritage and cultures and feature individuals with whom they can identify.

Quality and Verve of the Writing

In addition to the factors that have been presented thus far, one must consider the quality of the writing, the flair of the writing, the particular blend of topic, organization, and style that makes one piece of writing intriguing and memorable and another piece mundane.

Very little research has been done on the effects of the quality and verve of writing. However, in one relevant study with native-English learners, Beck et al. (1995) found that modifying textbook passages by giving them "voice" significantly increased fourth graders' comprehension of the passages. In revising the passages to give them voice, Beck and her colleagues attempted to make text situations more dynamic, make the language more conversational, and highlight connections between the reader and the text. Although voice is only part of what we mean by quality and verve, it is certainly a major part of it.

While texts students read should be lucid, clarity is only one criterion for good prose. Joseph Williams, author of a short text titled *Style: Ten Lessons in Clarity and Grace,* addresses the topic in this way:

> Let us assume that you can now write clear [and] cohesive . . . prose. That in itself would constitute a style of such singular distinction that most of us would be more than satisfied to achieve so much. But even though we might prefer bald clarity . . . the unrelenting simplicity of the plain style can finally become very flat and dry indeed, eventually arid. Its plainness invests prose with the blandness of unsalted meat and potatoes—honest fare to be sure, but hardly memorable and certainly without zest. Sometimes a touch of class, a flash of elegance can make the difference between forgettable Spartan plainness and a well-turned phrase that fixes itself in the mind of the reader.

Exposing English-language learners to the power and beauty of the language ought to be one of our aims in selecting texts. When selecting texts for English-language learners, quality and verve of writing deserve your consideration, for texts with energy help students to learn as much about language and language use as they do about their content and themes.

Interestingness

We left this factor for last because it is the most subjective factor and the factor most dependent on the reader. A poorly written piece on dogs is likely to be of great interest to a child who loves dogs, while even very well-written articles on the topic will not capture the interest of a child who doesn't care much about animals. Moreover, the results of studies of interesting material on children's comprehension in general are mixed. Some studies have shown positive effects of interesting material (Anderson, Shirey, Wilson, & Fielding, 1987; Asher, 1980). Others have failed to show such effects and have even found that interesting anecdotes in textbooks can sometimes focus children's attention away from more impor-tant parts of a selection (Duffy et al., 1989; Garner, 1992; Graves et al., 1991). Garner has aptly labeled these interesting, but tangential, topics that detract from comprehension "seductive details." Like the sirens of Greek mythology, they lure unsuspecting readers from their true course with their arresting call. Recall, for example, the adventure narrative that begins the fourth-grade expository selection on subways, a passage we mentioned in the section on coherence and unity. The narrative is very likely to capture students' interest, but their attention will be focused on solving the problem of helping a friend and not on the information about subways.

In general, texts with integrated interesting material are likely to facili-tate comprehension, while texts in which the interesting material is an add-on are likely to impede comprehension. The implications for teach-ing are threefold. First, although a great deal has been written about children's interests, the best way to find out about what interests your English-language learners is to spend a lot of time with them, sharing your interests and seeking to learn about and share theirs. Second, anno-tated bibliographies and other discussions of children's books abound. Selecting texts written by authors of the same ethnicities as your students is an important way to potentially boost text interestingness to students. We encourage you to spend some time reading children's books and pe-riodicals themselves. Finally, be particularly aware of seductive details in expository writing for children. Try to choose writing that makes the sub-ject matter itself interesting rather than writing that relies on irrelevant asides to gain its readers' interest, and alert students to the presence of irrelevant details in some texts. Their learning to deal with such matters is part of their becoming genuinely metacognitive in reading.

Concluding Comments

In all, we have listed 10 factors likely to influence text difficulty. Six of the factors—vocabulary, sentence structure, length, elaboration, coherence and unity, and text structure—are largely inherent in the text itself. Four factors—familiarity of content and background knowledge required, au-dience appropriateness, the quality and verve of the writing, and interest-ingness—definitely involve both the reader and the text.

We should note that a factor may be critically important for one text or situation but not very important for another. As one example, consider length. Length may be critically important in considering an expository selection that requires a great deal of background knowledge, that is not very interesting, and that is going to be used as a required reading for

English-language learners who are just beginning to learn English. Conversely, length may be unimportant in considering an interesting narrative selection that you plan to recommend as recreational reading for an advanced English-language learner who is an adept reader in the language of the text.

As another example, consider quality and verve. Quality and verve are likely to be extremely important when considering a lengthy social science selection to be given to less than avid readers as a required assignment. On the other hand, style and verve are not very important considerations in choosing documentation for some computer software that a student really wants to learn to use. In fact, straightforward and unadorned prose may well be preferable for the software documentation.

We should also note that with some texts you will probably consider only some of the factors before making a decision. For example, you might choose to discard a poorly organized selection on an unfamiliar and uninteresting topic without examining the piece in great detail. Or, you might plan to use a particularly interesting piece even though it displayed a number of difficult features. Of course, in the latter case, you may decide to give all students, and particularly your English-language learners, a good deal of assistance in dealing with the text.

More generally, in concluding we want to note again that as part of the task of matching texts and students, several elements deserve and require your consideration: the factors discussed here, the students who will be reading the selection, your purposes and their purposes for reading the selection, and the scaffolding you will provide to help them deal successfully with the selection.

References

Adams, M. L., & Bruce B. (1982). Background knowledge and reading comprehension. In J. A. Langer & T. M. Smith Burke (Eds.), *Reader meets author: Bridging the gap* (pp. 2–25). Newark, DE: International Reading Association. A very readable introduction to the importance of background knowledge.

Alexander, P. A., & Jetton, T. L. (2000). Learning from text: A multidimensional and developmental perspective. In M. Kamil, P. Mosenthal, P. D. Pearson, & R. Barr (Eds.), *Handbook of reading research*, (Vol. III, pp. 285–310). Mahway, NJ: Lawrence Erlbaum. Review of research on learning from text.

Anderson, R. C. (1984). The role of the readers' schema in comprehension, learning, and memory. In R. C. Anderson, J. Osborn, & R. J. Tierney (Eds.), *Learning to read in American schools* (pp. 243–257). Hillsdale, NJ: Lawrence Erlbaum. Another readable introduction to the importance of background knowledge.

Anderson, R. C., Shirey, L. L., Wilson, P. T., & Fielding, L. G. (1987). Interestingness of children's reading material. In R. Snow & M. Farr (Eds.), *Aptitude, learning and instruction: Cognitive and affective process analyses.* A brief analyses of interestingness. Hillsdale, NJ: Lawrence Erlbaum.

Anderson, T. H., & Armbruster, B. B. (1984). Content area textbooks. In R. C. Anderson, J. Osborn, & R. J. Tierney (Eds.), *Learning to read in American schools* (pp. 193–226). Hillsdale, NJ: Lawrence Erlbaum. Influential article on what is wrong with textbook writing and how it can be improved.

Asher, S. (1980). Topic interest and children's reading comprehension. In R. J. Spiro, B. C. Bruce, & W. F. Brewer (Eds.), *Theoretical issues in reading comprehension.* Hillsdale, NJ: Lawrence Erlbaum. Brief review of research suggesting that interest does positively affect reading comprehension.

Beck, I. L., & McKeown, M. G. (1989). Expository text for young readers. The issue of coherence. In L. Resnick (Ed.), *Essays in honor of Robert Glaser* (pp. 47–66). Hillsdale, NJ: Lawrence Erlbaum. Insightful overview of text characteristics that reduce coherence.

Beck, I. L., McKeown, M. G., & Gromoll, E. W. (1989). Issues that may affect social studies learning: Examples from four commercial programs. *Cognition and Instruction, 6,* 99–158. An extended and sophisticated examination of text factors affecting learning.

Beck, I. L., McKeown, M. G., & Worthy, J. (1995). Giving a text voice can improve students' understanding. *Reading Research Quarterly, 30,* 220–238. Empirical study of the effects of giving a text "voice"; includes sample materials illustrating the concept.

Bransford, J. D., & Johnson, M. K. (1972). Contextual prerequisites for understanding: Some investigations of comprehension and recall. *Journal of Verbal Learning and Verbal Behavior, 11,* 717–726. A classic article on the effects of elaboration.

Britton, B. K., & Black, J. B. (Eds.). (1985). *Understanding expository text: A theoretical and practical handbook for analyzing explanatory text.* Hillsdale, NJ: Lawrence Erlbaum. A comprehensive and fairly technical collection on expository text.

Carroll, J. M. (1990). *The Nurnberg funnel: Designing minimalist instruction for practical computer skills.* Cambridge, MA: MIT Press. Advances the intriguing concept that less detail is sometimes preferable for learning.

Chall, J. S., Bissex, G. L., Conard, S. S., & Harris-Sharples, S. (1996). *Qualitative assessment of text difficulty: A practical guide for teachers and writers.* Cambridge, MA: Brookline Books. A good source of passages representing various grade levels and several subject areas.

Chall, J. S., & Dale, E. (1995). *Manual for use of the new Dale-Chall readability formula.* Cambridge, MA: Brookline Books. Manual for the revised formula.

Chambliss, M., & Calfee, R. C. (1998). *Textbooks for learning: Nurturing children's minds.* Cambridge, MA: Basil Blackwell. An in-depth and insightful look at textbooks and textbook adoption.

Charney, D. H., & Reder, L. M. (1988). Studies in elaboration of instructional texts. In S. Doheny-Farina (Ed.), *Effective documentation: What we have learned from research* (pp. 47–72). Cambridge, MA: MIT Press. A summary of the authors' research on elaboration.

Coleman, E. B. (1971). Determining a technology of written instruction: Some determiners of the complexity of prose. In E. Z. Rothkopf & P. E. Johnson (Eds.), *Verbal learning research and the technology of written instruction.* New York: Teachers College Press. An early look at factors affecting text difficulty.

Cullinan, B., & Fitzgerald, S. (1984–1985). Background information bulletin on the use of readability formulae. *Reading Today, 2* (3). The source of the IRA/NCTE pronouncement against overreliance on readability formulas.

Droop, M., & Verhoeven, L. (1998). Background knowledge, linguistic complexity, and second-language reading comprehension. *Journal of Literacy Research, 30,* 253–271. A study of the impact of selected features of learners and text on second-language learners' reading comprehension.

Drum, P. (1984). Children's understanding of passages. In J. Flood (Ed.), *Promoting reading comprehension* (pp. 61–78). Newark, DE: International Reading Association. A very lucid examination of what children understand from narrative and expository texts.

Duffy, T. M. et al. (1989). Models for the design of instructional text. *Reading Research Quarterly, 24,* 434–457. Study showing the superiority of less adorned text.

Echevarria, J., Vogt, M. E., & Short, D. J. (2000). *Making content comprehensible for English language learners: The SIOP model.* Boston: Allyn &

Bacon. Describes the Sheltered Instruction Observation Protocol model for teaching English-language learners and provides many illustrations of its implementation using classroom scenarios.

Everson, M. G. (2002). *The effects of local and global coherence on the processing and recall of history and science texts.* Unpublished doctoral dissertation, University of Minnesota, Minneapolis. Contains an excellent review of research on text difficulty and text processing.

Fry, E. (1968). A readability formula that saves time. *Journal of Reading, 11,* 513–516. Complete instructions for this straightforward formula.

Garcia, G. E. (1991). Factors influencing the English reading test performance of Spanish-speaking Hispanic children. *Reading Research Quarterly, 26,* 371–392. An investigation of features that affected Latino students' performance on English reading tests.

Garner, R. (1992). "Seductive details" and learning from text. In K. A. Renninger, S. Hidi, & A. Krapp (Eds.), *The role of interest in learning and development.* Hillsdale, NJ: Lawrence Erlbaum. Review of research showing the negative effects of seductive details.

Gersten, R., & Baker, S. (2000). What we know about effective instructional practices for English-language learners. *Exceptional Children, 66,* 454–470. A synthesis of research and professional views on effective instructional practices with English-language learners.

Goldman, S. R., & Rakestraw, J. A., Jr. (2000). Structural aspects of constructing meaning from text. In M. Kamil, P. Mosenthal, & R. Barr (Eds.), *Handbook of reading research* (Vol. III, pp. 311–335). Mahwah, NJ: Lawrence Erlbaum. Review of research on structural aspects of text broadly conceived.

Graves, M. F. et al. (1991). Improving instructional text: Some lessons learned. *Reading Research Quarterly, 26,* 110–120. Reports a study and reviews a series of studies indicating the negative effects of seductive details.

Green, G. M., & Olsen, M. D. (1988). Preferences and comprehension of original and readability adapted materials. In A. Davison & G. M. Green (Eds.), *Linguistic complexity and text comprehension* (pp. 115–140). Hillsdale, NJ: Lawrence Erlbaum. Study showing that students prefer original text to supposedly more readable adapted versions.

Grobe, J. A. (1970). Reading rate and study time demands on secondary students. *Journal of Reading, 13,* 286–288, 316. Illustrates the huge task that lengthy readings pose for slow readers.

Linderholm, T. et al. (2000). Effects of causal text revisions on more- and less-skilled readers' comprehension of easy and difficult texts. *Cognition &*

Instruction, 18, 525–556. Empirical study demonstrating the effects on comprehension of certain sorts of revision.

McKeown, M. G., Beck, I. L., Sinatra, G. M., & Loxterman, J. A. (1992). The contribution of prior knowledge and coherent text to comprehension. *Reading Research Quarterly, 27,* 78–93. Study showing that both of these factors have significant effects on comprehension.

Muth, K. D. (Ed.). (1989). *Children's comprehension of narrative and expository text: Research into practice.* Newark, DE: International Reading Association. A teacher-oriented collection of articles on text comprehension.

Nagy, W. (1997). On the role of context in first- and second-language vocabulary learning. In N. Schmitt & M. McCarthy (Eds.), *Vocabulary: Description, acquisition and pedagogy* (pp. 64–83). Cambridge, England: Cambridge University Press. Discusses vocabulary learning in first and second languages.

Nation, I. S. P. (2001). *Learning vocabulary in another language.* Cambridge, England: Cambridge University Press. Detailed text on teaching and learning second-language vocabulary.

Otero, J., Leon, J., & Graesser, A. (2002). *The psychology of science text comprehension.* Mahway, NJ: Lawrence Erlbaum. A collection of quite technical articles about comprehending science text.

Pearson, P. D. (1974–1975). The effects of grammatical complexity on children's comprehension, recall, and conception of certain semantic relations. *Reading Research Quarterly, 10,* 155–192. Probably the first study to show that syntactically more complex text can sometimes be comprehended better than syntactically less complex text.

RAND Reading Study Group. (2002). *Reading for understanding: Toward an R&D program in reading comprehension.* Santa Monica, CA: Rand Education. Available: http://www.rand.org/multi/achievementforall/reading/

Reder, L. M. (1982). Elaborations: When do they help and when do they hurt? *Text, 2,* 211–224. Study indicating that elaboration does not always facilitate learning.

Reder, L. M, Charney, D. H., & Morgan, K .I. (1986). The role of elaborations in learning a skill from an instructional text. *Memory and Cognition, 14,* 64–78. Study indicating cases in which elaboration does facilitate learning.

Rouet, J., Vidal-Abarca, E., Erboul, A. B., & Millogo, V. (2001). Effects of information search tasks on the comprehension of instructional text. *Discourse Processes, 31,* 163–186. Experimental study of text comprehension.

Sawyer, M. H. (1991). A review of the research in revising instructional text. *Journal of Reading Behavior, 23*, 307–333. Comprehensive review of the literature on revising text to facilitate learning.

Schmidt, N. (2000). *Vocabulary in language teaching.* Cambridge, England: Cambridge University Press. Another full-length text on teaching and learning second-language vocabulary.

Spiro, R. J., & Taylor, B. M. (1987). On investigating children's transition from narrative to expository discourse: The multidimensional nature of psychological text classification. In R. J. Tierney, P. L. Anders, & J. N. Mitchell (Eds.), *Understanding readers' understanding* (pp. 77–93). Hillsdale, NJ: Lawrence Erlbaum. Sophisticated essay on factors influencing text comprehension.

Swanborn, M. S. L., & deGlopper, K. (1999). Incidental word learning while reading: A meta-analysis. *Review of Educational Research, 69*, 261–286. Provides a statistical analysis of data reported in studies of learning word meanings from reading.

Verhallen, M., & Schoonen, R. (1993). Vocabulary knowledge of monolingual and bilingual children. *Applied Linguistics, 14*, 344–363. Reports research comparing vocabularies of monolingual and bilingual children.

Verhoeven, L. T. (1990). Acquisition of reading in a second language. *Reading Research Quarterly, 25*, 90–114. Reports a study on learning to read in a second language.

Williams, V. M. (2000). *Style: Ten lessons in clarity and grace* (6th ed.). New York: Longman. A truly excellent little book on writing with style.

Children's Literature

Ancona, G. (1998). *Fiesta fireworks.* New York: Lothrop, Lee & Shepard.

Geist, W. (1987). The friends of trees. In M. W. Aulls & M. F. Graves (Eds.), *Quest: A Scholastic reading improvement program.* New York: Scholastic.

Kuralt, C. (1987). The butterfly mystery. In M. W. Aulls & M. F. Graves (Eds.), *Quest: A Scholastic reading improvement program.* New York: Scholastic.

Orwell, G. (1950). *Shooting an elephant and other essays.* New York: Harcourt, Brace.

GRADE LEVEL
INDEX OF ACTIVITIES

CHILDREN'S LITERATURE INDEX

ACADEMIC AUTHOR INDEX

Academic Subject Index

ABOUT THE AUTHORS

Jill Fitzgerald is Professor of Literacy Studies and Assistant Dean for Faculty Personnel at The University of North Carolina at Chapel Hill. She received her Ph.D. in Research and Evaluation in Education, specializing in Literacy, from State University of New York at Buffalo. She received her M.S. in Education from State University College at Cortland, New York, and her B.A. in General Literature from Harpur College, State University of New York at Binghamton. She has taught as a first, second, and third grade teacher and as a Title I Reading teacher and Title I Math  teacher in diverse settings, from upstate New York to rural Ohio to Appalachian West Virginia. Recently she won a university Kenan leave to enable a year-long reassignment from her university position to be a full-time first-grade teacher in a school where half of her students were Latino. Her research and writing currently focus on literacy for bilingual and English-language learners. In 1998 she won the American Educational Research Association Award for Outstanding Review of Research, and in 2000, she won (with George Noblit) the International Reading Association Dina Feitelson Award for Outstanding Research. Both awards celebrated her research on literacy for English-language learners. Dr. Fitzgerald has published widely in journals such as *Reading Research Quarterly*, *Research in the Teaching of English*, *JRB: A Journal of Literacy*, *The Reading Teacher*, *Language Arts*, *Kappan*, *Journal of Educational Psychology*, *Educational Psychologist*, *Written Communication*, *American Educational Research Journal*, and *Review of Educational Research*. Dr. Fitzgerald has also contributed service to various federal groups as a review panelist and presenter for bilingual and English-language learners' literacy issues, including the Office of Education's Office of Bilingual and Language Minorities Affairs and the National Institute of Child Health Development.

Michael Graves is Professor of Literacy Education and the Guy Bond Fellow in Reading at the University of Minnesota. He received his Ph.D. in Education from Stanford University and his MA and BA in English from California State College at Long Beach, and he has taught in both the Long Beach and Huntington Beach Public Schools. His research, development, and writing focus on comprehension development, vocabulary development, text difficulty, and effective instruction. His recent books include *Scaffolding Reading Experiences: Designs for Students Success* (2003, with Bonnie Graves, Christopher-Gordon), *Reading and Learning in Content Areas* (2003, with Randall Ryder, Wiley), *Teaching Reading in the Twenty-First Century* (2001, with Connie Juel and Bonnie Graves, Allyn & Bacon), and *Reading for Meaning: Fostering Comprehension in the Middle Grades* (2000, edited with Barbara Taylor and Paul van den Broek, Teachers College Press). He has also published widely in journals such as *Reading Research Quarterly, Research in the Teaching of English, Journal of Reading Behavior, Journal of Adolescent and Adult Literacy, Elementary School Journal, American Educator,* and *Educational Leadership.* Dr. Graves is the former editor of the *Journal of Reading Behavior* and the former associate editor of *Research in the Teaching of English.* He is currently developing a website of Scaffolded Reading Experiences, www.onlinereadingresources.com, with a grant from the U. S. Department of Education.